Entrepreneurship
and Self-Help
among
Black Americans

To Thojest Jefferson and Johnnie Mae Sibley Butler,
my mother and father, who are lights of encouragement;
and to Rosemary Griffey Butler, my wife,
who has given me additional encouragement

Entrepreneurship and Self-Help among Black Americans

A Reconsideration of Race and Economics, Revised Edition

John Sibley Butler

STATE UNIVERSITY OF NEW YORK PRESS

Published by
State University of New York Press, Albany

For information, address State University of New York Press,
90 State Street, Suite 700, Albany, NY 12207

Production by Michael Haggett
Marketing by Michael Campochiaro

Library of Congress Cataloging in Publication Data

Butler, John S.
  Entrepreneurship and self-help among Black Americans : a
reconsideration of race and economics / John Sibley Butler. — Rev. ed.
      p. cm. — (SUNY series in ethnicity and race in American life)
  Includes bibliographical references and index.
  ISBN 0-7914-5893-8 (harcover : alk. paper) — ISBN 0-7914-5894-6 (pbk. :
alk. paper)
  1. African Americans—Economic conditions. 2. African American
businesspeople. 3. Entrepreneurship—United States. I. Title. II. Series.

E185.8.B83 2005
338'.04'08996073—dc22

                                                                2004029877

10 9 8 7 6 5 4 3 2 1

Contents

List of Tables

Preface to the Revised Edition

The first edition of *Entrepreneurship and Self-Help Among Black Americans: A Reconsideration of Race and Economics,* was accepted well in both the academic and practical marketplace. When I spoke to people about a second edition, they asked me not to change the theoretical chapter in the book, or the community case studies on Durham, North Carolina and Tulsa, Oklahoma. They asked that I push hard on new case studies of immigrant groups and update the chapter that addresses the present status of black enterprise. This, essentially, is what I have tried to do in this present edition.

I have added new historical research on black enterprise in America, added a consideration of new research on groups that put entrepreneurship at the center of community, and presented an overview of the present status of black entrepreneurship in America. I would have loved to do a chapter on process, or the procedure for starting an enterprise, but that will have to be done separately. For my publisher, the number of pages in the book is already sufficient.

Over the years there have been hundreds of books and articles which address different aspects of race, ethnicity and economics. Because the country developed as a result of immigration of groups, these variables have remained central in any kind of analysis. Some years ago I began to read the research on ethnicity and enterprise. I found it quite interesting; the field seemed to develop systematically with different theoretical orientations guiding the research effort. One of the things that I found quite interesting was that the works hardly mentioned the Afro-American experience as being tied to entrepreneurship activities during the early part of their history. Certainly as ethnic groups came to America, they developed neighborhood enterprises. Of course some groups did it better than others. As I read the theory of these works, it dawned on me that most of it had already been specified by scholars as early as 1900. So I found myself confronted with an interesting situation. On the one hand the Sociology of Entrepreneurship, as I refer to it, completely neglects the Afro-American experience, although as we enter into a new century, people are more aware of the strong tradition of self-employment among black Americans, and how that tradition continues to influence the group today. We might also add that when this experience is mentioned, it is in a negative tone. But what I found ironic was that in this neglect scholars had simply re-thought old theories of race and entrepreneurship. For every book that has been written recently on entrepreneurship and ethnicity (e.g. *Latin Journey* by Alejandro Portes and Robert L. Bach and Bonacich and Model's *The Economic Basis of Ethnic Solidarity*,) there is one which parallels it in the Afro-American tradition of scholarship. It is not my purpose to match and compare such works, but simply to respecify the theory and the knowledge in this field by giving consideration to neglected work.

For the original edition, I read and talked to everyone I could about the development of Afro-American entrepreneurship. I was especially interested in speaking with older people, those who had been builders of business enterprises and communities when they were young. I also made it a point to talk to people who had attended traditional black schools in the south; I had a feeling that in a class in economics they could guide me to an old source on Afro-American enterprise. I was correct.

After reading for a couple of years, and incorporating materials in my course on Entrepreneurship, I decided to go back and read the history of one of the organizations to which I belong. In the History of Sigma Pi Phi, written by Charles H. Wesley, there is a picture of the manuscript entitled *Early History of Negroes in Business in Philadelphia* by Henry M. Minton, who was one of the founders of the organization. It was read before the American Historical Society in March of 1913. I immediately went to our library and discovered that the work was not there. More frightening, I was told that there were probably only one or two in the entire country. As always, the library staff at The University of Texas came through with flying colors and found a copy of the work. From then on I was excited about doing a manuscript on the topic. The more I researched, the more I found that the research brings about a different perspective on general race and ethnic relations. Thus in this manuscript I try to address the issue of race and sociological theory as it relates to entrepreneurship.

There are a host of people who contributed to the completion of this book. The Policy Research Institute of the Lyndon Baines Johnson School of Public Affairs funded my proposal on "Entrepreneurship in America." The University Research Institute at The University of Texas at Austin funded a faculty leave to allow me to pursue my interest. The African and African-American Research Program provided travel and general research support and anything else that I asked for. They were needed.

The Institute for Innovation Creativity and Capital (IC²) at The University of Texas at Austin provides a platform for the discussion of entrepreneurial ideas. As Director of IC², I have focused the organization on dynamic entrepreneurial research around the globe. This is in the tradition of George Kozmetsky, the original director of IC².I have also had the opportunity to discuss my ideas at Aoyama Gakuin University, School of International Politics, Economics, and Business, Shibuya, Shibuya-Ku, Tokyo, Japan, where I have been a Visiting Professor during the last seven summers (1995 and continuing). The National Center for Neighborhood Enterprise, headed by Robert Woodson, has provided an outlet for new ideas as communities continue to understand the importance of new ventures and entrepreneurship.

I extend special thanks to my Research Assistants who were so helpful during the project. For the original edition, Marsha Coleman, a graduate student in the School of Business, searched through many library stacks and rolled many micro-film reels during the early part of the research. She became so excited that she dropped her original research topic and switched to early Afro-American business. Gwendolyn Campbell, in addition to searching the library and ordering other works, read parts of the manuscript. Maria Zebonne, in addition to the help in search for materials, also performed a lot of the first round editing for the manuscript. Patricia Gene Greene, now a distinguished Professor at The University of Missouri Kansas City and holder of the Kauffman Chair in Entrepreneurship, was one of my graduate students when I began to think about doing a second edition of the book. I owe a lot of thanks to her. Also, a big round of thanks for Professor Margaret Johnson, who was also my graduate research assistant when the book was first published. I also owe a big thanks to Shannon Cormier, my present research assistant. Others who provided editorial comments were Rosemary Butler and Felice Coles.

Special thanks also goes to Patricia Bell, a professor of Sociology at Oklahoma State University and an original resident of Tulsa. She sent old newspapers, especially *The Oklahoma Eagle*, on the Tulsa race riots of the 1920's. On my trip to Durham, Professor Eugene A. Eaves of North Carolina Central University at Durham drove me around the old entrepreneur neighborhood and pointed out the houses which they constructed. A special thanks goes to Professor Nellie T. Hardy, a resident of Durham and Special Assistant to the Chancellor at Elizabeth City State University in North Carolina, for also driving me around Durham. I especially thank her for giving up her Saturday and helping me copy documents at the Durham Public Library. I am also grateful to Betty Nunley and Allen Martin. In their readings when they found something that might be of interest to me, I always received it gracefully. This edition has benefited from the eyes of Margaret Cotrofeld and Coral Franke.

I would also like to thank my colleagues for their support. Joe R. Feagin and Teresa Sullivan were always present to toss theoretical ideas around in the office. I also had the opportunity to speak with Daniel C. Thompson, a Professor at Dillard University in New Orleans. Professor Thompson was excited about the manuscript, and had agreed to review it. Unfortunately, he died three months later. I thank him posthumously for his input and his support. A special thanks to Charles C. Mokos, Jr., who has always shown a tremendous amount of encouragement throughout my academic career. Of course all of the content of the book is my responsibility.

John Sibley Butler
Austin, Texas
May, 2002

1

The Sociology of Entrepreneurship

This is a study in the sociology of entrepreneurship,[1] which takes as its subject matter the relationship between group characteristics and the development of business activity. Because major group characteristics examined revolve around race and ethnicity, this area of inquiry shares some of the same concerns as the study of race and ethnic relations. But the traditional field of race and ethnic relations concentrates on conceptualizing and measuring processes such as assimilation, colonialism, discrimination, racism, and prejudice. Indeed, the sociology of race and ethnic relations has produced one of the most massive and systematic research traditions within academia precisely by concentrating on these important topics.[2]

A general proposition which emerges from this massive effort is that, the more a group is assimilated into a society, the higher the probability of economic stability for that group. This research tradition assumes that economic opportunities are provided by the host society. As groups move into the society and years increase, they move up the economic ladder of success.

The sociology of entrepreneurship moves the analysis from a complete emphasis on topics such as assimilation and prejudice to the development of ethnic enterprises which generates economic stability for ethnic groups. Such an approach means that there is a concentration on the process by which ethnic groups develop, maintain, and expand business enterprises within the economic structure. In a real sense, it is the sociology of self-help, recognizing that groups develop economic stability as a result of entrepreneurship.

Sometimes, self-help means owning a pushcart, a small shop, or a small farm in a community. The emphasis is not on the prestige of the enterprise, but rather it is on simply owning an enterprise that will bring about economic stability. Indeed, entrepreneurial professionals, such as doctors and lawyers, because of the same ethnic experience of others in the group, find solidarity with the pushcart owner or the owner of a fruit stand in community organizations.

Because of economic stability, parents of self-help groups are more able to launch their children into professional occupations within the larger economic sector because of the importance that the group places on education.

Very often, offspring of these groups find themselves in the most prestigious occupations of American life. Thus, this field of inquiry is not only concerned with business activity, but the sociological outcomes that develop as a result of the ownership of enterprise. The developing literature has shown that members of some ethnic groups appear to generate business enterprises much better than others do. Thus, the documentation of business activity by ethnicity becomes a concern of the sociology of entrepreneurship. Sometimes, this field of inquiry is called the sociology of ethnic enterprise.

Although this approach appears to be relatively new, it is simply the restatement of an old issue using ethnic and racial groups rather than religious groups. Max Weber posed a similar question around the turn of the century.

> A glance at the occupational statistics of any country of mixed religious composition brings to light with remarkable frequency a situation which has several times provoked discussion in the Catholic press and literature, and in Catholic congresses in Germany, namely, the fact that business leaders and owners of capital, as well as the higher grades of skilled labor, and even more the higher technically and commercially trained personnel of modern enterprises, are overwhelmingly Protestant. This is true not only in cases where the difference in religion coincides with one of nationality, and thus, of cultural development, as in Eastern Germany between Germans and Poles. The same thing is shown in the figures of religious affiliation almost wherever capitalism . . . has had a free hand to alter the social distribution of the population in accordance with its needs, and to determine its occupational structure.[3]

Weber was perplexed by the fact that Catholics, a traditionally oppressed religious group, had not started a strong tradition of business enterprise. Laying the foundation for what I call the sociology of entrepreneurship. Weber noted that:

> The smaller participation of Catholics in the modern business life of Germany is all the more striking because it runs counter to a tendency which has been observed at all times, including the present. National or religious minorities which are in a position of subordina-

tion to a group of rulers are likely, through their voluntary or involuntary exclusion from positions of political influence, to be driven with peculiar force into economic activity. Their ablest members seek to satisfy the desire for recognition of their abilities in this field, since there is no opportunity in the service of the State. This has undoubtedly been true of the Poles in Russia and Eastern Prussia, who have without question been undergoing a more rapid economic advance than in Galicia, where they have been in the ascendant. It has in earlier times been true of the Huguenots in France under Louis XIV, the Nonconformists and Quakers in England, and, last but not least, the Jews for two thousand years. But the Catholics in Germany have shown no striking evidence of such a result of their position. In the past they have, unlike the Protestants, undergone no particularly prominent economic development in the times when they were persecuted or only tolerated, either in Holland or in England.[4]

Weber solved his problem by positing a relationship between the "Spirit of Capitalism," as measured by the will to take risk and enter the economic world, and the ideas of Protestant thinkers such as Luther and Calvin. As Weber noted, the explanation for this anomaly must be sought in the permanent intrinsic character of religious beliefs rather than in any historico-political situation.

Almost fifty years later, Werner Sombart entered the picture by arguing for the primacy of religious ideas found in Judaism rather than Protestantism. Building on Weber's statement that entrepreneurship had been a characteristic of the Jewish population because of oppression for thousands of years, Sombart posited the following:

One of the most important facts in the growth of modern economic life is the removal of the center of economic activity from the nations of Southern Europe . . . to those of the North-West. . . . Cannot we bring into connection the shifting of the economic center from Southern to Northern Europe with the wanderings of the Jews? . . . Israel passes over Europe like the sun: at its coming new life bursts forth; at its going all falls into decay. . . . My own view is . . . that the importance of the Jews was twofold. On the one hand, they influenced the outward form of modern capitalism; on the other, they gave expression to its inward spirit. Under the first heading, the Jews contributed no small share in giving to economic relations the international aspect they bear today; in helping the modern state, that framework of capitalism, to become what it is; and lastly, in giving the capitalistic organizations its peculiar features. . . . Under the second heading, the importance of the Jews is so enormous because they, above all others, endowed economic life with its modern spirit; they seized upon the essential idea of capitalism and carried it to its fullest development.[5]

Sombart, in a controversial and almost forgotten work, solved the issue by showing how major components of capitalism can be grounded in the old writings and teachings of Judaism. With respect to Weber's solution to the puzzle, Sombart notes that, in terms of religious ideas, Protestantism is Judaism.

Since the writings of Weber and Sombart, there have been advances in the conceptualization and specification of the relationship between economic activity and group characteristics. In a very real sense, these advances constitute the subject matter of the sociology of entrepreneurship. Also, in a very real sense, the inquiry remains the same while the groups change:

> Why should some foreign groups have higher rates of business enterprise than others, and why should the foreign born in general have much higher rates of business proprietorship than Mexicans and especially Blacks, the more disadvantaged of all?[6]

Thus, the question posed by Weber arises in America with the reemergence of the sociology of entrepreneurship. In order to solve the puzzle, scholars have developed a number of theoretical perspectives which serve as a guiding light for research. Although perspectives overlap considerably, they appear in the literature as distinct theoretical orientations. This chapter reviews these perspectives so that the reader can have an understanding of this subfield of sociology. In doing so, case studies which are a mixture of ethnic history and business activity are blended together. Such blending—a trademark of this research—allows the reader to capture the historical situations in which different ethnic groups developed business activity. Business activity in the early years is seen as a particular type of the adjustment to American life which leads to the development of an economic security, or what some call a *middle class*.[7] Although the literature is rich, for matters of exposition, the experiences of Japanese-Americans, Jewish-Americans, Greek-Americans, Amish Americans, and Pakistani Americans are presented.

I

The study of ethnicity and entrepreneurship in America was given life by a number of scholars. Edna Bonacich developed a "Theory of Middleman Minorities" which has served as the theoretical guide for many studies in this area. The theory began to take form in the work of Turner and Bonacich.[8] The major question is how ethnic groups succeed in America in the face of systematic discrimination and prejudice.

How is a degree of economic security carved out of a society which is hostile to the group?[9] Bonacich took the idea of middleman minorities from the theoretical shelf of sociological theory where it had lain dormant in the works of scholars such as Becker, Blalock, Schermerhorn, and Stryker.[10] These earlier works show that, in the international arena of race and ethnic relations, some groups play an interesting part in the economic structure. Unlike most ethnic groups and minorities who sink to the bottom of the economic structure within a society, these groups develop economic security by playing the middleman position within the structure of capitalism. As such, they are to be found in occupations such as labor contractor, rent collector, money lender, and broker. Playing the middleman position means that they negotiate products between producer and consumer, owner and renter, elite and masses, and employer and employee.[11]

European Jews, the Asians in East Africa, Japanese in the United States in the early 1900s, and Chinese in Southeast Asia are examples of middlemen in capitalist societies. Although trade and commerce are their "bread and butter," they are also found in bureaucratic organizations. Bonacich notes that, even here, they act as middlemen, interposed as they are between the consumer and his economic purpose. Put simply, minorities conceptualized as middlemen are less likely to be primary producers of goods and services. Their major purpose is to generate the flow of goods and services throughout the economy.[12] Because of this, middlemen minorities are viewed as *petit bourgeoisie* rather than members of the classic capitalist class.

Bonacich notes that early treatment of middleman minorities in the literature has produced two significant themes. The first emphasis is on the relationship between hostility directed toward the middleman minority and the loss of occupations and economic security, as they are pushed out of good occupations and are forced to develop economic security on the fringes of the economic system.

Another theme of the early sociological literature stresses the relationship between elites, masses, and middleman minorities. Here the concentration is on the types of society in which middlemen are found. Where there is a significant gap between elites and masses, middleman minorities plug this status gap by acting as go-betweens. Because elites feel that they may lose status by dealing with the masses, middleman minorities do it for them. These minorities are not concerned with status considerations, and they feel free to trade with anyone. Thus, they negotiate the economic relationships between elites and masses.[13]

Although the early literature on middleman minorities provided Bonacich with a concept which captured the economic relationship of minorities of host societies, it did not provide all of the answers. By concentrating solely on discrimination, prejudice, and hostility, Bonacich reasoned that only one side of the equation had been tapped. If these variables were so important, why is it that middleman groups create degrees of success from apparent failure? Bonacich explains:

> The prevalent themes are found to be inadequate for two chief reasons. First, discrimination and hostility against minorities usually have the effect of hurting group solidarity and pride, driving a group to the bottom rather than the middle of the social structure. How then can we explain the closing of ranks reaction of these particular groups, and their peculiar ability to create success out of hatred?[14]

In order to solve this puzzle, Bonacich retained the concept of middleman minorities but added a new twist, known as "A Theory of Middleman Minorities," to the old sociological concept.

Central to the understanding of middleman minority theory is the concept of sojourning, which is designed to capture the migration patterns of groups from a homeland to other parts of the world in their search for economic stability. Although people who sojourn can be classified as immigrants, they do not plan to stay permanently in a chosen land. Instead, the major goal is to engage in business enterprise, develop a pattern of systematic thrift or saving, and send money back to the original homeland.

As Bonacich notes, sojourners are interested in making money, not spending it. This orientation allows them to generate capital and build significant savings. In so doing, the group experiences deprivation and sacrifices tastes of the "good life." This approach to life is in marked contrast to other immigrant groups around the world who are interested in settling, becoming a permanent part of the new country, and enjoying prosperity. The Chinese in Indonesia, Indians in Malaya and Burma, and Indians in Central Africa have played the role of middleman minorities well.[15]

Because middleman groups sojourn from country to country, the problem of host hostility is also important in Bonacich's scheme. Hostility between middleman minorities and the host society revolves around economics and issues of solidarity. Economic issues are measured by concentrating on conflicts between clients, business, and labor.

For example, there has been systematic conflict—most recently in 1985 between Indians in South Africa and the native black population. The former can be conceptualized as a middleman minority because they serve as a buffer zone between the native black population and the white population.

Another example of conflict with members of the host business community is seen in the Japanese experience on the West Coast of the United States. White businessmen experience systematic business conflict with the Japanese because the latter price their products below market standards. This can also be seen in Jamaica, where the same activity was done by the Chinese; and in

Southeast Asia, where Chinese also conflict with the host business population over the pricing of goods.

Bonacich notes that this conflict has increased significantly with the emergence of nationalism throughout the world. Consider her analysis of the relationship between middleman minorities, business activity, and nationalism:

> Business conflict with emerging subordinate groups has increased in post-colonial times. As liberated nations try to gain control of their economies, they come into conflict with middleman groups. In Southeast Asia and East Africa attempts have been made to curb Chinese and Indian business, to establish native peoples in lines long dominated by these groups. The efficient organization of the middle-man economy makes it virtually impossible for the native population to compete in the open market; hence, discriminatory government measures (restrictions on the issuance of business licenses, special taxes, and the like) have been widely introduced.[16]

The final dimension of host conflict is related to labor relations. Because middleman minorities create their own firms and depend on immediate family or group members, the price of labor can be reduced significantly, and the workforce is very loyal, identifying with the ethnic labor force rather than the host labor force. As a result, the overall price of labor is reduced within a community, and conflict arises between host labor and the labor of middlemen. As noted by Bonacich, Modell describes a 1973 attempt by the Retail Food Clerks, Local 770, in Los Angeles to organize the sales force in the grocery business. Since white-run concerns could not concede a substantial advantage in labor costs to their Japanese competitors without suffering losses in trade, Local 770 believed that, if it was to organize the white portion of the industry, it could not ignore the Japanese. The Local 770 appealed to Japanese workers to stand up to their employers and fight for the American standard of living, but the appeal was rejected, and Japanese-owned farms were blacklisted and picketed by organized labor.[17]

In addition to labor conflict, Bonacich's theory notes that the host society develops anti-middleman plans in order to decrease their economic impact. For example, because the middleman minority moves from country to country, the label of disloyalty to the host country has been placed on them. This can be seen in the cases of Jews in Europe, Chinese in Southeast Asia, and Indians in East Africa. In essence, Bonacich's ideas center around groups which travel from country to country in search of economic security. Because they are strangers in societies which essentially put up with them, they develop economic security but pay the price of discrimination and other forms of hostility. As Bonacich's ideas formed a basic theory, research began to concentrate on the American experience, paying particular attention to people of color.

II

The Japanese experience jumps to the forefront as an ethnic group which could be utilized as a case study for middleman theory. Despite their non-European origin, members of the group have been successful within the American economy. Unable to change their names, change their accents, dye their hair, and assimilate, nevertheless they have been able to snatch economic security out of the jaws of a hostile society. Since the sociology of entrepreneurship by definition must interact strongly with ethnic history, after reviewing briefly the history of the Japanese, we can then turn to research which places the group in the middleman tradition of the sociology of ethnic enclaves.

The search for a "better way of life" has always been the ultimate motivating factor for groups to leave a country. In the classic concepts of sociology, push and pull factors interact to create migration. Push factors may be measured by famine or war, while indicators of pull factors can be opportunities, land, minerals, and occupations perceived to exist in another land. Unlike many groups who decided to leave a country of their own volition, the Japanese were forbidden by their government to leave Japan. It was not until 1853, when Japan dropped a policy of isolation which had been in effect for three and one-half centuries, that Japanese were able to migrate to search for economic security. In that year, U.S. Navy Commodore Matthew C. Perry sailed to Japan. A year later, he returned to sign a treaty which officially ended Japanese isolation. The signing of the treaty brought Japan into the arena of the Western World and signaled the search for economic stability in countries other than Japan.

But, unlike other groups who migrated independently of their government, Japanese migration in its early stages was supervised by the government. The first immigrants from Japan were contract laborers sent to Hawaii. Thus, began a tradition which would last for years to come. The Japanese abroad should not be treated simply as "another immigrant group." They were proud people with an outstanding historical experience. Their government played a major role in the protection of their rights as they migrated from the homeland. Consider the following quotation:

> The first emigration was in the year "Meiji One," or 1868, when 148 contract laborers went to Hawaii. Their experiences left an aftertaste of bitterness and distrust. Within a month of when they started work, complaints came to Hawaii's Board of Immigration both from them and from their employers, and reports of the trouble, considerably magnified, found their way back to Tokyo. An agent of the Japanese government, sent to investigate, arranged to have the most dissatisfied returned home at Hawaii's expense. The proud new regime was

determined that its country should not be regarded as another China, one more storehouse of coolie labor to be maltreated by foreign overseers. For seventeen years no more contract laborers were sent to Hawaii; and the emigration of Japanese to any destination was placed firmly under the control of a government bureau or, later, government-sponsored emigration companies, whose ostensible purpose it was to protect even humble workers abroad from any indignities. Often this protection was at best nominal, but the supervision by agents of the Japanese government set some of the conditions of acculturation.[18]

This relationship between Japanese abroad and the Japanese government would continue as emigration from Japan to other parts of the world increased over the years.

Because of the growing need for labor in the sugar plantations of Hawaii, Japan again allowed its citizens to migrate. In 1884, when there was an announcement for contract laborers in Hawaii, almost twenty-eight thousand people applied from all parts of Japan. However, only six hundred were allowed to go in the first wave. But, for the next ten years, about thirty thousand Japanese went to Hawaii in order to engage in contract labor. The stage was now set for systematic migration to the United States mainland.[19]

When one thinks of ethnic migration to America in the European tradition, what comes to mind is the idea of masses of immigrants showing up on the shores. For example, between 1820 and 1920, more than four million Italians migrated to the United States. Between 1881 to 1920, more than two million Jewish immigrants from Eastern Europe came to this country.[20] Japanese immigration to the U.S. mainland does not even begin to approach the numbers of Europeans who migrated here. As shown in Table 1.1, during the period between 1861 and 1870, Japanese made up only 0.01 percent of all immigrants to the United States. The largest percentage, during the period of 1915 to 1924, is 2.16. But the problems which they encountered in the process of developing economic security in America were gigantic. Because they concentrated on the West Coast, they became the ultimate "California problem."

Because of a practice called *primogeniture* in early Japan—the inheritance of the total estate by the oldest son—the search for a better way of life in America was spearheaded by second and third sons of Japanese families.[21] It is quite interesting that research has shown that most Japanese, who originally came to the U.S. mainland, came from more economically stable backgrounds and higher social classes than those who went to Hawaii and other areas, such as Latin America and the Philippines.

For example, Peterson presents data which show that, of the males who migrated from a village in Hawaii, almost half reported their occupations in Japan to be related to fishing, seamanship, casual labor, or agriculture. By

TABLE 1.1

Japanese "Immigrants" to Mainland United States* 1861–1940

Period	Number	Percent of All Immigrants
1861–1870	218	0.01
1871–1880	149	0.02
1881–1890	2,270	0.04
1891–1900	27,270	0.77
1901–1907	108,163	1.74
1908–1914	74,478	1.11
1915–1924	85,197	2.16
1925–1940	6,156	0.03

Sources: Calculated from U.S. Bureau of Census, Historical Statistics of the United States. Washington, D.C.: U.S. Government Printing Office, 1960. Series C-88, C-104; and Yamato Ichihashi, Japanese Immigration: Its Status in California. San Francisco: Marshall Press, 1915.9. Table adopted from William Peterson, Japanese Americans. New York: Random House, 1971:15.

*Not included migrants from Hawaii after its annexation.

contrast, those who applied to go to the mainland United States reported their occupations as merchants, students, and laborers. Each of these categories comprised more than 20 percent of the total. Agriculturalists and fishermen combined accounted for only 14.1 percent of those going to the U.S. mainland. But, as Peterson notes, there was not necessarily a relationship between occupational categories and economic stability. For, by American standards, Japanese immigrants were relatively poor.[22] But these occupational categories reflect the stratification which was present in Japan before the migration to America.

When the Japanese began to arrive in California, they found themselves in the midst of an anti-Chinese campaign. After the Civil War, more than a quarter of a million of Chinese nationals immigrated to the West Coast and worked in mining and service industries as well as in building railroads. As the percentage of Chinese immigrants increased and a certain amount of success came to the group, anti-Chinese sentiment began to emerge. They were viewed as inferior to white Americans, and vigilante groups emerged, posing a threat to life and civil rights.

By 1882, the government responded with the Chinese Exclusion Act which put an end to immigration of this group to the United States. But, in an interesting twist in Asian response, the first Japanese who arrived were separated from the Chinese. Just as the first Europeans were welcomed by native-Americans, the first Japanese, who formed the Wakamatsu colony, were welcomed. Consider the following analysis by the Sacramento Union, which compared Japanese immigrants to the hated Chinese:

These groups of Japanese are of the "better" class, talk English, and are very anxious to find a permanent home in this State. . . . It is in the interest of California to welcome and encourage these immigrants. . . . As the Indians learned much from the whites that was useful to them so there is probably much knowledge in the possession of these Asiatics that we could profit from, to compensate us in some measure from the very enlightened prejudice against their coppery color. They will at all events teach us how to produce teas and silk, some useful lessons in frugality, industry, and possibly in politeness.[23]

After the Japanese began to gain economic stability and compete with white labor, the positive attitudes of acceptance would turn to negative attitudes of rejection.

Japan continued the practice of looking out for its emigrants, handpicking those who left and supervising them once they reached their place of migration. This practice gave individuals leaving home for a strange place a sense of security. The Japanese Parliament, in 1896, passed an immigrants' protection law which required each laborer who was leaving the country to present evidence that someone would provide funds to care for him if he developed illness while in the United States. These "sponsors" would be responsible for returning the ill worker to Japan.[24] By 1940, there were about 6,156 Japanese immigrants in the United States (see Table 1.1).

The first generation of Japanese Americans, called the Issei, found employment in agriculture or established small businesses of their own. As a general observation, there was more of a tendency toward self-employment and interdependency within the group. But the second generation, the Nisei, took advantage of the American educational system and became more saturated in Americanism than did their parents. The third generation, or Sansei were born right after World War II. This group is now almost totally acculturated, with the exception of certain distinctions of religion and ethnic organizations which can be attributed to most ethnic groups.[25]

The road toward economic stability and general peace of mind for the Japanese was paved with systematic discrimination and constant struggle. Because of growing competition with Euro-Americans in the labor sector where Japanese-Americans would work for lower wages, hostility and racist ideology became a component part of the West Coast arena.

In 1890, members of the shoemaker's union assaulted Japanese cobblers. In 1892, members of the union for cooks and waiters attacked Japanese restaurateurs. Because the Japanese possessed exceptional skills in the cultivation of land, they found themselves in competition with Euro-American farmers. To remedy this situation, the California Legislature passed an alien landholding law in 1913, prohibiting persons who were ineligible for citizenship from owning land, but permitting them to lease it for only three years. This law derived its power from the U.S. Naturalization Act of 1790, which was still applicable at the time and which stipulated that citizenship was available to any alien, providing that he or she was a free white person. This, of course, excluded the Japanese. However, in a fascinating case, *Ozawa v. United States*, 1921, the Japanese claimed to be Caucasoid, but the case was not won, and the California law remained in effect.[26]

In order to place a cap on the "Japanese problem," the American Federation of Labor and the California Farm Bureau Associated fought for exclusion of the Japanese. In 1924, Congress granted the wishes of its citizens to exclude all undesirable immigrants by passing the 1924 Immigration Act. This Act gave preference to Northern European immigration to the United States, thus excluding the Japanese from entering the country.

Such policies satisfied the anti-Japanese groups which had emerged on the West Coast. The Mayor of San Francisco had campaigned against the "yellow peril." The California Legislature passed a resolution calling for exclusion of the Japanese on the grounds that they could not be assimilated. President Theodore Roosevelt developed a government prohibition on Japanese migrants coming in from Hawaii, Mexico, and Canada. In essence, this "gentleman's agreement" noted that no passports would be issued by the Japanese Government to workers except to those who had already been in the United States and to close relatives of those already here.[27]

Pearl Harbor and World War II served as the events which saw the ultimate solution to the "Japanese problem." When Japan attacked Pearl Harbor in 1941, there were approximately 127,000 Japanese in America, 94,000 of these in California. Since the individuals piloting the planes which bombed Pearl Harbor looked like the Japanese in California, more than 110,000 Japanese-Americans were taken to concentration camps. The camps were located in Arizona, Arkansas, California, Colorado, Utah, and Wyoming. During the evacuation, all liberal groups basically agreed with the program. For example, the Japanese-American Committee of New York, which had supported the Japanese in earlier conflicts, in 1942 stated:

> The Evacuation . . . may have seemed harsh. But we of the Japanese community must realize once and for all that this is a total war. . . . Surely it is not too much to ask the Japanese community to sacrifice, for the duration, some small portion of their civil rights . . . We realize that the evacuation is not foolproof or perfect, nor is it the complete solution to the Japanese problem.[28]

However, the Japanese-Americans in California and their "fellow Americans" suffered the full force of the experience:

> The evacuees loaded their possessions onto trucks . . . Neighbors and teachers were on hand to see their friends off. Members of other minority groups wept. One old Mexican woman wept, saying, "Me

next. Me next.". . . . People were starting off to 7 o'clock jobs, water-
ing their gardens, sweeping their pavements. Passers-by invariably
stopped to stare in amazement, perhaps in horror, that this could
happen in the United States. People soon became accustomed to the
idea, however, and many profited from the evacuation. Japanese
mortgages were foreclosed and their properties attached. They were
forced to sell property such as cars and refrigerators at bargain
prices.[29]

The Japanese-Americans lost almost everything during this experience,
except the most minimal of possessions.

This experience represents the building blocks for the study of Japanese-
Americans in the sociology of entrepreneurship. As noted earlier, the field
does not question traditional discrimination and prejudice, but concentrates on
the development of business activity which produces economic security in the
face of such historical experiences. After the war with Japan, scholars began to
notice the remarkable success of Japanese-Americans. William Peterson noted
that:

> Barely more than twenty years after the end of the wartime camps,
> this is a minority that has risen above even prejudiced criticism. By
> any criterion of good citizenship that we choose, the Japanese Amer-
> icans are better than any other group in our society, including native-
> born whites. They have established this remarkable record, moreover,
> by their own almost totally unaided effort. Every attempt to hamper
> their progress resulted only in enhancing their determination to suc-
> ceed. Even in a country whose patron saint is the Horatio Alger hero,
> there is no parallel to this success story.[30]

Edna Bonacich argues that this success can be explained by concentrating
on the Japanese as a middleman minority. Their historical experiences in the
United States fit well into her theory. Their solidarity as a group was strong.
They had an orientation at one time which concentrated on a return to the
homeland. They engaged in small businesses and faced hostility. Bonacich's
ideas are developed in a work with John Modell entitled *The Economic Basis of
Ethnic Solidarity: Small Business in the Japanese-American Community*.

Despite all of the problems discussed earlier, by 1909, there were about
3,500 Japanese businesses in the western states. They were created as a result
of hard work within communities. The majority of these businesses were in the
cities of Seattle, San Francisco, and Los Angeles. In the tradition of middleman minorities, these businesses tended to concentrate on service, including
hotels, restaurants, barber shops, pool rooms, supply stores, cobbler and shoe
shops and laundries. Of all Japanese on the West Coast, about 15 percent were

engaged in small businesses.[31] These types of businesses grew so rapidly that, by the outbreak of World War II, the majority of Japanese who resided in cities were engaged in small business activities, which brought about economic stability.[32]

Agriculture was a major mode of entrepreneurship for Japanese in rural areas. The literature shows that there was a movement from labor contracting or providing workers to other farmers, share tenancy or sharecropping, and leasing of the land, to ownership of the land.[33] Whether in the city or on the farm, businesses run by the Japanese provided economic security. As befitting the theory of middleman minorities, Japanese firms were family-oriented, depending on members for labor, and they were very small. Though grounded in the ethnic economy, they catered to the general market once the firms were established.

But as did all ethnic groups, the Japanese developed aspirations of upward mobility which would lead them out of their ethnic enterprises to prestigious positions in the larger society. This was especially true of the second generation—those who were coming of age during the pre-World-War-II period. However, the mental image of the American dream conflicted with the reality of the California experience.

> Extensive evidence suggests that the Nisei were dissatisfied with their role in the ethnic economy. Indeed, their dissatisfaction is what the prewar Nisei meant when they talked and wrote for the "Nisei problem." The picture was drawn as follows: The Nisei were highly motivated to obtain college education, and they hoped, after thus training themselves, to secure white-collar positions, particularly in the professions and at managerial levels in general community concerns. On attempting to gain employment in the non-ethnic world, however, they faced racism and discrimination. Consequently, they were forced back into seeking work in the firms run by their parents and their parents' colleagues. Now, not only were they over-educated for the menial jobs available, but they were forced to remain in unfortunate dependency to the same people upon whom they had always before been dependent. The paternalistic labor relations of the ethnic firm, its low pay, long hours, and expectations of loyalty, would seem suffocating to a western-educated young person who hoped to become a doctor or an engineer. It was only because they had no choice—or so the argument ran—that the Nisei entered the ethnic economy.[34]

Even with all of their business stability and educational status, the Japanese found that elements of the "American dream" were reserved only for individuals with certain racial characteristics.

Of course, the evacuation mentioned earlier destroyed the Japanese ethnic economy. The hardships experienced by the Japanese faded into a new beginning after 1944. But, nested within the new beginning, were harsh realities of property and dreams lost forever. Farm lands which had been owned by Japanese families could not be reclaimed. In urban areas, Euro-American businessmen did not have to worry about competing with the Japanese. For example, before the evacuation, Japanese-Americans in the city of Seattle owned 206 hotels, 140 groceries, 67 market stands, 94 cleaning establishments, and 57 wholesale produce houses. Only a handful of these enterprises were re-established in that city after the war.[35]

One of the most interesting and ironic findings by Bonacich and Modell relates to the impact of education on the decline of the Japanese as a middleman minority. As the experiences of World War II faded, the Japanese who did try to maintain the ethnic economy sent their children to institutions of higher education so that their lives could be improved within that economy. Indeed, the ultimate goal was to have their sons return to run the family business or farm with improved techniques. In fact, the opposite effect was generated. As hostility decreased against the Japanese, opportunities within the larger society became a reality, and, instead of realizing the wishes of their parents, Japanese began to enter the larger "American" labor force.[36]

As years passed, Japanese-Americans would serve as a model of success for ethnic and racial America. Perhaps the building blocks of this success lay in the "can-do" attitude of an early Japanese economy. Economic stability brings with it stable family relations, an appreciation for education, and the passing of these attributes to future generations.

III

Throughout work on the sociology of entrepreneurship, constant reference to the Jewish group is made along certain dimensions. This is especially true of the work of Bonacich and Modell, who utilize the experiences of Jews in the "Old World" in order to develop the middleman minority theory. Underlying the assumptions of middleman theory is the idea that the Jewish group only traded as they sojourned around the world. Historical accounts note, however, that the Jewish group not only participated in capitalism as a middleman minority, but they indeed helped to start it. Given this historical observation, middleman minority theory has shortchanged the Jewish contribution to the development of capitalism. The Jewish experience in America is not the same as that of other middleman groups nor does it begin with Jewish immigration at the turn of the century. The Jews simply are not another ethnic group which migrated to America and raised itself up by its boot straps. They are

too intertwined with the development of America and the Old World. Historical considerations will allow us to discuss the literature on Jews in the
sociology of entrepreneurship.

Ever since the exodus from Egypt in the thirteenth century, and the settlement of the Twelve Tribes in Canaan, Jewish history has been punctuated
by economic success and group suffering. This dichotomy was repeated in a
number of civilizations.

In the ancient city of Alexandria, Jews were prosperous artisans, forming
a middle class between the Egyptians, who were regarded as a subject people,
and the Greeks, who enjoyed all of the privileges of citizenship. In 33 B.C., a
clash among the population—sometimes called the first pogrom—saw the
destruction of property, synagogues, and the loss of life. The estimated eight
million Jews who were part of the Roman Empire repeatedly suffered under
the reign of Hadrian. Because Hadrian banned the practice of Judaism under
penalty of death, Jewish martyrdom—as a result of defiance of the law—
increased.

The fall of Rome saw the development of Christianity and systematic
anti-Semitism. As the Crusaders travelled across Europe, they left a trail of
Jewish blood.[37] Ironically, Christianity, which emerged from the rich writing
traditions of Judaism, was associated with anti-Semitism throughout the
European continent. Consider the following, which captures the dichotomy of
suffering and the economic success of the Jews:

> Spanish Jews had also suffered their tribulations, especially under the
> Almohades, a fanatical Moslem sect which invaded Spain in the
> twelfth century; but on the whole, Moslem rule tended to be enlight-
> ened and tolerant. Jews were able to prosper and rise to the highest
> offices of state and there was a flowering of Jewish culture such as had
> not been known in any of the previous centuries of exile. But as
> Christianity spread southwards across the face of the peninsula, their
> day darkened, their culture atrophied, their horizons narrowed. Per-
> secution elsewhere in Europe had been arbitrary and sporadic; in
> Spain it became systematic and formed part of an attempt to force
> them into the Church. Elsewhere in Europe most Jews killed them-
> selves rather than embrace the cross. In Spain, . . . entire congrega-
> tions opted for baptism. . . . The Crown yearned to witness the
> complete Christianization of Spain. . . . In 1492 the Jewish com-
> munity, numbering some two hundred thousand souls, was
> expelled.[38]

This experience was repeated throughout European history. For our purposes, it is important to realize that, nested within this historical suffering,
were periods of economic success. The experience in Hitler's Germany, or the

final solution to the Jewish problem, must be seen as a modern-day phenomenon which has its analog, albeit different, in earlier parts of European history. As Bermant notes, "It is good to be a Jew, which is a somewhat un-Jewish thing to say, for Jews are rather more accustomed to hugging their wounds than counting their blessings and are nervous of suggesting that things may be going well in case they should start going badly." Not every Jew is superstitious, but almost all are familiar with the Yiddish expression, *Kein-ein hor.* "Let not the evil eye behold it."[39]

The Jewish experience in America cannot be compared to the ugly experience in Europe. This has been recognized by scholars of the Jewish saga.[40]

The general idea is to view the evolution of American Jewish history within a general American framework. Such an approach has meant discarding the idea of the Jewish experience as a specialized case of suffering, and concentrating on the richness of the experience.[41]

Although most works on Jewish history place the beginning of their community in the United States in 1654, when twenty-three Jews of Dutch origin arrived in the harbor of New Amsterdam, in reality Jews were in the colonies as early as 1621. The arrival of the twenty-three Sephardic and Marranos Jews[42] received a welcome after leaving Recife, Brazil, where they unsuccessfully helped to defend Dutch possessions from Portuguese attack. When Portugal was successful in reconquering Brazil, the twenty-three Jews fled the territory because it had come under the jurisdiction of the Inquisition.[43]

Upon arrival in the colonies, Peter Stuyvesant, the governor of the New Netherlands, tried to prohibit their entrance. Even before the twenty-three had arrived, Stuyvesant had complained to his employers in Amsterdam (the Dutch West India Company) about Jewish competitors in the British colony. Within the protest, Stuyvesant argued that the settlement of a "deceitful race" who had an "abominable religion" would threaten and reduce the profit of loyal subjects of the company.[44] He noted that he had asked these "blasphemers of the name of Christ" to depart, but they had refused. He thought that their settlement would infect and trouble the new colony of New Amsterdam.[45]

But to Stuyvesant's surprise, a number of important stockholders of the Dutch West India Company were of the Jewish faith. In addition, the Jews sent their own petition to the Company, noting their loyalty to the Dutch in Brazil. In the final analysis, the Company allowed the Jews to stay, not deviating from their policy of fairness in the Netherlands. Thus, the early resistance by the governor was overruled by his employer, the Dutch West India Company.[46]

In 1664, the province of New Netherlands was conquered by the English, and renamed New York. By 1700, there were approximately three hundred Jews in the colonies, but they were beginning to gain economic security through commerce and were systematically involved in the developing prosperity of the English colonies.

Jews helped develop the country's colonial prosperity, largely as shop-keepers, traders, and merchants. The Trade and Navigation Acts limited colonial trade primarily to the British Empire, so the Jewish merchant exchanged local raw materials . . . for English consumer wares, hardware, textiles, and commodities such as rum, wines, . . . and sugar. . . . Jewish traders were among the first to introduce cocoa and chocolate to England, and at times they had a virtual monopoly in the ginger trade. . . . The typical Jew of this period lived in tidewater commercial and shipping centers like New York, Newport, Philadelphia, Charleston, Savannah, and Montreal. He was a small shopkeeper, or a merchant or merchant shipper who engaged in retailing, wholesaling, commission sales, importing, and exporting. . . . A number . . . were engaged in the slave trade on the North American mainland, participating in the infamous triangular trade which brought slaves from Africa to the West Indies, where they were exchanged for molasses, which was in turn taken to New England and converted to rum for sale in Africa.[47]

In addition, the group was involved in fur trading and land speculation as the new territory moved westward.

The Jewish experience in colonial America did not differ significantly from other groups. As Dimont notes:

Because the Jews in Colonial America, like their Christian brethren, were pioneers who grew up with the country, they learned how to innovate. Like the Puritans, the first Jews to arrive in Colonial America showed a willingness to amend the nonessentials in their Judaism but to hold on to the nonnegotiable items. . . . The same forces that created the Christian colonist also created the Jewish colonist, making him unique in the history of Judaism—a Jew differing as much from the European Jew as the European Jew differed from the biblical. Just as this frontier culture stripped the European Christian of his cultural vestments, so it stripped the European Jew of his. In the same way that the Christian colonist emerged from the wilderness not as a European but as an "American," so the Jewish colonist emerged not as a European Jew but as a distinctly "American Jew." Thus, for both, the frontier meant a steady turning away from the influences of Europe.[48]

Dimont also discusses reasons why American Judaism developed differently from the Judaism in Europe. For example, the twenty-three Sephardic Jews who arrived in the colonies were very different than those in Europe. They had no tradition of the ghetto, for there was never a place in Spain or

Portugal set aside exclusively for Jews. Sephardic Jews did not migrate to those countries—such as Germany, Eastern Europe, or Russia—which had ghetto traditions. Thus, these Jews in early colonial America wore the same clothes as others and were indistinguishable from them.

They were not as orthodox as European Jews; they would not die in order to worship at the synagogue three times a day. These Jews also brought with them a tradition of independence and a heritage of cosmopolitan life. They understood all kinds of religions and adapted to the influence of all. Quite interesting is the fact that the Puritans, which would eventually form, according to Dimont:

> the core culture of the developing country, followed a religious tradition which was basically Hebraic in nature. They followed the teaching of Moses, or the Ten Commandments, and called themselves Christian Israelites rather than British Christians. Thus, the continent of the Americans to the colonists was as much the Promised Land as Canaan was to the old Israelites.[49]

Another reason Dimont gives as to why American Judaism developed differently from its European counterpart has to do with the fact that there were no ordained rabbis serving permanently in America, and the European tradition never was systematically established. In Colonial America, being of the Jewish faith did not interfere significantly with the day-to-day lives of individuals, and Jews were accepted simply as colonists. Consider this letter written in 1791 by a Jewish immigrant who had settled in Virginia.

> One can make a good living here, and all live in peace. Anyone can do what he wants. There is no rabbi in all America to excommunicate anyone. This is a blessing here. Jew and Gentile are one. There is not galut [separation] here.[50]

From a sociological point of view, the colonial experience of Jews was one of assimilation. Studies of Jewish patterns of marriage show that, during this period, at least one in seven Jews and their descendants married Christians. Due to intermarriage, by the eve of the American Revolution, the pioneer Jewish families of New York had almost disappeared. Almost every Jew who settled in Connecticut married out of the religion and, thus, was completely assimilated.

This phenomenon was not the result of conscious assimilation on part of Jews, but rather reflected the fact that the Jewish population was small, had more men than women, and that the society was totally open to them. The typical American Jew, at this point in history, dressed, acted, and looked like their Gentile neighbors. They were more likely to be of German origin, and were very enterprising shopkeepers.[51] Although Jews played significant roles in the American Revolution, in the aftermath, a struggle began for civil liberties. As late as 1820, only seven of the thirteen original states recognized the Jews politically, although they continued to prosper economically. By the early nineteenth century, however, all traces of inequality in law had disappeared. Jews were elected or appointed as judges of lower courts, state legislatures, and town councils.[52]

Between 1820 and 1860, economic progress and social acceptance continued. During the Civil War, Jews generally sided with the region in which they lived. Like other Americans, some supported slavery and others were abolitionists. For example, Rabbi Morris J. Raphall of New York supported slavery on a national level, arguing that it was legitimated by the Bible. Rabbi David Einhorn of Baltimore upheld his abolitionist stand in a state which utilized slaves. About seven thousand Jews served with the Union Army and about three thousand served with the Southern rebels.[53]

During the 1870s, systematic anti-Semitism began. As exclusive social clubs began to form among the Protestant population, Jews were excluded. This was quite a reversal from the early experience:

> It appears that during the early development of American cities, Jews had the broadest opportunities for social mingling and political advancement. It was quite usual for a Jew, as one of the few literate, stable settlers, to become a mayor or a leading official of a frontier town. However, once these pioneer years ended and more fixed social groupings were formed, a tendency to exclude Jews from the elite social circles became evident.[54]

As the eighteenth century turned into the nineteenth century, the background of Jews coming to America changed significantly. As the population increased, and being Jewish became a visible characteristic, the entire relationship between Protestant and Jew altered.

In an article written in 1908, Alfred Stone noted that race relations were simply a matter of racial distribution.[55] As the number of minorities within a population increased, discrimination against the minority also increased. Between 1881 and 1914, Eastern European Jews came by the thousands to the shores of America. By 1918, there were almost three million Eastern European Jews in the United States, ten times the number of assimilated Jews of German origin.

Although of the same religion, according to Dimont:

> The German Jews in America watched with incredulity as the Russian Jews stepped off the boats. Were they apparitions from the middle-ages, these wild-bearded, earlocked, blackhatted caftaned,

Yiddish-speaking Jews? The Russian Jews stared with equal incredulity at the well-groomed, clean shaven, English-speaking German Jews, wondering if they were bona fide Jews or apostates. As the German Jews continued to watch this ambulant mass of poverty, reeking oppression, descend upon the land, their incredulity turned into fear, then into apprehension, and finally into pity. What should they do with them? What would the Christians think of this throw-back breed of Hebrews?[56]

Anti-Semitism increased in the Christians, regardless of when Jews arrived in America. In 1876, the New York *Tribune* carried an advertisement which noted that a certain resort hotel would no longer accept Jews. After 1880, it became a common practice to bar Jews from established summer vacation and resort areas. This practice spilled over into the cities, where the group was barred from private schools, social clubs, and other institutions which were measures of high status and prestige.[57]

Along with discrimination, old stereotypes and ideologies which had been absent or lain dormant began to emerge. Jews were viewed as conniving and grasping, attempting to rule the world through international financial networks, and a general threat to the country.[58] In addition, Jews were barred from colleges and universities, housing opportunities, the developing industrial occupational structure, and other occupations controlled by Christians.

In response, the Eastern-European Jews began to carve their economic place within the highly anti-Semitic sector. The 1890 Census shows that 58 percent of employed Jews were in trading or financial occupations, with 20 percent being office workers and 6 percent belonging to the professional category. They started small businesses within their communities, ranging from cart pushers to junk peddlers to clothing store owners.

The established Jewish community set up national and local organizations to help develop the economic security of the newcomers. Beginning in about 1895 in Boston, local Jewish charities established federations for fund raising. This practice spread throughout the United States with the founding, in 1917, of the Federation for the Support of Jewish Philanthropic Societies. In addition to economic help, Jewish leaders also founded organizations designed to fight anti-Semitism, including the American-Jewish Committee (1906), the Anti-Defamation League of B'nai B'rith (1913), and the American Jewish Congress (1920). In short, the entire group pulled together in order to make Jewish life as painless as possible within a hostile atmosphere. Thus, in 1977, Chaim Bermant could write:

Until a generation ago—or even less—no one was more inclined to share America's exalted view of itself than the Jew. He really did believe that it was God's own country, opened up just as the position

of European Jewry was becoming untenable, whose very creed might
have been laid down by the Prophets, a new world without the pho-
bias and dogmas of the old, where past histories were written off and
each individual could advance on his own merits. In Europe, the Jew
. . . liked to think of himself as a German, Frenchman or Englishman of the Mosaic persuasion, but to the Englishman, Frenchman or
German he was but a Jew who was trying to rise above himself. The
Jew could, however, be an American without presumption or abase-
ment and he gloried in the role. America had no more eager prose-
lytes than the Jew who had found prosperity and acceptance, so when
the 'huddled masses' came ashore toward the end of the nineteenth
century, they were met not only with soup kitchens set up by the earlier arrivals, but with a whole apparatus of schools and welfare institutions to bring them into the mainstream of American life. . . . By
the outbreak of World War II American Jewry was no longer an
immigrant community. . . . And so they beavered on and moved
from the slums into the suburbs, from the work-bench into the professions, from the small businesses into large. No Jew, even of the
Episcopalian persuasion, has become President of the U.S., or of
General Motors or of Chase Manhattan Bank, but Jews cannot, for
all that, be regarded as disadvantaged. They have come to the
forefront of American life, have savored its pleasures and enjoyed its
privilege.[59]

Although Jews gained economic success within the country, anti-Semitism has accounted for exclusion from certain occupations, as noted above.
Thus, the middleman minority has been the economic category within the tradition of the sociology of ethnic enterprises. Although the Jews have been
lumped with other immigrant groups in the literature of the sociology of
entrepreneurship and race and economics in general, this type of analysis can
be misleading. It treats the Jewish group as one without historical or ethnic
diversity within the group. Any cursory reading of the literature on the development of entrepreneurship and ethnicity will reveal that the Jewish group is
more than a middleman in the history of capitalism, especially in the development of capitalism within the United States. One cannot simply say, as Sowell
does in a recent work, that "There were some Jews in earliest American times,
but Jews became numerically and socially significant only in the nineteenth
century."[60]

The fact is that the Jewish group played a significant part in the economic
development of America. Scholars have noted that Jews perfected the navigation techniques which allowed Europeans to cross the ocean. They also played
a significant part in the financing of the American Revolution, provided the
philosophical base for the Constitution, and developed the very basis of the

mechanics of capitalism—for example, bank notes, securities, the stock market and other money markets.[61] Although our purpose in this book is not to give a systematic account of the relationship between Jews and capitalism, it is sufficient to say that accounts in the tradition of the sociology of ethnic enterprise do not give consideration to this history, thereby misinterpreting the Jewish tradition in the literature.

IV

Close to the theoretical approach of middleman theory is the body of literature concentrating on the relationship between collectivism and business activities of immigrant groups, the interaction of cultural attributes of ethnic groups and the development of entrepreneurship. As Light noted, the theory of middleman minorities developed by Bonacich lacked a hard cultural side, and thus, can be viewed as reactive in the sense that exclusion within a society enhances ethnic solidarity, which, in turn, creates a clannish cooperation in business. This also creates more hostility toward the ethnic minority, which further intensifies ethnic solidarity. Thus, middleman or sojourning groups engage in business activity because of the negative situation in which they find themselves.[62] A collectivist approach also represents a response to the idea of focusing on rugged individualism, which has its roots in Weber's work, *The Protestant Ethics and the Spirit of Capitalism*. This work examines the relationship between religious ideas and individual accomplishments within the capitalist system.

The collectivist approach is stressed in a collection of papers edited by Scott Cummings.[63] Written at a time when the importance of ethnicity was being rediscovered by assimilated America, the major purpose is to show that immigrants coming to America followed a collectivist approach to the problems of urban life. Cummings argued that the ethos of rugged individualism is a cornerstone of cultural folklore and has saturated the thinking of American scholars.

Although this line of thought can be traced to Weber, Weber recognized the importance of collectivism or communitarianism on trade in the world context. Thus, Cummings argues that post-Weberian scholars have actually misinterpreted elements of Weber's original writings. This misinterpretation can be traced to the fact that many scholars who contributed to the original literature were from small-town Protestant communities. On the other hand, many of the immigrant groups were of Jewish, Catholic, or Oriental origin.[64] The theoretical preoccupation of scholars with rugged individualism has led to a misinterpretation of the ethnic self-help experience. The collectivist approach, with an emphasis on self-help institutions, stresses the cultural side in explaining the economic stability of ethnic groups, and also brings to bear the idea that these institutions have more of an influence on the development of economic stability through business activity than through the process of assimilation. Unlike middleman theory, where hostility plays a major role in the interpretation of business success, collectivism concentrates on the "cultural baggage" of a group as the major explanatory variable. Research within the tradition tests the relative importance of collectivism and rugged individualism in the development of business activity.

An excellent example of the importance of collectivist cultural apparatuses on the development of business activity is the research on the development of businesses among Greek-Americans. Greek migration to America began in significant numbers around the turn of the century, with about 50,000 arriving between 1900 and 1924, and settling mostly in the cities of the Northeast and Midwest.[65] As did other immigrants, Greeks came to the United States in search of economic security. Their goal of economic stability was realized as a result of the development of small businesses.[66]

The importance of collectivism in the development of Greek-American business activity has been pursued by Lawrence A. Lovell-Troy,[67] who was also interested in the impact of individualism—such as starting a business without the help of one's ethnic group—during the development of Greek-American business. The small businesses which Greeks developed ranged from shoeshine parlor owners and general street peddlers to florists and confectioners. But the bread-and-butter of their activity lay in the restaurant business.

As the urban centers in which Greeks settled began to expand, there was a need for businesses which served lunch to workers. Thus, they were able to take advantage in the increase of disposable income among individuals as job opportunities increased.

Cities in which restaurants were found include New Haven, Chicago, Tacoma, and San Francisco. Census data from 1950 and 1970 show that the pattern of restaurant ownership was continuous for thirty years. In recent years, the group has adjusted its food businesses to follow the trends of society: instead of concentrating on full service restaurants, fast food businesses have become the order of the day.[68] Lovell-Troy was interested in how Greek food businesses develop and sustain themselves. His central question is the one which is at the center of the sociology of entrepreneurship: how "recent" immigrants initially find employment in America, gain the training needed to open small businesses of their own, and arrange for the financing of such businesses. From his studies emerges the importance of the clan, a major cultural component which enhances the development of business activity among Greek-Americans. Nested within the clan is the importance of the family which in a sense, gives rise to the clan structure.

> ... although the Greek entrepreneurial response is based fundamentally on the nuclear family and consequently might be conceived of as

a version of family capitalism, the sociocultural adaptation of Greeks to American society is based on the clan structure, which provides economic assets to Greeks that would have been unavailable to isolated family units.[69]

Lovell-Troy explains this clan structure:

The Greek clan itself is a loose structure formed through the migration process. When an immigrant family sponsors its relative for admission to Connecticut, a clan forms, centering on the original immigrant. Because of provisions in the U.S. immigration laws, sibling ties are the most important kinship ties for the migration of new immigrant families. The sibling tie, therefore, becomes the primary relationship by which various nuclear families are united into clans. Moreover, . . . the sibling tie also becomes the most important kinship bond by which Greeks fashion their economic adaptation.[70]

Small business education is one of the backbones of this economic adaptation. In analyzing data from Greek clans in Connecticut, Lovell-Troy found that immigrants with relatives who owned pizza establishments learned the business from them. If individuals were not family members, they also learned the business by participating in its everyday operation.

An interesting finding in this collectivist tradition is that the clan did not help in the generation of capital for business development. Unlike other studies showing that ethnic groups pooled their money in different ways in order to build capital, Lovell-Troy found little of this among the Greeks. His findings show the overlap of the collectivist approach with individualist approaches within the study of the sociology of ethnic enterprise.

. . . in the matter of capital formation, kinship ties within the clan structure do not appear influential. . . . it appears that thrift, hard work, savings, and investment provide Greek immigrants with the capital needed, and, although such values may be found in the Greek culture, each immigrant appears to solve the problem independently.[71]

Whether or not a Greek immigrant pursued an individual or collective route to the development of business activity depended on two conditions. If a new immigrant's sponsor had already developed a small business, then the collective response was followed. If, however, the sponsor of an immigrant did not have a small business, then the individualistic approach emerged. Sometimes, this latter approach took the immigrant outside the ethnic community into the developing factories of the city, where the traditional approach to economic stability was followed.

Lovell-Troy ends his analysis by contrasting his findings with the rich research on Oriental businesses. "The less collective entrepreneurial pattern displayed by Greeks, in comparison to the Orientals, may be explainable in terms of weaker family and clan obligations. Greek nuclear families operated businesses independently or, at most, in partnerships of two or three families, while Chinese and Japanese seem to have operated businesses which were tied together by a strong network of collective, ethnically based morality."[72] The Greek example is an excellent comment on the interaction between individual and collectivist responses to the development of businesses within the collectivist tradition.

The collectivist approach of Lovell-Troy has been demonstrated in the work of Light on Oriental groups. Augmenting the work of Bonacich on the Japanese, but stressing the contribution of cultural attributes to the development of capital, Light demonstrates the importance of the rotating credit system in the development of business enterprises.[73] It is essentially the practice of placing amounts of money in a pool, then lending that money through a system of rotation. Light notes that Japanese most likely adopted the system from the Chinese who had utilized it in San Francisco.

> The Chinese have a peculiar method of obtaining funds without going to commercial banks. If a responsible Chinaman needs an amount of money, he will organize an association, each member of which will promise to pay a certain amount on a specified day of each month for a given length of time. For instance, if the organizer wants $1,300 he may ask 12 others to join with him and each will promise to pay $100 each for 13 months. The organizer has the use of the $1,300 the first month. When the date of the meeting comes around again, the members assemble and each pays his $100, including the organizer. All but the organizer, who has had the use of the money, bid for the pool. The man paying the highest bid pays the amount of the bid to each of the others and has the money. This continues for 13 months. Each man makes his payment each month but those who have already used the money cannot bid for it again. By the end of the 13-month period, each will have paid in $1,300 and have had the use of the whole amount.[74]

More importantly, Light shows that this form of capitalization was adopted from the Chinese by the Japanese as early as the thirteenth century.

Among Japanese tenants in agriculture, partnership was encouraged by the owner simply because it made more than one individual responsible for the note. Such an arrangement made it easier for the Japanese to engage in agricultural enterprises. Finally, capital was generated by the use of cheap labor in Japanese firms. In addition to inexpensive labor, the labor force was held together by ethnic solidarity. Workers were loyal to the small firms in which they worked. Given the high degree of anti-Japanese sentiment in California, it is not surprising that this bond developed.

The collectivist approach was also used in the study of Ismaili Pakistani in America by Greene and Butler. [75] This study shows how this community developed a community business incubator for the development of enterprise and provide for the social welfare of the immigrant community. In a real sense, community incubators are the highest form of collectivism for the creation of business enterprise.

The number of studies on Pakistani entrepreneurs has increased as this group started to immigrate to different part of the world. Research in England has documented the rapid development of retail and service enterprises owned by the Pakistani group. The core of the majority of this work is on how business communities change from the host English group to the Pakistani.[76] Research by Greene and Butler, concentrating on the American experience, was reported in two articles which concentrate on the use of the collectivist approach for the building of a community incubator and the development for a strategy for economic stability through business enterprise.[77] As a relative new comer to the shores of America in large numbers, the Pakistani do not share in the great migration from Europe during the turn of the century; nor do these Asian Indians have a history of systematic exclusion like Asians from Japan. Their experience provides an excellent study of how new comers create economic stability in America.

Formal business incubators are designed to give birth to new ventures, providing a safe haven in which to launch the enterprise. In the overall non-ethnic literature, incubators have been seen as change agents for economic development. They address many of the problems that might cause a business to fail in the marketplace. These problems include difficulty in obtaining business services, a shortage of money or capital sources, and the lack of simple networks. Although incubators in the non-ethnic society, or general society may differ slightly, they all concentrate on launching an enterprise into the business.[78]

When enough English is mastered, the coordinator matches the immigrant with a person who is economically stable in the community. This person connects the immigrant with a job, often as a convenience store worker, and the immigrant is expected to work and save for two years. During this period training in the English language and business practices continues.

When the apprenticeship is nearing an end, selected members of the community start to help the immigrant look for enterprise opportunities. Ideas are evaluated systematically and sites for the located of an enterprise are developed. Once an opportunity is located, the immigrant combines savings with capital from the Pakistani community. This community controls an internally raised capital investment fund of over $1.2 million dollars.[79]

When the enterprise is started, community help is available on an on-going basis for business plans, general support, inventory control, expansion, security and additional capital needs. Pakistani enterprises include hotels, restaurants, high-tech companies, and a host of retail stores.

The rotating credit system has also been found among the cultural baggage of other groups such as the West Indian immigrants in Brooklyn, New York.[80] The study of rotating credit adds significantly to the understanding of the development of business enterprises.

V

The ethnic enclave theory brings to the sociology of ethnic enterprise a combination of elements contained in middleman and collectivist theory, but adds a consideration of theories relating to economic structures. It draws on labor market analysis in order to build models of economic structures of minority communities. While its fundamental concerns are with the development of minority business enterprises, its theoretical base takes advantage of ideas which have been applied to the larger economy. Central to an understanding of ethnic enclave theory are theoretical models of economic structures.

Kalleberg and Sorensen[81] note that interest in labor market analysis is due in part to the failure of orthodox economic labor theory to explain persistent poverty, discrimination, and income inequality. Unlike classical economic theory, which assumes that the marketplace is perfectly competitive, the sociology of labor markets is concerned with market segmentation. Key to the understanding of this segmentation is the idea of dual economies.

The idea of dual economic structures emerges from the work of Averitt.[82] Dual economy theory suggests structural idea types: (1) a center economy with a high degree of corporate and bureaucratic organization, great diversification, technologically progressive means of production and distribution, and national and international accounts; and (2) a peripheral economy. The peripheral economy contains firms which are small, dominated by one individual, use outdated techniques of production, and operate in small restricted markets. The center economy is structured to reduce or eliminate competitive forces, while the peripheral economy is somewhat powerless against, and subject to, forces of competition. Although the literature employs different names to specify center and periphery—for example, monopolistic/competitive and concentrated/unconcentrated—the characteristics noted by Averitt identify the basic distinctions.[83]

Such a conceptualization of the labor market has allowed scholars to ground their work in the rich tradition of Marxist analysis. Put differently, the dynamics of concentration and centralization mean that capital will be accumulated in large forms under firms which are in the center economy. This dynamic includes the processes of labor exploitation and the collection of other smaller firms during periods of economic stability. Thus, Marxism becomes the major theoretical explanation for the diversification of capital or the movement of the market.[84] The analog for the segmentation of the economy vis-a-vis workers finds realization in the idea of the dual labor market.

Labor markets have been defined by Kalleberg and Sorensen as ". . . the arenas in which workers exchange their labor power in return for wages, status, and other job rewards."[85] The idea of labor market segmentation grew out of ghetto studies of the 1960s.[86] The guiding descriptive light is that the labor market can be partitioned into two distinct sectors, each with its own unique characteristics:

> The primary sector offers jobs with relatively high wages, good working conditions, chances of advancement, equity and due process in the administration of work rules, and above all, employment stability. Jobs in the secondary sector, by contrast, tend to be low-paying with poorer working conditions and little chance of advancement; to have a highly personalized relationship between workers and supervisors which leaves wide latitude for favoritism and is conducive to harsh and capricious work discipline; and to be characterized by considerable instability in jobs and a high turnover among the labor force.[87]

In essence, the labor market is divided into good jobs and bad jobs which produce different outcomes for workers. Outcomes noted in the literature include pay, different rates of turnover or commitment, different types of discipline, and different returns to education. This growing literature has documented the fact that minority group members are more likely to be located in the bad jobs or the periphery economy.

Ethnic enclave theory, as developed by Wilson, Portes, and Martin, significantly advances our understanding of minority business.[88] Because it draws on existing ideas about labor markets, this theory brings to the sociology of entrepreneurship an analytical sophistication lacking in the theoretical approaches discussed above. However, as with the research discussed earlier, it must begin with the idea of an ethnic community which creates a certain amount of solidarity which also enhances the development of small businesses. Thus, an enclave is defined as a distinctive economic formation, characterized by the spatial concentration of immigrants who organize a number of enterprises to serve their own ethnic market and the general population.[89] In addition, it brings ideas from general labor market theory into the analysis:

> Since the majority economy has become organized into two alternative structural forms, the periphery and the center, minority enclaves can have economies that are structured primarily in the image of

either structural alternative. Enclaves can be composed of a group of relatively independent firms which compete with each other for supplies and minority consumers, or minority firms can theoretically be arranged in a fairly unified system of vertical and horizontal integration, employing one or more of the strategies for achieving both kinds of integration. In the former case, the enclave resembles, and may indeed be a part of, the periphery in the majority economy. In the latter case, the enclave resembles the center economy and should have many of the advantages which that form of economy enjoys. Stated as a formal hypothesis: enclave economies that are vertically and horizontally integrated yield higher initial profits per unit of demand, create higher levels of production in related industries . . . pay higher wages, and create more jobs . . . than enclave economies that are not vertically and horizontally integrated.[90]

The most systematic integration of theory and research within the ethnic enclave literature is provided by Alejandro Portes and Robert L. Bach in *Latin Journey*.[91] In the tradition of Bonacich's work on Japanese middleman theory, they apply enclave theory in order to understand Cuban and Mexican economic development in America. Our concern is with Cubans, since the authors argue that Mexican-Americans never did have the type of economic enclave that Cubans had in the United States.

The island of Cuba was acquired by the United States as a result of the Spanish-American War in 1898. After two years of military occupation, it emerged as an independent country with close ties to America. Given its physical proximity to the United States, there has always been some degree of migration. In 1930, there were an estimated 18,000 Cubans in the United States, a figure which increased to about 80,000 in 1960.[92] When Fidel Castro took power, the mass migration began, and, because of the political nature of the mass migration, Cuban-Americans can be called refugees as well as immigrants.

The emergence of Castroism can be traced to 26 July 1953, the date of the unsuccessful attack on the Moncada army post in Santiago de Cuba, a year and a half after Batista's seizure of power. From this conflict, Fidel Castro emerged as a significant political figure with a loyal personal following. During his imprisonment on the Isle of Pines from 1953 to 1955, Castro published "History Will Absolve Me," a document which shows the beginning of his ideas for a new Cuba. In a pamphlet which was secretly published in 1954, his ideas of reform began to show structure. The core of his policy was (1) the restoration of Cuba's 1940 constitution; (2) to hold popular elections; (3) develop agricultural cooperatives; and (4) to carry out land reform.[93] By 1959 the Cuban revolution was a success, and the connection to the United States and capitalism were severed. By 1973 there were 273,000 Cuban immigrants in this country, which planted the seed for the development of an economic enclave in Miami, Florida.

Portes and Bach utilized this natural laboratory to apply ethnic enclave theory. Overlapping with the collectivist approach discussed earlier, Portes and Bach realize that immigrants do not come to the United States as isolated individuals with personal resources or what is called human capital. They also have access to the resources of the larger social groups of which they are a part.[94] Thus, like collectivism, the failure of orthodox labor-market theories to explain the dynamics of ethnic mobility lies in their ignoring labor-market segmentation, an important explanatory tool for the incorporation of Cubans into the American economic sector:

> The organization of an immigrant enclave economy typically requires recent arrivals to take a tour of duty at the worst jobs. The willingness of immigrants to remain in this condition rather than move to higher-paid occupations in the open economy has been explained by such factors as lack of knowledge of the host-country language or inadequate skills. Such explanations fail to take into account the built-in mobility opportunities in this mode of labor-market incorporation. Immigrant workers willingly remain in subordinate jobs because these jobs open paths of mobility unavailable on the outside. These opportunities are connected with expansion of immigrant firms, which create managerial-level openings for members of the same minority, or with opportunities for self-employment.[95]

Such theoretical reasoning stresses the fact that good jobs, in the tradition of the primary sector in the dual economy, can be realized in the ethnic enclave.

Before empirically testing this idea, Portes and Bach described the Cuban enclave in Miami. Although only eight percent of refugees had begun their own businesses after three years in America, 21.2 percent had done so by 1979. Retail trade, business, and repairs—such as automobile repair shops and electrical repair stores—professional services, and construction account for three out of every four of the self-employed. Professional services such as doctors and dentists were more likely to be established in the early wave of middle-class Cuban immigrants. Like other immigrants, a small number (seven percent) of the entrepreneurs established firms in manufacturing where capital requirements are more demanding.[96]

> Also in the enclave were wage earners. Whereas manufacturing accounted for only seven percent of Cuban owned firms, 38 percent

of the wage earners in this sample worked in this field. A significant
number of individuals found employment outside of the enclave in
large firms . . . The wage earners in this sample worked in firms
that were much larger than those owned by their fellow refugees. In
textiles, for instance, the average firm employing a Cuban refugee
maintained a total workforce of more than one hundred workers. Frequently, these firms employed as many as five hundred. This size difference is particularly noticeable within the retail sector, which
ranked third as an employer of these refugees and first as a type of
firm with which to begin one's own business. In the latter case, the
total number of employees was often fewer than five. In contrast,
retail stores in which the refugees found jobs were major employers
in general. On the average, these retail stores hired close to one hundred workers. The larger stores also employed a majority of Anglo
workers.[97]

Such a stratification system by definition creates a class system within the
enclave. Portes and Bach divided this system into employees, self-employed
without workers, and self-employed with workers. Then, they examined
income by these work categories. They discovered that salaried workers earn
the least, followed by independent entrepreneurs without employees, and self-
employed with workers earned the largest monthly paycheck. This discovery
highlights the diversity of the Cuban enclave in Miami, which leads to an
analysis of the enclave based on labor market theory already discussed. However, in order to empirically test the distinctions between primary, secondary,
and enclave labor markets, the classification scheme utilized in labor market
segmentation analysis must be altered in order to encompass the peculiarities
of immigrant group data.

Because segmented labor theory associates the secondary sector with
ethnic groups, Portes and Bach placed individuals in a sector based on the
ethnicity of coworkers. Thus, the primary sector in this analysis is inclusive of
workers hired by Anglo employers and who worked in a predominantly
Anglo workforce. The secondary sector was composed of workers employed
by Anglos but who worked alongside other Cubans or other ethnic minorities. The enclave sector posed no problems and was defined as Cubans who
worked for Cuban firms and self-employed businessmen. Portes and Bach
found empirical support for the existence of three labor market sectors in
their data. Utilizing discriminant analysis, it was found that refugees incorporated into the enclave were not only distinct from those in the secondary
sector, but that their ethnically bounded support systems contributed to the
enhancement of their economic position. Put differently, the parallel to labor
segmentation of the larger majority Anglo labor market, in terms of economic
benefits, can be found in the Cuban enclave.

Ethnicity as the organizing principle of a class-differentiated enclave represents primarily a mechanism of economic support. Though the resulting ethnically enclosed labor market is quite different from the Anglo-dominated primary sector, both yield comparable benefits. Ethnicity in the secondary sector, on the other hand, reflects the lower rewards and subordinate social and economic positions characteristically found among immigrant minorities.[98]

This analysis shows that there is more than one way to economic stability, or incorporation into the labor market, for Cubans in Miami. One can achieve success by working in the ethnic economy in a good job. On the other hand, Cubans who work outside of the ethnic community in the secondary labor force receive few benefits. Indeed, they simply compete with other minorities for the "bad" jobs of the secondary labor market.[99]

For those Cubans who work in the primary sector of the larger society, their success is attributed to traditional variables such as education and degree of assimilation. In a similar paper, Wilson and Martin compare the Cuban experience with the Black experience in Miami. Like Portes and Bach, Wilson and Martin find that there is an active center economy, as characterized by general dual labor market theory. Although the effect is not very strong, this community is developing good jobs which may provide opportunities outside the good jobs found in the general economy, and industries within the Cuban enclave produced significant vertical integration—or (firms buying from other Cuban firms, thereby creating the flow of money in the community) which contributes to the strength of the community. On the other hand, the Afro-American community in Miami resembles the periphery of the general economy. There is no creation of good jobs, and vertical integration is absent.[100] This comparative research converges with Portes and Bach and provides an interesting analysis of the Cuban and Black experiences.

VI

Middleman, collectivist, and enclave theory is driven, for the most part, by immigration. Scholars trace how the first generation develop small shops for economic stability and educate their children for the professional labor market. The Amish in America is also a group which places enterprise at the very center of community. The interesting thing about this group, however, is that the movement into small-scale enterprise in large numbers took place after they had been in America for quite some time. The Amish experience is an excellent example of how a group made a decision to move into business enterprise in order to maintain their cultural traditions.

Donald B. Kraybill and Steven M. Nolt, in a work entitled *Amish Enterprise: From Plows to Profits,* blends original and past research to show how this group made a conscious decision to move from almost exclusive farming for economic stability to micro-enterprise.[101] The work brings together elements of middleman, collectivist, and enclave theory, and is an excellent example of what happens when a group decides to place new business ventures at the center of community.

Earlier it was noted that Max Weber connected the spirit of enterprise with the development of Protestant thinkers such as Luther and Calvin. Also, Werner Sombart challenged the ideas of Weber by arguing that the Jewish religion, as a body of ideas, was also important for the development of the spirit of capitalism. The Amish, and the religious ideas that guide their way of life, can also be traced to early religious conflict and resolution.

The Protestant Reformation which gave rise to Calvin and Luther also gave rise to the Amish church, which grew out of the Anabaptist movement of sixteenth-century Europe.[102] The Anabaptists were merchants and craftsmen who felt that the Reformation was moving too slow and wanted to discard traditions of infant baptism and the Mass, which they viewed as not having a biblical backing. Originally baptized as infants in the Catholic Church, they meet in a private home and rebaptised themselves (thus the term Anabaptist) and broke with both Catholicism and Protestantism. They established a religious institution that was based on voluntary choice with members accountable to each other who would live apart from the worldly society.[103]

The new religious order paid dearly for their ideas; Anabaptists were jailed, tortured, and killed. After 1525 thousands were beheaded, drowned and burned at the stake throughout Europe. In the Netherlands, where Anabaptist ideas were strong, a former Catholic priest named Menno Simmons emerged as a strong Anabaptist leader. Having broken with Rome in 1536, his writings and leadership made him a leader among the Anabaptists. Those Anabaptists who followed him became known as Mennonites.[104]

At the end of the seventeenth century another strong Anabaptist, Jakob Ammann, emerged within Mennonite congregations. He argued that the Mennonites were too lax and undisciplined. Ammann insisted upon strict discipline, simple living, untrimmed beards, and simple clothing. Those who followed Ammann became known as Amish and they maintained a separate identity from their Mennonite Anabaptist.[105]

Like other Europeans, the Amish left Europe in search of economic and religious freedom. By 1730 communities of Amish families began to arrive in Pennsylvania, settled in southern Berks County and Lancaster County. Over the last one hundred years the Amish population has doubled about every twenty years. At this time there are 230 Amish settlements in America.[106]

The Amish community studied by Kraybill and Nolt is located in Lancaster County, Pennsylvania. For generations their lives were dictated by the importance of closeness to the soil, with an emphasis on living separately from larger society. They shunned emerging important technological changes such as telephones, radios, and automobiles. The horse and buggy became their symbol within Lancaster County, and the family farm their means of livelihood. Unlike other immigrants who joined the industrial labor force, the Amish lived by the motto that the "lunch pail is our worst enemy."[107] By joining the factor work force, the family solidarity, the socialization of children, and the overall fabric of Amish society was threatened. Thus joining the labor force, like millions of other Americans, did not develop as part of the Amish tradition.

The family farm, or the plow, became the instrument for livelihood for the Amish. As noted by Kraybill and Nolt, "Agriculture . . . is a religious tenet, a branch of Christian duty. The divine injunction to Adam to till the ground from which he came provides a religious mandate for farming. The Amish believe that the Bible instructs them to earn their meanings, for it ushers them into the presence of God.[108] The farm is thus the best place to raise a family; fathers instruct children on the importance of hard work and the family is placed against the harshness of nature as they carve out a living. The glue which holds this society together is the religious book, Ordnung. It contains all of the rules, regulations, and boundaries for Amish people.

For over one hundred years the Amish tilled the soil in Lancaster County. Refusing to allow their children to continue after an eighth-grade education, most of which was performed in their own community schools, the Amish built a society based on continued agriculture. Their peaceful life was disturbed, however, by rapid population growth. Lancaster's population increased about seventeen percent between 1980 and 1990.[109] This population growth meant that the number of farms, and farmlands, began to decrease significantly. Couple this with the fact that the Amish population was also growing, and you have what Kraybill and Nolt calls the demographic squeeze or demographic crisis.

Given the reality of the decrease in farmland and the demographic squeeze, the Amish had seven possible responses. The first response was migration from their strong communities. Other responses included subdividing farms, buying new farmland, working in factories, birth control, higher education of children beyond eighth grade, and entrepreneurship. After much debate, the Amish chose to add entrepreneurship to their culture, with a strong emphasis on micro-enterprises.

This decision was made to preserve the Amish culture. Armed with the slogan, "The lunch pail is our worst enemy," they set out to transform their culture by placing enterprises at its very center. Some Amish tried the workplace outside of their community and found that they were pulled away from family, exposed to unproductive aspects of the American work force, and had to miss Amish holidays. Thus the transformation to enterprise had to maintain the closeness of the family that had been produced by farm work during past generations. Kraybill and Nolt explains:

> The Amish were willing to experiment with new occupations, products, and markets if they could control their newly created world of work. . . . Many new entrepreneurs tried to maintain the patterns and virtues of farm life in their new commercial context. Moreover, they remembered the lessons from their foray into factory employment in the seventies. And so the ethnic enterprises, burgeoning in the eighties, were located at or near home as much as possible. No travel to far-off industrial parks would separate fathers from their families. Working at or near home preserved family values by blending spouses and children into the world of business. Parents working alongside their children could pass on the virtues of Amish life in the context of work, albeit at the edge, not the center, of the farm.[110]

The transformation of the Amish culture to enterprises, as noted by the authors of this excellent study, turned into a constant negotiation between the demands of a culture and the tools necessary for engaging in business enterprise.

Like the immigrant groups discussed earlier, the development of enterprises among the Amish was rapid. Although they were not a recent immigrant group, they shared the cultural and ethnic solidarity of middleman groups and, of course, used collective action to start their enterprises. Also, through the years they had maintained the fundamental aspects of Amish culture developed since their arrival in the America and thus had not gone through the process of assimilation. Within two decades (starting in 1970) the Amish produced over 300 micro enterprises. Although few owned agriculture related enterprises prior to 1970, sixty percent of all enterprise were started after 1980 and thirty-one percent started after 1990.[111]

Kraybill and Nolt divide the variety of Amish enterprises into four categories. They are (1) sidelines (2) cottage industries (3) manufacturing and (4) mobile crews.[112]

Sideline businesses provide supplemental income for the Amish and can be home based, occupy an old storage barn, an unused tobacco shed, or a roadside stand. Wherever space can be converted to retail, many Amish families create an opportunity to sell to the public. Included in the hundreds of sideline enterprises are bakeshops, hardware stores, greenhouses, show stores, carpenter shops, and small-engine repair shops.[113]

The opportunity for a nuclear family or an extended family to work together provides the glue for Kraybill and Nolt's cottage industries category. They note that these industries resemble the mom-and-pop grocery stores that were so prevalent in American communities in past decades. Included in this category are grocery stores, bulk food stores, and at-home harness shops.[114]

The manufacturing category is made of large-scale enterprises that also can depend on non-Amish for labor and have characteristics that are non-ethnic in nature. They contract with other non-Amish firms, and family members are less likely to play a significant role. Included in this category are cabinet shops, household appliance enterprises, and machine shops (servicing horse-drawn equipment).

Mobile work crews are carpenters who, in addition to working within the community, also contract in non-Amish communities. Woodworking and construction are ranked second to farming as the occupations of choice for the Amish.[115] Mobile crews create the most tension between traditional Amish culture and the world of work. Traditionally a horse and buggy transportation culture, mobile crews (some with non-Amish drivers) are allowed to utilize trucks and vans daily. Others contract transportation means to non-Amish people.[116]

The Amish were able to move into enterprises by using personal savings and limited borrowed money. The story of the Amish, however, is that they were able to preserve most of their old cultural traditions within the context of business enterprises which created hundreds of jobs for members of their communities. They never had to join the American work force, a work force that they considered a threat to their way of life. Kraybill and Nolt explain this negotiation between culture and enterprise:

> This astute compromise enabled the Amish to harness their work within an ethnic subculture. Employment within the context of kin and church reinforced Amish values, fortified the Pennsylvania German dialect, and accommodated the calendar of ethnic holidays and celebrations. Finally and most important, the implicit terms of the agreement enabled the Amish to work within the moral boundaries of their faith. They could now easily avoid Sunday sales, fringe benefit packages, and other dubious influences that sometimes accompany factory employment—blaring music, profane language, and organized labor.[117]

The Amish maintain their enterprises through community organizations, managing the growth of the enterprises, teaching their children entrepreneurial skills in their own private schools, and maintaining the quality of products and service. Within this community that once depended almost exclusively on the plow, there are part-time enterprises as well as those that gross millions of dollars a year.

Although the Amish tradition is not driven by recent migration, it is an excellent example of how groups can consciously switch from the plow to the development of enterprise, based on their cultural decisions.

Although the above theoretical perspectives have provided a pathway for research in this area, they are by no means exhaustive. There is, however, an excellent edited work which examines ethnic entrepreneurship from an international perspective,[118] discussing issues such as opportunities for ethnic business in Britain, small entrepreneurs in Europe, the vulnerability of small businesses in the United States and Europe, and the research agenda for ethnics in business. Business activities of West Indians, Jews, Asians, Pakistani, and Turkish Cypriots in Great Britain are also explored in a systematic way.[119] In addition, the work on immigration and its implications for the American and international communities has made significant contribution to the literature.[120] Although we cannot review all of the developing literature, we will utilize it as we proceed with the task at hand, that is, the reconstruction of the sociology of entrepreneurship.

CONCLUSION

The purpose of this chapter has been to introduce the sociology of entrepreneurship. Although this field has been revived recently in America and other countries, it represents a classic question in the history of sociology.

Max Weber, one of the most celebrated scholars of his time, raised a similar question in relation to religious groups in the 1800s. Werner Sombart also raised the question in the religious arena. The basic question was: Why is it that certain religious groups show more of a propensity toward entrepreneurial activities than others?

Both Weber and Sombart concentrated on doctrines found in the religious traditions of Catholicism, Protestantism and Judaism in order to solve the question. The same type of question is asked today, but with special reference to ethnic and racial groups. Rather than relying on strictly religious explanations, there is an emphasis on entrepreneurship which develops as a result of discrimination, oppression, and racism. However, unlike orthodox race relations research, these processes are not the major concern. Rather, the research is concerned with the business activity itself.

Although there are a number of theoretical orientations, we chose to concentrate on: (1) middleman theory, (2) collectivism, and (3) ethnic enclave theory to introduce this area of sociology.

Middleman theory, an outgrowth of early sociological theory, is concerned with the relationship between host hostility, ethnic solidarity, sojourning, and the development of business activity.

The collectivist tradition stresses the interaction of group members when considering the development of business enterprise. It does not view entrepreneurship as an individualist phenomena. Individualism is replaced with group self-help and institutional building guides.

Ethnic enclave theory introduces the idea of labor markets when studying ethnic communities. Just as the sociology of labor markets divides work into primary and secondary occupations for the society at large, ethnic enclave theory does this for ethnic communities. For matters of exposition, the history of Japanese-Americans, Jewish-Americans, Greek-Americans, Latin-Americans, and Amish-Americans were woven into the theoretical cloth.

The sociology of entrepreneurship is always in the becoming, with new studies appearing almost daily. But the construction of this discipline has, for the most part, omitted the story of constructive Afro-American entrepreneurship. For this reason, the field must be reconstructed and its theory renegotiated.

2

Race and Entrepreneurship

A Respecification

It is quite interesting that the sociology of entrepreneurship has not utilized the Afro-American experience in the theory building process. However, a search of any library reveals that much of the early research on business activities by minority groups employs the Afro-American experience as data. The literature on the sociology of entrepreneurship leads to the assumption that Afro-Americans did not develop a strong business tradition—but this is far from being correct. The historical business tradition developed by this group, when measured by theories which guide the sociology of entrepreneurship, was quite strong.

Nested within the realities of racism, prejudice, and discrimination is a history of business enterprise which has been overlooked by contemporary scholars of race relations in general. In reality, some Afro-Americans exhibited the same type of entrepreneurial spirit as other groups who immigrated to this country, but in a curious kind of way, scholars have reacted differently. When the Afro-American tradition has been recognized, it has been misinterpreted and scandalized.

In a real sense, this reveals the combative approach often taken toward this group as it developed a degree of economic stability. We will return to this issue in a later chapter. Our task now is to reconstruct, as is done in the literature on ethnic enterprises, the historical development of Afro-American business activity.

In the previous chapter we presented a review of the major works which have come to define the sociology of entrepreneurship. Edna Bonacich's and

41

John Modell's *The Economic Basis of Ethnic Solidarity,* Ivan Light's *Ethnic Enterprise in America,* and Alex Portes's and Robert Bach's *Latin Journey* are excellent examples of works which have contributed to this area. But what is most interesting is that *almost* every theoretical idea which appears in these works was specified in earlier works on Afro-Americans. This is especially true if you remove from these theories the idea of sojourning, of moving from country to country in order to engage in business activity.

These ideas began to take form in W. E. B. Du Bois' seminal work published in 1898 and entitled *The Negro In Business.* They were nurtured in Henry M. Minton's *Early History of Negroes in Business in Philadelphia,* which was published in 1913, and became full-blown in Joseph A. Pierce's *Negro Business and Business Education* which was published in 1947.

Although Pierce's work contains ideas which have been used in the work of scholars such as Bonacich, Portes, Bach, and Light, none of these authors acknowledges his contribution to the field.[1] Indeed, it will be somewhat a surprise when we present data which show that in 1910, Afro-Americans were just as likely as white Americans to be employers, and almost as likely as whites to be self-employed. Abram Harris' outstanding work *The Negro as Capitalist* is also untapped. It is not clear why this occurs; perhaps it is because these contemporary scholars' early training did not allow them to explore Afro-American history in its totality.

Whatever the reasons, there are many misconceptions and historical untruths about the Afro-American experience. Scattered throughout the literature on minority enterprise are references to the failure of Afro-Americans to generate business activities. For example, Bonacich, in her work on middleman theory, asks "How can we explain the closing of ranks reaction of these particular groups, and their peculiar ability to create success out of hatred? (Or to cite cases, why have Japanese Americans been able to overcome racism, while blacks have not?)."[2] Ivan Light asks a similar question: "and why should the foreign-born in general have much higher rates of business proprietorship than Mexicans and especially blacks, the more disadvantaged of all?"[3]

As this analysis unfolds, it is hoped that answers to such questions as these will develop and advance knowledge in this field. The analysis begins by examining entrepreneurship activities of Afro-Americans prior to the Civil War. We then move from historical considerations to the theoretical idea of an economic detour, a concept which will help us to understand the types of problems associated with Afro-American enterprise after the Civil War. Because of the importance of inventions in Afro-American entrepreneurship, we also consider examples of this activity. In subsequent chapters of this book, we will return to the history of self-help and the continued thriving of Afro-American enterprise.

I

Anthony Johnson was probably the first person of African descent to become an entrepreneur in the New World. Having arrived in America before the pilgrims, he accumulated property in Jamestown, Virginia.[4] The first wholesaler, merchant, and settler of Chicago, Jean Baptist DuSable, was also a businessman and capitalist. As America began to take shape as one of the leading capitalist countries, Afro-Americans tried to carve out a business place for themselves.

Of course, slavery constituted the dominant form of Afro-American existence, but despite this harsh reality, free Afro-Americans were able to generate a measure of economic stability. Indeed, at every level, the quest for economic stability through the practice of entrepreneurship during the colonial period revolved around the presence of this group. It has been estimated that the number of Afro-Americans who were free during this period was around sixty thousand.[5] Table 2.1 shows the proportions of free blacks and slaves in the United States for the years 1790 and 1860. It shows that, in 1790, the percentage of free blacks to the black population was 7.9 and, in 1860, it was 11.0.

TABLE 2.1
Proportion of Free Blacks and Slaves in the United States, 1860

Year	Number of Blacks	Percentage of Blacks to U.S. Population	Number of Free Blacks	Percentage of Free Blacks to Black Population
1790	757,208	19.3	59,557	7.9
1860	4,441,830	14.1	488,070	11.0

Source: Robert H. Kinzer and Edward Sagarin, *The Negro in American Business*. New York: Greenberg Publisher, 1950. 27.

Before the Civil War, Afro-American businesses fell into two categories. The first was composed of free Afro-Americans who accumulated capital with which to generate business activity. They developed small marginal businesses as well as enterprises that were far from peripheral to mainstream American business activity. Indeed, these Afro-Americans developed enterprises in almost every area of the business community prior to the Civil War, including merchandising, real estate, manufacturing, construction trades, transportation, and extractive industries.[6] This underscores the fact that Afro-Americans are woven historically into the economic fabric of America and cannot be looked upon, in totality, as a recently arrived ethnic group.

The second group consisted of slaves who—as a result of thrift, native intelligence, industry and the liberal paternalism of their masters—were able

to engage in business enterprise. Table 2.2 presents the geographical distribution of free Afro-Americans and those who were slaves, and the percentage of
free blacks to the total Afro-American population for 1860. Table 2.3 presents
the geographical distribution of slaves and free blacks in the United States in
1860.

TABLE 2.2

Geographical Distribution of Free Afro-Americans and Afro-American Slaves
in the United States, 1860

States	Slaves	Free Negroes	Percentage of Free to Total Negro Population
Texas	182,566	355	0.19
Missouri	114,931	3,572	3.01
Delaware	1,798	19,829	91.6
Maryland	87,189	83,942	49.05
District of Columbia	3,185	11,131	77.5
Virginia	490,865	58,042	10.57
North Carolina	331,059	30,463	8.43
South Carolina	402,406	9,914	2.40
Georgia	462,198	3,500	0.75
Florida	61,745	932	1.48
Kentucky	225,483	10,684	4.52
Tennessee	275,719	7,300	2.57
Alabama	435,080	2,690	0.61
Mississippi	436,631	773	0.16
Arkansas	111,115	144	0.12
Louisiana	331,726	18,647	5.32

Source: Robert H. Kinzer and Edward Sagarin, *The Negro in American Business.* New York: Greenberg Publisher, 1950. 59.

TABLE 2.3

Geographical Distribution of Slave and Free Negroes in the United States by
Section of the Country, 1860.

Section of Country	Slaves	Free Negroes
New England	0	24,711
Middle Atlantic	18	131,272
East North Central	0	63,699
West North Central	114,948	5,592
South Atlantic	1,840,445	217,753
East South Central	1,372,913	21,447
West South Central	625,407	19,146
Mountain	29	206
Pacific	0	42,224

Source: Robert H. Kinzer and Edward Sagarin, *The Negro in American Business.* New York: Greenberg Publisher, 1950. 30.

The reality of slavery was that the slaves, despite acquired skills, could not
become entrepreneurs in the true sense of the word. The majority of blacks

were excluded from the possibility of being businessmen. Indeed, slaves could not even act as customers or patrons of Afro-American businesses, not only because of a lack of money, but also because of the fact that all their money was directed toward purchasing their freedom or that of their relatives.[7]

Nevertheless, the fact that some degree of Afro-American entrepreneurship has been documented as existing during slavery is testimony to the fact that this form of capitalism is able to exist under the most extreme conditions.[8] But it was also difficult for free Afro-Americans to engage in business because they actually had only a half-free status. The fear of being captured and enslaved was always with them. Wherever they resided, states passed laws to restrict their movement, and thus, their possible business success:

> There was a mass of legislation designed to ensure the white community against threats and dangers from the free Negroes. Virginia, Maryland, and North Carolina were among the states forbidding free Negroes to possess to carry arms without a license. . . By 1835 the right of assembly had been taken away from all free Negroes in the South . . . Benevolent societies and similar organizations were not allowed to convene. . . A number of proscriptions made it especially difficult for free Negroes to make a living.[9]

This kind of governmental restrictions continued to mitigate the development of Afro-American business as the country developed; but despite these hardships, wherever there were free Afro-Americans, a business tradition was developed. Because historical Afro-American scholars studied this development, we have excellent documentation of its existence.[10]

In the North, Pennsylvania was one of the early states to witness the development of Afro-American business enterprise. This is not surprising since, in 1780, this state was the first to emancipate slaves by legislative action. In 1838, a pamphlet, perhaps the first of its kind, was published. Entitled "A Register of Trades of Colored People in the City of Philadelphia and Districts," it listed 656 persons engaged in fifty-seven different occupations.[11] In that year, there were eight Afro-American bakers, twenty-three blacksmiths, three brass founders, fifteen cabinetmakers and carpenters, and five confectioners. There were also two caulkers, two chair bottomers, and fifteen tailoring enterprises. The register also lists thirty-one tanners, five weavers, and six wheelwrights.[12]

The business register of 1838 also listed the businesses which were independently run by women of Afro-American descent. There were eighty-one dressmakers and tailoresses, four dyers and scourers, two fullers, and two glass or paper makers. As noted by Minton in his review of the register, hairdressers were greater in number than any other occupation, and their enterprises were very lucrative:

When I noted in this directory that there were ninety-eight Hair Dressers, greater than any other classification, I felt that here it was that we should stop and consider. And when I note under it such names as those of Thomas Bowers, David Bowser, John P. Burr, and ...James Needham, I felt that we can but realize that at that time, as well as for many years afterwards, this was a business which the colored man controlled. That it was a business which was lucrative and one in which many laid the foundation of fortunes is indisputable.[13]

Another profitable business controlled by Afro-Americans in Philadelphia in the 1820s and 1830s was that of sail making. Nineteen were recorded in the business register of 1838. Indeed, sail making provided the foundation for one of the most successful Afro-American entrepreneurs in the period prior to the Civil War. James Forten, who lived between 1766 and 1841, ran a major manufacturing firm that made sails and, in 1829, employed some forty black and white employees.[14]

Matching Forten's entrepreneurial spirit in Philadelphia in manufacturing was Stephen Smith, who lived between 1796 and 1873. Smith was a lumber merchant who, by the 1850s, was grossing over $100,000 annually in sales, a sum which was viewed as the magic number that earned one the status of *wealthy*. In fact, when Moses Beach published, between 1842 and 1855, a series of twelve handbooks about New York's wealthy citizens, he set $100,000 as the lower limit of wealth.[15] By 1864, Smith's net worth was placed at $500,000. An indication of his wealth and race can be seen by the fact that, in an 1857 credit entry, he was described as the "King of the Darkies w. 100m."

Although several individuals succeeded in manufacturing trades, the business which brought prosperity to the largest number of Afro-Americans in Philadelphia was catering. Robert Bogle, a black waiter, conceived the idea of contracting formal dinners for those who entertained in their homes. Catering spread rapidly across the newly developing country, but it was in the city of its birth that it was king.

The catering business has been intimately linked with the history of Philadelphia from the earliest times down even to today [1913]. No other city in America has been so famed for its efficient and successful caterers as this, whose patronage was not confined by any municipal, state or even national borders. Those men before the Civil War brought such fame to Philadelphia are probably more easily recalled to mind than any other class of business men who lived in this community. One of the first of these was Peter Augustine, who came from the West Indies and started business on 3rd Street above Spruce in 1816. His fame was world-wide, often sending his terrapin as far as Paris. Augustine and Baptist of today are his successors, furnishing a remarkable example of the continuance of one business by one family for but a few years than a century. . . . Among others of the old guild of caterers was Thomas J. Dorsey, who achieved fame and fortune in his art.[16]

Robert Bogle, the founder of this business, was honored for his entrepreneurship ideas by Nicholas Biddle, the leading financier of Philadelphia at the time and President of the Bank of the United States. He honored him by writing an "Ode to Bogle" in 1829. Bogle died eight years later in 1837.

The historical record of the material progress of blacks in Philadelphia is also documented in the pamphlet. "They owned fifteen meeting houses and burial grounds adjacent, and one public hall. Their real estate holdings were estimated at $600,000 and their personal property at more than $667,000 dollars."[17] But, this was all accomplished within an atmosphere which had elements of racial hostility.

There are records which show that, as early as 1789, Afro-Americans found it difficult to borrow money in order to establish business establishments. Nevertheless, through hard work and thrift, many were able to do so. For example, it is recorded that in 1771, Sara Noblitt was refused a license to keep a public house.[18] In addition to service businesses, there were also those engaged in entertainment. The Walnut Street Theatre was opened in 1808 and served as one of the focal points for "night life" in the city.[19]

We may pause to note here that most of the businesses discussed were in the service area. This is one of the major points of middleman theory. Middleman minorities are seen as developing an economic niche by concentrating on small enterprises. But this fact was established by Abram Harris as early as 1936 in his study of *The Negro As Capitalist*, some forty years before the development of middleman theory.

> In personal service enterprises the free Negroes had practically no competition. . . . And the fact that white persons tended to avoid enterprises of this character because of their servile status gave free Negroes an advantage in this sphere. Hence, personal service occupations were open freely to black enterprisers and constituted a source of considerable income. Their success in these lines has been looked upon as a shrewd capitalization of social proscription. A second important advantage offered by personal service was the small amount of capital required to begin businesses.[20]

In order to generate capital, blacks organized for mutual assistance. These mutual-aid societies were a combination of secular fund raising and religious ceremonies. There was also an element of insurance attached to these societies. Philadelphia was the setting for one of the first of these mutual-aid societies.

It was founded by Richard Allen and Absolom Jones in 1778. After ten years of operation, the treasurer reported that daily applications for membership were being received and the balance was "L42,9s.ld." By 1813, Philadelphia sported eleven benevolent societies, and, by 1838, this number had increased to one hundred with a total membership of 7,448. During this same year,societies in Philadelphia had taken in $18,851 and expended $14,172. Their primary responsibility was mutual improvement and assistance. There is no doubt that part of this assistance was to help to develop business enterprises in the city of Philadelphia during this period.[21]

But in addition to mutual-aid societies, and because of the success of many Afro-Americans, there was a trade in money lending. Abram Harris summarizes this important business venture in his seminal work entitled *The Negro As Capitalist*.

> Closely paralleling the development of mutual aid associations, a beginning was made in banking and money lending. The first dealers in money and credit were individual money lenders who were regularly engaged in other pursuits as the chief source of income. Surpluses accumulated from these sources were lent at interest. In Berne, North Carolina, John C. Stanley, a barber by trade, and also a farmer and slaveholder, made a small fortune by discounting notes. His backers were white men in the town who shunned the social stigma attached to sharp practices. Stanley amassed property worth more than $40,000. . . . In Philadelphia, Joseph Cassey conducted a profitable money-lending business for many years prior to 1852. At his death he left an unencumbered estate of $75,000. Stephen Smith, the lumber merchant of Columbia, Pennsylvania, also engaged in private money lending. From this and other ventures he amassed property amounting to a half million dollars. In New York City, Peter Van Dyke accumulated a fortune of $50,000, a considerable amount of which was gained from lending money at interest. In New Orleans, [in the 1840s] there were eight free Negro brokers who speculated in cotton futures and, at times, performed many of the services of the commercial bank. The richest of them, Lafon and Recaud, were not professional financiers in the strictest sense of the term. Recaud was primarily a planter who had a subordinate interest in real estate and money lending. Thomas Lafon was first of all a merchant, but one who conducted a real estate and money lending business. His business career began sometime before the [Civil] War and continued for many years after. At his death, his estate was assessed at a half million dollars.[22]

It should be pointed out that, although free black entrepreneurs engaged in money lending, it was very difficult for them to invest their money. The developing large Euro-American banks (which accepted money from people of European descent despite ethnicity) and home building associations denied Afro-Americans the opportunity to become investors. For instance, a Maryland Act of 1852, based simply on racial discrimination, was designed to limit Afro-American investments.

Additionally, Afro-Americans experienced especially strong racial discrimination when it came to dealing with brokers. During this time period, blacks were not allowed to deal in the stock market.[23] Given the history of capital accumulation by Afro-Americans, it is surprising that the literature on the sociology of ethnic enterprise has not recognized this strong tradition. One wonders how Ivan Light could write, in *Ethnic Enterprise in America*, "The single most prominent argument advanced to explain the black American's underrepresentation in small business has fastened on his special difficulty in securing business loans from lenders, especially from banks. This explanation is 200 years old."[24]

Also given the massive historical data on Afro-American business during the period before the Civil War, one wonders how Light could note that "there is a very old tradition of successful Negro businessmen in the United States. This tradition is, to be sure, one of successful individuals, rather than one based on collective experience."[25] Instead of analyzing the collective efforts of Afro-American businesses, and giving them significant praise, Light concentrates on the rotating credit system of various ethnic groups. This primitive system does not compare with the efforts of capitalization by free Afro-Americans during the late 1700s and 1800s.

The fact that free Afro-Americans as a group developed enterprises in the North can be seen throughout this time period in a variety of locations. In addition to Philadelphia, Cincinnati was the center of enterprise for the free black population of the Middle West. In 1835, this city's black population was 2,500. Of these, 1,195 or about 48 percent had been slaves. But, by 1840, the free blacks had accumulated, not including personal and church property valued at $19,000, a total of $209,000 in real property. By 1852, their property holdings had increased to more than half a million dollars.

> Of a population of 3,500 at the time, 200 were owners of real estate. . . . There were . . . 300 Negroes in Cleveland in 1895, 20 of whom owned real estate valued at $36,000. Eight years prior to this date, 1837, Columbus had twenty-three free Negroes whose real estate investments amounted to $17,000, while that of twenty Negroes living in Lancaster amounted to $17,000 in 1840.[26]

The free Blacks also dominated the restaurant business before the Civil War. They were famous for their ability to prepare a meal and serve it in the "right" way. Their clientele in the North were leading white citizens. In 1769,

Emanuel, an emancipated slave, established the first oyster-and-ale house in Providence, Rhode Island. In 1800, Thomas Downing opened a restaurant near Wall Street in New York. He was successful for thirty years at this location, serving members of New York's professional and commercial classes. George Bell and George Alexander also operated a successful restaurant business near Wall Street.[27] Throughout the North, the restaurant business was a significant source of income for Afro-American business people.

Taken as a whole, however, the largest industrial undertakings in which Afro-Americans participated were related to manufacturing and building. Fascinating narratives are part and parcel of this neglected history of Afro-American enterprise. Typical of the rise to business prominence was Henry Boyd. His story is worth recounting because it exemplifies some of the key issues in the struggle of Afro-Americans to capitalize a business—racial cooperation, business success, and the reality of racism.

> Boyd was born a slave in Kentucky on May 14, 1802. He was bound out to a master from whom he learned cabinet making. In 1826 he settled in Cincinnati, hoping to obtain employment in one of the shops of that city. Unable to find employment because of the restrictions of the workingmen's associations and the prejudices of the community, he hired himself out as a stevedore on the river front. Here he worked for four months and later found work as a carpenter. After six months he formed a partnership with a white man whose duty apparently was to obtain the work that his Negro partner was to do. In this way they successfully avoided the barrier which Boyd had originally encountered as an independent job-seeker. With the savings from this venture Boyd was able in 1836 to practice his own craft as a master cabinet maker and woodworker. He began to make bedsteads on a small scale. Within six years he enlarged his plant and erected a building at Eight and Broadway and began to manufacture all kinds of furniture. At the height of his trade Boyd hired from twenty to fifty black and white workmen. His factory was equipped with improved machinery and the Boyd Bedstead had a national market. Boyd also invented a machine for turning the rails of a bed, but failed to obtain a patent for it. His success aroused the antagonism of his fellow townsmen and they burned him out four times. Three times he rebuilt, but the fourth blaze compelled him to yield since insurance companies refused to underwrite his risk.[28]

The experiences of Henry Boyd are more than interesting. They alert us to a very important aspect of competition within the American business world—namely, the tendency of Euro-Americans to view significant profits in an enterprise to be reserved for themselves. Their reaction to Boyd's success repeats itself systematically in the literature on race and business experience.

In the South, free blacks also built a business tradition despite the presence of slavery. Since slavery represented the grounds for sources of income, some free Afro-Americans engaged in it in order to run plantations. In 1830, there were 3,777 slave owners in America who were black. The state of Louisiana, which had large numbers of free blacks, was one of the places where Afro-Americans generated economic stability that resulted from slavery.

> In Louisiana there were large numbers of wealthy colored families many of whom owned plantations and slaves. . . . Recaud, head of one of these families, purchased in 1851 an estate in Iberville Parish stocked with ninety-one slaves. Marie Metoyer of Natchitoches Parish left an estate of two thousand acres of land and fifty-eight slaves in 1840. Charles Rogues of the same parish left forty-seven slaves and a thousand acres at his death in 1854, and Martin Donate of Saint Landry owned his wife and seven children at his death in 1848, and also eighty-nine other slaves, 4,500 acres of land, and notes and mortgages valued at $46,000. Nowhere in America was there a black planter aristocracy comparable with that of Louisiana. However, there had been in Saint Paul's Parish, South Carolina, a black planter who was reported before the close of the eighteenth century to have two hundred slaves, as well as a white wife and son-in-law and the returns of the first federal census appear to corroborate it. Such persons were also to be found infrequently in North Carolina, Virginia and Maryland.[29]

In addition to wealthy families, the state of Louisiana had the largest number of successful businessmen during this period, and they were involved in almost all phases of business activity. One of the most successful was Pierre Andre Destrac Cazenave, a merchant and commission broker. Between 1850 and 1857, he increased his income from $100,000 to $400,000.[30]

Another of the most interesting entrepreneurs in Louisiana was Madame Cecee McCarty, who made her money in merchandising. Once a slave herself, she owned, by 1830, more than thirty slaves. She purchased goods from importers, and her slaves served as a sales force. They were assigned territories outside New Orleans in rural parishes. In Plaquemines Parish, she owned a depot that provided a base for the sale of goods outside her New Orleans territory. By 1848, she was worth more than $155,000.[31]

But it was in the skilled trades that free southern blacks established themselves as businessmen in the South. While Afro-Americans were denied the possibilities of formal education—which was also true of the great majority of white southerners—the slaves' main work was confined to agriculture on the plantations, and they were forced to accomplish all other tasks for their master. Therefore, every type of craft was open to a slave. He learned trades and crafts so that masters would not have to pay white labor to perform certain duties.

As Kinzer and Sagarin note, "The Negro in the South was not only proficient as a carpenter, blacksmith, shoemaker, barber, tailor, and cook, but as a result of almost two and a half centuries of slavery, up to the outbreak of the Civil War, the knowledge of these skills was concentrated almost exclusively in the hands of the Negroes, free and slave."[32]

One of the interesting comments made on the development of Afro-American business in general, and this time period in particular, concerns the idea that they did not have the skills to run a business. As has been pointed out, a knowledge of reading and writing was not needed by businessmen during this time period:

> ... A knowledge of reading, writing, and elementary arithmetic was not as important to the conduct of a small business a century ago as it would be today [1950]. If one were able to count the money, and knew how to give the proper change, the mathematics problem was frequently solved. Few of the smaller businessmen, Negro or white, kept books or records of any kind to aid them in the conduct of their businesses.[33]

In North Carolina there was a free black boat builder who employed both white and black labor in his plant. In the state of South Carolina, two mulattos owned one of the finest factories for the manufacture of agricultural machinery, and Anthony Weston was a famous millwright for thirty years prior to the Civil War. His wealth was generated by perfecting a thrashing machine. In Alabama, the most enterprising black contractor and bridge builder was deemed so essential to the welfare of the state that the Legislature passed a special enactment to allow him to practice his business unmolested.[34]

Further south in New Orleans, in 1852, a Mr. Cordovall was the leading mercer and tailor, and the styles created by him were very popular among the white elite. Albert and Freeman Morris were respected tailors in New Berne, North Carolina. An interesting story is that of Robert Gordon, who began in the South but ended up in Cincinnati. Gordon's story is worth putting into narrative form because it captures the spirit of entrepreneurship among free Afro-Americans before the Civil War:

> As a slave in Richmond, Virginia, Gordon had charge of his master's coal yard. He was given the privilege of keeping the profits from the sale of coal slack. By 1846 he had saved several thousand dollars. He purchased his freedom and moved to Ohio where he invested

$15,000 in a coal yard and built a private dock on the waterfront. White coal merchants attempted to force him to the wall by ruthless price-cutting. Gordon craftily filled all of his orders from his competitors' suppliers by hiring light mulattos to act as his agents. When he retired from business in 1865 he invested his profits in real estate. His fortune passed eventually into the hands of his daughter.[35]

As noted earlier, capitalism allows for entrepreneurship even under extreme conditions such as slavery. Slave entrepreneurs before the Civil War were bondsmen who purchased or hired their own time. They depended on ingenuity, resourcefulness, and business sense in order to run successful enterprises. The profits generated by these enterprises were first utilized to pay slave owners for allowing the slave to hire his own time. Remaining profits were used as venture capital to purchase freedom for family members, friends, and themselves.[36]

Other examples of slave entrepreneurship include Free Frank, a bondsman who, in 1812, hired his own time from his master and developed a saltpeter manufactory in Kentucky. Saltpeter was the major ingredient in the manufacture of gunpowder. As a result of Frank's enterprise, he was able to purchase his wife's freedom in 1817 and his own in 1819, at a total cost of $1,600. Historically, this reflects the fact that the purchase of freedom occurred primarily among slave entrepreneurs. For example, in the state of Ohio in 1839, more than one-third, or 476 of 1,129, Afro-Americans who had been slaves had purchased their freedom for a total amount of $215,522.04. In Philadelphia, in 1847, of the 1,077 former slaves, 275 bought their freedom for $60,000.[37]

Because slaves often ran their owners' businesses, there existed a phenomenon known as *intrapreneurship*. This was when a slave was given decision-making authority in the management of the owner's business in industry, commerce, or agriculture. A spin-off of such an arrangement was, at times, the development by the slave of a separate enterprise. The example of Robert Gordon given above is an excellent example of this process.[38]

The literature on Afro-American entrepreneurship, both slave and free, is systematic testimony to the spirit of enterprise even under troublesome conditions. It is also testimony to the fact that Afro-Americans began early to build a tradition of business enterprise.[39] Although our discussion of Afro-American business before the Civil War merely scratches the surface, it is clear that historical documents show that a very impressive business class evolved wherever there were free Afro-Americans. In the North and South, their clients were interracial. Whenever they became very successful, Euro-Americans tried to disrupt their businesses. There were laws passed by some states which made it very difficult to make their enterprises successful. As suggested by many scholars who studied Afro-American business—ideas that were later included in Bonacich's theory of middleman minorities—"The lines of business in which Negroes met with greatest success were those which whites did not wish to operate. [As can be seen from previous discussion] these were mainly of the labor and service types. Negro barbers, mechanics, artisans, and restaurant and hotel operators could be found in most southern cities."[40] The growth of these businesses was limited by capital and by the fact that the Afro-American market was not strong.

In their analysis of Afro-American business, Kinzer and Sagarin suggest that the following factors were advantageous to Afro-Americans in business during the antebellum period:

1. Widespread knowledge of craftmanship
2. Frequent lack of such knowledge among whites
3. Relatively less significance for literacy and education in the conduct of business
4. Tolerant attitude of southern whites, arising from general contempt for laborers

Kinzer and Sagarin also suggest that the following factors operated against Afro-American business during this time period:

1. Population distribution of slave and free Negroes
2. Slave status of the majority of Negroes
3. Lack of education and business training, and lack of opportunities to obtain such education and training
4. Restrictive laws and customs, and opposition and restrictive activities on the part of Negro leadership
5. Lack of basis for the emergence of national Negro-sponsored banking, insurance, building and loan, or newspaper industries
6. Depressed economic status of free Negroes, involving lack of capital for investment and poverty of market.[41]

The accomplishments of Afro-American businessmen before the Civil War must be appreciated within the context of the economy at that time. When the war for independence ended, the United States was an agricultural nation. As late as 1800, only 4 percent of the population lived in cities with populations of eight thousand or more. When available, capital was invested in land, commerce, shipping, and, of course, slaves. What is now referred to as industrial production was carried on by artisans in small shops. Manufacturing as we know it today was not even a dream. The beginnings of iron and coal mining, iron smelting, and textile making were a developing part of the scene. It was not until 1788 that the first woolen mill was created. Later, in 1791, the cotton mill was developed. Lumbering, flour milling, and ship-building were somewhat more developed, but were carried on in small shops.[42]

The important capitalist factions in the developing nation, or the new American bourgeois, were the Northern merchants and the Southern slaveholders. The larger merchants combined the activities of merchandising, transporting, and banking. The genuine, wage-earning working class was relatively small, consisting mostly of seamen, dockers, day laborers, clerks in government and commerce, and agricultural laborers. As industry developed, even the small town shopkeepers became wage earners.[43]

The significant point is that Afro-American business people were squarely in the tradition of small shops and artisans, but, as entrepreneurs, they were simultaneously involved in almost every major industry during this time period. This was especially true in the North where they exalted in all of the important occupations and formed an impressive and cohesive business class.

This was also a time when the ethnic groups had not begun to migrate to America in significant numbers. Thus, there was hardly any competition from such groups in the field of small enterprises.

II

In addition to the development of business enterprise during this early period, Afro-Americans displayed an active role in the area of inventions. Because they grew up with America, as opposed to coming in massive numbers during waves of migration, they participated in significant numbers in the development of the nation during its early years.

SECTION 8 of the Constitution of the United States notes that "The Congress shall have Power . . . to promote the Progress of Science and useful Arts, by securing for limited Times to Authors and Inventors the exclusive Right to their respective Writings and Discoveries." This constitutional reality gave rise to our copyright and patent laws.[44] Unlike business activity—which has a certain collective sense to it—invention is an art. It is an intellectual activity which requires systematic reason and logic, as well as trial and error. As ideas became inventions and inventions became income, Afro-Americans made significant contributions.

These contributions, however, were made within the face of constant discrimination because of race. As long as there has been an application of an idea to a product, Afro-Americans have had a difficult time securing their patents. Before the Civil War, for example, slaves were not able to secure patents. Therefore, no record exists of the numerous black inventors whose work was stolen by their masters. In addition to the monetary loss, these individuals were robbed of their intellectual credit, and their identity as sentient human beings was stripped.[45] But despite these realities, research in this area reveals that Afro-American inventors made significant contributions.

Lack of formal schooling, the many legal and illegal obstacles, and his isolation from the centers of research and industry, all combined to exclude the Negro from the fields of science and invention. Yet, despite these awesome barriers, many forged ahead and obtained patents for their discoveries and creations. Some are widely in use today: there is the familiar potato chip, invented by the Saratoga chef, Hyram S. Thomas; ice cream, invented in 1832 by Augustus Jackson, a Philadelphia confectioner; the common mop-holder, created by Thomas W. Stewart; and the player piano invented by J. H. Dickinson. . . Many thousands of inventions . . . were lost to whites who affixed their own names to the patent applications. Nevertheless, even the verifiable inventions, also in the thousands, represent a remarkable Negro achievement, individually and collectively, when one considers odds that confronted them.[46]

TABLE 2.4
Afro-American Inventors, 1860–1900

Inventor	Invention	Date of Invention	Patent Number
Allen, C. W.	Self-leveling table	Nov. 1, 1898	612,436
Allen, J. B.	Clothes line support	Dec. 10, 1895	551,105
Ashbourne, A. P.	Process for preparing coconut for domestic use	June 1, 1875	163,962
Bailes, William	Ladder scaffold-support	Aug. 5, 1879	218,154
Bailey, L. C.	Combined truss and bandage	Sept. 25, 1883	285,545
Bailey, L. C.	Folding bed	July 18, 1899	629,286
Beard, A. J.	Rotary engine	July 5, 1892	478,271
Beard, A. J.	Car-coupler	Nov. 23, 1897	594,059
Becket, G. E.	Letter box	Oct. 4, 1892	483,525
Bell, L.	Locomotive smoke stack	May 23, 1871	115,153
Benjamin, M. E. (Miss)	Gong and signal chairs for hotels	July 17, 1888	497,747
Binga, M. W.	Street sprinkling apparatus	July 22, 1879	217,843
Blackburn, A. B.	Railway signal	Jan. 10, 1888	376,362
Blackburn, A. B.	Spring seat for chairs	Apr. 3, 1888	380,420
Blair, Henry	Corn planter	Oct. 24, 1834	*
Blair, Henry	Cotton planter	Aug. 31, 1836	*
Blue, L.	Corn shelling device	May 20, 1884	298,937
Boone, Sarah	Ironing board	Apr. 26, 1892	473,653
Bowman, H. A.	Flag-making equipment	Feb. 23, 1892	469,395
Brooks, C. B.	Street-sweepers	Mar. 17, 1896	556,711
Brown, Henry	Receptacle for storing and preserving papers	Nov. 2, 1886	352,036
Brown, L. F.	Bridle bit	Oct. 25, 1892	484,994
Brown, O. E.	Horseshoe	Aug. 23, 1892	481,271
Brown and Latimer	Water closets for railway cars	Feb. 10, 1874	147,363
Burr, J. A.	Lawn mower	May 9, 1899	624,749
Burr, W. F.	Switching device for railways	Oct. 31, 1899	636,197
Butler, R. A.	Train alarm	June 15, 1897	584,540

TABLE 2.4—*Continued*

Inventor	Invention	Date of Invention	Patent Number
Butts, J. W.	Luggage carrier	Oct. 10, 1899	634,611
Byrd, T. J.	Apparatus for detaching horses from carriages	Mar. 19, 1872	124,790
Carrington, T. A.	Cooking range	July 25, 1876	180,323
Carter, W. C.	Umbrella Stand	Aug. 4, 1885	323,397
Certain, J. M.	Parcel carrier for bicycles	Dec. 26, 1899	639,708
Cherry, M. A.	Velocipede	May 8, 1888	382,351
Church, T. S.	Carpet beating machine	July 29, 1884	302,237
Cook, G.	Automatic fishing device	May 30, 1899	625,829
Coolidge, J. S.	Harness attachment	Nov. 13, 1888	382,351
Cooper, A. R.	Shoemaker's jack	Aug. 22, 1899	631,519
Cralle, A. L.	Ice cream mold	Feb. 2, 1897	576,395
Creamer, H.	Steam feed water trap (six more patents granted)	Mar. 17, 1895	313,854
Cosgrove, W. F.	Automatic stop plug for gas oil pipes	Mar. 17, 1885	313,993
Darkins, J. T.	Ventilation valve	Feb. 19, 1895	534,332
Davis, W. D.	Riding saddles	Oct. 6, 1896	568,939
Davis, W. R., Jr.	Library table	Sept. 24, 1878	208,378
Dickinson, J. H.	Pianola (in Detroit, Michigan)	—— 1899	*
Dorticus, C. J.	Device for applying dye to shoe soles and heels	Mar. 19, 1895	535,820
Dorticus, C. J.	Equipment for embossing photos	Apr. 16, 1895	537,442
Dorticus, C. J.	Photographic print wash	Apr. 23, 1895	537,968
Downing, P. B.	Electric switch for railroads	June 17, 1890	430,118
Elkins, T.	Refrigerating apparatus	Nov. 4, 1879	221,222
Evans, J. H.	Convertible settees	Oct. 5, 1897	591,095
Falkner, H.	Ventilated shoe	Apr. 29, 1890	426,495
Ferrell, F. J.	Steam trap (8 valves patented between 1890 and 1893)	Feb. 11, 1890	420,993
Fisher, D. A.	Joiners' clamp	Apr. 20, 1875	162,281
Fisher, D. A.	Furniture castor	Mar. 14, 1876	174,794
Goode, Sarah E.	Folding cabinet bed	July 14, 1885	322,177
Grant, G. F.	Golf tee	Dec. 12, 1899	638,920
Gray, R. H.	Baling Press	Aug. 28, 1894	525,203
Gregory, J.	Motor	Aug. 26, 1887	361,937
Gunn, S. W.	Boot or shoe cutter	Jan. 16, 1900	641,642
Hammonds, J. F.	Apparatus for holding yarn skeins	Dec. 15, 1896	573,985
Harding, F. H.	Extension banquet table	Nov. 22, 1898	614,468
Hawkins, J.	Gridiron	Mar. 26, 1845	3,973
Headen, M.	Foot power hammer	Oct. 5, 1886	350,363
Hearness, R.	Sealing attachment for bottles	Feb. 15, 1898	598,929
Hilyer, A. F.	Water evaporator attachment for hot air registers	Aug. 26, 1890	435,095
Hunter, J. H.	Portable weighing scales	Nov. 3, 1896	570,553
Hyde, R. N.	Composition for cleaning and preserving carpets	Nov. 6, 1888	329,205
Jackson, B. F.	Heating apparatus	Mar. 1, 1898	599,985
Jackson, B. F.	Gas burner	Apr. 4, 1899	622,482

TABLE 2.4—*Continued*

Inventor	Invention	Date of Invention	Patent Number
Jackson, W. H.	Railway switch	Mar. 9, 1897	578,641
Jackson, W. H.	Automatic locking switch	Aug. 23, 1898	603,436
Johnson, D.	Grass receivers for lawn mowers	June 19, 1890	429,629
Johnson, I. R.	Bicycle frame	Oct. 10, 1899	634,823
Johnson, W.	Velocipede	June 20, 1899	627,335
Johnson W.	Egg beater	Feb. 5, 1884	292,821
Johnson W. H.	Overcoming dead centers	Feb. 4, 1986	554,223
Jones and Long	Caps for bottles	Sept. 13, 1898	610,715
Joyce, J. A.	Ore bucket	Apr. 26, 1898	603,143
Latimer, L. H.	Manufacturing carbons	June 17, 1882	252,386
Latimer, L. H.	Apparatus for cooling and disinfecting	Jan. 12, 1886	334,078
Lavslette, W. A.	Printing press variation	Sept. 17, 1878	208,208
Lee, H.	Animal trap	Feb. 12, 1867	61,941
Lee, J.	Bread crumbing machine	June 4, 1895	540,553
Leslie, F. W.	Envelope seal	Sept. 21, 1897	590,325
Lewis, A. L.	Window cleaner	Sept. 27, 1892	483,359
Lewis, E. R.	Spring gun	May 3, 1887	362,096
Linden, H.	Piano truck	Sept. 8, 1891	459,365
Love, J. L.	Pencil sharpener	Nov. 23, 1897	594,114
Marshall, T. J.	Fire extinguisher variation	May 26, 1872	125,063
Marshall, W.	Grain binder	May 11, 1886	341,599
Martin, W. A.	Lock	July 23, 1889	407,738
Matzeliger, J. E.	Nailing machine	Feb. 25, 1896	421,954
Matzeliger, J. E.	Lasting machine	Sept. 22, 1891	459,899
McCoy, E.	Lubricator for steam engines (plus 26 other inventions for lubricators, lawn sprinklers, ironing tables, and drip cups)	July 2, 1872	129,843
McCree, D.	Portable fire escape	Nov. 11, 1890	440,322
Miles, A.	Elevator	Oct. 11, 1887	371,207
Mitchell, J. M.	Cheek row planter	Jan. 16, 1900	641,462
Murray, G. W.	Cotton chopper (plus 5 other inventions involving fertilizer distributors, planters, and reapers)	June 5, 1894	520,888
Newson, S.	Oil heater or cooker	May 22, 1894	520,188
Nichols and Latimer	Electric lamp variation	Sept. 13, 1881	247,097
Nickerson, W. J.	Mandolin and guitar attachment for pianos	June 27, 1899	627,739
O'Connor and Turner	Alarm for boilers	Aug. 25, 1896	566,612
Outlaw, J. W.	Horseshoes	Nov. 15, 1898	614,273
Phelps, W. H.	Apparatus for washing vehicles	Mar. 23, 1897	579,242
Pickering, J. F.	Air ship	Feb. 20, 1900	643,975
Pickett, H.	Scaffold	June 30, 1874	152,511
Purdy and Sagwar	Folding chair	June 11, 1889	405,117

TABLE 2.4—*Continued*

Inventor	Invention	Date of Invention	Patent Number
Purvis, W.	Fountain pen (additional patents for bag fastener, hand stamp, electric railway improvement and switch, magnetic railway car balancing device, and 10 patents between 1884 and 1894 for bag machines)	Jan. 7, 1890	419,065
Queen, W.	Guard for ship's companion ways and hatches	Aug. 18, 1891	458,131
Ray, L. P.	Dust pan	Aug. 3, 1897	587,607
Reed, J. W.	Dough kneader and roller	Sept. 23, 1884	305,474
Reynolds, H. H.	Safety gate for bridges	Oct. 7, 1890	437,937
Reynolds, R. R.	Non-refillable bottle	May 2, 1899	624,092
Rhodes, J. B.	Water closets	Dec. 19, 1899	639,290
Richardson, A. C.	Churn (additional patents for casket lowering device, insect killer, and bottle)	Feb. 17, 1891	445,470
Richardson, W. H.	Cotton chopper	June 1, 1886	343,140
Richardson, W. H.	Child's carriage	June 18, 1889	405,559
Rickman, A. L.	Overshoe	Feb. 8, 1898	598,816
Robinson, E. R.	Electric railway trolley	Sept. 19, 1893	505,370
Robinson, J. H.	Life saving guards for locomotives	Mar. 14, 1899	621,143
Robinson, J.	Dinner pail	Feb. 1, 1887	356,852
Sampson, G. T.	Clothes drier	June 7, 1892	476,416
Scottron, S. R.	Curtain rod	Aug. 30, 1892	481,720
Smith, J. W.	Lawn sprinkler	May 4, 1897	581,785
Smith, P. D.	Potato digger	Jan. 21, 1891	445,206
Spears, H.	Portable shield for infantry	Dec. 27, 1887	110,599
Standard, J.	Oil stove	Oct. 25, 1889	413,689
Standard J.	Refrigerator	July 14, 1891	455,891
Stewart and Johnson	Metal bending machine	Dec. 27, 1887	375,512
Stewart, E. W.	Punching machine	May 3, 1887	362,190
Stewart, T. W.	Mop	June 13, 1893	499,402
Sutton, E. H.	Cotton cultivator	Apr. 7, 1874	149,543
Sweeting, J. A.	Device for rolling cigarettes	Nov. 30, 1897	594,501
Taylor, B. H.	Rotary engine	Apr. 23, 1878	208,888
Thomas, S. E.	Waste trap (additional patents for casting, pipe connections, water trap for basins, etc.)	Oct. 16, 1883	286,746
Toliver, George	Propeller for vessels	Apr. 28, 1891	451,086
Tregoining and Latimer	Globe supporter for electric lamps	Mar. 21, 1882	255,212
Walker, Peter	Machine for cleaning seed cotton	Feb. 16, 1897	577,153
Washington, Wade	Corn husking machine	Aug. 14, 1883	288,173
Watts, J. R.	Bracket for miner's lamp	Mar. 7, 1893	493,137
White, J. T.	Lemon squeezer	Dec. 8, 1896	572,849

TABLE 2.4—*Continued*

Inventor	Invention	Date of Invention	Patent Number
Winn, Frank	Direct acting steam engine	Dec. 4, 1888	394,047
Winters, J. R.	Fire escape ladder	May 7, 1878	203,517
Woods, G. T.	Steam boiler furnace (22 additional patents for electricity and railway devices)	June 3, 1884	299,894

Source: Henry D. Spaulding, *Encyclopedia of Black Folklore*. New York: Middle Village Jonathan David Publishers, 1972. 417.

*Data Not Available

Aaron Klein calls Afro-American scientists and inventors in America hidden contributors.[47] Table 2.4 presents only a partial listing of known patents held by Afro-American inventors. Inventions include the locomotive smoke stack, the railway signal, the street sprinkling apparatus, the lawn mower, golf tee, and ice cream. Stories of Afro-American scientists and inventors are just as interesting as those of their counterparts in the business world; indeed, they are stories of personal triumph within a harsh, discriminating environment. While it is not our purpose to develop a major thesis on Afro-American inventors, a review of the accomplishments of a few of these men and women will afford the reader a glimpse of the significance of their roles.

One of the earliest Afro-American scientists was Benjamin Banneker. Born in 1731, he attended school in the colonies until he was fifteen. Reading every book available, he developed an interest in mathematics, astronomy, and other sciences. Before the American Revolution, there was little scientific activity in the colonies. All of the support for scientific activity was located in European governments. Euro-Americans, inventors such as Benjamin Franklin and David Rittenhouse (creator of the first telescope in America), had the opportunity to travel to Europe in order to share intellectual ideas. In the early 1700s, the American Philosophical Society was founded as a scientific society in Philadelphia. But, with the exception of the work of Franklin, European scientists did not feel that individuals in their colonies could make any contributions to science.[48]

Banneker's first application of his scientific knowledge revolved around the making of a clock. His idea for making a clock came from his first contact with a watch. He studied the workings of the watch and decided that he would utilize it as a model for making a clock. The few clocks that existed in the colonies had been imported from Europe or assembled from parts shipped from Europe. Banneker's clock was made entirely from wood. He began around 1758 and completed the job in 1761. Gears had to be carved exactly and put together in the proper balance. When he finished, he had constructed the first completely American-made clock.[49]

News of the unique clock made by Banneker spread throughout the colonies, and it became somewhat of a tourist attraction. He became known for his problem-solving abilities in mathematics and astronomy. He wrote and published significant almanacs which sold well throughout the colonies. But it was his participation in the platting of Washington, D.C., which earned him a place in the history books.

On 12 March 1791, the *Georgetown Weekly Ledger* noted that Andrew Ellicott (Banneker's friend and colleague) had arrived in Georgetown "attended by Benjamin Banneker, Etheopian, whose abilities as surveyor and astronomer already prove that Mr. Jefferson's concluding that the race of men were void of mental endowment was without foundation. The southerner, Jefferson had earlier noted that blacks were inferior to whites in a series of essays entitled *Notes on Virginia*."[50] Thus, even in his glory, Banneker had to fight the idea of racial inferiority. During his leisure time in Washington, he completed an almanac and decided to send a copy of it to Thomas Jefferson, the person who had written the words all men are created equal, but who had also noted that Afro-Americans were biologically inferior. In a letter that is probably the first of its kind, Banneker addressed the issue in a straightforward manner:

Maryland, Baltimore County,
(August 19, 1771)

Sir,

I am fully sensible of the greatness of the freedom I take with you on the present occasion; a liberty which seemed to me scarcely allowable, when I reflected on that distinguished and dignified station in which you stand, and the almost general prejudice and prepossession, which is so prevalent in the world against those of my complexion.

I suppose it is truth too well attested to you, to need a proof here, that we are a race of beings, who have long laboured under the abuse and censure of the world; that we have long been looked upon with an eye of contempt; and that we have long been considered rather as brutish than human, and scarcely capable of mental endowments.

Sir, I hope I may safely admit, in consequence of the report which has reached me, that you are a man less inflexible in sentiments of this nature, than many others; that you are measurably friendly, and well disposed toward us; and that you are willing and ready to lend your aid and assistance to our relief, from those many distresses, and numerous calamities, to which we are reduced.

Now, Sir, if this is founded in truth, I apprehend you will embrace every opportunity, to eradicate that train of absurd and false ideas and opinions, which so generally prevail with respect to us; and that your sentiments are concurrent with mine, which are, that one universal

Father hath given benefit to us all; . . . and endowed us all with the same faculties; and that however variable we may be in society or religion, however diversified in situation or colour, we are all of the same family, and stand in the same relation to Him. . . .

Sir, I freely and cheerfully acknowledge, that I am of the African race, and in that colour which is natural to them, of the deepest dye; and it is under a sense of profound gratitude to the Supreme Ruler of the Universe, that I now confess to you, that I am not under the state of tyrannical thralldom, and inhuman captivity, to which too many of my brethren are doomed, but that I have abundantly tasted to the fruition of those blessings, which proceeded from that free and unequalled liberty with which you are favored . . .

Sir, suffer me to recall to your mind that time, in which the arms and tyranny of the British crown were exerted, with every powerful effort, in order to reduce you to a state of servitude; look back, I entreat you, on the variety of dangers to which you were opposed; reflect on that time, in which every human aid appeared unavailable and you cannot but be led to a serious and grateful sent of your miraculous and providential preservation. . . .

This, Sir, was a time when you clearly saw into the injustice of a state of slavery, and in which you had just apprehensions of the horrors of its condition. It was then that your abhorrence thereof was so excited that you publicly held forth this true and invaluable doctrine; which is worthy to be recorded and remembered in all succeeding ages: "We hold these truths to be self-evident that all men are created equal; that they are endowed by their creator with certain inalienable rights, and that among these are life, liberty, and the pursuit of happiness."

Here was a time, in which your tender feelings for yourselves had engaged you thus, to declare; you were then impressed with proper ideas of the great violator of liberty, and the free possession of those blessings, to which you were entitled by nature, but sir, how pitiable it is to reflect, that although you were so fully convinced of the benevolence of that Father of Mankind, and of His equal and impartial distribution of these rights and privileges, which he hath conferred upon them, that you should at the same time counteract His mercies, in detaining by fraud and violence, so numerous a part of my brethren under groaning captivity, and cruel oppression, that you should at the same time be found guilty of that most criminal act, which you professedly detested in others, with respect to yourselves.

And now, Sir, although my sympathy and affection for my brethren has caused my enlargement thus far, I ardently hope that your candour and generosity will plead with you in my behalf, when I make known to you that it was not originally my design; but having taken up my pen in order to direct to you, as a present, a copy of an Almanac which I have calculated for the succeeding year, I was unexpectedly and unavoidably led thereto.

This calculation is the product of my arduous study, in this my advanced stage of life . . . I have taken the liberty to direct a copy to you which I humbly request you will favorably receive and although you may have the opportunity of perusing it after its publication, yet I desire to send it to you in manuscript previous thereto, thereby you might not only have an earlier inspection, but that you might also view it in my own handwriting.

And now, Sir, I shall conclude, and subscribe myself, with the most profound respect.

Your most obedient humble servant,

Benjamin Banneker [51]

Thomas Jefferson was quite moved by the work of and letter from Banneker. Writing to Marquis de Condorcet, an official of a scientific society who was active in the antislavery movement, he noted:

I am happy to be able to inform you that we have now in the United States a Negro, the son of a black man in Africa and of a black woman born in the United States, who is a very respectable mathematician. I procured him to be employed under one of our chief directors in laying out of the new federal city on the Potomac, & in the interval of his leisure while on the work, he made an Almanac for the next year, which he sent me in his own handwriting, & which I am enclosing to you. I have seen very elegant solutions of Geometrical problems by him. Add to this that he is a worthy and respectable member of society. He is a free man. I shall be delighted to see these instances of moral eminence so multiplied as to prove that the want of talents observed in them is merely the effect of their degraded condition and not proceeding from any difference in the stature of the parts on which intellect depends.[52]

Banneker produced an almanac every year, and they were published until 1787. He also wrote manuscripts on bees and carried out a study of the seventeen-year locust. Indeed, he was the first to note the seventeen-year periodicity of this insect. He also wrote on international affairs. In one of his almanacs, he wrote an essay entitled "A Lasting Peace." The major thesis of the essay was a proposal to establish an organization such as the present United Nations. Banneker died in 1806 and was recognized as a national treasure with a great scientific mind.[53]

The year that Banneker died, Norbert Rillieux was born in New Orleans, Louisiana. He was the son of Vincent Rillieux, a wealthy sugar cane plantation owner, and Constance Vivant, who was his slave. At his birth, his father chose to free him. He joined the large population of people who were called *Creoles, quadroons,* or simply *gens de colour.* In the tradition of Creoles of color, Rillieux attended Catholic schools in the early years and then went to France. There, he studied engineering at L'Ecole Central in the city of Paris. After graduation at the age of twenty-four, he was asked to become a faculty member at L'Ecole Central. During his appointment, he published a number of papers on steam engines and the steam economy. His work was grounded in the ideas and aspirations of what people would later call the Industrial Revolution.[54]

Rillieux never had to slave on sugar plantations, nor did he have to work on what was called the "Jamaica Train," where slaves stood over boiling hot kettles of cane juice, dipping it from kettle to kettle as it became thicker—yet during his days as a professor in Paris, he worked on a way to make that process safer and more efficient.

> He conceived of an idea that would put the steam to better use than making slaves sweat. Rillieux felt that heating the juice in open kettles wasted fuel. The principle that the boiling point of liquids is reduced as the atmosphere pressure is reduced had been established. Rillieux, therefore, proposed that if the cane juice was heated in a partial vacuum in a closed container, it would boil at a lower temperature with a consequent saving of fuel. This idea did not originate with Rillieux, but he carried the concept several steps further. He saw that the steam from one vessel could be used to heat the juice in the next vessel in the series. The device he formulated in his mind consisted of several enclosed vacuum pans connected by pipes that led the juice and steam from one container to the next. Rillieux called his device the multiple effect vacuum pan evaporator. . . .[55]

Rillieux returned to Louisiana and, as a free man, was able to patent his invention.

A few years later, an Attorney General of the United States ruled that, because they were property, slaves could not obtain patents. Inventions of slaves were therefore ruled to be the property of the master just as was any other product of the slave's labor. The ruling came about because one of the slaves of Jefferson Davis invented an improved ship propeller. When Davis attempted to get a patent for his slave, he was denied. When he later became President of the Confederacy, he suggested a clause in the Confederate Constitution noting that masters could take out patents for any inventions of their slaves.[56] This was a crucial ruling, since it was slaves who actually worked as laborers, engineers, builders, and at similar tasks. They were more likely than anyone else to come up with ideas of how to improve an object or develop an invention.

Elijah McCoy was born in 1844 in Colchester, Ontario. His parents had fled to Canada in 1840 when the Fugitive Slave Act was passed after the compromise of 1850. The compromise meant a strict enforcement of the fugitive slave law, which meant that slave catchers could return any black to the South and to slavery. Fearing that they would be returned to the South unjustly, many blacks left the country.[57]

When the Civil War was over, McCoy's family moved back to the States and settled in Ypsilanti, Michigan. He developed an interest in engineering and went to Scotland where he learned mechanical engineering while working as an apprentice. With a skill in hand, he returned to America but was unable to find a job simply because he was black. He was forced to take a menial job as a fireman on the Michigan Central Railroads, where his job was to shovel coal into the firebox and to oil the moving parts of the engine whenever the train came to a stop. At that time, heavy machinery, such as locomotives and those in the factories, had to be shut down in order to be lubricated.

Making the most of his situation, McCoy turned his intellectual energy to the problem of lubricating machines when they were still turned on. In 1872, McCoy applied for his first patent on a device called a lubricating cup. In the application for the patent McCoy described his new invention: ". . . provides for the continuous flow of oil on the gears and other moving parts of a machine in order to keep it lubricated properly and continuously and thereby do away with the necessity of shutting down the machine periodically."[58]

McCoy's ideas became reality as locomotives and other large machinery were soon being lubricated without having to be shut down. In the course of his creative life, he obtained more than fifteen patents. Included among these were a new type of ironing board and the lawn sprinkler.

As Klein notes, most of the people who referred to the "real McCoy" may have been factory owners or railroad owners who discriminated against blacks. They perhaps never knew that, when they insisted on the "real McCoy," they were reconstructing the creativity of an Afro-American.

In 1880, the *American Catholic Tribune*, a nationally distributed newspaper, noted the following:

> Granville T. Woods, the greatest colored inventor of the race and equal, if not superior, to any inventor in the country is destined to revolutionize the mode of the streetcar transit. The results of his experiments are no longer a question of doubt. He had excelled in every possible way in his inventions. He is master of that situation

and this name will be handed down to coming generations as one of the greatest inventors of his time. He has not only elevated himself to the highest position among inventors but he has shown beyond doubt the possibility of a colored man inventing as well as one of any other race.[59]

The newspaper clipping is speaking of Granville T. Woods, the inventor who patented and improved the steam boiler furnace for steam engines. He then turned his interest to problems of an electrical nature.

Alexander Bell was so impressed with Wood's ability that he purchased a device from him which combined the features of the telephone and telegraph.

Woods called the device *telegraphony*, which captured the nature of the entire system. Essentially, the device made it possible for inexperienced operators to send and receive messages at a rate almost as fast as experienced operators working with older equipment could. It could also be used for voice or Morse code transmission. In 1885, Woods obtained a patent for his device, and the Bell Company purchased it for an undisclosed but large sum of money. This purchase created financial independence for Woods.[60]

Woods was also instrumental in improving the operation of electrical streetcars after they were introduced. There was a need for continuous electrical contact with the source of power and the car as it made its turns. Woods made a device that revolved at the end of a pole and extended from the top of the car to the overhead wire. The grooved wheel fit onto the wire and revolved, making continuous contact possible as the car moved along. This grooved wheel was called a *"troller"* or *"trolley."* It was from this device that the name *"trolley car"* was born.[61]

In 1887, Woods invented his most important device. It was called the *multiplex telegraph* or the *induction telegraph system*. Its major use was in the business of railroading in which it improved safety. Woods had to go through three patent suits to protect his rights. Two of these suits were filed by Thomas Edison and the third by an inventor named Phelps. Woods was successful in all three legal actions brought against him. So impressive was his device that an article in the *American Catholic Tribune* called him "the greatest electrician in the world." In 1887, the paper gave a vivid description of Woods's most celebrated device.

Mr. Woods who is the greatest electrician in the world still continues to add to his long list of electrical inventions. The latest device he invented is the synchronous multiplex railway telegraph. By means of this system, the railway despatcher [*sic*] can note the position of any train on the route at a glance. The system also provides for telegraphing to and from the train while in motion. The same lines may also be used for local messages without interference with the regular train signals. The system may also be used for other purposes. In fact, 200 operators may use a single wire at the same time. Although the messages may be passing in opposite directions, they will not conflict with each other. In using the device there is no possibility of collisions between trains as each train can always be informed of the position of the other while in motion. Mr. Woods has all the patent office drawings for these devices as your correspondent witnessed. The patent office has twice declared Mr. Woods prior inventor. The Edison and Phelps Companies are now negotiating a consolidation with the Woods Railway Telegraph Company.[62]

Woods refused to consolidate with Edison. After Woods's legal battle with Edison, he was widely called the "Black Edison." As the *Cincinnati Sun* noted, "Mr. T. Woods, a young colored man of this city has invented a new system of electrical motors for street railroads. He also invented a number of other electrical appliances and the syndicate controlling his inventions think they have found Edison's successor."[63]

Although we cannot consider in depth all Afro-American inventors, their hidden experiences are testimonials to their participation in the art of inventiveness despite the limits imposed by racial discrimination. Their individual accomplishments are testimony to the fortitude of human will.

The 1850s saw the emergence of a high degree of prosperity for America. Although there were political tensions between the North and South, they complemented each other economically. The raw materials for the industrial North were taken from Southern plantations. As Senator Thomas Hart Benton of Missouri noted, "the two halves of this Union were made for each other as much as Adam and Eve."[64]

In the South, cotton was "king." Tobacco and other cash crops also did well. Between 1849 and 1859, the annual yield of cotton soared from 2 million bales to 5.7 million bales. This amounted to seven-eighths of the total world's cotton and more than half of all American exports. But the beneficiaries of this boom were the very small population of Southern planters. In fact, the great majority of white Southerners were very poor and lived in rural areas.

This explains, in part, the fact that all of the southern cities, with the exception of New Orleans, were quite small. Both Richmond and Savannah had populations of less than 40,000, in contrast to New Orleans whose population topped 150,000. The slavery system was firmly intact, and planters felt secure in their Southern way of life.[65]

On the other hand, the North was becoming crowded. The great migration, which was generated by Europeans, was beginning to take shape. In 1850, New York's population increased from 515,000 to 814,000. Chicago, which developed as a sleepy hamlet of 4,170, had 112,000 inhabitants in 1860. By the 1850s, the Irish dominated politics in Boston and the Germans controlled St. Louis and Milwaukee.[66] Although the great migration of Euro-peans would continue in years to come, the Euro-ethnic diversity of America was beginning to take shape.

Although the two sections of America complemented each other, the country was nevertheless divided. The conflict between industrialism and agrarianism, the issue of slavery, and the southern will to protect a way of life led to the Civil War. On December 20, 1860, South Carolina seceded from the Union. Other Southern states followed, and the United States was no longer one nation, under God, and indivisible.

The Civil War struck at the roots of slaveholder power, making Afro-Americans among the strongest supporters of Union troops. Throughout the North, free blacks who had secured a degree of economic stability along with others, responded with enthusiasm to the first call for volunteers. Some left their business enterprises, seeking to help end slavery as a way of life. But when Afro-Americans responded, the Secretary of War said bluntly that "This Department has no intention to call into service any colored soldiers."[67] It was not until after the Emancipation Proclamation that blacks were finally allowed to fight the Southerners who had for so long kept them in bondage. War Department Order G0143 signed on the eve of May 22, 1863, allowed black enlistment for the first time.

Eventually, nearly 200,000 Afro-Americans fought on the Union side and were formed into the separate army units designated as United States Coloured Troops. Their units fought in pivotal battles; individual members of their units won fourteen Congressional Medals of Honor, and played major roles in the liberation of Petersburg and Richmond.[68]

History shows that Afro-American troops took part in more than 198 bat-tles and skirmishes. Although in segregated units, their commanders were white. The logs of these commanders are replete with praise for these soldiers. General Rufus Saxton, noting a campaign in Georgia, stated that Afro-Americans fought with the most determined bravery. Colonel Thomas Wentworth Higgin-son noted that "it would have been madness to attempt with the bravest white troops what he successfully accomplished with black." General Banks, speaking of Afro-American soldiers at the battle of Port Hudson, said that "Their con-duct was heroic; no troops could be more determined or more daring."[69]

The end of the Civil War brought both hope and despair for the new freedmen. The promises of Reconstruction, in which Afro-Americans would engage in politics, send congressmen to Washington, and become governors and senators of Southern States, were replaced with the realities of the black codes as white Southerners engaged in the redemption of the South. Because of the existence of free Afro-Americans during slavery, the group had begun to develop an intellectual class. There were many proposals of what to do with the freedmen, but the clearest program came from Afro-Americans them-selves. Leaders such as Douglas, Langston, Purvis, Wier and Martin had, for years, demanded emancipation, full equality, and land for slaves. These demands were supported by the Afro-American population.

In Nashville in 1865, a convention of Afro-Americans demanded that they be given full rights as citizens and that Tennessee's representatives be barred from Congress unless that state recognized equal rights. Also in the same year, the North Carolina Negro Convention approved the Thirteenth Amendment, recognition of Liberia and Haiti, cash wages for labor, free education for children, a repeal of the black codes, and the endorsement of the radical Republicans. In South Carolina in 1865, the South Carolina Negro Convention demanded the repeal of the black codes, the right to serve on juries and testify in court, the right to the land in the Sea Islands, the right to vote and bear arms, the right of full civil liberties, and free schools. The same types of platforms were drawn up in other Southern states such as Louisiana. Given that Afro-Americans had just emerged from slavery, their conventions are a testimony to their political unity during that time period.[70]

The Reconstruction period, then, represents one of the most interesting periods of race relations. The conflicts between radical Republicans and Democrats, Southerners and carpetbaggers, and the presence of federal troops have been examined systematically by scholars.[71] The hope of Afro-Americans at this time rested on the fact that the South was a conquered people, under military rule. That hope faded in 1877, when Rutherford B. Hayes betrayed the Afro-American people. In exchange for the support of Southerners during his campaign for the presidency, he promised to withdraw federal troops from the South. In 1877, troops were withdrawn only from South Carolina and Louisiana. Hayes never considered the Afro-American people who had been loyal supporters of the Republican party. As noted by Foster, it was a cold-blooded sell-out that was to cause misery and hardship to Afro-Americans and problems for American democracy.[72]

After the compromise, the entire governmental structure was returned to the white South and a system of legal segregation and racism was instituted. By 1890, Afro-Americans in the South had lost all legal and civil rights. In 1833, the Supreme Court held that the Fourteenth Amendment gave Congress the right to stop states, but not individuals, from acts of discrimination. In 1877, in *Hall* v. *deCuir*, the court ruled that a state could not prohibit segregation on a common carrier, and in *Plessy* v. *Ferguson* (1896), "separate but equal" became the law of the land. The pattern of race relations was set for the next one hundred years.[73]

III

The development of a rigid pattern of segregated race relations after the Civil War produced the most significant ideological and practical conflict ever to occur between Afro-American scholars. Afro-American business was shaped by this segregation as scholars debated the future of the group. Within the context of segregation and disenfranchisement, W. E. B. Du Bois saw the complete destruction of democracy and constitutional rights of Afro-Americans. His ideas stressed the importance of the reestablishment of civil rights without regard to race. His platform stressed the right to vote and the intellectual development of the most talented Afro-Americans.

Booker T. Washington also saw these things in segregation and disenfranchisement. But he also saw a captured black market and the possibility of Afro-American economic stability through business development. Because of Washington's compromise on civil rights, most scholarly treatment of his ideas relegate him to the status of "Uncle Tomism." Although his ideas on civil rights were conservative and "Tomish," he laid the foundation for economic nationalism and the analog of today's ethnic enclave theory within the black community. As a matter of fact, there is hardly any idea within the ethnic enclave theory which is not nested within the writings of Washington. Of course, scholars within this tradition do not recognize the contributions of Washington.

The ideas and actions of Washington appear both simple and complex at the same time. As W. E. B. Du Bois noted, the ascendancy of Washington commenced when memories of the Civil War were passing, the days of commercial development were emerging, and a sense of hesitation developed within freedmen. His program emerged at the correct psychological moment; the nation was ashamed of giving so much sentiment to Afro-Americans and was turning to the task of making money.[74] The keystone of Washington's ideas was a triple alliance consisting of the "new South's" white leading class, Afro-Americans, and Northern capitalists. He offered to trade Afro-Americans' demand for equal rights, or the maintenance of segregation, in return for a promise by whites to allow Afro-Americans to share in the economic growth of the South.[75] But this economic growth was designed to take place only in those fields which allowed the freedmen to develop and utilize skills which were developed during slavery. This led Washington to stress the importance of industrial education over higher education.

Given the historical events which made it possible for Washington to become a leader in the South, it is quite ironic that he developed his position on civil rights. In 1880, during reconstruction when Afro-Americans could vote, the people of Macon County, Alabama, utilized their political power to establish an Afro-American school. W. F. Foster, a former Confederate colonel, was a candidate for the Alabama legislature on the Democratic ticket. Needing the Afro-American vote, he went to Lewis Adams, the local Afro-American political leader. He suggested a deal: if Adams would convince his people to vote for him, he would, if elected, push for a state appropriation to create a school for Afro-Americans in that county of Alabama. Foster won and delivered, appropriating the money to create Tuskegee Institute. Adams then wrote to Hampton Institute in Virginia, seeking someone to come to Alabama and start the school. The president of Hampton recommended one of his best professors, Booker T. Washington.[76] Tuskegee Institute was established in 1881.

As Afro-American disenfranchisement spread throughout the South, Washington's voice was hardly heard from Tuskegee. He finally burst upon the national scene in 1895 during the Atlanta Exposition, a showcase for industrial development and inventions. When Washington rose to the platform, he spoke the words which condemned the short-lived political experience of Afro-Americans during reconstruction and hammered home his point:

> . . . [The] opportunity afforded will awaken among us a new era of industrial progress. Ignorant and inexperienced it is not strange that in the first years of our new life we began at the top instead of at the bottom; that a seat in Congress or the state legislature was more sought than real estate or industrial skill; that the political convention or stump speaking had more attractions than starting a dairy farm or truck garden. . . Our greatest danger is that in the great leap from slavery to freedom we may overlook the fact that the masses of us are to live by the productions of our hands, and fail to keep in mind that we shall prosper in proportion as we learn to draw the line between the superficial and substantial. . . . No race can prosper till it learns that there is as much dignity in tilling a field as in writing a poem. *In all things that are purely social we can be separate as the fingers, yet one as the hand in all things essential to mutual progress.*[77]

Washington believed, however, that civil rights would be forthcoming when Afro-Americans developed economic stability.

> The wisest among my race understand that the agitation of questions of social equality is the extremist folly, and that progress in the enjoyment of all the privileges that will come to us must be the result of severe and constant struggle rather than of artificial forcing. No race that has anything to contribute to the markets of the world is long in any degree ostracized. It is important and right that all privileges of law be ours, but it is vastly more important that we be prepared for the exercise of these privileges. The opportunity to earn a dollar in a factory just now is worth infinitely more than the opportunity to spend a dollar in an opera house.[78]

Washington's major goal was to develop a substantial propertied class of Afro-American businessmen and landowners. These "captains of industry," as he envisioned them, would not have to be subordinate to white businessmen in the economy. This belief was based on two key assumptions: (1) since Afro-Americans were not protesting for civil rights, there would be little hostility toward them; and (2) Afro-Americans would be welcomed if their business talents were directed in certain salient areas.

The first assumption has been reiterated in the work of Edna Bonacich on the Japanese. One of the characteristics of middlemen groups is that they pay attention to politics only if issues apply specifically to their community. Although Afro-Americans were forced to give up the ballot and could not pay attention to issues pertaining to their community, Washington incorporated the idea that the group could develop enterprise in areas where whites were not active. This would afford them an economic niche. The following quotation captures Washington's idea that racial conflict, and even prejudice would not exist if Afro-Americans developed business activity within certain economic niches:

> The Negro was also fortunate enough to find that, while his abilities in certain directions were opposed by the white South, in business he was not only undisturbed but even favored and encouraged. I have been repeatedly informed by Negro merchants in the South that they have as many white patrons as black, and the cordial business relations which are almost universal between the races in the South proved . . . *there is little race prejudice in the American dollar*. . . A merchant, unlike a physician, for example, is not patronized because he is white or because he is black; but because he has known how to put brains into his work, to make his store clean and inviting . . . and to foresee and provide the commodities which his patrons are likely to desire. I am convinced that in business a man's mettle is tried as it is not, perhaps, in any other profession. [Italics added][79]

Clearly, Washington drew ideas from the experiences of Afro-American businessmen who had already attained a certain degree of success. Stories of successful businesses run by the free Afro-Americans in both the North and South since the 1700s had been passed down through the decades.

Although many scholars view Washington as the guiding force behind Afro-American business, he simply took an old experience and added an element of national organization. In 1900, he spearheaded the development of the National Negro Business League to encourage enterprise. The league was founded on certain fundamental assumptions which were designed to: (1) generate high character; (2) develop racial respect; (3) develop economic stability; and (4) lay the economic groundwork for future generations.

As noted, Washington was very soft on the generation of "equality" through the political process. Instead, he believed that, if there was a black man who succeeded in business, paid his taxes, and had high character, there would be respect from whites who were also of high character. It is interesting to note that Washington did not link all whites together when he spoke of equality. As a matter of fact, he argued that one of the problems with the South was that poor whites without ingenuity were allowed to participate in the political process. Thus, Washington connected the right to vote, for example, to the ownership of property regardless of a person's race. During the first meeting of the National Negro Business League, the delegates concluded that:

> A useless class is a menace and a danger to any community, and that when an individual produces what the world wants, whether it is a product of hand, heart or head, the world does not long stop to inquire what is the color of the skin of the producer. It was easily seen that if every member of the race should strive to make himself the most indispensable man in his community, and to be successful in business, however humble that business might be, he would contribute much toward smoothing the pathway of his own and future generations.[80]

Washington noted that, as long as Afro-Americans are able to secure an education and employment and are treated with respect in the business or commercial world, then the race problem could be worked out in the South.[81]

In terms of economic stability, Washington's motto was that there is "No Job-Hunting for Those Who Are Able To Do Something Useful." In his writings, he noted that you rarely see a man idle who knows all about house-building, who knows how to draw plans, or how to test the strength of materials that enter into the making of a first-class building. He asks, "Did you ever see such a man out of a job? Did you ever see such a man as that writing letters to this place and that place, applying for work?" He noted that people who can do work well are wanted all over the world; men and women are wanted who understand the preparation of food—not in the small menial sense—but as people who know all about it.[82] Put simply, Washington believed that business activity was the key to economic stability and independence. Racial integration was not as important as the right to establish business enterprises, no matter how small, and to have them be successful.

It is very clear that in his original conceptualization, Washington was banking on an integrated clientele for Afro-American business development. After all, this had been the case for Afro-American business in the pre-Civil War North and South. But the system of complete segregation, which we will call complete governmental control of Afro-Americans, ultimately doomed Washington's economic plans for the south.

It is significant to point out that the system of segregation which was implemented as a program in the South applied exclusively to Afro-

Americans. For Chinese-Americans, Mexican-Americans, Jewish-Americans, or Native Americans, the system did not apply. Thus, in the South and as late as the 1960s, Mexican-Americans did not have to drink, eat, and sleep at segregated fountains or in segregated hotels. This is also true for other ethnic groups such as Italians and Jews who moved into the Southern states.

Although there was conflict based on ethnicity, there were never explicit ethnic programs developed by state governments to control their every movement. This governmental control took away the opportunity for Afro-American business to compete in a truly open market. This is one of the fundamental differences between Afro-American business and ethnic American business. For example, while the Japanese in California were able to develop a white clientele, Afro-Americans were forced to find clients from within their own communities. Such a governmental policy negatively impacted the program which Washington designed for business development in the South. This reality was also taking place in the North. As ethnic groups continued to migrate to America, and as Afro-Americans from the South began to go North, the relationship between Afro-American businessmen and white clients began to change. Most importantly, the strong Afro-American service businesses which had been developing since the 1700s were being replaced with other ethnic businesses.

With regard to this problem, W. E. B. Du Bois in 1888 completed a major study of the city of Philadelphia. His work shows the importance of the impact of business activity on the class structure of the Afro-American community. He distinguished four social classes or grades within Philadelphia. The top 10 percent he called an upper class or aristocracy. These families were primarily entrepreneurs and professional people, native Philadelphians who were descendents from families who had established the service businesses which were discussed earlier. Wives within this class were not labor-force participants, and the children were enrolled in the best schools. This class was, at most, assimilated into the developing middle-class American culture.

The respectable working class made up Du Bois' next group. These were, for the most part, servants (waiters and porters) and laborers. They were ambitious and anxious to accumulate property and engage in upward mobility. The next group, Du Bois termed the poor. It was made up of recent immigrants who could not find steady work, unreliable persons, widows, and wives of broken families. The lowest class—or about 6 percent of the population—Du Bois classified as criminals.[83]

It is very important to point out that the entrepreneur class of Afro-Americans were able to distinguish themselves from other classes within the city. Class has always been a distinguishing feature of American society, especially among Euro-Americans. But it is also true that, in the unpredictable arena of race and ethnic relations, class effects can easily turn into race effects. This is something that scholars of race and ethnic relations have not realized.

Thus, class is not a stagnant variable, but one which can change and interact with a status variable such as race. In Philadelphia, as the racial characteristics of the city began to change, and as immigrant groups began to compete with one another, the old Afro-American business class was doomed to an uncompetitive segregated market. Du Bois described the transformation vividly:

> The new industries attracted the Irish, Germans, and other immigrants; Americans too, were fleeing to the city and soon, to natural race antipathies, were added a determined effort to displace Negro labor—an effort which had the aroused prejudice of many of the better classes; and the poor quality of the new black immigrants to give it aid and comfort. To all this was soon added a problem of crime and poverty. Numerous complaints of petty thefts, housebreaking, and assaults on peaceful citizens were traced to certain classes of Negroes. In vain did the better class protest by public meetings, their condemnation of such crimes. The tide had set against the Negro strongly. . . A mass of poverty-stricken, ignorant fugitives and ill-trained freedmen had rushed to the city, swarmed in the vile slums which the rapidly growing city furnished, and met in social and economic competition equally ignorant but more vigorous foreigners. These foreigners outbid them at work, beat them on the streets, and were able to do this by the prejudice which Negro crime and anti-slavery sentiments had aroused in the city.[84]

Given the development of legal segregation in the South and racial distinctions in the North, the pattern of racial interaction was set for decades to come. While Japanese, Italians, Jews, and other ethnics developed business activities and were free to place their enterprises in the major growth areas of the city (and, of course, in their own neighborhoods) and take full advantage of the free enterprise system, Afro-Americans found themselves limited by law and unable to pursue this simple tenet of free enterprise.

When the first meeting of the Negro Business League was called, the reality of a one-race market was on the agenda. Although Booker T. Washington had called for a concentration on integrated marketing, Fred Moore, the paid organizer for the league, faced reality. When he rose to speak he considered the question of the possibility of whether any kind of Afro-American business success was possible. He said:

> [W]e must . . . require every person who joins a local league to pledge himself to support all worthy enterprises managed by men and women of the race, and when I [find] him doing otherwise I would fire him out of the organization. . . All business enterprises should be

supported. How else can we expect to be respected . . . if we do not
begin to practice what a great many of us preach? How can we otherwise succeed? Some would say that this was drawing the color line.
I do not believe it. Jews support Jews; Germans support Germans;
Italians support Italians until they get strong enough to compete with
their brother in the professions and trades; Negroes should now begin
to support Negroes, . . . The white man . . . would respect Negroes if
they were organized in support of each other and thus, demonstrated
faith in the capacity of the race. Instead of constantly appealing to
whites, Negroes should create their own opportunities. What a
mighty power we shall be when we begin this, and we shall never be
a mighty power until we do begin.[85]

Implicit in the words of Fred Moore are strains of what is called economic
nationalism or the "Buy Black" slogan. Although Moore alluded to the fact
that different ethnic groups turn within during the establishment of business
enterprise, he failed to point out that they also cooperated with each other.
Indeed, different ethnic groups form the basis of what is now called white
America. Although whites could enter ethnic neighborhoods to dine, buy
goods, and the like, in the South it was against both law and custom for Afro-
Americans to do so. Afro-American businessmen throughout the country
resented the fact that governmental regulations in the form of "Jim Crow" laws
in the South and informal segregation in the North excluded them from the
overall market.

IV

It is at this point that we begin to reconstruct the sociology of entrepreneurship. We commence by resurrecting a concept which was developed in the
1930s and appeared in published form in 1940. The concept is that of *economic
detour* and it emerged because of the business activities of those groups which
the theoretical literature refers to as middleman minorities. This term was created by M. S. Stuart, an Afro-American scholar who published a major work
on entrepreneurship.[86]

The idea came at a time when segregation had assumed its most rigid
form, and Stuart was searching for the solution to many of the problems of
Afro-American enterprise. Interestingly, when one juxtaposes Stuart's ideas to
the framework of the sociology of entrepreneurship, one finds that the theory
of economic detour contains elements which are direct criticisms of groups
that are the subject matter of middleman theory. We should recall that middleman groups are those which go from country to country, from city to city,
in pursuit of enterprise development.

The Chinese in Mississippi or the Japanese in California are examples. They often encounter hostility because the host group accuses them of showing no loyalty to the nation or of making money so that they can return it to their homeland. As a result of societal hostility, these groups turn to business enterprise.

Max Weber had also noted this trend among groups which had been oppressed by a nation. Indeed, entrepreneurship is a form of reaction to hostility. But the middleman groups who are discussed in the literature were able to enter the open market and compete. They were able, if possible, to expand their businesses as much as the market and their risks would allow. In short, they were able to find an economic niche in the market and sell their products.

The idea of economic detour is that Afro-Americans, especially in the period following the Civil War, were restricted by law from operating their business enterprises in an open market. The expansion of the economic detour concept into a theoretical construct allows us to reconstruct the framework of the sociology of entrepreneurship and understand the historical problems of Afro-American enterprise.

Let us transform this concept into a theoretical construct. The first element of a theory of economic detour has to do with the fact that the institution of segregation laws, as developed by southern states, represented a governmental program. As such, it involved the interference of government into the normal operation of the marketplace. The policies of the government had a detrimental effect on the development and operation of Afro-American business. In the North, de facto segregation produced the same type of effect as in the South. This must be seen in light of the tremendous business effort that Afro-Americans had developed prior to the Civil War and in light of the entrepreneurship of slaves in bondage. A man-made barrier such as segregation prohibited free commercial intercourse among people.

The next component to the theory is that Afro-Americans were the only group to which this policy of segregation applied. Thus, any ethnic group— albeit developing economic niches in certain enterprises—could feel free to operate in the open market. Other ethnic groups were not restricted to developing a market only among their own people.

As Bonacich and Modell's work on Japanese-Americans shows, the Japanese were able to develop a clientele outside of the Japanese community. Indeed, as noted in that work, when they had to rely on only a Japanese market, they failed considerably.[87] Similarly, it is true that throughout history, when Afro-American business enterprises developed a clientele outside of their community, they were more likely to be successful. This was true of the successful operations in Providence, Rhode Island, by the ex-slave Emanuel in 1769. It was also true of Thomas Downing's eating house near Wall Street in New York which catered to the leading members of New York's professional and commercial classes. Also note the large number of Afro-American saloon keepers, restaurant owners, and caterers who operated in the early 1800s[88] before the influx of ethnic America.

The fact that such a policy applied to Afro-Americans only was enhanced by the reality that the U.S. Department of Commerce recognized a separate Afro-American market. This department released statistical data on the affairs of Afro-American businesses. In 1939, the president of an Afro-American insurance company wrote to the Department of Commerce in order to get information on the business activities of other ethnic groups such as the Japanese, Jews, and Italians. The Bureau of the Census, a part of the Department of Commerce, answered as follows:

> We have received your letter of August 3, requesting information as to whether special releases have been issued relating to retail stores, service establishments, hotels, etc., for any other group of native Americans with the exception of whites and Negroes. These are the only two groups for which we issue statistics of that character.[89]

This indicates that, while other ethnic groups were free to roam the marketplace without governmental control or interference, Afro-Americans were singled out and expected to operate only within their own group.

Segregation has been examined extensively in the literature.[90] However, the major point is that, for Afro-Americans, it was similar to living in a communist society. In addition to basic rights being abridged, there was an element of fear based on the weapons power of the police. As would be the case in the Soviet Union, they were not allowed to travel comfortably in all parts of a city, and they could be picked up and detained without due process. Even more analogous to a communist society, the government told blacks where to drink water, where to sit on the bus, which schools they could attend, which bathrooms they could visit, and which communities they could live in. All of these rules were enforced by law. There was total governmental interference in the lives of Afro-Americans.

Most significantly, it was not until the 1960s that any white person was convicted of a crime against Afro-Americans. Although there have been many attempts to describe segregation, the best analogy is the system of communist societies. Such a segregation policy was disaster for Afro-American business.

The third element of the theory of economic detour is that foreign groups which traveled the free-market world and ended up in America had no service-to-country to their credit.

As noted by Bonacich and Modell, the concept of "the stranger" has been central to the concept of middleman. Stuart's original idea stressed the relationship between service-to-country and enjoying the rewards of that country. This is why, in this work, we mentioned the participation of Afro-Americans in all major conflicts of the nation since the Revolutionary War.

What puzzled Stuart was that, despite the loyalty of Afro-Americans to the country, they were excluded, by policy, from participating in the economic market. Obviously, this was not the wish of Afro-American businesses which sought to develop clientele wherever possible. Stuart captures the essence of his idea of economic detour in the following quotation:

> This [to be excluded from the business market] is not his preference. Yet it seems to be his only recourse. It is an economic detour which no other racial group in this country is required to travel. Any type of foreigner, Oriental or "what not," can usually attract to his business a surviving degree of patronage of the native American. No matter that he may be fresh from foreign shores with no contribution to the national welfare of his credit; no matter that he sends every dollar of his America-earned profit back to his foreign home and uses it to help finance organizations dedicated to the destruction of the government that furnishes him his new golden opportunity; yet he can find a welcome place on the economic broadway to America. But the Negro, despite centuries of unrequited toil to help build and maintain that highway, must turn to a detour that leads he knows not where. Following this doubtful economic trail, he knows that he will have to find most of his customers within his own race in any enterprise he attempts. Yet, within this limited scope, if only he had an even chance at this approximate 9 percent of the population, a not too discouraging field might lay before him.[91]

Thus, Stuart viewed new ethnic businesses, or what the sociology of entrepreneurship calls middleman minorities, as having distinct advantages in a business world from which Afro-Americans were excluded as a result of law and custom. Because of the economic detour, Afro-Americans were forced into the role of consumer. Although Afro-Americans developed businesses, if they could share in the total market, their businesses would increase. But other businesses did not restrict their sales to members of their own groups. The Chinese in Mississippi, the Jews in the South, and the Japanese developed markets outside their own groups. Stuart understood the effects of such a policy.

> . . . that brazen type of American prejudice which in effect says: We will sell to you: we want your money. But we will not employ you to sell to others; we will not even employ you to sell to your own kind. More than that, you and your kind, when you come to buy from the hands of others, may, at any time, expect discourtesies and insults. Moreover, we will send agents of other races into your homes seeking business and there, across your threshold, around your own fireside,

in the presence of loved ones, you may expect the same kind of humil-
iation. *Seeking a way, therefore, to have a chance at the beneficial reaction
of his spent dollars in the form of employment created; seeking a way to
avoid buying insults and assure himself courtesy when he buys the necessities of life; seeking respect, the American Negro has been driven into an
awkward, selfish corner, attempting to operate racial business-to rear a
stepchild economy.*[92]

The theory of economic detour is presented in Table 2.5. Governmental
programs forced Afro-American business people to develop separate enterprises and to sell in a restricted race market. This had the effect of decreasing
the total amount of business activity among Afro-Americans. Other ethnic
groups were free to operate in the larger market, thus, shared an advantage that
Afro-Americans did not. As noted by Bonacich and Modell, the classic middleman minority serves more than its own ethnic community. The primary
clientele for Japanese-Americans prior to World War II, when ethnic solidarity was high because of hostility from the larger society, was the larger white
community.[93] This was done despite the fact that they had no prior history of
service to this country. Afro-Americans, however, were forced into a consumer
role and, as entrepreneurs, were forced to operate under a system of segregation. They were forced to utilize their talents to create a separate economy
because of the economic detour. This model can be applied fully to the Afro-
American business person from after the Civil War to the 1960s. Although in
altered form, it is still applicable today.

When Booker T. Washington stepped into the picture with his overall
plan for business enterprise, he entered into a situation unlike any other in
American society. Certainly he deserves the criticisms he has received from
scholars over the years,[94] but what is interesting is that the major component
of Washington's political ideas, abstaining from politics, is part and parcel of
middleman theory. For example, Bonacich and Modell note that:

> middleman groups are noted for not participating in local politics
> except as they impinge on the affairs of their own groups.... The core
> of the community ... tends to focus its political energies internally
> and to deal with the surrounding polity as a corporate entity, its main
> concern being the way in which that polity is treating the minority.[95]

In effect this means that as long as a group is able to develop economic
security in an open market, political activity is unnecessary. It might even be
said that there is no necessary relationship between political activity and the
development of business activity. As long as a group is able to function in an
open market, economic stability will be forthcoming. This is precisely what
Booker T. Washington had in mind when he argued that the dollar was "color

Societal hostility (North & South)	Enterprises forced to move from central business district
Governmental programs in the form of "Jim Crow laws" are passed in the South*	The development of a one-race market for Afro-American enterprises
	A significant decline in the number of Afro-American enterprises
	Completely removing Afro-American entrepreneurials from the competitive marketplace

TABLE 2.5
Heuristic Model of the Theory of Economic Detour

*Although "Jim Crow" laws were a southern program, as noted in the text, the increasing number of ethnic groups and hostile racial attitudes contributed to an economic detour in the North. Thus, the overall model is not southern specific.

blind." But Washington's ideas could not be put into practice because, although the dollar might have been color blind, the market participation was based on race. Thus, segregation as a program took away both political rights and the right to compete in the marketplace. This is why the theory of economic detour is so important. It helps us to understand the ways in which ethnic and racial groups relate to the overall marketplace. The theory of economic detour argues—and rightly so—that exclusion from the overall marketplace applied only to Afro-Americans.

A neglect of previously cited historical circumstances is the single most important reason why theories in the sociology of entrepreneurship must be reconstructed. Hostility from the host society, which is so much a part of the middleman theory, fades in comparison to being excluded from the overall economic marketplace. Indeed, marketplace exclusion is the most powerful form of hostility in which questions of racial and ethnic discrimination are concerned. As noted earlier, if middleman minorities had been restricted to selling only to members of their own groups, they would certainly have failed in their efforts to create viable enterprises. But, despite the economic detour which Afro-Americans were forced to follow—mainly because of the large percentage of blacks in the South and some northern communities—they were able to develop business activities which created a degree of economic security.

It is very important to realize that the Afro-American business experience, in the tradition of the sociology of entrepreneurship, is a tradition of self-help and small (and in some cases, large) business development. One of the overall tragedies of the literature on race and economics is that it refers to the Afro-American business experience as a failure because it did not develop enterprise which matched those of the larger society. E. Franklin Frazier calls the tremendous efforts of Afro-American entrepreneurs under hostile conditions a "myth." In his *Black Bourgeoisie*, he dedicates an entire chapter to showing that business development by Afro-Americans constituted the major element in a make-believe world that they created.[96] James Boggs pursues a similar line of reasoning when he discusses Afro-American entrepreneurship in "The Myth and Irrationality of Black Capitalism"; Earl Ofari regenerated the theme in a comprehensive way in a book entitled *The Myth of Black Capitalism*, and in *Black Metropolis*, St. Clair Drake and Horace Clayton were somewhat confused and tried to distinguish the myth from the fact as they examined a major American city.[97]

Although these works are interesting, they suffer from a basic methodological flaw—the tendency to compare the Afro-American business experience with that of the larger assimilated business experience and economy. No ethnic group—whether Japanese-Americans, Italian-Americans, Vietnam-Americans, German-Americans, or Mexican-Americans—has ever developed a business tradition which compares with corporate America as a whole. This is true whether you examine the late 1800s and early 1900s, the heyday of European migration, or the present time period which is characterized by studies of recent immigrant groups such as the Cubans and Vietnamese. But all groups have developed economic niches in the business community in order to develop a form of economic security.

All groups have developed self-help agendas, the business experience being only part of the total experience. This can be seen in studies of ethnicity since these immigrant groups began to arrive on the shores of America as well as since the inception of our nation.[98] Afro-Americans also have a strong tradition of self-help but, like that group's business activity, it has been overlooked and tucked under the historical carpet. Why this is so will be explored in a later chapter. This is related to the inability of Afro-American scholars and people in general to be comfortable with the development of an economically secure group within the race. It is also related to the unrealistic use of the Marxist perspective when applied to an understanding of Afro-American history. A reconstruction of race and economics—as with the reconstruction of the sociology of entrepreneurship—means that the experiences of the Afro-American middle class is placed within a comparative perspective of other groups which developed a middle class. As noted at the beginning of this chapter, entrepreneurship activities among groups produce a class structure within those groups. It is the middle class of different groups which is able to provide educational benefits to their children which produce upward mobility in later generations. The masses of all groups have developed economic stability as a result of working in the expanding larger economy. As we continue to reconstruct the sociology of entrepreneurship, race, and economics in general, it is important to have an understanding of the history of Afro-American self-help, and of race and economics in general.

CONCLUSION

The purpose of this chapter has been to reconstruct the sociology of entrepreneurship. Although the literature has overlooked the Afro-American experience, the group has been involved in enterprise since the inception of the nation. Free Afro-Americans in the 1700s and 1800s laid the foundation for the Afro-American business tradition. Even under the system of slavery, there are historical accounts of enterprise by Afro-Americans. In addition to entrepreneurship activities, a system of scholarship developed which analyzed this business activity. Although this literature is systematic and scholarly, what is called the sociology of entrepreneurship has neglected it. This research tradition has not considered the Afro-American experience as germane to an understanding of minority business. A reconstruction of this field, and the resurrection and augmentation of the theory of economic detour, shows that, throughout history, Afro-American business operated in a market atmosphere that was very hostile. They were forced, as was no other group, to operate in a segregated marketplace.

3

"To Seek for Ourselves"

Benevolent, Insurance, and Banking Institutions

The tradition of Afro-American business prior to the Civil War was augmented by a tremendous tradition of self-help institutions. This chapter documents the beginning of self-help among the group as it adjusted to hostility
within America. As has business enterprise, self-help by Afro-Americans has
been overlooked in the literature.

Indeed, the standard procedure among scholars is to treat the Afro-American experience as if it went totally from slavery to freedom to the ghettos of
American cities. But, as with other ethnic groups, Afro-Americans developed
massive efforts of self-help. Also, as did other ethnic groups, the religious institutions played an important role in this process.[1] Religious institutions were
connected to the development of benevolent and insurance societies. The
Afro-American tradition of banking—perhaps the most formal kind of self-
help—is also discussed in this chapter.

As is the case with business activity, the development of Afro-American
self-help must always be viewed in reference to the environment in which the
enterprises operated. Despite the fact that different ethnic groups migrated to
American and had an original period of difficulty, no other racial or ethnic
group (which did not wage war against Europeans) has had to face the total
constitutionally sanctioned exclusion from the larger society that Afro-Americans have experienced. There have never been "German-only," "Irish-only," or
"Italian-only" facilities. Despite the fact that sociologists have drawn interesting parallels between the Afro-American experience and that of European
ethnic groups, the Afro-American experience stands in a different historical
light. Put another way, the most divisive force in America has always been race,
especially as regards black/white relations. Certainly, there were alien land laws

in California that attempted to regulate the life of Japanese immigrants, and Chinese in Mississippi faced certain forms of discrimination. But Europeans have spent a great amount of time excluding Afro-Americans from basic participation in the social and economic sector of America. In an interesting way, this exclusion was not based on divisive activities, such as fighting against them in a war or the nonpatriotic activities of the group.

It is obvious that it was based on differences in phenotype. In an environment that totally shut them out, Afro-Americans placed more emphasis on self-help. This meant creating, almost from scratch, significant institutions which could have a positive effect on the lives of Afro-Americans.

I

The fundamental institution for self-help among Afro-Americans was the church. Beginning with slavery in America, the church traditionally has held center stage. On plantations, formal church services always required the attendance of whites. Slaves, however, held secret services choosing their own ministers and creating their own internal organizations.

These religious gatherings also provided a forum for the discussion of grievances and for the organization of insurrections. After the Nat Turner incident of 1831—which sent shock waves through slave society and feelings of revenge throughout the slave community—some southern legislators developed laws which curtailed the activities of Afro-American preachers and churches.

For example, in Virginia in 1831, a law was passed forbidding Afro-Americans to preach. In Maryland, groups of more than five Afro-Americans were prohibited from meeting together, especially in church. Other slave states passed similar laws. Such historical laws stand as indicators of the importance of the church in the struggle against chattel slavery.[2]

As Afro-Americans began showing more of an interest in Christianity, they sometimes attended white churches. These services served as models for the development of Afro-American churches. In 1871, the Methodist Church of the South officially set aside their black members into the Colored Methodist Episcopal Church, and, in similar fashion, the other Southern churches drove their members into other black churches. But it was in the North, where free Afro-Americans served, that religious independence was created.

In the early 1700s, Afro-Americans were accepted into white congregations of the Methodist Church. But, in the fall of 1787, when George Mason was putting the final touches on the Bill of Rights of the Constitution, Afro-Americans experienced the reality of discrimination and racism within a religious institution in the city of Philadelphia.

A number of us usually attended St. George's Church in Fourth Street; and when the colored people began to get numerous in attending the church, they moved us from the seats we usually sat on, and placed us around the wall, and on Sabbath morning we went to church and the sexton stood at the door, and told us to go in the gallery. He told us to go, and we would see where to sit. We expected to take the seats over the ones we formerly occupied below, not knowing any better. We took those seats. Meeting had begun, and they were nearly done singing, and just as we got to the seats, the elder said, "Let us pray." We had not been long upon our knees before I heard considerable scuffling and low talking. I raised my head up and saw one of the trustees . . . having hold of the Rev. Absalom Jones, pulling him off of his knees, and saying, "You must get up and must not kneel here." Mr. Jones replied, "Wait until prayer is over." Mr. . . . said, "No, you must get up now, or I will call for aid and force you away." Mr. Jones said, "Wait until prayer is over, and I will get up and trouble you no more." With that he beckoned to one of the other trustees, Mr. L-S-, to come to his assistance. He came, and went to William Whit to pull him up. By the time prayer was over, and we all went out of the church in a body, and they were no more plagued with us in the church.[3]

These words were written by Richard Allen who had converted to Methodism in 1777, when he was writing about trials and suffering in the White Methodist Church. Because of this experience, he became one of the founders of the African Methodist Church. Cofounders were Rev. Absalom, mentioned in the quotation, and Peter Williams. It was on this foundation that a tradition of self-help through religion was born. It is interesting to note that by 1909, seven-eighths of the entire Afro-American population were included in self-sustaining, self-governing religious institutions.

Although Allen and others had been treated with disrespect by the White Methodist Church, that same church did not approve in their "going it alone." As Afro-Americans tried to organize the African Methodist Episcopal Church, they encountered tremendous pressures of persecution from the white Methodist community. "We will disown you all," the elder white Methodists shouted again and again. Allen, Jones, and Williams adopted the radical slogan which had been created for the Free African Society, another organization created by Allen in the 1700s. The slogan simply was "To Seek For Ourselves."[4] The church became active in antislavery campaigns, fighting racism in the North, and developing an interest in the importance of education for the Afro-American community. It published *The A.M.E. Review*, the leading magazine among Afro-Americans during that time period, which included articles that stressed economic development, moral development, racial solidarity, and self-

help.[5] Thus, any discussion of self-help among Afro-Americans must begin
with this institution.

Table 3.1 shows the prosperity of the Afro-American Church between
1787 and 1903. Panel I concentrates on members and ministers. Panel II
shows the property held by the church, and its worth, and Panel III indicates
the total income or pastors' support of the church. It can be seen that, between
1787 and 1903, the number of members in the African Methodist Episcopal
church increased from 42 to 759,590. The property value of the church, during
the same time period, increased from $2,500.00 to $9,404,675.00, and
between 1822 and 1903, pastors' support increased from $1,000.00 to
$986,988.96. By 1903, there were 5,831 churches, 2,527 houses for ministers,
and 25 schools. The total value of the property was $9,404,675.00.

TABLE 3.1
Selected Statistics of the African Methodist Episcopal Church

Panel I

Year	Members	Ministers
1787	42	2
1818	6,778	7
1822	9,888	15
1826	7,937	17
1836	7,594	27
1846	16,190	67
1856	19,914	265
1866	73,000	265
1876	206,331	1418
1886	403,550	2857
1888	452,782	3569
1890	466,202	3809
1895	497,327	4125
1896	618,854	4680
1900	663,746	5659
1903	759,590	5838

Panel II

Year	Number of Churches	Valuation of Property	Annual Conferences	Number of Bishops
1787	1	$ 2,500.00	—	—
1816	7	15,000.00	2	1
1826	33	75,000.00	3	1
1836	86	125,000.00	4	2
1846	198	225,000.00	6	4
1856	210	425,000.00	7	6
1866	286	825,000.00	10	3
1876	1833	3,164,911.00	25	6
1886	3394	5,341,889.00	44	7
1888	4009	6,391,577.00	48	10

TABLE 3.1—*Continued*

Panel II

Year	Number of Churches	Valuation of Property	Annual Conferences	Number of Bishops
1890	4069	7,772,284.00	48	9
1896	4850	8,650,000.00	52	9
1900	5775	9,043,391.00	64	9
1903	5831	9,404,675.00	69	13

Panel III

Year	Pastors' Support	Average per Pastor
1822	$ 1,000.00	$ 66.60
1826	1,017.00	63.35
1836	1,126.00	41.70
1846	6,267.00	93.50
1856	18,040.00	109.33
1866	85,593.00	322.99
1876	201,984.96	142.44
1886	583,557.79	204.25
1888	601,785.00	168.61
1890	619,547.00	158.49
1895	682,421.00	141.19
1896	956,875.00	204.00
1900	935,425.58	204.00
1903	986,988.96	168.00

Source: W. E. B. Du Bois, *Economic Co-Operation Among Negroes,* Atlanta, Ga.: The Atlanta University Press, 1907. 57.

TABLE 3.2

Receipts, Extension, Loans, and Donations of the African Methodist Episcopal Church

Panel I

Church Extension Receipts

1892–1893	$4,817.07
1893–1894	11,896.56
1894–1895	11,568.12
1895–1896	12,119.55
1896–1897	14,426.60
1897–1898	17,252.99
1898–1899	15,403.25
1899–1900	17,391.17
Total	$104,875.28

Panel II

	Loans	Donations	Total
1897	$10,407.17	$1,149.48	$11,556.66
1898	11,614.30	719.00	12,433.80
1899	11,150.25	656.98	11,807.23
1900	9,070.96	1,142.83	10,213.79
Total	$42,242.68	$3,668.29	$46,011.48

TABLE 3.2—*Continued*

Panel III
Sunday School Union Receipts

Year

1882–1888	$40,271.72
1888–1892	82,623.26
1892–1896	69,714.62
1896–1900	72,835.42
1900–1902	68,814.05
Total	$334,259.07

Source: W. E. B. Du Bois, *Economic Co-Operation Among Negroes*, Atlanta, Ga.: The Atlanta University Press, 1907. 5.

What is important for our purposes is the relationship between the A.M.E. church and the Afro-American community. In 1892, at the A.M.E. annual conference in Philadelphia, the church organized the Department of Extension. The money coming into this department consisted mostly of savings from church funds that had been previously spent without a definite purpose. Between 1892 and 1900, the church extension increased from $4,817.07 to $17,391.17. Over the years the extension receipts totalled $104,875.28 (Table 3.2). One can also see from Table 3.2 that between 1897 and 1900, the church made $42,242.68 worth of loans. There is no doubt that significant amounts of these loans went to capitalize small enterprises, especially in the northeastern part of the country. Donations and loans totaled more than $45,000.

Perhaps the most lasting tradition started by the A.M.E. Church was the founding of and support of institutions of higher education. Given that Afro-Americans could not attend church services with whites on an equal basis, the founders of the A.M.E. Church reasoned that this would also be true of education. In the tradition of the slogan "to seek for ourselves," universities were founded.

TABLE 3.3
Expenditures for Education, African Methodist Episcopal Church by Years

1847–1903, Union Seminary	$20,000.00
1863–1903, Wilberforce University	440,164.77
1891–1903, Payne Seminary	44,800.00
Total for Wilberforce Plants	$504,964.77
1891–1903, Connectional money	$1,021,558.49
1900–1904, By Endowment	48,000.00
1900–1904, by 8 percent	40,000.00
Total for connectional	$1,109,588.49
Total for education	$1,614,553.26

Source: W. E. B. Du Bois, *Economic Co-Operation Among Negroes*. Atlanta, Ga.: The Atlanta University Press. 1907. 62.

TABLE 3.4

Schools Supported by the African Methodist Episcopal Church by Year Established (if available), Receipts for Four Years, and Other Descriptive Data, 1856–1896

School and Location	Established in Year	Schools	Teachers	Property	Receipts (4 yrs.)
Payne Theological Seminary, Wilberforce, Ohio	1891	37	3	$13,000	$15,360.48
Wilberforce University, Wilberforce, Ohio	1856	311	20	158,000	85,923.23
Morris Brown College, Atlanta, Ga.	1880	350	17	75,000	35,248.69
Kittrell College, Kittrell, N.C.	1896	136	8	30,000	31,372.46
Paul Quinn College, Waco, Tex.	1881	203	8	80,000	28,510.56
Allen University, Columbia, S.C.	1880	285	8	35,000	19,365.05
Western University, Quindan, Kan.	—	90	10	75,000	15,637.53
Edwards College, Jacksonville, Fla.	1883	172	8	25,000	12,873.85
Shorter University, North Little Rock, Ark.	1887	110	4	10,250	11,929.44
Payne University, Selma, Ala.	—	233	9	3,000	5,981.00
Campbell-Stringer College, Jackson, Mo.	—	100	2	10,300	4,272.85
Wayman Institute, Harrodsburg, Ky.	1891	50	1	2,760	2,618.08
Turner Normal Institute, Shelbyville, Tenn.	1887	79	3	3,500	2,030.36
Flagler High School, Marion, S.C.		161	3	1,500	700.00
Delhi Institute, Delhi, La.		57	3	3,000	—
Sisson's High School, South McAlister, I.T.		35	2		322.78
Blue Creek and Muskogee High School, I.T.					
Morsell Institute, Haiti					
Bermuda Institute, Bermuda					
Zion Institute, Sierra Leone, Africa					
Eliza Turner School, Monrovia, Africa					
Cape Town Institute, Cape Town, Africa					

Source: W. E. B. Du Bois, Economic Co-Operation Among Negroes. Atlanta, Ga.: The Atlanta University Press, 1907. 81.

Wilberforce University became the first college owned and operated by Afro-Americans. It grew from the 1863 merger of the Union Seminary, founded by the African Methodist Episcopal Church and a college founded by the Cincinnati Conference of the Methodist Episcopal Church.

Table 3.3 shows the amount of money given to these institutions by the A.M.E. church. Between 1847 and 1904, the church gave more than one million dollars to educational efforts. It also had over a million dollars in connectional or general operating funds. By 1907, the African Methodist Episcopal Church supported twenty-two schools. These schools, including dates of establishment (where available), teachers, properties, and receipts (for four years) are listed in Table 3.4. It is interesting to note that this educational effort by the A.M.E. had an international flavor. In addition to schools established in the United States, there was one in Monrovia, Africa; Cape Town, Africa; Sierra Leone, Africa; Bermuda; and Haiti. The idea of self-help vis-a-vis education was not simply limited to America.

Other churches which were also developing were active in promoting the importance of education. The Colored Methodist Episcopal Church developed five schools. They were Payne College of Augusta, Georgia; Texas College of Tyler, Texas; Lane College of Jackson, Tennessee; Homer Seminary of Homer, Louisiana; and Haygood Seminary of Washington, Arkansas. The African Episcopal Zion Church was also quite active during this period. The schools supported by this institution are listed also in Table 3.5.[6] By 1901, this institution had physical plants which were valued at more than $100,000, had collected in excess of $71,000 per quadrennium, and had 32 teachers and 959 students.

The most extensive educational self-help program, however, was instituted by the Afro-American Baptists. Table 3.6 shows that by 1909, they

TABLE 3.5
School of The African Methodist Episcopal Zion Church, 1901

Name of School	Number of Teachers	Number of Students	Amount Collected per Quadrennium	Vaue of Plant
Livingston College	14	267	$57,193.05	$117,950
Clinton Institute	5	202	3,450.00	5,000
Lancaster Institute	6	277	5,038.00	4,500
Greenville College	3	125	2,705.66	3,000
Hannon and Lomax	2	80	300.00	1,500
Walters Institute	2	72	300.00	1,000
Mobile Institute	—	—	1,500.00	2,000
Jones University	—	—	530.00	—
Money raised by Secretary	—	—	568.00	—
Totals	32	1,023	$71,884.71	

Source: W. E. B. Du Bois, Economic Co-Operation Among Negroes. Atlanta, Ga.: The Atlanta University Press, 1907. 81.

helped to support a total of 107 schools at different educational levels and had established property which was worth more than $600,000. As can be seen from the table, in addition to schools in the United States, the church established five schools in Africa.

Added to this effort were a number of private schools, some supported by churches and others by benevolent societies. By 1907, the total cost to operate these schools (which numbered 74) over a nine-year period was estimated to be $11,537,099. If missing figures were included in the estimate, then it would total to $11,610.00.[7] These are listed in Table 3.7.

TABLE 3.6
Schools Supported by the Afro-American Baptist Church, 1909

States	Institution	Location
Alabama	Baptist University	Selma
	Normal College	Anniston
	Eufaula Academy	Eufaula
	Marion Academy	Marion
	Opelika High School	Opelika
	Thomsonville Academy	Thomsonville
	Stokes Institute	Montgomery
	Autauga Institute	Kingston
Arkansas	Aouchita Academy	Camden
	Baptist College	Little Rock
	Arkadelphia Academy	Arkadelphia
	Brinkley Academy	Brinkley
	Magnolia Academy	Magnolia
	Wynne Normal and Industrial Institute	Wynne
	Southeast Baptist Academy	Dermott
	Fordyce Academy	Fordyce
Florida	Florida Baptist College	Jacksonville
	Florida Institute	Live Oak
	West Florida Baptist Academy	Pensacola
	Institutional Church School	Jacksonville
	Fernandina Bible College	Fernandina
Georgia	Americus Institute	Americus
	Walker Academy	Augusta
	Jeruel Academy	Athens
	Central City College	Macon
Illinois	Southern Illinois Polytechnic Institute	Cairo
	New Livingstone Institute	Metropolis
Indiana	Indiana Colored Baptist Institute	Indianapolis
Indians Territory	Dawes Academy	
	Sango Baptist College	Muskogee
Kansas	Topeka Industrial Institute	Topeka
Kentucky	State University	Louisville
	Cadiz Theological Institute	Cadiz
	Female High School	Frankfort

TABLE 3.6—*Continued*

States	Institution	Location
	Glasgow Normal Institute	Glasgow
	Western College	Weakly
	Hopkinsville College	Hopkinsville
	Eckstein Norton University	Cane Springs
	Polytechnic Institute	Danville
	London District College	London
Louisiana	Baton Rouge Academy	Baton Rouge
	Houma Academy	Houma
	Morgan City Academy	Morgan City
	Howe Institute	New Iberia
	Opelousas Academy	Opelousas
	Central Louisiana Academy	Alexandria
	Cherryville Academy	Cherryville
	Baptist Academy	Lake Providence
	Monroe High School	Monroe
	Ruston Academy	Ruston
	Shreveport Academy	Alexandria
	Mansfield Academy	Mansfield
	North Louisiana Industrial High School	Monroe
	Thirteenth Dist. Nor. and Col. Institute	Shreveport
Maryland	Clayton Williams Institute	Baltimore
Mississippi	Natchez College	Natchez
	Gloster High School	Gloster
	Central College	Kosciusko
	Meridian High School	Meridian
	Ministerial Institute	West Port
	Nettleton High School	Nettleton
	Greenville High School	Greenville
	New Albany High School	New Albany
	Kosciusko Industrial College	Kosciusko
	Baptist Normal and Industrial School	Friar Point
	Springer Academy	Friar Point
Missouri	Western College	Macon
North Carolina	Latta University	Raleigh
	High School	Wakefield
	Shiloh Industrial Institute	Warrenton
	Thomson's Institute	Lumberton
	Addie Norris's Institute	Winston
	Training School	Franklinton
	Roanoke Institute	Elizabeth
	Albermarle Training School	Edenton
	Bertie Academy	Windsor
	New Berne Institute	New Berne
	Rowan Institute	Charlotte
	Burgaw Normal Institute	Burgaw
	Colon Training and Industrial School	Faison
Ohio	Curry School	Urbana

TABLE 3.6—*Continued*

States	Institution	Location
South Carolina	Peace Haven Institute	Broad River
	Friendship Institute	Rock Hill
	Morris College	Sumter
	Seneca Institute	Seneca
	Charleston Normal and Indus. Institute	Charleston
Tennessee	Howe Institute	Memphis
	Nelson Merry College	Jefferson City
	Lexington Normal School	Lexington
Texas	Guadalupe College	Seguin
	Central Texas Academy	Waco
	Houston Academy	Houston
	Hearne Academy	Hearne
	Pine Valley Institute	Pine Valley
	New Home Academy	Oakwood
Virginia	Virginia Seminary and College	Lynchburg
	Union Industrial Academy	Port Conway
	Keyesville Industrial Institute	Keyesville
	Halifax Institute	Houston
	Spiller Academy	Hampton
West Virginia	Bluefield Institute	Bluefield
	West Virginia Institute Farm	Kanawha county
Africa	Hope Institute	Lagos, W. Africa
	Rick's Institute	Monrovia
	Jordan's Industrial School	Cape Mount
	Miss De Laney's School	Blantyre, W. C. A.
	Queenstown Institute	South Africa
Total number of schools	107	
Valuation of property	$600,000	

Source: W. E. B. Du Bois, *Economic Co-Operation Among Negroes.* Atlanta, Ga.: The Atlanta University Press, 1907. 82–83.

As noted by the author of the study that produced these tables, it is clear that primary and grammar schools for blacks were supported, for the most part, by blacks themselves. Almost all of the institutions whose students paid 50 percent or more of the cost in cash were schools of this type. The schools for higher training got a smaller proportion of cash from their students, and the industrial schools the smallest proportion. But the latter schools received a very large payment in work hours from their students.[8]

In addition to private schools, other state schools were established because of the separate-but-equal ruling handed down as a result of *Plessy v. Ferguson* in 1896. Some of the private schools were taken over by the state. For example, Jackson State College was founded in 1877 by the American Baptist Home Mission Society in Natchez, Mississippi. It was moved to Jackson in

TABLE 3.7

Private Schools Supported by Afro-Americans, 1898–99 to 1906–07

School	Place	Cash Paid Students	Cash Value of Work	Total Cost of Conducting Institution	Percent Paid by Students	Remarks
Straight University	New Orleans, La.	$110,702	$4,916	$153,000	72.3	
Utica Institute	Utica, Miss.	5,019	13,164	42,446	11.8	5 years, 1902–07
Claflin University	Orangeburg, S.C.	51,570	16,643	343,522	15.1	
Kowaliga School	Irma, Ala.	1,156	9,121	36,730	4.1	
Shaw University	Raleigh, N.C.	168,241	5,161	301,241	55.8	
Paine College	Augusta, Ga.	17,361	—	87,607	19.8	Donated $22,386.04
Tougaloo University	Tougaloo, Miss.	58,366	23,340	265,370	21.9	1905–06 short: epidemic
Calhoun Colored School	Calhoun, Ala.	8,751	40,886	205,924	4.2	Bldg. cost not included
Mary Holmes Seminary	West Point, Miss.	63,000	—	108,000	58.3	Approximate
Brainerd Institute	Chester, S.C.	13,293	—	45,075	29.4	
Alabama Baptist Colored Institute	Selma, Ala.	63,370	9,668	92,938	73.5	Cost raised by Negroes
Tidewater Institute	Cheriton, Va.	8,760	1,697	18,281	47.9	
St. Augustine's School	Raleigh, N.C.	24,842	—	110,341	22.4	6 years
Bishop College	Marshall, Tex.	81,793	12,587	146,538	55.7	5 years: 1902–03 to 1906–07
Samuel Houston School	Austin, Tex.	33,700	8,150	53,157	63.3	1900–01 to 1906–07
Jos. K Brick Agricultural, Indus., Normal School	Enfield, N.C.	19,791	24,800	98,000	20.1	7 yrs., 1900–01. estimated
Allen University	Columbia, S.C.	5,988	—	34,323	17.4	1904–06. board not included
New Orleans University	New Orleans, La.	49,835	7,779	87,459	56.9	5 yrs., 1902–07
State A & M College for Colored Race	Greensboro, N.C.	22,122	9,278	154,767	14.2	1901–07. $7,533.15 bldgs.
Paul Quinn College	Waco, Tex.	43,238	7,081	64,222	67.3	All raised by Negroes

Virginia Union Univ.	Richmond, Va.	$53,128	$17,593	$226,983	23.4	1899–1907. Approx. total
Lincoln School	Meridian, Miss.	7,050	2,281	10,510	67.0	Rent $300
Pilgrim High School	Guyton, Ga.	1,147	15	1,512	75.8	3 years
Albion Academy, Normal Industrial School	Franklinton, N.C.	18,761	4,889	32,050	58.5	5 years
Bennet College	Greensboro, N.C.	9,494	1,183	16,521	57.4	5 years
Emerson N & I Institute	Mobile, Ala.	11,668	2,077	39,124	29.8	
Livingstone College	Salisbury, N.C.	38,755	7,719	247,609	23.4	Supported by Negroes
Northern Neck Academy	Ivondale, Va.	2,076	2,380	7,052	29.4	7 years
Wiley University	Marshall, Tex.	154,896	28,500	232,346	66.6	
Colored Agricultural and Normal University	Langston, Okla.	28,470	13,308	72,790	39.1	
Meridian Academy	Meridian, Miss.	6,100	1,300	9,400	64.8	2 years
Bowling Green Academy	Bowling Green, Va.	3,357	638	4,927	68.1	4 years
Rust University	Holly Springs, Miss.	83,790	3,641	115,682	53.8	
Morris Brown College	Atlanta, Ga.	20,450	180	59,500	34.3	3 yrs. supported by Negroes
Penn Normal, Industrial, Agricultural School	Frogmore, S.C.	1,667	283	38,619	4.3	
Kentucky Normal, Indus., Institute for Colored Persons	Frankfort, Ky.	5,095	10,070	11,700	4.3	Negroes pay 1 to 15% taxes
Virginia N & I School	Petersburg, Va.	127,695	12,595	279,824	45.6	
Lincoln University	Chester, Pa.	19,783	22,000	387,000	5.1	Student work not reduced
Hartshorn Mem. College	Richmond, Va.	49,708	—	115,720	42.9	
Trinity School	Athens, Ala.	1,700	800	9,000	18.8	3 years
Allen N & I School	Thomasville, Ga.	16,275	4,212	38,906	41.8	
Howard University	Washington, D.C.	211,988	15,927	743,788	28.5	
King and Queen Indus. High School	Cauthornville, Va.	6,385	1,280	7,650	83.4	Many men earn their way

TABLE 3.7

Private Schools Supported by Afro-Americans, 1898–99 to 1906–07

School	Place	Cash Paid Students	Cash Value of Work	Total Cost of Conducting Institution	Percent Paid by Students	Remarks
Washburn Seminary	Beaufort, N.C.	361	106	2,801	12.8	2 years
Gregory Normal Institute	Wilmington, N.C.	10,890	1,954	37,964	28.6	
Biddle Institute	Charlotte, N.C.	24,885	22,829	286,408	8.6	
Louisville State Univ.	Louisville, Ky.	65,680	550	76,345	86.0	
Cabin Creek	Griffin, Ga.	344	71	1,146	30.0	2 years
M.T. & I. College	Holly Springs, Miss.	$ 10,611	$ 1,300	$ 15,876	66.8	2 yrs.: equip. not included
Tuskegee N & I Institute	Tuskegee, Ala.	217,798	707,285	1,416,417	15.3	
Knoxville College	Knoxville, Tenn.	109,450	24,000	257,250	42.5	
LeMoyne Normal Inst.	Memphis, Tenn.	52,376	—	87,750	59.6	
Cookman Institute	Jacksonville, Fla.	14,950	2,700	30,600	48.8	
Walker Baptist Institute	Augusta, Ga.	2,435	237	9,414	25.8	Negroes give $3,841
Scotia Seminary	Concord, N.C.	64,588	48,330	157,675	40.9	
Lane College	Jackson, Tenn.	47,601	4,500	95,500	49.8	Negroes give $8,500
Arkansas Baptist College	Little Rock, Ark.	52,854	7,064	119,729	44.1	
Leland University	New Orleans, La.	38,331	8,260	130,467	29.3	
Franklin Junction Inst.	Franklin Junction, Va.	4,490	870	9,370	47.9	Bldg. cost not included
Florida State Normal, Industrial School	Tallahassee, Fla.	502,338	—	139,703	35.8	
Spelman Seminary	Atlanta, Ga.	53,434	—	844,460	15.5	Student labor not included
Jeruel Academy	Athens, Ga.	19,112	423	22,218	57.3	
Atlanta University	Atlanta, Ga.	82,487	16,362	460,562	17.9	
Clark University	South Atlanta, Ga.	116,757	7,084	253,877	45.9	
Franklinton Christian College	Franklinton, N.C.	11,701	1,691	23,889	48.9	
Jackson College	Jackson, Miss.	45,686	3,941	89,738	50.9	

Waters Normal Institute	Winston, N.C.	13,195	—	23,992	54.9	Negroes give $7,760.31
Ballard Normal School	Macon, Ga.	39,314	8,100	90,000	43.6	
Southern Christian Inst.	Edwards, Miss.	30,514	18,721	118,940	25.6	
Tillotson College	Austin, Tex.	42,466	3,700	61,030	69.5	
Fisk University	Nashville, Tenn.	261,576	22,500	—	—	Total cost unknown
Hampton Institute	Hampton, Va.	91,228	549,618	1,695,678	5.3	
Atlanta Baptist College	Atlanta, Ga.	50,160	13,794	147,033	34.1	
Fort Valley H & I School	Fort Valley, Ga.	2,260	5,440	17,630	12.8	

Source: W. E. B. Du Bois. 1907. *Economic Co-Operation Among Negroes.* Atlanta, Ga.: The Atlanta University Press, 1907. 86–87.

1882 and was eventually taken over by the state in 1930. These colleges, as will be seen later, played an important role in the development of the class structure and business opportunities of Afro-Americans.

The building of educational institutions, then, represented a major task for Afro-Americans and must be seen in the total context of southern education. White southerners had no strong history of building successful educational institutions for the masses of people. The introduction of the northeastern public school system in the South was a major aim of white Northerners during the Reconstruction period. If the South was to be a part of the United States, it would have to develop a good educational system for its people. Thus, as Louis Harlan wrote:

> The Schoolma'am and the carpetbagger rode into the South together, Yankees both, one to uplift, the other to exploit. Though the carpet-bagger often spoke of developing the country, he was primarily concerned with the opportunities available in a colonial area. The Northern teacher in the South, on the other hand, modeled her program after that of the Massachusetts town public school, which had developed in an area of high population density and expanding industry. The Schoolma'am ideal, though not impossible, was difficult to develop in the South.[9]

Regardless of race, there was little education in the South during the years before or after the Civil War. Though there were some schools for whites before the conflict, supported by State Literary Funds or local taxation, universal education was not accepted as a state obligation until after the period of Reconstruction. On the eve of the Civil War, there was only one elementary school per forty square miles in South Carolina. The typical antebellum school system was exemplified by the pauper school, rather than the free school, and illiteracy was symbolic of an ethical failure of the old society of the planter system. Thus, this aristocratic rule of the planter class had not developed educational institutions in the South.[10]

As noted by the following analysis, white Southerners, when compared to the rest of the country, left a lot to be desired when it came to education:

> ... the contrast is clear between Southern and other American school systems. The average term in the Southern seaboard was less than 100 days, only three-fifths of the children in the Southern seaboard were enrolled, and less than three-fifths of those enrolled were included in average daily attendance. Thus, barely over one-third of the children of school age in these states were normally in school. The average North Carolina child attended school 21.9 days a year, or one-fifth as long as the Massachusetts child. In school finance the

contrast was equally striking. The average daily expenditure per pupil in attendance in 1900 ranged from 8.2 cents in Virginia to 5 cents in South Carolina, while it was 20 cents in Massachusetts. The difference in school terms made annual expenditures more divergent, ranging in the Southern seaboard from $9.70 in Virginia to $4.34 in North Carolina, whereas the national average was $20.29 and the Massachusetts total was $37.76 per pupil. On a basis of school population regional discrepancies were wider. For each child of school age in South Carolina $1.80 was expended, and in North Carolina $1.65; the amount in Massachusetts was $21.55, over twelve times as large.[11]

By any measure, the educational system of the white South did not measure up to that of the country as a whole, a fact that the region still suffers from today. We can add to the dilemma that, in the late 1800s, the average salary for teachers in Virginia was $165.19 while in North Carolina it was $82.87. In Massachusetts the average teacher's salary was $566.09. In marked contrast, a teacher's salary in the agricultural state of Kansas was only $236.26 a year.[12] Given these statistics, it is not surprising that in the four Southern seaboard states in 1900, there were 1,517,450 illiterates who were ten years of age or older. More than one-fourth of these illiterates were native whites.[13]

It was in this environment that Afro-Americans engaged in self-help in terms of education. While it was true that white Southerners had an education system that was inferior to the rest of the country, the developing black educational system of the South also fell beneath northern educational standards. Thus, neither of these two school systems could compare to the rest of the country. It has been estimated that, in 1900, in sixteen former Confederate states, the average Afro-American student was allotted only half as much money as the average white student. In these states, although Afro-Americans made up 32.8 percent of the school population, they received about 20 percent of the school funds. When one looks at individual states, the statistics look even worse. For example, in South Carolina, Afro-Americans made up 61.0 percent of the school population but received only 22.6 percent of the funding.

After examining the literature, it is difficult to judge whether one system was better than the other. One indication of quality was the amount of money which a state allotted to black and white school systems respectively. For example, in Georgia, the average Afro-American student received about one-fourth as much as the average white child, and, in Virginia, they received about one-third as much.[14]

These comparisons are based on federal studies done around the turn of the century. Other studies show that state money allocated to Afro-American education was augmented by private efforts. Thus, it is interesting that one of the major findings of an Atlantic University Study on economic self-help among Afro-Americans was that they supplemented the funding provided by the state to black schools. In addition, there was a certain relationship between high schools and the developing Afro-American universities, a sort of college-prep training. Consider the following finding from studies done by Atlantic University:

> To overcome these poor conditions [funding from the states], and to provide reasonably ample opportunities for effective training, the Negroes are working in several different directions. They are not only supplementing the public funds and lengthening the school term, but are establishing private schools and consolidating with the public schools nearby; they are rebuilding independent private schools; and they are supporting in larger measure the great schools established by Northern philanthropy. One of the most conspicuous cases of consolidating with the public school is furnished by the Keyesville Industrial School in Charlotte Country [Virginia]. This is an industrial school, founded in 1898 and supported almost entirely by Negroes, through the Baptist organizations of that neighborhood. They have a plant, including 100 acres of land, worth $2,600. . . . The curriculum includes such instruction as will fit a pupil to enter Virginia Union University, with which school it is affiliated, and such manual and industrial training as will fit them for useful lives and for trade schools like Hampton. This school succeeded in having the public school and the public funds placed in its hands. It gets only $175 formerly given by the county to the public school, but it gives the children a term of seven instead of five months, and it pays two well trained teachers of its own appointing $20 each and board per month instead of $15 and $20, respectively, without board, as was the case formerly. The children are better housed and better taught and maintain higher attendance than was known before, to say nothing of having the benefit of effective manual training. This is made possible by the contributions of Negroes to this school. It is a positive effort on the part of the Negroes there about [70,000 within a radius of 75 miles] to improve their educational facilities.[15]

The study notes that, in nearly all of the Southern states there were town and city systems where the cost of Afro-American schools was more nearly equal to that of the whites. In 1899, the contribution to public education for Afro-Americans was partitioned in the following way: (1) the total cost of black education was $4,617,5054; (2) from direct taxes blacks contributed $1,336,291; (3) from indirect taxes, blacks contributed $2,426,266; (4) the estimated total was $3,762,557; and (5) white taxes paid $912,887 of the total spent on black education.

The above statistics point to the fact that blanket statements about the inferiority of Afro-American schools are extremely misleading. One can say that Afro-Americans, like white Southerners, developed an educational system which was mixed in quality. There were good schools and bad schools in both traditions.

As one examines the documents which speak to education in the South, it is clear that Afro-Americans engaged in a tremendous amount of self-help. It must be remembered, however, that, no matter how much education they received, whether in the developing schools of the South or in the established Ivy League schools of the North, they still could not exercise political and civil rights. Nevertheless, their educational efforts served as one of the backbones for the development of Afro-American business.

II

The insurance business represents one of the most continuous enterprises for Afro-Americans. This industry grew out of the self-help organizations which developed in the 1700s. The Free African Society (1787), mentioned in the previous chapter, was the prototype of such self-help societies. Originating in churches, these organizations gave relief to Afro-Americans in terms of sickness, health care, and death benefits in the free North. The major benevolent societies which followed the Free African Society were the New York Society (1810), the Clarkson (1812), the Wilberforce Benevolent (1820), the Union Society of Brooklyn (1820) and the Woolman Society of Brooklyn (1820).[16] Without these self-help societies, life would have been much more difficult for Afro-Americans in the North.

The Emancipation Proclamation and the dawn of freedom saw the spread of beneficial societies to the South. By definition, there was a great deal of uncertainty, privation and suffering within the Afro-American group following slavery. Although scholars have mentioned the importance of the Freedmen's Bureau—the only governmental attempt to deal with problems of emancipation—it was the Afro-American Church which was most effective in dealing with those problems. For more than a quarter of a century, church relief societies increased their memberships in the South and served the purposes for which they were organized.[17] Of course, as Afro-Americans began to move throughout the country, new societies were established. Let us take a step back in history and examine the nature of these societies.

Table 3.8 presents data on beneficial societies found in the cities of Petersburg, Virginia, and Atlanta, Georgia, for the year 1898. In Petersburg, there were twenty-two societies as of 1898. These societies were all organized in the late 1800s. Membership ranged from 22 to 163 persons. Their annual assessments per year ranged from $.60 to $7.00. They paid sick and death benefits

TABLE 3.8
Beneficial Societies of Petersburg, Virginia, and Atlanta, Georgia, 1898[1]

Petersburg, Virginia

Name	When Organized	Number of Members	Assessments per Year[2]	Annual Income	Sick and Death Benefits	Cash and Property
Young Men's	1884	40	$7.00	$ 275.00	$ 150.00	$ 175.00
Sisters of Friendship, etc.[3]	—	22	3.00	68.55	43.78	—
Union Working Club	1893	15	3.00	45.00	23.00	—
Sisters of Charity	1884	17	3.00	51.00	30.00	—
Ladies' Union	1896	47	3.00	135.00	—	123.25
Beneficial Association	1893	163	5.20	1,005.64	806.46	440.00
Daughters of Bethlehem	—	39	3.00	129.48	110.04	—
Living Sisters	1884	16	3.00	22.50	30.50	62.00
Ladies Working Club	1888	37	3.00	95.11	52.65	214.09
St. Mark	1874	28	3.00	84.00	32.00	150.00
Consolation	1845	26	3.00	68.00	27.00	100.00
Daughters of Zion	1867	22	3.00	66.00	40.00	36.00
Young Sisters of Charity	1869	30	3.00	90.00	30.00	100.00
Humble Christian	1868	26	3.00	68.00	35.50	75.00
Sisters of David	1885	30	3.00	90.00	60.00	130.00
Sisters of Rebecca	1893	40	3.00	120.00	85.00	175.00
Petersburg	1872	29	3.00	85.00	11.00	99.53
Petersburg Beneficial	1892	35	5.20	182.00	158.00	118.00
First Baptist Church Ass'n.	1893	100	.60	60.00	40.00	80.00
Young Men's	1894	44	3.00	211.00	202.25	100.00
Oak Street Church Society	1894	38	1.20	42.60	112.63	50.00
Endeavor, etc.	1894	98	3.00	120.00	96.00	43.00
Total		942		$3,113.88	$2,177.81	$4,275.87

Atlanta, Georgia

Name	When Organized	Number of Members	Annual Income	Remarks
Helping Hand, First Congregational Church	1872	40	$ 120	Benefits paid in 5 years, $225; benevolence, $25
Rising Star, Wheat Street Baptist Church	1879	168	250	Benefits paid in 5 years, $370; donations, $50; owns cemetery lot for poorer members
Daughters of Bethel, Bethel Church	1874	175	525	Donations in 5 years, $125; benefits in 5 years, $580
Ladies' Court of Calanthe	1891	15	72	Benefits $590 since 1891
Daughters of Friendship, Union No. 1, Friendship Baptist Church	1869	150	450	Benefits 5 years, $430; donates much to the church
Fort Street Benevolent Mission	1897	—	390	Benefits 1 year, $190
Daughters of Plenty	1892	115	250	Benefits 4 years; $200; secession from Daughters of Bethel
Pilgrims Progress, Park Street Church	1891	120	360	Benefits 5 years, $600
Sisters of Love, Wheat Street Baptist Church	1880	190	570	Has $600 in bank
Nine organizations		973	$2,978	

Source: W. E. B. Du Bois, *Economic Co-Operation Among Negroes.* Atlanta, Ga.: The Atlanta University Press, 1907. 94.

[1] Atlanta University Publication, No. 3

[2] Assessment upon each member in case any member dies.

[3] Organized before the war.

to their members. As can be seen from the table, Atlanta, Georgia, had eight organizations that paid benefits. Members paid an annual assessment and, in return, received benefits for sickness and death.

Note that these types of societies flourished in large measure as a result of racial discrimination by white insurance companies. In the late 1800s, scholarly works argued that Afro-Americans represented poor insurance risks. The work which had the greatest impact was Frederick L. Hoffman's *Race Traits and Tendencies of the American Negro* published in 1896.

Hoffman argued that, because of social diseases, living conditions, and undesirable circumstances, insurance companies should not insure Afro-Americans. While white insurance companies willingly insured incoming ethnic groups who could afford the service, Afro-Americans were excluded on the basis of race. Thus, Afro-Americans in Atlanta and Petersburg, Virginia, like blacks in other cities, had to seek for themselves.

In the 1890s, Baltimore, Maryland, had the greatest number of self-help beneficial societies. In a city of 67,000 Afro-Americans, its first society was formed in 1820. In order to create the society, Afro-Americans had to be exempted from a state law which forbade their assembly.

Before the Civil War, twenty-five organizations had been formed. Between 1865 and 1870, seventeen or more were founded. More than twenty were added between the years 1870 and 1875.[18] In 1884, the societies of Baltimore held a conference to increase interest in their efforts and to present the status of their societies.

More than forty of these societies had memberships in excess of 2,100. Almost 1,400 members had been buried, which cost the societies more than $45,000 dollars. Sick dues accounted to $125,000, and $27,000 had been given to widows by about thirty societies. Well over $10,700 had been given to members toward house rent, and more than $11,300 had been paid for incidental expenses. In addition, after all the expenses had been paid, the society was able to pay dividends to its members in excess of $40,000. Still more than $21,400 remained in the bank, which was an indication of the effectiveness of the societies. About five societies had invested well, and one had a sum of $5,642 after expenses. The total amount of money handled by the benevolent societies of Baltimore had been nearly $290,000.[19] Note that all dollars are expressed in 1890 dollars.

The Free African Society of Philadelphia which was mentioned earlier generated a number of societies in that city. By 1838, there were 100 societies in Philadelphia, with 7,448 members. They paid in $18,851, distributed $14,172 in benefits, and had $10,023 dollars saved. Ten years later, by 1848, it has been estimated that 8,000 members belonged to 106 societies. Seventy-six of these societies produced a total membership of 5,187. The members contributed 25 cents to 37.5 cents a month. Sick members received $1.50 to $3.00

per week, and death benefits of $10 to $20 were allowed. The total income of these seventy-six societies amounted to $16,841.23.[20]

New York City's Benevolent Society was founded in 1808 and chartered in 1810. By 1900, it had real estate which was valued at more than $40,000. Examining one of its accounts which included the time period 1813 to 1814, receipts were $1,148.17; between 1852 and 1855, receipts jumped to $2,628.68. The 1891 total receipts equaled $3,162.15. For 1892, the receipts from all sources (rents, dues, and the fee) equaled $2,735.64. As with most societies of its kind, the objectives of the society were to "raise a fund to be appropriated exclusively toward the support of such of the members of said society as shall by reason of sickness or infirmity, or either, be incapable of attending to their usual vocation or employment, and also toward the relief of the widows and orphans of deceased members."[21] There were a large number of these societies in New York, although the exact number is not known.

In addition to benevolent societies, secret societies were instruments of self-help. Although historical records show that there was some overlap between the two, secret societies were more secular. As noted by Stuart, while secret societies also engaged in charity and self-help, they were steered away from the paths of true charity to serve ends that were highly commercialized and mercenary in nature and practice.[22]

Unlike the benevolent societies which revolved around a religious flavor for recruitment of members, secret societies stressed the importance of ritual and flashiness. During the period of Reconstruction, Northern politicians introduced Afro-Americans to brilliant regalia in which they sported sharp uniforms as members of Negro State Militias. The secret societies adopted the regalia of the militia and presented themselves in a flashy way. Although these societies eventually evolved into excellent self-help organizations, people were originally attracted to them because of: (1) the love for pompous ceremonies and the spectacular; (2) the human craving to take part in governmental and political affairs; and (3) a desire for the advantages of the deep secrets of these societies.[23] Since the educational elite and other leaders of the community were more likely to participate in secret societies, there was a definite prestige associated with membership.

The largest and most prestigious of all secret societies were the Masons. Although the organization of Masons has been traced back as far as Egypt, Western scholars trace the organization back to England and Scotland. Masonry grew out of builders' guilds in these countries. When a work project ended, some workmen left their guilds in search of other projects. Others continued their association as a fraternal group and formed lodges which adopted a policy of admitting only men as members.

In 1717, four lodges in London met and formed the first Masonic Grand Lodge. Freemasonry was transplanted to the English colonies of America in

1730, and lodges were formed in Philadelphia and Boston. As a charitable organization, the Masons enjoyed a relative degree of prosperity. It was an exclusive organization which selected its membership according to recommendations from existing members. Nine signers of the Declaration of Independence and thirteen signers of the Constitution belonged to the organization. The first President of the United States, George Washington, was a member in good standing.[24] Afro-Americans trace their origins in the association to 1775 when a Masonic lodge which was attached to one of the English regiments near Boston initiated fifteen blacks into the mysteries of Freemasonry. Among those fifteen men was Prince Hall. According to the customs of that day, they were allowed to assemble as a lodge, "walk on St. John's Day" and bury their dead in acceptable manner and form. Yet, they were not allowed to initiate other people into the organization until they developed their own lodge.

On March 2, 1784, they applied to the Grand Lodge of England for a warrant and were successful. The warrant was issued to them as African Lodge, No. 459, in 1784. Prince Hall was named Master of the new lodge. A person of exceptional ability, Prince Hall served in the American Army during the Revolutionary War. Until his death in 1897, he dedicated himself to the organization.[25] This is why, today, among Afro-Americans, the organization is called the Prince Hall Masons.

The number of Masons grew rapidly after the Civil War. The research during that period is not consistent in terms of the actual numbers of the group. In 1897, in a paper published in *The North American Reader* on black and white secret societies, it was estimated that there were 224,000 black Masons in America. Another source, *The Encyclopedia of Fraternities*, published in 1899, put the number at 55,713.[26] Given the rapid growth in this secret society, actual numbers are hard to estimate, but it is certainly true that there were significant numbers of this group in the country, enough to have an impact on the Afro-American community.

In 1907, the financial status of the various lodges was estimated. The figures are presented in Table 3.9 by state. The table is divided into income and expenditures. Under income is money taken in by the Grand Lodge of that state and money generated by subordinate lodges. Under expenditures is a category for charity and other purposes. Then there is the amount of property owned by Afro-American Masons for each state. For this study, data are not available for all lodges. This study estimated that the total income in 1909 was about $500,000 and that the property was valued well over $1,000,000.[27]

In addition, one must also consider insurance features which fell under benefits within the organization. The method of insurance operation was by assessment of all members on the death of a fellow Mason. In 1905, the Grand Master of Mississippi explained the procedure as follows:

We have 7,000 craftsmen in our ranks, and with such a number it is not surprising that we should have fourteen deaths a month, or 168 per annum. The present assessment rate is 7 1/7 cents for each death, and fourteen assessments are paid for $1; thus, we pay $7,250 per month or $87,000 per year. This is the greatest amount collected and paid out by any institution operated and controlled by our race variety known to us in the civilized world. This is a startling statement, but no doubt true. This institution has $19,132.65 to its credit in three banks. They have also recently purchased 1,000 acres of land. Governor Vardaman and all the other devils this side of Hades cannot stay this kind of prosperity.[28]

TABLE 3.9
Financial Status of Masonic Lodges, Income, and Expenditures

| | Income | | | Expenditures | |
State	Grand Lodge	Subordinate Lodges	Charity	Other Purposes	Property
Arkansas	$1,597	$51,157	$22,055	$23,683	$217,247
California	1,385	—	—	—	—
Colorado	—	—	—	—	16,000
District of Columbia	683	5,755	1,600	—	5,475
Florida	3,037	—	—	—	3,000
Georgia	—	32,400	—	—	110,000
Illinois	2,300	—	—	—	80,000
Indiana	681	—	—	5,173	10,352
Iowa	2,400	—	—	—	1,715
Kentucky	1,400	—	—	—	40,000
Louisiana	—	—	—	—	55,900
Maryland	—	7,500	5,000	—	17,500
Massachusetts	373	—	—	—	1,650
Michigan	—	—	389	1,757	4,225
Mississippi	2,896	—	—	—	80,855
Missouri	—	31,707	—	27,705	61,948
New Jersey	—	—	—	—	3,103
New York	1,000	—	—	—	7,000
North Carolina	2,520	14,000	—	—	68,560
Ohio	—	—	—	—	80,000
Oklahoma	—	3,000	—	—	—
Pennsylvania	2,000	48,000	—	—	28,000
South Carolina	1,576	—	—	—	—
Tennessee	—	—	—	—	7,000
Virginia	—	45,284	—	—	80,610
West Virginia	—	—	—	—	25,000

Source: W. E. B. Du Bois. Economic Co-Operation Among Negroes. Atlanta, Ga.: The Atlanta University Press, 1907. 110.

The latter part of the quotation is a direct comparison to the property held by whites in a county of Mississippi. This led the Grand Master of Mississippi to feel a sense of accomplishment for his organization.

The above pattern was repeated throughout states where Afro-Americans resided and organized Masonic Temples. Other examples are presented in Table 3.10, which presents the financial reports of selected lodges of Arkansas, Florida, and Louisiana. In the state of Arkansas, at the top of the financial statement, is stated that this Masonic Temple paid $125,000 to widows and orphans. Their receipts increased from over $4,000 in 1892 to over $27,000 in

TABLE 3.10
Financial Statement of Masonic Lodges of Arkansas, Florida, and Louisiana

Arkansas
(Total Insurance Paid to Widows and Orphans, $125,000)

	Receipts	Expenditures	Balance
1892	$4,187.83	$5,187.83	—
1893	7,422.90	6,063.37	$1,359.54
1895	4,912.29	4,500.00	474.88
1896	5,600.00	5,600.00	—
1897	6,691.20	5,568.32	1,122.88
1898	8,509.56	8,478.90	30.66
1899 (deficit)	8,331.17	8,387.64	56.47
1900	336.88	—	—
1901	14,107.59	12,873.90	1,233.69
1902	14,817.27	13,689.17	2,361.79
1903	16,214.21	13,605.00	4,071.00
1905	27,092.49	18,868.75	8,223.74

Florida

Receipts, 1906		$6,976.08
Claims	$4,001.00	
Expenses	910.44	4,911.44
Balance		$2,064.57
Other funds		444.65
Total		$2,509.22
Claims unpaid:		
Approved	$ 600.00	
Unapproved and filed	2,700.00	3,300.00

Louisiana

Year	Receipts	Claims Paid	Balance	Unpaid Claims
1899	$3,120.00	$ 1,451.00	$1,668.00	—
1904	—	11,950.00	—	$2,400.00
1905	—	13,100.00	—	2,540.00

Source: W. E. B. Du Bois, *Economic Co-Operation Among Negroes.* Atlanta, Ga.: The Atlanta University Press, 1907. 111.

1905. In a Florida Temple in 1906, their receipts totaled over $6,000 and their expenses totaled over $4,000. One can also see the receipts collected for a Louisiana Temple in 1899 totaled $3,120.00 and the claims paid amounted to $1,451.00. These examples are excellent testimonies to the practice of self-help exercised by Afro-Americans in general and the Masons in particular.

Another very active self-help group was The Odd Fellows. In 1842, Afro-Americans applied for membership in the International Order of Odd Fellows. They were refused because they were not European. Peter Ogden, an Afro-American who already had membership in the Grand United Order of Odd Fellows of England, secured a charter for the first Afro-American lodge. The lodge began operation in 1843 as number 646 in the city of New York. Between 1843 and 1904, the order grew from one lodge and only a few members to 4,643 lodges and 285,000 members. In 1886 alone, the amount paid to sick members was $37,757.82. Funeral expenses were $21,002.45, and the society paid widows $6,957.20. Also in the tradition of self-help organizations, $4,326.95 was donated to charity. For the same year, the society invested $100,993.15, held property, and had a balance of funds which totaled $343,197.70. Table 3.11 presents the reports of the Grand Secretary (Grand and Subordinate) for the years starting in 1845. Panel I shows Receipts and Disbursements by years for the grand and subordinate lodges. Panels II and III show receipts and disbursements by states. What is important is the increase in receipts and disbursements by years, the latter utilized to solve problems in communities. For example, Panel IV shows that in 1907 the subordinate lodge in Ohio paid $3,285.50 in sick funeral benefits, $329.88 to widows and orphans, and $8,317.30 to charity. This organization also had over $61,000.00 in invested property and in funds.

TABLE 3.11
Reports of Grand and Subordinate Lodges of the Old Fellows

Panel I

Term	Receipts	Disbursements
1845	$ 109.00	$ 97.01
1845–1846	175.99	169.90
1846–1847	163.18	120.03
1847–1848	899.10	419.61
1848–1849	209.98	210.34
1849–1850	321.37	250.28
1851	236.34	307.85
1852	416.36	372.28
1853	263.59	260.94
1854	361.67	329.06
1855	350.65	371.02
1856	363.34	359.95
1857	283.62	297.05
1858	329.61	273.06

TABLE 3.11—*Continued*

Panel I

Term	Receipts	Disbursements
1859	460.27	532.56
1860	385.11	352.01
1860–1862	581.91	565.14
1863	297.41	273.77
1864	365.33	377.07
1865	436.80	412.93
1866	673.99	585.53
1867	646.77	650.58
1868	684.58	625.89
1869	713.16	676.46
1870	812.97	856.62
1871	1,043.78	778.41
1872	1,869.36	1,365.83
1873	2,893.15	1,768.37
1874	3,000.00	3,598.56
1874–1888	—	—
1888–1890	16,413.44	18,625.02
1890–1892	17,159.64	17,086.67
1892–1894	24,026.90	13,717.59
1894–1896	35,517.59	25,951.26
1896–1898	35,275.64	28,948.71
1898–1900	37,471.33	28,722.53
1900–1902	48,727.32	34,589.69
1902–1904	52,196.63	33,843.12
1904–1906	58,976.06	37,750.01

Panel II
Grand Lodge Reports

State	Receipts	Disbursements
Kentucky (1906)	$ 445.98	$ 401.71
Georgia (1903–04)	1,215.39	1,157.45
Colorado and Jurisdiction		
(1904)	74.48	45.00
(1905)	64.35	64.15
Illinois and Wisconsin		
(1904)	359.61	285.25
(1905)	370.24	126.51
Missouri (1907)	3,284.00	2,475.00
Florida (1906)	1,938.31	1,421.22
Louisiana (1907)	783.62	623.99
Ohio (1907)	1,193.93	1,069.08

TABLE 3.11—*Continued*

Panel III
Subordinate Lodge Reports (Lodge Reports Simply Sent to the Central Office and Filed)

State	Receipts	Disbursements
Georgia (1904–05)	$27,718.33	$21,594.22
Ohio (1907)	12,960.83	13,813.53
Kentucky (1907)	—	25,503.37
Colorado and Jurisdiction		
(1904)	—	2,460.47
(1905)	—	8,409.30
Missouri (1907)	10,806.33	11,825.00
Illinois and Wisconsin (1905)	—	8,016.75
Florida	16,782.90	14,796.18
Louisiana	42,127.83	43,104.30

Panel IV
Subordinate Lodge Reports (Lodge Reports Simply Sent to the Central Office and Filed)

State	Date	Sick and Funeral Benefits	Widows and Orphans	Charity	Whole Amount Paid Out	Invested Property and in Funds
Ohio	1907	$ 3,285.50	$ 329.88	$8,317.30	$13,813.53	$61,780.03
Florida	1906	12,344.30	2,398.74	1,836.36	—	14,337.63
Illinois and Wisconsin	1905	6,961.55	664.00	391.20	—	54,637.11
Missouri	1907	5,925.00	5,600.00	300.00	11,825.00	117,372.65
Kentucky	1907	12,668.47	1,532.31	606.69	25,503.37	103,843.38
Colorado and Jurisdiction	1907	1,000.40	19.00	64.65	2,992.53	5,752.12
Georgia	1905	12,385.70	2,725.06	3,973.96	39,139.38	120,377.99

Source: W.E.B. Du Bois. *Economic Co-Operation Among Negroes.* Atlanta, Ga.: The Atlanta University Press, 1907. 116.

Table 3.12 shows a summary financial sheet for the Odd Fellows for the years 1904–1906. This historical record shows cash on hand, receipts, disbursements, cash expenses and a recapitulation. During this period of self-help, different segments of the black community depended upon contributions from groups such as the Odd Fellows for assistance in many areas.

The Knights of Pythias also has an interesting history of self-help in the Afro-American experience. In the city of Washington in 1864, the order was organized by J. H. Rathbone and others. During the meetings of the Supreme Lodge of the Knights of Pythias of the World in 1869 (the white organization), an application requesting a charter for blacks from Philadelphia was turned down. Because of this request, the white organization created a Supreme Grand Council of the Knights of Pythias, to be known as the Supreme Lodge of North America, South America, Asia, and Europe, for the

TABLE 3.12

Financial Sheet of the Odd Fellows

Cash balance on hand, 1904 August 31	$40,811.47
Receipts from all sources during term	58,976.06
Total	$99,787.53
Disbursements for all purposes	37,750.01
Balance cash	$62,037.52

Details of Receipts, 1904–1906

Receipts from lodges	$40,734.03
Receipts from households	13,964.47
Receipts from councils	1,398.54
Receipts from patriarchies	161.88
Receipts from district grand lodges	75.23
Receipts from district households	106.79
Receipts from juvenile societies	77.26
Receipts from interest on deposits	1,907.05
Receipts from *Odd Fellows' Journal*	500.00
Receipts from rentals	150.81
Total	$58,076.06

Disbursements, 1904–1906

Odd Fellows' Journal	$11,823.47
Salaries and clerk hire	10,167.05
Traveling expenses of the S. C. M. and grand auditors	5,787.70
Postage, express charges, telephone service	2,767.09
Office rent, gas, ice and laundry	640.70
Watson & Hazlehurst	2,500.00
Committee of Management, England, and custom duties	1,211.36
Officers, 12 B. M. C., 3 grand household and 17 triannual conference	758.50
Miscellaneous purposes	2,094.44
Total	$37,750.01

Total Receipts

Total receipts	$57,018.20
Interest on deposits	1,807.05
Rentals	150.81
Total	$58,976.06

purpose of extending its membership to individuals regardless of race. Lightfoot Lodge No. 1 in Vicksburg, Mississippi, was the first Afro-American lodge established under this arrangement.[29]

In an address to the lodge in 1905, the leader (the Supreme Chancellor) made the following statements that effectively capture the spirit of self-help among these types of organizations:

Up to this time I think we have demonstrated the Negro's ability to successfully conduct an organization with a representative form of

TABLE 3.12—*Continued*

Cash Expenses

1904

		Brought forward	$19,604.25
September	$ 1,151.66	September	731.34
October	1,732.18	October	978.47
November	1,565.94	November	1,543.87
December	1,477.29	December	2,683.34

1905		1906	
January	$ 2,347.89	January	$ 2,862.68
February	892.55	February	611.01
March	812.60	March	1,990.95
April	493.18	April	1,035.69
May	927.53	May	1,162.79
June	563.81	June	1,503.17
July	6,692.39	July	566.95
August	947.23	August	2,475.53
Carried forward	$19,604.25	Total	$37,750.01

Recapitulation

Balance on hand, 31 August 1904	$40,811.47
Receipts for term, 1904–1906, from all sources	58,976.06
Total	$99,787.53
Disbursements for all purposes	37,750.01
Cash balance, 31 August 1906	$62,037.52

Source: W. E. B. Du Bois. *Economic Co-Operation Among Negroes.* Atlanta, Ga.: The Atlanta University Press, 1907. 120.

government. The history of our order for the past few years is known to all of you. The manner in which we have risen from nothing, as it were, a few years ago to the high and respected position we occupy today, with 26 grand Lodges, 1,536 subordinate lodges. 68,462 members, with $211,899.46 in our various treasuries, $33,268.37 of which belong to the Supreme Lodge itself, is the wonder of the age. With this growth and prosperity come great responsibilities. I wish to say frankly, as I have said before, that my great interest in the order is due to the fact that I consider it one of the greatest agencies now employed in the work of uplifting the race to which we belong.[30]

From the 1700s to 1915, fraternal and beneficial societies served the masses of Afro-Americans and helped to bring a sense of security to a people who were going through one of the most trying times in their history. Although these societies had a distinguished record, they also had their problems. For example, Table 3.13 shows the number of fraternal buildings lost by state. Hard economic times and bad management contributed to this loss.

TABLE 3.13

Fraternal Buildings Lost* to Afro-Americans, by States

Building	City	Estimated Cost
Arkansas		
Mosaic National Temple	Little Rock	$ 250,000
Mosaic State Annex	Little Rock	50,000
Mosaic Hospital	Little Rock	100,000
H. L. Bush Building and Hotel (Mosaic connections)	Little Rock	100,000
Pythian Building	Little Rock	100,000
Taborian Building	Little Rock	200,000
Sisters of Mysterious Ten and United Brothers of Friendship	Little Rock	50,000
Century Life Insurance Company (not fraternal)	Little Rock	110,000
Woodmen of Union Bathhouse, Hospital, Office Building**	Hot Springs	497,000
Georgia		
Odd Fellows Building	Atlanta	303,000
Wage-Earners Building	Savannah	100,000
Illinois		
Pythian Temple Building	Chicago	more than 1,000,000
Louisiana		
Masonic Building	Shreveport	150,000
Court of Calanthe	Shreveport	200,000
Mosaic Templar Building	Shreveport	50,000
Tennessee		
Masonic Building	Nashville	150,000
Masonic Building	Memphis	75,000
Taborian Building	Memphis	10,000
Texas		
Odd Fellows Building	Houston	385,000
Pilgrims Building	Houston	285,000
District of Columbia		
Masonic Temple	Washington	950,000
Total Loss		$5,222,500

Source: M. S. Stuart. An Economic Detour. New York: Wendell Malliett and Company, 1940. 116–117.

* According to Attorney J. L. Lewis, $50,000 in state and county back taxes is owed on the Masonic Temple in Jacksonville, Florida, which cost approximately $300,000. The order has an approximate monthly income of $20,000, but it is reputed to owe $60,000 in unpaid death claims.

** Foreclosed and possessed by the United States of America.

Although loss of a building did not mean that services were also lost, it is an indication of the difficulties that some of the societies faced. Of course, some of the buildings were reclaimed after difficult economic times. As noted by Stuart, fraternal failures can be traced to the fact that a lot of money was tied up in "brick and mortar." Thus, some societies lost sight of their original purpose, which was to take care of their members during times of need.[31]

But, without question, the experiences gained within these organizations were priceless. Here, Afro-Americans practiced the values and techniques of organization. They also practiced lessons in discipline, cooperation, and loyalty to authority. They taught and practiced teamwork. The techniques of salesmanship and canvassing campaigns for members also provided reliable knowledge. Indeed, these organizations were the only places where leaders could come in contact with very large sums of money.

This experience helped them to develop financial institutions in connection with some of the organizations. The budding legal talent of the race was also utilized and given experience. Given the amount of money involved, most of the organizations retained lawyers.

Perhaps more important, as a result of the millions of dollars collected, thousands of young Afro-American families were helped in getting an education, hundreds of homes were paid for, and mortgages were satisfied in places where these societies operated.[32]

Although these societies were helpful in the "uplift" of the race, they cannot be strictly classified as *businesses*. They did not produce or move a product, had no systematic program of investment of assets for profits (although some societies did invest), and did not provide an array of employment opportunities. But, they were very successful in what they set out to do. They represented a massive contribution of self-help in the Afro-American tradition. More importantly, they laid the groundwork for one of the first successful business enterprises among Afro-American entrepreneurs—the insurance business.

III

As can be seen from the previous discussion, self-help within Afro-American history can be related to racial discrimination. Despite the fact, as scholars noted, that blacks were not good insurance risks, some white insurance companies began to insure them. Because of racial discrimination and unfair treatment, however, Afro-American entrepreneurs saw the need to develop their own insurance industry. Consider the analysis which was a part of the "Report of the Hampton Conference" in the late 1800s and which examined the shift from benevolent societies to insurance enterprise:

> As soon as the colored man became free he formed all kinds of associations for mutual protection, many of which exist today though in somewhat modified forms. These organizations were founded for the purpose of caring for the sick and furnishing decent burial at death.

No attention was paid to difference of age, and very little to health conditions. The same joining fee was charged regardless of age, and the same monthly dues paid. . . . Regalia of all kinds were worn and the society having the greatest amount of regalia was the most popular. . . . From paying no attention to the laws of health and taking in persons without medical examination, many of these organizations found themselves loaded down with large amounts of money due on account of unpaid sick dues and death benefits. Many of them have gone to the wall and there remains little to tell that they ever existed . . . In the early eighties the colored people began to take out insurance in white companies requiring a small weekly payment and giving in return therefore a death benefit and in some instances sick dues . . . Some of these persons being more inquisitive than others found that the amounts paid on accounts of colored persons were smaller than the amounts paid to whites for the same premiums. Deciding at once that this was unjust, the more enterprising members of the race began to devise ways and means to break down the discrimination by the establishing of colored insurance companies and by attaching an insurance feature to societies [such as secret societies] already organized. The promoters of these various companies had no experience whatever in insurance, and it never occurred to them that all successful insurance is based on some well established mortality table. No investigations were made in order to find out the relative death rate of the colored and white races. In order to secure the business from white companies the common attempt was to adopt a rate lower than that charged by the white companies and to pay therefore more benefits. The woods are full of the graves of these earlier companies which failed for the want of knowledge of business.[33]

The first Afro-American insurance enterprise was founded in Philadelphia in 1810 as a response to discrimination by Euro-American companies, and was called the African Insurance Company. Although it had a capitalization stock of $5,000, it collapsed in 1833.[34] It was not until after the Civil War, when governmental control in the form of segregation ran rampant, that Afro-American insurance companies took root. In the late 1800s then, as the analysis in the above quotation makes clear, discrimination by white companies actually helped the development of Afro-American insurance businesses.

All analyses of this period stress the fact that white agents who visited black homes did not show common courtesy, and they frequently abused the property of their clients. As noted by a scholar of the period, "Nothing has more greatly aided Negro agents in meeting the competition of their more experienced competitors than the abundance of examples of insults to and abuses of Negro policy holders at the hands of white agents which could nearly always be pointed out in every community."[35]

When a white agent participated in the lynching of an Afro-American in a Southern state, struggling Afro-American companies increased their debit more than 800 percent within a month. In Vicksburg, Mississippi, during the late 1800s, the collection book of a white agent was found under a lynch tree. Sixty percent of his debit was lost, and his company lost Afro-American business in that city. During this period of racial uplift, Afro-Americans were also upset by the placing of calendars with white females' pictures on them by agents in their homes.

In addition to conflict between the races, Afro-American insurance companies began to flourish because they made prompt payment of death claims; premiums paid into their companies had the effect of creating employment; and there was more frequent payment of disability claims.[36] Thus, the insurance industry was a natural extension of self-help organizations with an enterprising factor added to it.

If one were to choose a secret society which had a direct impact on the establishment of Afro-American insurance, it would be the Grand United Order of True Reformers which was organized in Virginia. This was a secret society which especially stressed the insurance business. Not only did persons receive sick and burial benefits, but they were able to leave substantial sums of money to their dependents.

By 1932, Afro-Americans had established an insurance industry which was well-organized and functional for the community. As one would predict from the theory of economic detour, there was a direct relationship between the numbers and successes of these insurance companies and the number of Afro-Americans. This is shown in Table 3.14, where the name of company, state and number of Afro-Americans in that state is presented (Panel I). Also presented are states where there were no insurance companies (Panel II).

TABLE 3.14
Operating Territories of Negro Life Insurance Companies, 1931–32

Panel I

State	Company	Negro Population
Alabama	Atlanta Life North Carolina Mutual Life Pilgrim Health and Life	944,834
Arkansas	Universal Life	478,834
California	Golden States Mutual Life	81,048
Florida	Afro-American Life Atlanta Life Central Life	431,828

TABLE 3.14—*Continued*

Panel I		
State	*Company*	*Negro Population*
Georgia	Atlanta Life	1,071,125
	North Carolina Mutual Life	
	Pilgrim Health and Life	
	Afro-American Life	
	Guaranty Life	
Illinois	Supreme Liberty Life	328,982
	Unity Independent Life	
	Victory Mutual Life	
Indiana	Mammoth Life	111,982
	Supreme Liberty Life	
Kansas	Atlanta Life	66,344
Kentucky	Domestic Life	226,040
	Mammoth Life	
	Atlanta Life	
	Supreme Liberty Life	
Louisiana	Louisiana Industrial Life	776,326
	Unity Industrial Life	
	Universal Life	
	The Douglas	
	The Victory Independent Life	
	Good Citizens Benefit Association	
	Liberty Industrial Life	
	People's Industrial Life	
	Safety Industrial Life	
	Standard Industrial Life	
Maryland	North Carolina Mutual Life	276,379
	Southern Life	
Michigan	Great Lakes Mutual Life	169,453
	Supreme Liberty Life	
	Western Union Association	
Missouri	Atlanta Life	223,840
	Supreme Liberty Life	
	Universal Life	
Mississippi	Universal Life	1,009,718
New York	Victory Mutual Life	412,814
	United Mutual Benefit Association	
North Carolina	North Carolina Mutual Life	918,647
	Winston Mutual Life	
Ohio	Supreme Liberty Life	309,304
	Atlanta Life	
	Mammoth Life	
	Domestic Life	
	Fireside Mutual Life	
	Dunbar Mutual Insurance Society	

TABLE 3.14—*Continued*

Panel I

State	Company	Negro Population
Oklahoma	Universal Life Security Life	173,198
Pennsylvania	North Carolina Mutual Life Provident Home Benefit Society Key Stone Aid Society	431,257
South Carolina	North Carolina Mutual Life Pilgrim Health and Life	793,681
Tennessee	Universal Life Atlanta Life North Carolina Mutual Life Supreme Liberty Life Union Protective Assurance Company	477,646
Texas	Excelsior Mutual Life Atlanta Life Universal Life Western Mutual Life Watch Tower Mutual Life	854,964
Virginia	Southern Aid Society Richmond Benefit Life North Carolina Mutual Life Virginia Mutual Benefit Life	650,16
West Virginia	Supreme Liberty Life	114,893
District of Columbia	Federal Life Richmond Benefit Life Southern Aid Society North Carolina Mutual Life	132,068 *
Total		11,463,889

Panel II
States In Which No Negro Companies Operate

States	Negro Population
Arizona	10,749
Colorado	11,828
Connecticut	29,354
Delaware	32,602
Idaho	668
Iowa	17,380
Maine	1,096
Massachusetts	52,365
Minnesota	9,445
Montana	1,256
Nebraska	13,752
Nevada	516
New Hampshire	790
New Mexico	2,850

TABLE 3.14—*Continued*

Panel II
States In Which No Negro Companies Operate

States	*Negro Population*
New Jersey	208,828
North Dakota	377
Oregon	2,234
Rhode Island	9,913
South Dakota	646
Utah	1,108
Vermont	568
Washington	6,840
Wisconsin	10,739
Wyoming	1,250
Total	427,154

Source: M. S. Stuart. *An Economic Detour.* New York: Wendell Malliett and Company, 1940. 59–60.

For example, in the State of Louisiana in 1931–32, there were 776,326 Afro-Americans and ten insurance companies. In Florida, there were 431,828 Afro-Americans and three companies.

Although there is a great variation between the number of Afro-Americans and the number of insurance companies in a state, it is also true that states such as Massachusetts, Minnesota, New Jersey, Wyoming, and Maine (Panel II), or other states with a relatively small population of blacks were less likely to have insurance companies. The total black population in states where companies operated was 11,463,889; the total Afro-American population where they did not operate was 427,154.[37]

All studies of Afro-American insurance during the early 1900s stress the fact that this business was industrial. Put differently, Afro-Americans have always been weekly wage earners. Thus, they were looking, as were other Americans, for services which provided them with medicine and medical services in times of physical disability. Investment in insurance is also a measure of the willingness to plan and save.

The total industrial debit of twenty-nine companies in 1938 was $248,910. This meant that blacks paid into Afro-American insurance companies almost this amount each week for industrial insurance coverage. In 1938, white companies also had a substantial portion of the Afro-American business. It has been estimated that the $248,910 paid to black companies during that year represented no more than 25 percent of the amount paid by them to white companies for the same coverage. Thus, the total industrial premiums paid into white companies each week by blacks was not less than $995,640. This makes the total paid by blacks into all companies for industrial insurance $1,224,550. By 1939, the total amount paid weekly by Afro-Americans exceeded per week, $1,250,000.[38] These figures are an excellent indicator of thrift and planning by a group which had been excluded by the larger society.

One can measure the commitment to general economic improvement through insurance by Afro-Americans by comparing them with other groups. In an interesting study, this comparison was made with blacks and other nations in 1940. Undoubtedly, this had to be done because white ethnic groups in America never had to develop their own national insurance companies but, rather, were brought into insurance as they were able to afford it. Table 3.15 shows this comparison. The $340,000,000 insurance in force for Afro-Americans compared well with many countries of the world.

The table reflects only insurance in force for black-owned companies. Controlling for population size, one can see that there was more insurance in force for Afro-Americans in 1940 than the countries of Brazil, Poland, Mexico, Romania, Siam, and Yugoslavia. Although no systematic data were available on Afro-Americans who were insured by white companies, it has been estimated that the total life insurance on the lives of blacks amounted to $1,360,000,000. This study noted that such an estimation placed the Negro race ahead of all of the smaller national groups except Canada, Sweden and Australia.[39]

TABLE 3.15

Afro-American Insurance in Force: Compared with Selected Nations of the World

Group	Population[1]	Insurance in Force[2]
France	42,000,000	$2,891,422,000
The Netherlands	8,400,000	2,004,470,000
Italy	42,625,000	1,953,109,000[3]
Argentine Republic	12,000,000	500,000,000
Belgium	8,275,000	341,631,320
Negroes (African-Americans)	13,891,143[4]	340,000,000
Brazil	41,500,000	179,186,000
Poland	33,500,000	136,389,000[5]
Mexico	18,000,000	102,966,000
Rumania	19,000,000	76,658,000[6]
Thailand (Siam)	13,000,000	45,000,000
Yugoslavia	15,000,000	41,398,000

Source: M. S. Stuart. An Economic Detour. New York: Wendell Malliett and Company, 1940. 42.

[1]Latest available statistics. Foreign Commerce Yearbook, 1935. U.S. Department of Commerce.

[2]As of 31 December 1936. John A. Stevens, vice-president, Penn Mutual Life. Address to 32nd Convention of Life Insurance Presidents, 2 December 1938.

[3]Includes government insurance.

[4]Estimated for 1938.

[5]Includes insurance on lives of both domestic and foreign residents.

[6]Includes insurance on lives of both domestic and foreign residents.

For Afro-American insurance companies, income was estimated at $2,525,000 in 1921. By 1931, it had grown to $13,966,839. In 1932, when the Great Depression occurred, income from premiums dropped to $8,587,954 and the total income to $9,685,564. The Great Depression caused a decrease of $4,281,275 in total income.[40]

The developing insurance businesses also provided jobs and opportunities for people interested in working in this field. Actually, some white insurance businesses which were started after 1900 employed Afro-Americans as agents, but these individuals were all fired after a few years of service. In a tradition which would become "par for the course" in dealing with denied opportunities for blacks, the reason for their dismissals was cited as incompetence.

In his work on the insurance business, M. S. Stuart reflected on this treatment of Afro-Americans who tried to work in white insurance companies.

> These officials knew at the outset that there were no Negroes trained in the business of life insurance; but there was an absence of that degree of persistence that would have established a sincerity of purpose or desire to continue Negro agents in their employ. If it be remembered that of the nearly 500 life insurance organizations now operating in the United States and Canada, no more than 25 were incorporated prior to 1865 and less than 60 others chartered before the beginning of the present century, it will become plain that there was no abundance even of trained white agents in 1900; and patently, these white companies must have been willing to pay the price of training white agents by practice and experience—a price they declined to pay to use Negro agents.[41]

With no opportunity available in white insurance companies, blacks worked exclusively for black-owned companies. By 1937, there were more than 9,000 persons employed by the industry (Table 3.16). Agents' commis-

TABLE 3.16

Number of Employees of Afro-American Insurance Companies and Compensations

Year	Number of Employees	Agents' Commissions	Agency Supervision	Salaries	Medical Fees	Total Compensation
1931	7104	$ 2,116,842	$ 376,319	$ 913,027	$ 74,503	$ 3,480,692
1932	6388	2,078,138	280,133	773,445	46,140	3,167,856
1933	7656	1,959,452	478,111	843,599	53,620	3,334,783
1934	7874	2,341,602	529,391	860,215	61,864	3,793,072
1935	8150	2,606,099	654,811	858,992	66,891	4,186,795
1936	8694	2,859,054	682,188	953,500	78,348	4,753,093
1937	9010	3,249,784	574,436	978,774	87,809	4,809,803
Total		$17,210,971	$3,775,389	$6,181,552	$2,649,185	$27,346,094

Source: M. S. Stuart. An Economic Detour. New York: Wendell Malliett and Company, 1940. 49.

sions totaled $17,210,971, and those who supervised agents were paid a total of $3,775,389. Total salaries were more than six million dollars, medical fees more than two million, and total compensation more than 27 million.

As the years passed, this self-help, protection, and savings institution began to increase. At the twenty-ninth annual session of the National Negro Insurance Association held in Philadelphia in 1949, the state of the enterprise was assessed. In 1948, there were sixty-two member companies of the associ-ation with a little less than one billion dollars worth of insurance in force. Assets were well over $108 million. The annual income of these companies was more than $55 million. Between 1937 and 1948, the membership of the association showed a fourfold increase in assets and a similar increase in income.[42] These figures do not include all Afro-American insurance compa-nies because all were not members of the association. The association included sixty company members.

In 1947, there were a total of 211 insurance companies (not all members of the National Negro Insurance Association) exclusively owned by Afro-Americans. In these companies, the group had a total of 5,213,259 policies in force, an increase of 37.6 percent over 1945.[43]

Although we noted earlier that insurance companies grew from benevo-lent and secret societies, these societies did not disappear completely. Although they did not play a major role after the introduction of the insurance enter-prise, they nevertheless remained a part of Afro-American culture. Table 3.17 gives data that allows us to make a comparative statement on the condition of all Afro-American-owned associations, societies, and insurance companies for the years ending 31 December 1941–1947. The data are reflective of the number of companies reporting each year. By 1947, there were 211 companies reporting. As a measure of self-help, between 1941 and 1947, the total amount of claims paid increased from $7,294,241 to $12,749,931. Total liabilities increased from $26,790,960 to $75,553,981; for the same years, capital reserves, though showing an increase, hovered well above the two million mark.

In order to assess how different types of associations contributed to the total bottom line, the study by Kinzer and Sagarin divided the insurance com-panies into several types (Table 3.18). Statements of assets, liabilities, capital, and other data are shown. It can be seen that the legal reserve life insurance companies account for a tremendous amount of the total business of these companies. Their premium or assessment income is $40,791,576. Burial com-panies and traditional fraternal benefit societies combined account for $4,889,786 for the same category.

Of course, life insurance is a business and is designed to generate profits. As with all businesses, Afro-American life insurance companies were inter-ested in the bottom line and profits for its stockholders. In his classic study entitled *Negro Business and Business Education*, Pierce sampled Afro-American

TABLE 3.17

Comparative Statement of Conditions of All Negro-Owned Insurance Companies, Associations, and Societies

	1941	1942	1943	1944	1945	1946	1947	Increase—Decrease** 1947 over 1941	
								Amount	Percent
Number of Reporting Companies	202	203	196	199	191	202	211		
Total admitted assets	$36,447,561	$42,189,143	$51,750,181	$61,985,921	$72,787,542	$85,824,105	$101,973,906	5,526,345	179.8
Total liabilities	26,790,960	29,859,567	36,213,809	43,496,594	46,175,063	58,548,764	75,553,981	48,763,021	182.0
Capital	2,141,770	2,189,415	2,897,373	2,959,912	3,398,010	3,721,740	4,695,890	2,554,120	119.3
Surplus (exclusive of capital)	5,687,222	6,032,617	8,550,618	12,498,338	18,606,901	21,898,814	24,155,796	18,468,574	324.7
Statutory policy reserves	20,216,335	22,443,766	28,323,918	34,193,742	44,186,981	54,350,408	66,371,485	46,155,150	228.3
Premium or assessment income	22,214,318	25,416,988	27,171,529	35,470,133	36,219,504	45,023,746	32,240,345	30,026,027	135.2
Total income	25,338,459	28,589,021	33,435,306	41,639,924	43,990,225	52,703,038	57,239,412	31,900,953	125.9
Total disbursement	20,129,802	22,799,965	25,426,617	30,183,835	30,352,437	38,377,796	45,296,125	25,166,323	125.0
Total claims paid	7,294,241	6,773,708	7,689814	8,887,803	8,565,236	10,0006,522	12,749,931	5,455,690	74.8
Total amount of policies in force	471,328,921	540,627,298	595,312,053	717,211,163	745,310,805	888,400,733	1,035,136,094	563,807,173	119.6
Total number of policies in force					3,789,989	4,611,889	5,213,259	1,423,270***	37.6***

*** Comparative Period, 1945–1947

Source: Robert H. Kinzer and Edward Sagarin. *The Negro in American Business.* New York: Greenberg Press. 1950. 96.

TABLE 3.18

Recapitulation of Data on Negro-Owned Insurance Companies, 31 December 1947

	Total Admitted Assets	Total Liabilities	Capital	Surplus (Exclusive of Capital)	Statutory Policy Reserves	Premium or Assessment Income
Legal reserve life companies	$ 83,742,815	$61,644,739	$4,090,920	$19,922,156	$60,474,564	$40,791,576
Assessment legal reserve life companies	328,887	268,431	—	60,456	242,117	332,477
Assessment life companies	1,429,487	1,015,062	—	284,012	1,107,023	808,958
Limited life company	426,908	350,898	—	76,010	322,820	451,899
Assessment health and accident companies	110,812	13,291	—	97,521	870	220,610
Fire and casualty companies	378,554	30,320	200,000	148,233	12,366	203,785
Mutual aid companies	241,300	150,003	5,000	69,822	2,475	306,680
Industrial life companies	4,465,988	3,207,387	345,000	930,499	2,900,576	4,234,574
Burial companies	1,990,812	1,310,456	54,970	544,814	166,634	2,852,384
Fraternal benefit societies	8,858,343	7,563,394	—	2,022,273	1,142,040	2,037,402
Totals	$101,973,906	$75,553,981	$4,695,890	$24,155,796	$66,371,485	$52,240,345

	Total Income	Total Disbursement	Total Claims Paid	Total Policies or Certificates in Force	
				Amount	Number
Legal reserve life companies	$44,639,494	$33,965,142	$9,369,664	$792,664,641	3,771,383
Assessment legal reserve life companies	349,152	314,710	53,736	10,988,923	37,828
Assessment life companies	954,483	696,341	172,648	16,119,966	73,889
Limited life company	470,219	440,570	109,400	7,884,444	35,165
Assessment health and accident companies	246,999	239,746	60,746	—	31,073
Fire and casualty companies	227,040	208,550	63,587	—	—
Mutual aid companies	330,276	304,434	90,786	5,041,978	13,261
Industrial life companies	4,390,797	4,142,245	1,050,962	69,565,104	527,444
Burial companies	3,006,237	2,844,027	941,516	79,827,173	446,034
Fraternal benefit societies	2,624,715	2,140,360	836,752	53,043,865	277,182
Totals	$57,239,412	$45,296,125	$12,749,931	$1,035,136,094	5,213,259

Source: Robert H. Kinzer and Edward Sagarin. The Negro in American Business. New York: Greenberg Press, 1950. 95.

insurance companies and included a section on returns to stockholders. In 1945, sixteen stock companies (of the seventeen listed) paid cash dividends to their stockholders (Table 3.19). They ranged from 4.0 percent of the capital stock of two firms to a high of 90 percent of the capital stock of a rather small company. All companies in the sample paid cash dividends equal to 7.9 percent of their total capital stock. The data in Table 3.19 also reveal that three of the companies paid stock dividends of $300,000, $100,000 and $75,000; respectively, this represented 60 percent, 50 percent, and 75 percent of their capital stock. One large company reported a dividend to policyholders of more than $2,000. Pierce notes that this was not a dividend in the strict use of the word, but rather represented payment in liquidation of guaranteed coupons.[44]

In a rare but important comparison, Pierce's study also examined the investment practices of 44 member companies of the National Negro Insurance Association to those of companies that belonged to the Life Insurance Association of America, an association that owned about 94 percent of the assets of all companies in America. Afro-American companies were in the tradition of ethnic enterprise and, as a consequence, were small. They also were mostly industrial insurance, a fact which affected their investment practices.

Table 3.20 shows that Afro-American life insurance companies invested more of their assets in real estate than did other American companies in gen-

TABLE 3.19
Dividends Paid to Stockholders of Negro Life Insurance Companies, 1945

| | Cash Dividend | | Stock Dividend | |
Company	Amount	Percentage of Capital Stock	Amount	Percentage of Capital Stock
A	$ 5,372.78	5.4	—	—
B	4,500.00	90.0	—	—
F	4,730.40	4.0	—	—
G	8,962.50	4.5	—	—
H	60,000.00	6.0	—	—
I	30,000.00	15.0	$100,000.00	50.0
K	12,000.00	12.0	—	—
N	—	—	1,249.96	5.0
R	10,000.00	20.0	—	—
S	7,500.00	5.0	—	—
U	2,656.80	17.7	—	—
W	5,000.00	5.0	—	—
GG	2,000.00	40.0	—	—
JJ	8,000.00	4.0	—	—
MM	25,000.00	25.0	75,000.00	75.0
NN	39,915.00	8.0	300,000.00	60.0
QQ	949.00	9.5	—	—

Source: Joseph A. Pierce. Negro Business and Business Education. New York: Harper & Brothers Publishers. 1947. 127.

TABLE 3.20
Percentage Distribution of Physical Assets of 44 Member Companies of The National Negro
Insurance Association and of The Member Companies of the Life Insurance Association of
America, 31 December 1945

| | *Percentages of Physical Assets of:* | |
Physical Assets	Member Companies of the National Negro Insurance Association	Member Companies of the Life Insurance Association of America*
Mortgages	13.7	14.7
Bonds	60.7	77.5
Stocks	3.7	1.9
Real estate	6.5	1.9
Collateral loans	0.1	—
Cash	14.0	1.6
All other	1.3	2.4
Total Physical Assets	100.0	100.0
Policy Loans and Premium Notes	2.6†	4.2†

Source: Joseph A. Pierce. *Negro Business and Business Education.* New York: Harper & Brothers Publishers. 1947. 128.

Source: Best's Life Reports. New York: Alfred M. Best Company, 1946. v.

†Percentage of admitted assets.

eral. The percentage of real estate investments made by these companies was almost three and a half times that of white companies in America.

There is not a great deal of difference between the two categories, however, when investments in mortgages are considered. One can also see from Table 3.20 that Afro-American companies invested less in bonds than did their white counterparts.

This study also revealed that cash accounted for only 1.6 percent of the physical assets of white companies as a whole. For Afro-American companies, cash accounted for 14.0 percent of their assets. However, the author of the study was careful to note that cash-on-hand figures can be misleading because the data reflect year-end positions of the companies. Sometimes, bonds were sold at the end of the tax year in order to help the company avoid certain types of tax payments. Bonds were then repurchased—hopefully at a profit—at the beginning of the next tax year.[45]

As we will see when we examine retail enterprises in the next chapter, the insurance business was the "cream of the crop" of Afro-American entrepreneurship. Consequently, as it developed, the insurance business was able to take advantage of the increasing educational level of the Afro-American community. Pierce's classic study allows us to look back at this development. It also allows us to examine the significance of the types of gender and personality traits that were considered to be desirable by these companies.

All of the companies studied by Pierce had a policy of hiring qualified beginners who were expected to occupy, at some point in their careers, the most important positions in the company. These companies concentrated on individuals who had collegiate business educations and, thus, were considered to be promotable. Of the 27 companies examined, twenty-three used this method. The other four companies simply promoted through the ranks, regardless of education.

Managers of insurance companies paid considerable attention to sex, age, personality traits, and, of course, education when seeking qualified promotable employees. Of the twenty-four companies that reported their hiring preferences as regards gender, eleven stated that gender was unimportant, eleven companies desired males, and one company wanted only males. There were no companies that requested only female employees, and only one company preferred most of its promotable employees to be women.

The inevitable conclusion is that these companies were not excited about the hiring of women into positions that might lead to the exercise of authority. Pierce also noted, however, that a significant number of the companies were willing to play down their gender prejudices and hire qualified persons regardless of gender.[46]

As far as age was concerned, the typical company preferred to employ people who were no younger than twenty and no older than forty. The personality traits considered to be most important were honesty, friendliness, cooperativeness, reliability, appearance, enthusiasm, loyalty, and sincerity.

In terms of education, eleven companies (or 44 percent) stated that the minimum educational requirement was a high school diploma. Five companies (20 percent) considered a junior college education as a necessity, and nine companies (36 percent) noted that a college education was most desirable for its upper-level promotable employees. The high school completion category was most emphasized for those people who worked at lower levels.[47] All of the companies—except for two—favored business education as a prerequisite for employment in positions which would lead to advancement.

When compared to the responses of the companies, the actual data compiled by Pierce showed the importance of education.

> The average employee of life insurance companies has considerably more education than the average employee in general business. The median extent of education of home-office employees is 13.6 years, which represents about one and one-half years in college. . . . The median education of employees in general business (retail stores, service establishments, and miscellaneous businesses) is only 10.8 years. Only about 20 percent of the employees of life insurance companies have less than that amount of education. . . . The business edu-

cation of employees . . . may be studied with respect to type of training and place; and where the training was received . . . Of the 144 employees who took courses in business, 105, or 72.9 percent, majored in business. Of those who majored in business, 40 percent took their training in high school, 32.4 percent in a private business school, 25.7 percent in a college, and 1.9 percent in graduate school. The average time spent by persons who took a business major in high school was 2.5 years; in private business school, 1 year; in college, 2.5 years; and each of the two employees who took business in graduate school studied 4 years. The 39 employees who had taken business subjects but had not majored in the field generally took a few business subjects in high school, a private business school, or in college.[48]

The metamorphosis of Afro-American insurance companies from the self-help associations of the 1700s is a remarkable untold story in the sociology of ethnic enterprise. As William K. Bell noted in his classic book entitled *A Business Primer for Negroes*, the strength and durability of Negro insurance companies was made apparent by the way in which they weathered the Great Depression with a creditable record. These Afro-American enterprises came through the Depression in much better economic shape than did the white companies. Although Afro-Americans lost two outstanding companies because of the Depression,[49] the survival rate of Afro-American insurance companies, and the question of how they managed that survival, is one of the most interesting topics to emerge during that time period. Consider the following analysis by W. J. Kennedy, Jr., which Bell quoted:

> For purpose of comparison, we now turn the spotlight on the records of life enterprises operated by white people in the United States. According to current issues of *Insurance Year Book* published by The Spectator Company of New York City, and other insurance publications, the business of 109 white companies was taken over by other companies during the last four years, and twenty-seven white companies were forced into receiver ship during this period; ten of them having failed since January 1, 1933.[50]

Bell noted that this analysis showed that—in comparison with big white companies—the management of the Negro life insurance companies was outstanding. He also noted that the failure of white companies meant a big loss to many blacks who held their insurance in those companies. As Bell said, "All of this will go to show 'Doubting Thomases' in the race that their life insurance is as safe, if not safer in some cases, with Negro life insurance companies."[51]

IV

One of the central problems of the sociology of entrepreneurship is to examine how institutions generate capital for the development of business activity. Ivan Light presented a noncomparative analysis of the Afro-American banking experience.

Relying on old stereotypes rather than comprehensive analysis with white bankers, he noted that Afro-American banks experienced a crisis in management due to receiving education from inferior institutions. He suggested that Afro-Americans had an "object ignorance of elementary banking principles." Although Light pointed out that Afro-American banks in California did much better than did Oriental banks, this point was made without much discussion.[52]

Light's analysis, like most in this tradition, is most interesting because education was a struggle throughout the South. Research has revealed that it was a toss-up as to which group was more interested in educational attainment—black or white Southerners.

One could easily argue that, although developing white institutions of the South had better facilities (though that was not always the case), objective standards show that professors at black colleges had degrees from more prestigious institutions and published more than did their white counterparts. Put another way, white Southerners had no more of a tradition of excellence in education than did their black counterparts.

More importantly, comparative analyses, that do not automatically infer an institution's excellence simply because it is white, make Light's comments on Afro-American banks seem even more elementary, and, indeed, biased. Although Afro-Americans had their troubles in the banking business, these problems were similar to those facing American bankers in general.

In his analysis of the Afro-American banking experience, Pierce was careful to take a comparative approach.[53] He noted that whites had organized thousands of banks without much regard to their need for the equipment and capital that management would require to be successful. Indeed, between 1865 and 1920, 3,108 banks operated by whites experienced failure. When one examines failures by type of bank, one finds that 594 were national banks and 2,514 were state and private banks. Between the years 1921 and 1932, 10,816 white banks failed in America; 1,612 of these were national banks; 8,716 were private, and 476 were mutual savings banks.

We will not make the theoretical leap, as Light does, and say that white banks failed because the whites who were in charge of them had inferior education and lacked managerial skills. We will say, rather, that all businesses—whether banking or otherwise—are subject to factors such as the marketplace and the success of individuals which interact with them. This is true even today.

For example, bank failures in the oil states of Oklahoma, Texas, and Louisiana, in 1987 pushed bank closings in that year to a post-Depression record. The Federal Deposit Insurance Corporation reported 187 bank closings among the 14,000 commercial banks that it had insured. More than half of the failures (95) were in Texas, Oklahoma, and Louisiana. In Texas, 50 banks failed; Louisiana counted 14 failures; and Oklahoma recorded 31. The Federal Deposit Insurance Corporation expected the failures to continue.[54] These banks were full of managers with college degrees and Masters of Business Education (MBAs).

As of yet, no studies have been done which attempt to draw a relationship between the quality of the schools that employees attended with bank failures. Because Light knew nothing about the Afro-American experience in banking and enterprise, his analysis will forever stand as misleading.

At any rate, the sociology of entrepreneurship is concerned with the activities of ethnic groups under hostile environments, and, in this tradition, the history of Afro-Americans in banking provides an excellent case study. The creation of banking by Afro-Americans took place at a time in American history when things were changing rapidly. Let us now take a look at this period and then consider the banking experience of Afro-Americans.

During the middle of nineteenth century, America was on the verge of the Industrial Revolution. There was westward expansion and a general feeling of economic progress. Although Afro-Americans had established beneficial societies, they began to think about forming banking institutions which would enhance economic development. Euro-Americans practiced a policy of racial exclusion in economic development. Regardless of their European ethnic background, if persons had funds to invest in the developing economic prosperity, they were welcome to do so. But, despite the relative scarcity of cash in the country, even Afro-Americans with large amounts of money to invest were not welcomed.

In the 1850s, there is a well-documented case of an Afro-American who attempted to deal on the New York Stock Exchange and who was denied the privilege to do so. Put another way, although Europeans of all ethnic origins were allowed, Afro-Americans were excluded from participation in the more lucrative dimensions of the economic marketplace.[55]

During the early 1850s, interested Afro-Americans began to think about establishing a major banking institution in the country. The 29 March 1851, issue of *The New York Times* reported the organization of what was perhaps the first major think-tank developed to tackle this problem.

In the early months of 1851, Afro-Americans met in New York City to discuss plans for forming a bank. The guiding premise of the meeting was the development of an institution which could help in the creation of homesteads for Afro-Americans—especially in the developing West—and enhance the development of business for Afro-American enterprise.

Drawing on their early experiences with benevolent societies, the members of this think-tank made a plan to set the bank up on a mutual principle in order to deal in real estate, bonds, mortgages, and commercial paper. People at the meeting were aware that Afro-Americans had on deposit some forty thousand dollars in New York banks in 1851. The plan was to capitalize the original Afro-American bank by convincing depositors to transfer their money to the developing Afro-American bank. There were other similar meetings held in 1855 in New York City and in Philadelphia.[56]

These efforts by blacks were hampered, however, by the realities of race and the national conscience during this time period. In addition to the problem of obtaining capital and credit—a major obstacle for developing banking enterprises—the racial climate imposed perhaps the most important obstacle.

The 1850s, or the pre-Civil War period, saw Euro-Americans debating the economic and social implications of slavery. In 1857 the Dred Scott case further increased white consciousness about the race problem. Only twenty years earlier, Nat Turner had struck fear in the hearts of all Euro-Americans, and that episode was still fresh in their minds.[57]

In a very real sense, all efforts of Afro-Americans to organize on their own behalf were closely watched and monitored by Euro-Americans. Because of the racial climate, and the outbreak of the Civil War in 1860, efforts initiated in the 1850s never materialized. It took the Civil War and the Emancipation Proclamation to instigate changes in the character and nature of race relations, especially where business enterprise was concerned.

As they had done in the American Revolution, free Afro-Americans responded to the call to fight for the country. Despite the reality of discrimination and racism within the civilian sector, Afro-Americans responded with enthusiasm, perhaps because this war struck at the very roots of the slave society. Overall, they were among the most fervent supporters of the war. But when Northern blacks reported to duty, the Secretary of War said bluntly, "This department has no intention to call into service any colored soldiers."[58]

As noted earlier, it was not until after the Emancipation Proclamation, when manpower was badly needed, that Afro-Americans were allowed to enlist for duty.[59]

At the conclusion of the Civil War, the country returned to the traditional pattern of race relations. The military reversed its policy allowing black enlistment. Those who remained in service were formed into four units: the Ninth and Tenth Cavalry and the Fourteenth and Fifteenth Infantry. During the war, there had been 120 colored units or troops. Still, these units played major roles in the settlement of the West, fighting native Americans and ensuring the safe migration of covered wagons between 1870 and 1890.[60]

Afro-Americans had their first organized banking experience while serving in the military. During the Civil War, Union officers encouraged saving and thrift among their Afro-American troops. In order to facilitate this process, banks were established so that soldiers could deposit part of their pay.

In 1864, the first of such banks—called the Free Labor Bank—was established. When the war ended, it was the first to serve blacks during the "dawn of freedom." These types of banks were located where large percentages of black soldiers were stationed. There were banks in Beaufort, South Carolina, and Norfolk, Virginia. When the war ended, although there are no records for all such banks, the Beaufort Bank had on hand about $200,000.[61]

Unlike earlier beneficial societies which were private ventures, the first organized bank after the defeat of the Confederacy was established by the Federal government. The end of the war and emancipation had increased the need for a financial agency to meet the economic needs of the new freedman. In March of 1865, the National Congress incorporated the Freedmen's Savings and Trust Company. Section Five of the Act noted the following:

> And be it further enacted, that the general business and object of the corporation hereby created shall be received on deposit such sums of money as may, from time to time, be offered therefore by or on behalf of persons heretofore held in slavery in the United States, or their descendants, and investing the same in the stocks, bonds, treasury notes or other securities of the United States.[62]

Given that Afro-Americans were just released from slavery, their response to the Freedmen's Bank was quite remarkable. Table 3.21 shows branches of the bank and deposits made as of March 1872. The banks were located in mostly Southern states, and blacks responded by depositing, as of 1872, close to four million dollars. Such a response showed that Afro-Americans were: (1) well aware of the importance of saving and thrift; (2) understood the importance of economic security and making a better life in America; and (3) were willing to trust economic institutions designed to organize for a collective effort.

Unfortunately, the Freedmen's Bank did not deliver on its economic promise. It turned out to be one of the most massive failures in the history of Afro-American financial institutions. Historical analysis reveals that, within the Afro-American community, it had an effect similar to the 1970 Watergate affair—complete with hearings, blame, and dishonesty. Like Watergate, the transcripts of the hearings became an interesting commodity within the Afro-American community. The historical account, with all testimonies and hearings, can be found in Congressional Records.

The Freedmen's Bank was organized and controlled by whites for the benefits of Afro-Americans. Although there was no governmental backing, Afro-Americans were led to believe that the government was responsible for the funds. In *The Negro As Capitalist*, which is the most interesting analysis of the bank, Harris noted that while officers of the bank were not totally responsible

TABLE 3.21
Branches of the Freedmen's Bank*

Branches	Dates of Organization	Deposits as of March 1872
Atlanta, Ga.	Jan. 14, 1870	$23,632.57
Augusta, Ga.	March 8, 1866	75,482.87
Baltimore, Md.	March 12, 1866	212,588.79
Beaufort, S.C.	Oct. 16, 1865	46,480.92
Charleston, S.C.	Jan. 11, 1866	291,018.42
Chattanooga, Tenn.	May 10, 1869	328.41
Columbus, Miss.	Aug. 1, 1870	14,432.38
Columbia, Tenn.	——, 1871	16,879.55
Huntsville, Ala.	Dec. 11, 1865	45,946.89
Jacksonville, Fla.	March 10, 1866	83,623.82
Lexington, Ky.	Oct. ——, 1870	37,279.27
Little Rock, Ark.	Nov. 25, 1870	22,469.83
Louisville, Ky.	Sept. 1, 1865	127,404.33
Lynchburg, Va.	June ——, 1871	12,741.73
Macon, Ga.	Oct. 14, 1868	39,721.43
Memphis, Tenn.	Dec. 30, 1865	134,884.77
Mobile, Ala.	Jan. 1, 1866	106,741.39
Montgomery, Ala.	June 14, 1870	27,414.00
Natchez, Miss.	March 29, 1870	21,101.73
Nashville, Tenn.	Oct. 28, 1865	101,342.10
New Berne, N.C.	Jan. 11, 1866	60,262.13
New Orleans, La.	Jan. 7, 1866	255,260.39
New York, N.Y.	July 21, 1866	337,911.92
Norfolk, Va.	June 3, 1865	123,447.01
Philadelphia, Pa.	Jan. 4, 1870	73,624.79
Raleigh, N.C.	Jan. 9, 1869	19,459.82
Richmond, Va.	Oct. 13, 1865	130,984.30
Savannah, Ga.	Jan. 11, 1866	134,087.17
Shreveport, La.	Nov. 15, 1870	31,710.81
St. Louis, Mo.	June 27, 1868	66,173.38
Tallahassee, Fl.	Aug. 22, 1866	44,221.89
Vicksburg, Miss.	Dec. 3, 1865	155,946.29
Washington, D.C.	Aug. 1, 1865	760,797.12
Wilmington, N.C.	Oct. 24, 1865	51,689.95
Total		$3,684,739.97

* Report of the Senate Select Committee to investigate the Freedmen's Savings Bank and Trust Company, 1880. Appendix, 41–42.

for this belief, their actions, public utterances and literature promoted this idea. In addition to literature, which bore the picture of a likeness of Lincoln and General Grant, two heroes of the Civil War, the American flag was draped over the building which housed the Freedman's Bureau. Believing that their funds would be protected, more than 70,000 Afro-Americans rushed to deposit their money. Table 3.22 shows how the deposit grew each year from 1866 and 1874. As can be seen from the table, by 1874 deposits had reached $55 million.

Du Bois noted, in his Atlanta Papers, that "Of all disgraceful swindles perpetrated on a struggling people, the Freedmen's Bank was among the worst, and the Negro did well not to wait for justice, but went to banking himself as soon as his ignorance and poverty allowed.[63]

This Watergate-type affair had a devastating effect on the willingness of Afro-Americans to invest their savings in any institution. Because they had been led to believe that the Freedmen's Bank was a government institution, they lost a tremendous amount of confidence in the whole federal apparatus in Washington. Even after the memories faded, they turned to the creation of private banks in attempt to "seek for themselves." This plan created the most tremendous effort at private banking by any ethnic or racial group in the history of America that experienced systematic discrimination. The history of this effort—as with the history of banking in America—was filled with triumphs and failures, but it was this banking industry which provided the seed money for business enterprises in the period following the Civil War.

Historical records show that the first Afro-American private bank with any substance was organized on 17 October 1888. It opened with a capital of $6,000, which increased to $50,000 during the sixteen years of its business life. The bank endured the difficult financial panic of 1893, and did an excellent commercial business for those sixteen years. During the 1800s, it served as an excellent example of private enterprise by Afro-Americans. It was located at 609 F Street, N.W., in the heart of the business district of Washington. Although little is known about the bank, scholars have noted three reasons for its failure in 1904. These reasons are central to bank failures in general and include:

1. Long-term and unprofitable commercial loans, which resulted in the freezing of assets
2. Speculative schemes of officers
3. The misappropriation and embezzlement of funds by one of the high officials.[64]

TABLE 3.22
Growth of Deposits in Freedmen's Bank

Year	Total Amount of Deposits	Deposits Each Year	Balance Due Depositors	Gain Each Each Year
1866	$ 305,167	$ 305,167	$ 199,283	$ 199,283
1867	1,624,835	1,319,686	366,338	167,054
1868	3,582,378	1,957,525	638,299	271,960
1869	7,257,798	3,675,240	1,073,465	435,166
1870	12,605,782	5,347,983	1,657,000	582,541
1871	19,952,947	7,347,165	2,455,836	798,829
1872	31,260,499	11,281,313	3,684,739	1,227,927
1873	—	—	4,200,000	—
1874	55,000,000	—	3,013,670	—

Source: Abram L. Harris. *The Negro As Capitalist*. McGrath Publishing Company. 1936. 29.

The next important banking venture by Afro-Americans was begun in 1888. In March of that year, the Virginia Legislature granted a charter for a bank to the Grand Foundation of the United Order of True Reformers. The bank had its first business day on 3 April 1889, and received a total of $1,268.69 on that day.

When the idea of an Afro-American bank was presented to the Legislature of Virginia, it was not treated seriously. But Afro-Americans, again in response to the actions of Euro-Americans, had a determination to seek for themselves. The action which caused the idea for the bank was detailed in the 1890s at a conference at Hampton College:

> It might be interesting to know . . . that this bank, founded by William W. Browne, had its origin in a lynching which occurred in Charlotte County at a point called Drake's Branch. A branch of the organization of True Reformers had been founded at Mossingford and the fees of the members, amounting to nearly $100, had been deposited in the safe of a white man, who had thus, an opportunity to see that the Negroes of the county had some money and that they were organizing for some purpose. We decided that this was an unwise thing and so determined to break up the organization. This fact was reported to Mr. Browne and by a personal visit to the place he succeeded in saving the organization and at the same time had his attention called to the need of a colored bank, where colored people could carry on their business and not have it exposed to unscrupulous whites. The idea of a bank was first advanced by a countryman named W.E. Grant and immediately adopted by Mr. Browne. Thus it came to pass that because of an unpleasant race feeling in Charlotte Country, Virginia, the oldest incorporated Negro bank came into existence.[65]

It should be pointed out that early ventures in the banking business had their origins in the same religious benevolent societies which were discussed earlier. For example, the True Reformers Bank was a subsidiary organization of the Grand Fountain United Order of True Reformers. Other examples were the Alabama Penny Savings Bank, founded by a minister; and the Nickel Saving Bank, founded in 1896 in Richmond, Virginia, as a part of the People's Insurance Company. This pattern was systematic in the early formation of Afro-American banks.[66]

The most impressive study of the Afro-American banking tradition was done in 1936 by Abram L. Harris, entitled *The Negro As Capitalist: A Study Of Banking and Business Among American Negroes*. Although the banking experiences of all Afro-Americans were not involved in the analysis because significant numbers deposited in white banks, the analysis is an overlooked classic in the sociology of entrepreneurship. Harris's analysis is clear in terms of history;

quantitative analysis of deposits, growth, earnings, assets, loans and discounts; and it shows how and why banks failed or succeeded. His analysis covers the years 1899–1934 and greatly informs our understanding of Afro-American banks. His findings are worth reviewing.

In his survey, Harris found that, from 1888 to 1934, no less than 134 banks were founded and organized by Afro-Americans. Under this classification are private banks doing a general banking business and banks operating under state or national charters. It does not include credit unions, industrial loan associations, or building and loan societies. Table 3.23 shows Harris' data which reflect the names of Afro-American banks, the year and place of organization, and the date of failure.

In addition to Harris' work, the work of Walter L. Fleming, entitled *The Freedman's Savings Bank: A Chapter in The Economic History of The Negro Race*, published in 1927; and Arnett Lindsay's seminal article published in the *Journal of Negro History* in April 1929 and entitled "The Negro in Banking"[67] are also valuable.

As in a case reviewed earlier, the banking enterprise in different cities related to unpleasant racial situations, but it is also true that the spirit of capitalist enterprise lay behind the establishment of these banks.

Table 3.24 shows the relationship between the number of banks and the development of resources. In 1899 there were two Afro-American banks with total resources equaling $22,917.55. By 1926, during the Roaring 1920's, resources reached a height of $12,831,384.05. There were thirty-three banks in operation during this year. Table 3.24 shows that the number increased rapidly between 1907 and 1908, going from eleven to twenty-nine. Between 1921 and 1927, the number hovered around thirty. By the time the Great Depression was in full swing, the number had dwindled to one, with resources of only $406,012.34.

Table 3.24 also shows the liabilities of these banks. In an interesting analysis, Harris creates ratios based on the rules for analyzing bank statements in order to understand exactly why there was failure. The ratios were used as norms published in "Bank Credit Problems Department" of the *Bankers Magazine*, and are not absolute.

The results of Harris' analysis are presented in Table 3.25. Using the normative ratio of one to two for the categories in the table, he found that Afro-American banks, taken in the aggregate, had too large of a capital structure given the amount of deposits that they received. This conclusion is measured by the fact that the ratio of capital investment to total deposits from 1903 to 1930 averaged 32.9 percent. As can be seen from the normative ratios expected, the anticipated ratio (as measured by state banks), was 18 percent.

Harris judged the financial structure by examining the ratio of loans and discounts to earning assets; the ratio of fixed assets to capital investment; and the ratio of fixed assets to surplus and undivided profits. For the same time period, the ratio of loans and discounts to earning assets ranged from 99.8 percent to 64.1 percent, with the average ratio being 85.8 percent. The norm for this category was 75 percent.

This finding points to the fact that the financial structure of Afro-American banks included few stocks and bonds and was confined almost totally to loans and discounts. Harris attributes this finding—the high ratio of loans and discounts to earning assets—to the absence of government and other good securities in the portfolios of these banks.[68]

Harris further notes that real estate or chattel property secured the loans and discounts of banks that failed. This meant that the bank structure was frozen, unable to liquidate if it became necessary. Harris concludes the following about Afro-American banks for this time period:

> In one year between 1903 and 1930 was the ratio of fixed assets to capital investment as low as 30 percent. While the normal ratio to be expected of state banks is at about 21 percent of capital, surplus and undivided profits, the ratio of Negro banks fluctuated between 109.7 percent and 31.7 percent. It was highest in 1920 and lowest in 1903. The average was 72.8 percent. This means that in almost every year, the fixed assets of Negro banks were over 50 percent of their capital investment. This condition has an important bearing upon the ability of the banks to liquidate on one hand, and to remain in a healthy condition by accumulating a surplus, on the other. Thus, when we compare the fixed assets with the surplus and undivided profits of these banks, rather startling results appear. The ratio of fixed assets to surplus and undivided profits averaged 428.3 percent from 1903 to 1930 and ranged from a low of 65.5 percent to a high of 1104.5 percent. The non-liquid character of these banks, their high ratio of loans to earning assets and the heavy fixed investment are the direct and indirect results of the small volume of business which was essentially non-commercial in character.[69]

Although there were banks which were successful, Harris' analysis captures the experiences of most Afro-American banks. As we consider his conclusions, it is necessary to examine banking in general during this time period.

The experience of Afro-American banks represented a mirror of the banking industry in general around the turn of the century. In an analysis of white banks, T. Bruce Robb noted that these banks failed first of all because of poor management. In an article entitled "Safeguarding the Depositor," he concluded:

TABLE 3.23
Directory of Negro Banks

State	Name	City	Organized	Failed
Alabama	Alabama Penny Savings and Loan	Birmingham	1880	1915
	Safety Banking and Realty Company	Mobile	1909	1911
	Prudential Savings	Birmingham	1910	—
	Tuskegee Institute Savings	Tuskegee	1919	—
	Alabama Savings	Selma	—	—
	Anniston Penny Savings	Anniston	—	—
	Montgomery Penny Savings	Montgomery	—	—
	People's Investment and Banking	Birmingham	—	—
Arkansas	Capital City Savings	Little Rock	1883	—
	Penny Savings	Edmonston	—	—
	Unity Savings and Trust	Pine Bluff	—	—
District of Columbia	Capital Savings	Washington	1883	1902
	Industrial Savings	Washington	1913	1939
	Prudential Bank	Washington	1923	1929
	Union Laborers Savings	Washington	1923	1926
Florida	S. H. Hart and Son	Jacksonville	1912	—
	Metropolitan Savings	Ocala	1913	1936
	Anderson and Company	Jacksonville	1914	1931
	Progress Savings Bank	Key West	—	—
	Ocala Savings	Ocala	—	—
Georgia	Knights and Ladies of Honor of the World	Greenville	1904	—
	Metropolitan Savings	Savannah	—	1906
	Atlanta State Savings	Atlanta	1913	1923
	Wage Earners Savings	Savannah	1916	1936
	Citizens Trust and Savings	Atlanta	1931	—
	Savannah Savings and Real Estate Corp.	Savannah	1915	—
	Auburn Savings Corporation	Atlanta	—	—

TABLE 3.23—*Continued*

State	Name	City	Organized	Failed
	Penny Savings, Loan and Investment	Augusta	—	—
	Fidelity Loan and Trust Company	Savannah	—	—
	Middle Georgia Savings and Investment Company	Macon	—	—
	Laborers Savings and Loan	Columbus	—	—
	Mechanics Investment Company	Savannah	—	—
	Union Savings Bank	Savannah	—	—
	Afro-American Investment Company	Savannah	—	—
Illinois	Binga State Bank	Chicago	1908	1930
	Douglass National	Chicago	1922	1963
	Douglass Park State Bank	Chicago	1919	—
	Merchant and People's Bank	Chicago	—	—
	Hunter Banking Company	Chicago	1917	1919
	Woodfolk Banking Company	Chicago	1918	1919
Kentucky	American Mutual Savings	Louisville	1931	1933
	Peoples Savings and Trust	Hopkinsville	—	—
	First Standard	Louisville	1931	1933
Louisiana	Citizens State Banking Company	New Orleans	—	—
Maryland	Hatchett and Lewis, Bankers	Baltimore	—	—
	Wingate and Brown, Bankers	Baltimore	—	—
	Taylor and Jenkins, Bankers	Baltimore	—	—
	J. Winfield Thomas Bank	Baltimore	—	—
	Harry O. Wilson Bank	Baltimore	—	—
	Houston Savings	Salisbury	—	—
Michigan	D. C. Northcross and Company, Bankers	Detroit	—	—
Mississippi	Lincoln Savings	Vicksburg	1902	1909
	Delta Penny Savings	Indianola	1904	1936
	American Trust and Savings	Jackson	1904	1911

State	Bank	City		
	Union Savings	Vicksburg	1903	1909
	Bank of Mound Bayou	Mound Bayou	1904	1922
	Peoples Penny Savings	Yazoo City	1905	1914
	Penny Savings	Columbus	1906	1911
	Southern Bank	Jackson	1906	1914
	Bluff City Savings	Natchez	1906	1914
	Delta Savings	Greenville	1906	1913
	Magic City	Hattiesburg	1910	1912
	Peoples Home	Shaw	1911	1912
North Carolina	Mutual Aid Banking Company	New Bern	1897	1914
	Dime Bank	Kinston	1896	1908
	Mechanics and Farmers	Durham	1907	—
	Forsyth Savings and Trust	Winston-Salem	1907	1939
	Albermarle	Elizabeth	1919	1934
	Citizens Bank and Trust	Winston-Salem	1929	1934
	Fraternal	Durham	1920	1931
	Peoples	Kinston	1921	1928
	Commercial	Wilson	1921	1928
	Holloway, Borden, Hicks and Company	Kinston	1903	1920
	Isaac Smith's Bank and Trust	New Bern	—	—
Oklahoma	Farmers and Merchants	Boley	1907	1930
	Peoples Bank and Trust Company	Muskogee	1908	1914
	Boley Bank and Trust Company	Boley	1906	1910
	First National	Boley	1906	1914
	Creek Citizens	Muskogee	1904	1910
	Gold Bond	Muskogee	1902	1909
Pennsylvania	First Northern Colored Cooperative Banking Company	Philadelphia	1901	1902
	Peoples Savings Bank of Philadelphia	Philadelphia	1907	1917
	Modern Savings and Trust	Pittsburgh	1920	1922
	Keystone Company Operative Banking Association	Philadelphia	1922	1926
	Citizens and Southern Bank and Trust Company	Philadelphia	1925	—

TABLE 3.23—*Continued*

State	Name	City	Organized	Failed
	Brown and Stevens Banking Company	Philadelphia	1924	1925
	Cosmopolitan Bank	Philadelphia	1924	1925
	Steel City Banking Company	Pittsburgh	1919	1926
South Carolina	Charleston Mutual Savings	Charleston	1920	1930
	Peoples Federation	Charleston	1920	1926
	Workers Enterprise	Bennettville	1920	1924
	Victory Savings Bank	Columbia	1921	—
Tennessee	Mutual Bank and Trust Company	Chattanooga	1889	1893
	One Cent Savings	Nashville	1903	—
	Solvent Savings and Trust Company	Memphis	1906	—
	Fraternal Savings and Trust	Memphis	—	—
	Peoples Savings and Trust Company	Nashville	—	—
	Citizens Bank and Trust Company	Nashville	—	—
	Fraternal and Solvent Bank and Trust Company (merger of Solvent and Fraternal Banks)	Nashville	1923	—
Texas	Provident Bank and Trust	Forth Worth	1907	—
	Penny Savings	Dallas	—	—
	Farmers and Citizens Savings	Palestine	—	—
	Farmers Improvement	Waco	—	—
	Farmers and Mechanics	Tyler	—	—
	Fraternal Bank and Trust Company	Fort Worth	1923	—
	Workmen's Savings and Loan Company	Galveston	—	—
	Orgen Realty and Savings	Houston	1904	1912
Virginia	Savings Bank of the Grand Fountain, U.O. True Reformers	Richmond	1888	1910
	Nickel Savings	Richmond	1896	1910
	Galilean Fisherman	Hampton	1901	1910
	Mechanics Savings	Richmond	1901	1922

Bank	Location	Organized	Closed
Surrey, Sussex and Southampton—			
American Home and Missionary Banking Association	Courtland	1903	—
Sons and Daughters of Peace—			
Penny, Nickel, Dime Savings Bank	Newport News	1904	1925
Knights of Gideon	Norfolk	1905	1910
Star of Zion Banking and Trust	Salem	1905	1906
People Savings	Petersburg	1907	1913
Peoples Dime Savings Bank and Trust Association	Staunton	1908	1930
Crown Savings	Newport News	1908	—
Brickhouse Banking Company	Have Valley	1910	1913
Brown's Savings	Norfolk	1910	1925
Mutual Savings	Portsmouth	1916	1920
Tidewater Bank and Trust Company	Norfolk	1919	1921
Savings Bank of Danville	Danville	1919	—
Phoenix Bank of Nansemond	Suffolk	1919	1930
Commercial Bank and Trust	Richmond	1920	—
Consolidated Bank and Trust (merger of Second Street Savings with St. Luke)	Richmond	1920	—
Community Savings Bank	Portsmouth	1920	1924
Metropolitan Bank and Trust Company	Norfolk	1921	1930
Acorn Banking Company	Roanoke	1925	1927
American Home and Missionary	Courtland	—	—
Negro Savings Bank	Manchester	—	—
Southern One-Cent Savings	Bane City	—	—

Source: Abram L. Harris. *The Negro As Capitalist.* McGrath Publishing Company, 1936. 29.

TABLE 3.24

Resources and Liabilities of Afro-American Banks in the United States

Resources

Year	Number of Banks	Loans and Discounts	Overdrafts	Stocks, Bonds and Securities	Banking House Furniture and Fixtures	Other Real Estate	Due from Banks	Cash on Hand	Cash Items	Reserve with Federal Reserve	Other Resources	Total Resources
1899	2	$ 3,635.38	$ 1,711.53	—	$ 2,217.65	$ 12,287.03	$ 773.19	$ 2,292.77	—	—	—	$ 22,917.55
1900	4	15,942.97	3,959.15	188,814.72	24,707.65	111,838.00	99,250.07	2,807.15	—	—	—	447,319.71
1901	5	24,415.04	4,327.55	396,578.79	25,582.50	101,138.00	73,195.61	2,142.02	—	—	—	627,379.51
1902	6	27,201.16	3,005.17	444,521.96	35,347.12	35,077.77	80,972.35	2,293.25	—	—	958.30	629,377.08
1903	6	493,590.83	412.40	915.00	35,726.64	37,682.21	65,303.22	1,560.22	—	—	—	635,190.52
1904	8	604,905.82	1,588.83	3,106.44	14,419.13	76,703.97	102,758.23	29,377.76	1,104.11	—	7,350.50	841,314.79
1905	7	560,275.82	1,536.45	4,967.18	12,163.65	104,857.26	86,121.74	1,133.14	13.28	—	13,910.77	784,979.29
1906	9	724,753.19	2,736.21	9,572.36	76,080.55	88,021.11	153,056.40	20,051.12	218.08	—	23,321.85	1,097,810.87
1907	11	797,228.67	4,838.78	23,141.73	82,041.51	131,557.46	106,816.66	84,511.17	4,767.06	—	35,979.60	1,270,882.64
1908	29	1,157,693.65	11,692.30	35,698.06	135,145.29	214,319.41	119,795.87	99,361.56	5,885.89	—	13,196.84	1,792,788.87
1909	29	1,312,410.15	15,638.47	45,114.65	147,369.34	219,928.46	114,020.66	90,432.34	11,373.94	—	22,574.13	1,978,862.14
1910	28	1,016,931.90	53,805.63	58,247.18	207,146.99	205,949.36	193,655.65	99,406.36	8,212.23	—	22,618.06	1,865,973.36
1911	28	1,456,434.44	24,785.03	76,534.12	208,171.69	257,365.99	236,777.81	91,201.62	5,550.84	—	19,330.25	2,376,151.79
1912	27	1,746,385.98	23,596.36	149,005.66	295,425.14	200,320.42	213,102.96	90,173.11	8,566.79	—	26,905.87	2,753,483.29
1913	26	1,321,711.25	19,548.43	92,552.71	278,235.89	276,555.74	195,658.89	89,500.79	13,104.88	—	12,872.97	2,299,741.55
1914	24	1,248,714.56	6,259.61	107,058.78	236,831.61	227,010.81	155,875.60	79,390.00	12,186.37	—	11,069.88	2,084,397.22
1915	21	1,056,107.09	3,383.52	32,685.13	199,954.54	157,761.80	199,805.36	63,275.73	15,755.36	—	22,931.62	1,751,660.15
1916	19	1,099,604.51	4,469.06	23,121.71	264,205.29	132,858.26	361,609.75	70,305.95	11,406.75	—	12,347.46	1,979,928.74
1917	18	1,239,470.02	5,077.99	119,482.26	259,710.45	163,632.62	423,153.38	105,857.02	18,579.18	—	16,920.28	2,351,883.20
1918	18	1,793,997.71	6,462.41	550,023.53	266,457.37	191,068.07	769,369.12	118,419.93	35,706.98	—	72,377.08	3,803,882.20
1919	22	3,520,497.29	5,092.87	899,035.56	382,233.20	244,734.78	898,395.78	114,069.61	50,165.43	—	100,991.70	6,245,216.22
1920	29	4,668,819.06	8,857.74	930,946.76	502,304.15	806,452.26	821,212.28	237,523.18	46,220.28	—	158,053.37	8,180,389.08
1921	35	5,581,982.27	46,310.58	1,251,805.94	1,024,681.55	725,959.49	870,672.57	194,867.42	52,108.99	18,866.89	92,427.39	9,840,816.20
1922	34	4,966,852.54	8,565.58	1,023,993.69	951,595.43	595,545.31	747,778.33	307,384.38	48,015.62	33,467.49	351,949.84	9,020,547.61
1923	34	6,205,827.94	11,958.03	1,440,785.90	1,051,083.38	165,739.71	929,561.15	245,912.27	186,383.06	50,391.35	292,184.73	10,562,903.66
1924	35	6,834,107.91	9,984.08	2,122,861.62	1,075,424.27	238,683.26	1,006,028.53	370,199.26	91,818.90	75,728.92	237,252.73	12,036,751.91
1925	33	7,043,696.69	6,571.34	2,059,326.60	1,134,538.77	352,877.29	1,146,622.26	237,378.12	97,069.93	62,808.71	138,788.90	12,292,598.82
1926	33	7,059,987.40	9,377.69	2,267,373.89	1,313,485.26	218,923.61	1,304,910.04	164,468.41	103,838.95	67,808.97	326,210.09	12,831,384.05
1927	30	7,098,057.53	29,198.59	1,979,109.12	1,312,027.30	173,265.30	1,005,088.28	177,787.10	86,521.88	79,438.84	210,062.93	12,138,927.00
1928	28	6,094,864.27	11,659.18	1,870,371.10	1,133,246.85	237,743.19	1,135,440.54	184,810.71	116,104.80	62,405.51	188,128.51	11,051,807.99
1929	21	5,438,596.90	4,071.77	2,021,498.28	1,040,503.31	279,553.10	857,990.41	151,269.13	154,613.63	76,339.10	245,128.75	10,255,630.79
1930	14	2,631,146.27	11,699.64	1,423,349.38	792,534.03	227,057.99	476,321.65	257,087.56	55,740.16	7,144.08	55,424.51	6,006,700.29
1931	3	812,372.37	3,096.88	697,917.61	479,258.57	58,368.40	190,195.19	8,953.10	30,600.70	—	155,625.68	2,443,532.58
1932	1	128,086.02	504.53	185,888.75	72,813.72	4,710.00	12,798.63	—	475.69	—	735.00	406,012.34

Liabilities

Year	Number of Banks	Capital	Surplus	Undivided Profits	Dividends Unpaid	Due to Banks	Demand Deposits	Savings Deposits	Time and Demand Certificates of Deposit	Bills Payable and Rediscounts	Cashiers' Checks	Certified Checks	Other Liabilities	Total Liabilities
1899	2	$ 591.22	$ 10,401.90	$ 401.75	—	—	$ 6,234.39	—	$ 998.19	$ 4,185.00	$ 105.10	—	—	$ 22,917.55
1900	4	94,605.92	93,108.43	7,522.75	—	159.47	9,178.71	—	238,040.63	4,685.00	18.80	—	—	447,319.71
1901	5	99,669.61	132,615.84	7,789.78	—	—	124,415.11	—	249,786.20	13,013.28	62.69	—	27.00	627,379.51
1902	6	115,042.20	132,380.47	9,268.60	27.20	3,927.73	150,792.76	—	211,088.12	6,750.00	100.00	—	—	629,377.08
1903	6	119,405.08	101,411.73	10,665.28	43.40	2,917.21	147,657.27	—	251,380.60	—	1,709.95	—	—	635,190.52
1904	8	160,461.89	97,443.25	10,693.78	189.43	3,500.00	304,608.90	—	254,325.42	10,084.37	7.75	—	—	841,314.79
1905	7	151,532.18	95,838.73	43,749.09	235.50	3,900.00	180,698.93	—	298,948.16	10,069.87	6.83	—	—	784,979.29
1906	9	191,515.76	106,144.95	38,091.49	937.77	1,144.83	397,443.68	—	355,594.93	4,204.87	17.25	—	2,715.34	1,097,810.87
1907	11	221,801.70	115,082.53	40,770.91	1,256.35	694.88	461,773.24	—	408,288.81	15,376.46	152.98	125.00	5,559.78	1,270,882.64
1908	29	381,216.61	114,778.34	48,532.88	778.61	1,224.38	649,877.66	11,273.10	484,577.70	84,069.94	1,642.66	3,018.58	11,798.41	1,792,788.87
1909	29	438,964.72	121,273.19	56,996.20	3,080.84	3,716.42	671,581.42	325,517.32	231,206.33	113,819.99	2,591.64	77.95	10,036.12	1,978,862.14
1910	28	369,895.01	10,108.49	25,700.77	9,913.71	9,525.09	1,052,589.53	31,960.50	233,447.62	96,202.63	2,726.68	413.47	23,489.86	1,865,973.36
1911	28	586,919.58	5,910.54	35,137.84	1,098.45	19,372.68	1,179,347.89	80,112.38	293,773.04	145,687.00	6,551.31	1,357.20	20,883.88	2,376,151.79
1912	27	612,088.30	23,072.47	28,128.21	819.76	17,595.54	1,327,273.47	232,201.58	322,453.47	101,287.05	6,661.64	7,451.20	74,450.60	2,753,483.29
1913	26	492,443.52	40,164.16	24,918.02	1,951.20	12,803.67	967,742.91	294,488.47	293,245.36	135,420.50	2,551.24	313.40	33,699.10	2,299,741.55
1914	24	424,781.62	35,126.20	19,443.46	644.68	21,098.75	852,039.99	340,333.67	219,839.75	136,836.10	5,068.02	168.53	29,016.45	2,084,397.22
1915	21	350,608.29	41,348.32	12,311.40	707.97	1,055.87	580,474.78	455,066.93	127,405.30	162,878.79	1,518.97	136.86	18,146.67	1,751,660.15
1916	19	323,788.09	48,374.36	23,518.62	1,033.22	202.04	873,457.68	529,213.58	47,980.94	113,905.00	4,811.81	264.59	13,378.81	1,979,928.74
1917	18	324,882.99	46,387.72	17,463.01	1,177.57	21,046.56	1,035,194.57	690,408.35	79,485.01	108,800.00	5,098.81	265.02	21,673.59	2,351,883.20
1918	18	386,126.09	78,891.38	36,009.27	1,460.87	19,643.96	1,646,461.19	1,184,303.21	110,217.25	149,995.00	7,872.31	295.60	182,606.07	3,803,882.20
1919	22	593,917.59	188,873.02	54,541.06	1,168.02	103,661.04	2,264,254.50	2,439,565.50	184,071.09	214,980.50	8,810.30	5,144.34	186,229.26	6,245,216.22
1920	29	871,525.76	248,716.79	67,756.56	3,967.86	188,718.86	2,745,328.46	2,930,269.02	436,446.98	540,064.68	11,608.92	11,764.98	124,220.21	8,180,389.08
1921	35	1,610,691.50	366,815.94	63,018.37	7,647.93	29,916.34	2,606,348.13	3,202,523.94	983,364.61	588,566.65	16,420.36	10,456.16	355,046.27	9,840,816.20
1922	34	1,734,671.75	459,071.31	97,741.52	2,711.98	132,542.05	2,079,480.31	3,167,450.90	956,055.44	311,593.85	5,662.33	5,949.14	67,617.03	9,020,547.61
1923	34	1,573,263.34	436,943.75	96,681.08	2,759.78	6,959.31	3,017,482.36	4,186,619.98	518,596.12	362,696.98	88,180.80	11,380.97	261,339.19	10,562,903.66
1924	35	1,897,638.99	342,351.85	64,283.20	3,653.13	28,974.36	2,792,647.47	4,622,602.31	1,479,438.65	466,615.41	22,530.27	10,693.61	305,322.66	12,036,751.91
1925	33	1,743,222.24	286,602.33	80,884.61	8,822.58	15,192.90	3,198,829.32	5,292,811.82	862,925.60	437,301.79	15,565.26	9,510.55	340,929.82	12,292,598.82
1926	33	1,766,228.27	324,004.33	114,823.42	7,675.81	11,180.43	3,332,144.30	5,564,620.51	864,611.00	412,338.03	36,116.67	13,412.85	384,228.43	12,831,384.05
1927	30	1,700,264.24	308,496.01	52,216.50	6,743.56	10,819.92	2,991,197.36	5,395,898.63	786,019.85	391,033.28	13,850.19	19,724.67	453,662.81	12,138,027.00
1928	28	1,671,381.16	332,564.12	189,537.61	2,791.74	28,278.66	3,001,310.81	4,675,635.36	429,201.73	242,928.16	15,071.56	19,172.84	443,934.24	11,051,807.99
1929	21	1,518,017.28	342,891.10	59,353.04	9,722.37	11,848.32	3,128,571.20	4,011,769.19	284,200.25	139,479.65	11,359.50	10,658.21	727,760.68	10,255,630.79
1930	14	1,011,013.28	206,344.59	49,462.91	5,701.91	12,426.84	1,427,948.98	2,507,566.50	158,317.63	277,079.94	2,354.41	7,362.13	341,121.17	6,006,700.29
1931	3	463,725.00	222,500.00	3,453.36	105.00	8,318.19	461,411.56	922,253.01	32,780.14	219,439.00	—	1,723.39	307,823.93	2,443,532.58
1932	1	100,000.00	—	1,605.51	—	6,929.87	169,798.51	94,678.45	—	33,000.00	—	—	—	406,012.34

Source: Abram L. Harris. *The Negro As Capitalist*. McGrath Publishing Company, 1936. Appendix IV.

TABLE 3.25

Ratio of Capital Investment to Total Deposits for Afro-American Banks, 1903–1930

1	2	Ratio of 1 to 2 in Percentages
Loans and discounts	Earning assets	75.0
Capital investment	Total deposits	18.0
Total cash	Demand deposits	35.0
Total cash	Total deposits	22.0
Fixed assets	Capital investment	21.0
Bills payable and rediscounts	Capital investments	25.0
Loans and discounts	Total deposits	56.0

Source: Abram L. Harris. *The Negro As Capitalist*. McGrath Publishing Company, 1936. 57–58.

Equally important with the excessive number of banks was the weakness of management. No serious effort could be made to select competent management for this multitude of new banks, for a trained bank in any genuine sense did not exist. The dangers inherent in this inexperience and incompetent management were accentuated by the excessive and more often cutthroat competition resulting from the superfluity of banks. Five percent was commonly paid for time deposits, and loans grossly lacking in security were made through fear that the business would be lost to a competitor.[70]

Poor management practices on the part of white banks was also the theme of systematic research by Robert Weidenhammer, who examined fifty bank failures in the state of Minnesota in the 1920s. Forty-seven of these banks failed because more than 60 percent of deposits were tied up in loans which could not be liquidated. These banks also had loans in excess of deposits, and secondary reserves of less than 20 percent of what the deposits on hand totaled.[71]

Of course, our major purpose is not to analyze bank failures in America, but to show that Afro-American banks experienced normal problems while engaging in the banking businesses in the United States. As previously noted, literature in the sociology of entrepreneurship—especially the work of Ivan H. Light—treats Afro-American banks as if they were the only ones to have failed. In general, however, even with the inception of the Federal Deposit Insurance Company, today's banks fail for the same reasons that caused the banks at the turn of the century to fail. As we pointed out, banks in Texas, Louisiana, and Oklahoma in 1987 were failing at record rates. This was true because of bad loans, especially in the real estate industry. As with business in general, the banking industry is affected by the forces of the marketplace in any historical period.

The banking experience for Afro-Americans represented a natural evolution from the beneficial societies of the early 1700s. As the data show, savings and thrift institutional building was strong in the Afro-American community as they attempted to seek for themselves. One should also note that other groups which comprise the subject matter of the sociology of entrepreneurship—Japanese, West-Indians, and Chinese—do not have a structured tradition of banking such as the Afro-Americans possessed.

Part of this difference is due to the fact that Afro-Americans have such a long history in America. But it is also due to the intensive discrimination against Afro-Americans. As noted by the theory of economic detour, what distinguishes Afro-Americans from other groups is the reality of total segregation in the marketplace. Just as important is the fact that they developed a system of financial institutions such as the rotating credit system, that went well beyond primitive saving system, noted frequently in the literature. In the next chapter we will examine the relationships between economic institutions such as banking and the development of Afro-American business activity more generally.

CONCLUSION

The purpose of this chapter has been to explore the tradition of self-help in the history of Afro-Americans. As early as the 1700s, this group had engaged in self-help activity, which originated in the church and in beneficial societies. The group showed an early interest in the development and support of educational institutions. Banking and insurance institutions developed as business enterprises which contributed to the economic growth of entrepreneurs in the Afro-American community. One can trace the development of these institutions to those which originally were founded to allow members of the group to seek for themselves.

4

Entrepreneurship under an
Economic Detour

The development of financial institutions discussed in the previous chapter
was accompanied by a tremendous amount of business development at the
retail level. One can say with confidence that the rapid growth of Afro-
American business activity and entrepreneurship had a direct impact on the
growth of banks and savings and loans at the turn of the century. The purpose of this chapter is to discuss the development of retail trade enterprises
during this time period.[1] As before, we take advantage of the excellent literature of that time period which has been overlooked by students of the sociology of entrepreneurship.

I

As noted in the first chapter of this book, it is very important to understand
that the Afro-American experience cannot fit the definition of middleman
theory because Afro-Americans, unlike other groups, were not allowed to participate in the larger economy, especially after "Jim Crow" laws were instituted
following the Civil War. This economic segregation—called an *economic
detour*—is what makes the Afro-American experience unique.

In a real sense, the sociology of ethnic enterprise stresses the relationships
between economic solidarity, ethnic solidarity, and business development. From
a historical point of view, ethnic groups developed "little Polands," "German
Towns," "China Towns," and, more recently, "little Havanas." However, the
non-Afro-American groups all shared the ability to take advantage of the
broader market. Japanese restaurants, Chinese laundries, Italian restaurants,

Jewish enterprises, and others were never strictly limited to their ethnic groups in terms of marketing their products. Although restaurants and other businesses might maintain an "ethnic flavor," they were patronized by members of the larger society.

On the other hand, it was against the law—especially in the South—for whites to mingle with Afro-Americans. In Chapter One we noted that governmental interference (in the form of Jim Crow laws) helps to account for the fact that Afro-Americans could not utilize the open market. A telling point is that, after the development of such laws and despite the fact that Afro-Americans began a business tradition in the 1700s, it was not until the passage of the Fourteenth Amendment to the Constitution that Afro-Americans anywhere in the country were allowed to engage in any occupation in which white persons worked.[2] But, despite this economic detour, Afro-Americans developed businesses by any means available.

We must also reiterate a point made in chapter 1. In the tradition of the sociology of ethnic enterprise, all Afro-Americans represent the development of small businesses which allowed the group to develop a certain amount of economic stability. Thus, we are talking about small shops rather than large-scale capitalist enterprise, which is the experience of ethnic enterprise in America in general. People developed enterprises which allowed them to buy homes, live comfortably, send their children to college, purchase certain luxury items, and develop a sense of economic dignity. Such activities generate different classes within a group. In this sense, Afro-Americans were no different than other groups, with the exception that they were legally segregated from the larger society.

As we proceed with the analysis, we must take regional effects into consideration. Put another way, the development of ethnic enterprise was different in the South than in the North due to different support systems and the availability of land to build retail centers. We take into consideration the years approximately beginning with 1900 and ending with the Great Depression.

Before ethnic groups arrived in the North in large numbers, Afro-American businesses were able to serve clients on a nonracial basis. In the South, ten years following the Civil War, Afro-American businesses did not serve only black clientele. But the passage of Jim Crow laws in the 1890s changed this pattern and forced all Afro-American businesses into one section of the business world. In an interesting article entitled "Negro Main Street as a Symbol of Discrimination," William Carter shows how the residence of Afro-American businesses changed:

> A decade after the Civil War Negro businesses were concentrated in the same artisan and craftmen's lines as before the War. Dispersion made them downtown, but not main street, businesses. The very nature of Negro businesses in the 1880–90 period . . . accounted for

their continued location on downtown "front streets" rather than back ones. Moreover, this was a period of limited Jim Crow and little forced segregation, since it was in the 1890s that the majority of Jim Crow laws were passed. Basement and upstairs locations of barber shops and restaurants, even when all customers were white, served to point up color-line distinctions between Negroes and whites. . . . When the occupational group was composed solely of Negroes who served both Negro and white customers in the same physical plant, a mutual downtown, front-street location developed. Such was the case with butchers and dance bands. But when Negroes served both races in separate physical plants, distinctions were made through location.[3]

Throughout the nation, Afro-American businesses were forced to concentrate into race-specific business districts. They were forced to move businesses which had served the community for years from the central point of town. When Afro-American businessmen arrived in a city, they had to settle in the Afro-American district. It was simply against the law to settle their business in the developing downtown district of a major section.

As Afro-American "main streets" developed, they took different forms based on whether they were located in the South or North. In the former, because of the availability of land, their main streets developed as an almost new entity. Afro-Americans built the places of business themselves. In addition, because of the availability of land in the South, owners of businesses in those states were able to develop their own middle-class communities without having to purchase homes from immigrant groups who were moving out because blacks were moving in.

In the North, however, as blacks migrated to already established cities, problems emerged in creating main streets because immigrant groups owned the property. For example, in Chicago in 1938, Afro-Americans had difficulty in obtaining space. The principal shopping centers were located on 43d, 47th, 51st, and 57th streets. A large percentage of the property belonged to whites, most of whom were Jewish. This group made it difficult for Afro-Americans to develop businesses as they moved into what was known as "Bronzeville." Leases had clauses forbidding Afro-American tenants. If Afro-Americans did manage to secure a lease, the rent was always tripled when the lease came up for renewal.[4]

As Jim Crow Laws became crystallized in the South and the custom of racial segregation in the North became stronger, the complete separation of the races was defined in concrete. This governmental interference in the lives of blacks in general and of businessmen in particular had a devastating effect on the development of black business. Indeed, they had to develop separately. Consider the words by the governor of North Carolina around the turn of the century:

The law that separates you from the white people of the state socially always has been and always will be inexorable, and it need not concern you or me whether the law is violated elsewhere. It will never be violated in the South.... We are willing to give our energies and best thought to aid you in the great work necessary to make you what you are capable of and to assist you in that elevation of character and virtue which tend to the strengthening of the state, but to do this it is absolutely necessary that the race should remain distinct and have a society of its own.[5]

This experience is in sharp contrast to that of other ethnic groups. In a real sense, other ethnic groups were allowed to develop businesses, usually restaurants or other service businesses, which developed clients from the entire community. Although they faced systematic discrimination along a number of fronts, they were never legally separated from the larger society, a factor which discourages starting successful businesses that look forward to growth. Consider the following quotation from a work which examines the experiences of Jews in the Old South:

No wonder then that anthropologists and sociologists studying the region in the twentieth century have stumbled across Jews. . . . For example, in Indianola, Mississippi, the *mise en scène* of John Dollard's *Caste and Class in a Southern Town*, the seven department stores on the main street were almost entirely owned by Jews. In Natchez, the locale of another classic, *Deep South*, by Allison Davis, Burleigh B. Gardner, and Mary R. Gardner, "the wholesale merchants . . . who once rivalled the banks as credit agencies for planters were, with one exception, Jews. Most of them were socially of the middle class," . . . "but few had risen into the upper class." No wonder then that, even in the White House, the label on Jimmy Carter's suits had read: "Hart Schaffner & Marx, A. Cohen and Sons, Americus, Georgia." For Southern Jewry has been, as Napoleon is supposed to have said of England, a nation of shopkeepers.[6]

Scholars have also noted that it was an anomaly that anti-Semitism was not strong in the South.

It is a remarkable fact that large masses of Southerners were free of feelings of anti-Semitism. This was true for several reasons: they were so deeply prejudiced against Negroes and Catholics that they had little room to hate the Jews. Too, they were schooled in the Old Testament and much of their religious imagery was the same as the Jews' religious imagery. Jews were quiet and unobtrusive in the practice of their religion, and never offered competition to the rockribbed

Protestant South. Economically the Jew seldom if ever competed directly with the Southerner in his main economic activities.[7]

Most importantly, however, it was not against the law or custom to patronize Jewish merchants' enterprises. This has been true of all middleman minorities; they were not forced into an economic detour. As the quotation just cited notes, Jews in the South were able to compete, albeit in a certain economic niche.

One of the most systematic studies of Afro-American enterprises for this time period was done by Margaret Levenstein.[8] Her finding were major, especially given the treatment of Afro-American enterprise in the ethnic entrepreneurship literature, because show notes the rapid increase in the number of enterprises and compares them to other groups. Her research appears in an article entitled "African American Entrepreneurship: The View from the 1910 Census," and is important to present her conclusions in full:

> One of the most striking findings of this study is that in 1910 African-Americans were more likely than white Americans to be employers, and almost as likely as whites to be self-employed. This contrasts with the current period in which African-Americans are only a third as likely as whites to work in their own businesses. This raises questions about claims that African-American culture is unsupportive of entrepreneurial activity, or that cultural differences may explain black white differentials in self-employment. If cultural differences are to explain the 20th century differentials in self-employment, they must be a twentieth century development.[9]

In her analysis, Levenstein shows how blacks, which were mostly southern at that time, took advantage of the kind of agricultural market in which they found themselves. Although white entrepreneurs were concentrated in agriculture, Afro-American men were more concentrated.

An interesting part of the Levenstein analysis had to do with gender. Overall in 1910, men were more likely to be self-employed than women. Afro-America women, however, were more likely to be self-employed than white females and also made up a much larger proportion of the Afro-American labor force.[10] Levenstein's analysis was done in part to challenge the notion so popular in the ethnic entrepreneurship literature that self-employment was not part of the cultural experiences of black America. She notes that ". . . in contrast to contemporary findings, entrepreneurship is significantly more common among both whites and African-Americans in 1910 than among Asians (those of Japanese, Chinese, or Hawaiian decent)."[11]

Juliet Walker, in her work, *The History of Black Business in America,* calls this time period the golden age of black business.[12] Jake Simmons Jr. was busy creating a company that would make him the most successful black in the history of the oil business.[13] Turnbo-Amalone became America's first female millionaire, regardless of race, as she developed products in the care of hair.[14] Mademe C.J. Walker would follow in Turnbo-Analone's millionaire tracks, also by concentrating on hair care.[15] Individual entrepreneurs who became millionaires, during this time of Booker T. Washington, are some of the more interesting American stories.[16]

Between 1867 and 1917, the number of Afro-American enterprises increased from four thousand to fifty thousand. Table 4.1 shows business enterprises in which two hundred or more Afro-Americans were engaged. In the tradition of other groups, the largest category is that of restaurant, cafe and lunchroom keepers. Unlike the 1700s, these restaurants served an exclusive Afro-American clientele. It was never fashionable for white Americans to go

TABLE 4.1
Business Enterprises in which 200 or More Negroes Are Engaged, 1918–1919

Stock Raising	202
Jewelry	206
Dairying and farming	208
Ice dealers	208
Saw and planing mill proprietors	219
Wholesale merchants and dealers	241
Dry goods, fancy goods, and notions	280
Manufacturing and proprietors of clothing factories	310
Fruit growers	316
Livery stable keepers	323
Buyers and shippers of grain, livestock, etc.	357
Candy and confectionery	384
Proprietors of transfer companies	632
Saloon keepers	652
Drugs and medicines	695
General stores	736
Produce and provisions	756
Real estate dealers	762
Junk dealers	794
Billiard and pool room keepers	875
Undertakers	953
Hotel keepers and managers	973
Coal and wood dealers	1,155
Butchers and meat dealers	2,957
Builders and contractors	3,107
Hucksters and peddlers	3,434
Truck gardeners	4,466
Grocers	5,550
Restaurant, cafe, and lunchroom keepers	6,369

Source: Monroe N. Work. Negro Year Book, 1918–1919. Tuskegee, Ala.: Tuskegee Institute. 359.

out to eat Afro-American food. Even if they desired to do so, social customs would make it very difficult.

In 1938, following the Great Depression, a survey of retail businesses in which Afro-Americans engaged as of 1932 (Table 4.2) showed that 25,701 Afro-American retail merchants did an annual business of more than $101 million, and employed 28,243 proprietors and firm members plus 12,561 full-time employees. Their total payroll for these businesses was $8,528,306. Food and allied industries were the strongest retail businesses.

Although one cannot say that Booker T. Washington was the complete cause of the development of Afro-American businesses, he clearly represented the main intellectual force during this time period. In contrast to the period before the Civil War, when Afro-American business was developing from the self-help benevolent organizations, a systematic national organization appeared for the development of Afro-American business. In 1900, Booker T. Washington organized the National Negro Business League (NNBL) to encourage the development of Afro-American business. Meeting for the first time in Boston, the NNBL drew delegates from thirty-four states. Table 4.3 shows the number of those business leagues by state. All present embraced Washington's philosophy of gospel and wealth, noting that, whether in the North or South, if a black man succeeded in business, paid his taxes, and had high character, he earned respect from members of the white group, especially if those whites were businessmen themselves. They came to the conclusion that:

> a useless . . . idle class is a menace and danger to any community, and that when an individual produces what the world wants, whether it is a product of hand, heart or head, the world does not long stop to inquire what is the color of the skin of the producer. It was easily seen that if every member of the race should strive to make himself the most indispensable man in his community, and to be successful in business, however humble that business might be, he would contribute much toward smoothing the pathway of his own and future generations.[17]

At this first meeting, the reality of segregation and the economic detour was on the minds of the delegates. But it wasn't until the 1904 convention that delegates faced the reality of open economy—a reality which noted that Afro-American businessmen could not enjoy the development of clientele in the larger society. At that point, the group turned to the importance of racial solidarity as a major component of a business to be successful. As noted earlier, they required every person who joined the league to pledge themselves to support all enterprises owned by members of the race. The reasoning was that all ethnic groups supported their own enterprises in America.[18]

TABLE 4.2
Retail Stores Operated by Negro Proprietors in the United States, 1929–32

Type of Business	Number of Stores	Proprietors, Firm Members (Not On Pay Roll)	Number of Employees (Full Time)	Total Pay Roll (Including Part Time)	Stocks on Hand, End of Year (At Cost)	Net Sales Amount	Net Sales Percent of Total Sales
Totals	25,701	28,243	12,561	$8,528,306	$10,657,000	$101,146,043	100.00
Food stores	10,755	11,594	2,139	$1,341,671	$ 3,240,610	$ 36,662,523	36.25
Candy, confectionery	1,137	1,193	230	124,841	207,480	2,584,053	2.55
Grocery (without meats)	6,248	6,690	707	336,608	1,709,750	14,714,500	14.55
Combination (groceries and meats)	2,202	2,428	768	520,643	1,147,940	13,654,678	13.50
Meat (and sea foods)	537	576	252	188,200	68,150	2,829,147	2.80
Other	631	707	182	171,379	107,290	2,880,145	2.85
General stores—Groceries with dry goods, apparel, general merchandise	761	892	229	151,947	1,161,880	4,828,700	4.78
General merchandise	128	153	81	67,496	323,790	979,799	.97
Dry goods	61	76	33	27,418	165,900	381,111	.38
General merchandise	37	47	37	31,048	139,270	456,156	.45
Variety, 5 and 10, To-a-Dollar	30	30	11	9,030	18,620	142,532	.14
Automotive group	1,679	1,873	1,059	1,058,269	819,040	9,793,196	9.68
Motor Vehicle Dealers (new and used)	39	46	166	245,535	334,750	3,149,837	3.11
Filling stations	799	869	302	258,220	217,100	3,429,826	3.39
Garages, repair shops	732	838	525	481,317	184,310	2,543,898	2.52
Other	109	120	66	73,197	85,880	669,635	.66
Apparel Group	477	519	355	322,620	698,830	3,027,917	2.99
Men's, boys', furnishings	66	71	59	59,816	266,660	915,500	.90
Family—men's, women's and children's	32	37	27	29,295	149,040	426,756	.42
Women's ready-to-wear apparel, accessories	57	62	33	28,237	72,290	315,762	.31
Women's accessories	54	57	28	32,649	56,080	308,710	.31

Other	220	240	176	139,385	62,960	715,764	.71
Shoes	48	52	32	33,238	91,800	345,425	.34
Furniture, household group	149	174	125	133,500	240,290	1,160,120	1.15
Furniture	54	62	53	56,410	104,250	401,056	.40
Floor coverings, draperies, curtains, upholstery	7	7	6	3,588	2,220	19,450	.02
Household appliances	3	3	1	500	1,030	7,800	.01
Other	30	33	19	15,414	25,770	79,364	.08
Radio, music	55	69	46	57,588	107,020	652,450	.64
Restaurants, eating places	7,918	8,530	5,425	2,727,883	572,050	21,333,198	21.09
Restaurants, cafeterias, lunch rooms	5,729	6,209	4,742	2,358,331	431,950	17,284,126	17.09
Lunch counters, refreshment stands	2,189	2,321	683	369,552	140,100	4,049,072	4.00
Lumber, building group	96	112	170	202,778	180,380	1,268,024	1.25
Lumber, building materials	26	31	72	73,175	98,070	589,155	.58
Electrical (without radio)	23	29	30	36,565	18,010	159,862	.16
Heating, plumbing	26	30	45	69,147	29,020	354,537	.35
Paint, glass	21	22	23	23,891	35,280	164,470	.16
Other retail stores	3,365	3,994	2,858	2,411,120	3,231,540	21,109,630	20.87
Hardware	40	49	22	34,606	179,110	476,048	.47
Hardware, farm implements	11	16	22	20,284	92,160	335,348	.33
Farmers' supplies	107	123	50	45,880	97,850	927,859	.92
Books	8	9	9	4,933	22,120	52,661	.05
Cigar stores, stands	704	764	320	236,597	140,960	2,052,958	2.03
Coal, wood yards—ice dealers	549	594	337	250,079	125,900	2,117,474	2.09
Drug	712	852	955	790,465	1,566,750	7,253,921	7.17
Jewelry	67	74	33	45,596	231,650	388,282	.39
Miscellaneous	1,167	1,513	1,110	982,678	775,040	7,505,079	7.42
Secondhand stores	373	402	120	111,022	188,590	982,936	.97

Source: Monroe N. Work. *Negro Year Book*. Tuskegee Ala.: Tuskegee Institute, 1937–1938. 90–91. (Originally extracted from the Retail Distribution Summary for the United States, U.S. Department of Commerce, Table 12-B 88.)

TABLE 4.3
Number of Chartered Negro Business Leagues, by State, 1918–1919

State	Number
Alabama	20
Arkansas	7
California	5
Colorado	4
Delaware	1
District of Columbia	1
Florida	10
Georgia	21
Illinois	7
Indiana	4
Kansas	10
Kentucky	14
Louisiana	10
Maryland	6
Massachusetts	5
Mississippi	12
Missouri	6
Nebraska	1
New Jersey	9
New York	3
North Carolina	26
Ohio	4
Oklahoma	15
Pennsylvania	4
Rhode Island	2
South Carolina	11
Tennessee	15
Texas	24
Virginia	19
West Virginia	7

Source: Negro Year Book, Monroe Work, 1918–1919. Tuskegee Ala: Tuskegee Institute.

This doctrine originally created a conflict between the old Afro-American business upper class and the new Afro-American business class. For example, the Boston upper class had always been dependent on white customers and thus opposed the doctrine of racial solidarity vis-a-vis business. But as discrimination toward the upper class in Boston and other cities increased, they were forced to become congruent with the racial economic solidarity policies of the League, making the economic detour the complete Afro-American experience.[19]

As the NNBL crystallized, it adopted a program to guide Afro-Americans through the economic detour. The first part of the program created a national organizer to travel, organize local leagues and strengthen those already established. The qualifications for this field worker was knowledge of modern business systems and business promotion. He was to avoid any entertainment by various leagues; his only function was to strengthen and develop their enterprises so that they could be more efficient.

The second part of the program was to promote National Negro Trade Week through newspaper and magazine articles and establish a national advertising plan. The League wanted to utilize every means possible to sell Afro-American business to both blacks and whites. The third part of the program was to maintain an exchange and information bureau which would keep businessmen abreast of opportunities among their interests. More specifically, the bureau sought to: (1) maintain sources of information on business problems; (2) keep a record of names and addresses of trained workers who might be available for positions; and (3) note positions open in all establishments which hired Afro-Americans. The fourth part of the program was to publish a monthly bulletin to provide brief but comprehensive reports of the activities of the League and the achievements of the race in the field of business.[20]

As was the case in the 1700s, self-help in the face of intense racial restrictions became the guiding light of the League. As noted at the 1928 meeting by the president, R. R. Moton:

> We must demonstrate our capacity to cooperate among ourselves, before demanding any cooperation where the resources of others are at stake. Business is the ultimate test of our ability to cooperate. Somehow we must learn this fundamental lesson. It will be costly; there will be some loss in the process, but we must keep it up until we have developed within the race a group of men of definite capacity and unquestioned integrity, who can lead the way to larger achievements for the benefit of the whole race.[21]

In addition to Booker T. Washington's League, there were other national associations in specialized fields, including the National Negro Press Association, the National Negro Insurance Association, and the National Association of Bankers. At the governmental level, Emmer R. Lancaster, special advisor to the U.S. Department of Commerce for Negro Affairs, proposed in 1940 the formation of a National Negro Business Advisory Council. The following year, a national committee on the Negro in Business, helped plan the Department's first conference.[22]

Organizations also included the youth. By 1930, the spirit of enterprise led to the formation of the Young Negro Cooperative League, with, branches in New York, Pennsylvania, Ohio, Arizona, Louisiana, South Carolina, Virginia, and the District of Columbia. Although some members opened their own businesses, their main goal was educational. Their first national meeting was held in Pittsburgh in 1931 with thirty delegates attending. Another league, though not youth oriented, developed and operated in Connecticut, Florida, Indiana, and New York state.[23]

In addition to business-specific leagues, other Afro-American organizations—such as the National Urban League and the National Council of Negro Women—included a business agenda. The Greek-letter college fraternities and sororities were also involved. The most active was Phi Beta Sigma fraternity, which sponsored an annual program entitled "Bigger and Better Businesses." Iota Phi Lambda sorority, composed of women in business, conducted different types of celebrations during Negro Business Week. Alpha Kappa Alpha sorority, an organized lobby for projects, took the initiative in integrating Afro-Americans into commercial occupations. The Young Women's Christian Association also sponsored a Business and Professional Women's League.[24]

From the very beginning, the business organizations—and especially the Negro Business League—were criticized for maintaining that economic stability could be gained through a concentration on small business and thrift.[25] This criticism predates the work of scholars such as E. Franklin Frazier, who downgraded the efforts of Afro-American entrepreneurs on the grounds that their activities were insignificant when compared to the larger economy.

Similar to the leagues was the establishment of Chambers of Commerce in different cities. A study by Joseph R. Houchins, then assistant business specialist for Negro Affairs, Division of the Bureau of Foreign and Domestic Commerce of the United States, listed more than forty such organizations throughout the country as of 1938.[26] Their goal was to increase the amount of business activity among Afro-Americans and to support such businesses.

The most systematic study of Afro-American business—*Negro Business and Business Education* by Joseph A. Pierce, the analog of Bonacich's Japanese study—is clearly the most important contribution to the literature on racial/ethnic enterprise.[27] As noted earlier, it contains most of the theoretical ideas which guide the sociology of entrepreneurship. It is an intellectual and research tragedy that scholars who now write in this field do not build upon the work of Pierce. Because of its importance, it is necessary to examine Pierce's work in a systematic fashion.

Pierce's landmark study included both Northern and Southern cities and was based on a survey of 3,866 businesses in twelve cities in 1944. The cities chosen for study, with their total number of businesses and businesses in his sample are presented in Table 4.4. Pierce then engaged in a more extensive study of 384 of those businesses. Thus, his sample for the city of Atlanta, showed 843 businesses. He then chose 102, or 12.1 percent, to study extensively.

Pierce then classified his sample into (1) Retail stores and service establishments, following the classifications at that time in the U.S. Census; and (2) miscellaneous enterprises, covering all enterprises not found under retail stores

TABLE 4.4

Distribution of Total Businesses and Businesses in Pierce's Sample by Cities, 1944

City	Total Number of Businesses	Number	Businesses in Sample Percent of Total in City
Atlanta	843	102	12.1
Baltimore	124	—	—
Cincinnati	185	25	13.5
Durham	170	—	—
Houston	242	28	11.6
Memphis	506	80	15.8
Nashville	162	20	12.3
New Orleans	252	38	15.1
Richmond	241	17	7.1
St. Louis	244	—	—
Savannah	203	26	12.8
Washington	694	48	6.9
Total	3,866	384	9.9

Source: Joseph A. Pierce. Negro Business and Business Education . New York: Harper & Row, 1947. 33.

and service establishments. Table 4.5 shows Pierce's classification by line of business for the twelve cities.

Pierce found that 65.2 percent of his sample entered business for economic reasons, while 15.5 percent entered because of special interest and ability. Family connections and influence was given as a reason to begin enterprises in 10.1 percent of the sample, and 9.2 percent chose business as a career in order to meet a racial economic need. Pierce compared these results with a major study of white graduates from the Wharton School of Finance, which found that only 4 percent of the graduates entered business because of its economic possibilities and 24 percent because of family influence.

Thus, Afro-Americans were more likely to enter business in order to gain economic stability. In contrast, graduates from the Wharton School of Finance, who were more likely to come from established families, entered business in order to carry on a family tradition. It was obvious that Afro-Americans were really concerned with changing their economic position through business activity.

One of the more interesting topics in the sociology of entrepreneurship is the capitalization of business activity. For example, Bonacich found that, in the early 1900s, the average Japanese business was started on an average capitalization of $200. Pierce found that 15.8 percent of Afro-American businesses were begun on less than $100, and about 41 percent on less than $400. However, it was also true that 35.6 percent of the enterprises had a start-up capitalization of more than $1,000; 8 percent of the enterprises were capitalized in

TABLE 4.5
Classification by Line of Business for Twelve Cities, 1944

Line of Business	Number	Line of Business	Number
Accounting offices	1	Hotels, inns	30
Apartment houses and office buildings	10	House cleaning	1
		Insurance life, branch offices of	21
Auto accessories	1	Insurance, other	5
Bakeries	9	Insurance brokers	3
Barber colleges	2	Jewelry stores	8
Barber and beauty shops	10	Junk dealers	3
Barber shops	404	Laundries	15
Beauty schools	17	Liquor stores	13
Beauty shops	600	Loan and investment companies	7
Beauty shops and schools	6	Locksmiths	4
Bicycle shops	3	Men's clubs and recreation places, pool rooms	52
Blacksmith shops	5		
Booking agencies	2	Meat markets	2
Book stores	7	Music studios	7
Bottling works	2	Millinery shops	8
Bowling alleys	2	Moving and hauling	47
Building and loan associations	2	Manufacturing, cabinet	1
Business schools	3	Manufacturing, casket	5
Carnivals	1	Manufacturing, chemical	2
Gift shops	3	Manufacturing, cosmetic	8
Cemeteries	7	Manufacturing, flower	1
Grocery stores	293	Manufacturing, hair	1
Cleaning and pressing shops, alterations, repairs	288	Manufacturing, food	1
		News stands	19
Coal, ice, and wood dealers	61	Newspapers	8
Coin operated machines, rentals, repairs	5	Nurseries	2
		Optical stores	2
Concessions	1	Orchestras	5
Confectioneries	114	Photographers	29
Contractors, builders	14	Plumbers	9
Clinics	3	Printing and publishing	39
Dairies	1	Public stenographers	1
Decorators	6	Radio repair shops	39
Delicatessens	8	Real estate agencies	51
Dress shops	5	Record shops	14
Dressmakers	2	Restaurants	627
Drug stores	67	Secondhand stores	12
Dry-goods stores	5	Shoe-repair shops	130
Egg and poultry dealers	3	Shoe-shine shops	53
Electrical appliance stores	5	Shoe stores	2
Employment agencies	4	Sign-painting shops	7
Filling stations	75	Stocking shops	3
Fish and poultry markets	31	Tailor shops	42
Five-and-ten cent stores, variety, sundries	28	Taverns, cabarets, etc.	88
		Taxicabs and taxicab companies	36
Florists	33	Theaters	1
Fruit and vegetable stores	30	Toilet preparation stores	3
Furniture stores	10	Undertakers	126
Garages	66	Upholstery, furniture repairs	8
Hardware stores	2	Uniform shops	1
Hospitals	4	Watch and jewelry stores	3
Total			3,866

Source: Joseph A. Pierce. *Negro Business and Business Education.* New York: Harper & Row, 1947. Appendix.

excess of $5,000; 3.6 percent more than $10,000; and 1.1 percent of the businesses began with $20,000 or more. Pierce's data reveal that the median initial capitalization of miscellaneous businesses was $999.50; $543.73 for retail enterprises; and $446.38 for service establishments.

In Pierce's business sample, those who entered into business were very thrifty: 86.3 percent of the entrepreneurs began their businesses with their own savings accounts, and the median amount utilized was $500. Of the sample, 4.8 percent received their initial capital from relatives, the median being $586. Although Afro-American banks were present, only 3.3 percent of business owners generated initial capital from them, while 4.4 percent of the sample sold stock to go into business, with the median amount being $1,000.

Pierce found that the length of establishment of businesses showed variations by types. When retail stores were considered by these types, drugstores had been established on the average of nine years; apparel stores, an average of 7.8 years; furniture-household-radio stores, an average of 7.8 years; food stores, an average of 5.8 years; filling stations, an average of 5.7 years; and liquor stores, an average of 5 years. The highest average length of establishment came from the service category—such as blacksmith shops, beauty schools, undertaking establishments, employment agencies, printing and publishing shops, and photographic studios. Businesses in this category had an average length of establishment that ranged from 12.0 to 22.6 years. The shortest median length of establishment was for shoeshine parlors, which averaged 3.2 years.

By the 1940s when the study was done, Pierce found that miscellaneous businesses had the longest tenure of establishment. For example, burial plot companies had been established for an average of 29.5 years; hospitals, 24.5 years; branch offices of life insurance companies, 23.9 years; and building contractors, 13.7 years.

Pierce's work also examined the number of employees by type of business. Tables 4.6, 4.7 and 4.8, taken from the appendix of his *Negro Business and Business Education*, present data on the number of employees for retail, service, and miscellaneous enterprises, respectively. Retail stores had a total of 4,318 employees, and the average number of employees for the retail stores per business was 2.8. Within this category, clubs (drinking places) had the highest average number of employees at 8.3. Drug stores came in second with 4.7 employees. Hardware stores, eating places, and furniture-household-radio stores employed three or more people. In terms of the total number of employees for retail stores, eating places reported the highest number 1,867, which represents 43.2 percent of all people employed in retail stores. Food stores were second in this category, and drinking places ranked third. It is also interesting that the food group, restaurants or eating places, drinking places, and other retail stores reported significant numbers of unpaid employees, which probably reflects the family nature of these small businesses.

Table 4.7 shows that all service establishments, as did retail stores, averaged 1.7 employees. Looking more closely at these enterprises, laundries had the highest average number of employees: 12.2. Beauty shops and schools were second with 8.0 people employed. Of all the enterprises in this category, beauty parlors had the highest percentage of employees, 30.6. Barber shops employed 20.1 percent of people in service enterprises, and cleaning and pressing firms employed 15.0 percent. Funeral parlors employed 10.9 percent of individuals in these enterprises.

The average number of employees per business in the miscellaneous business category was 9.1 percent. Insurance firms headed the list with the average number of employees with 24.4. Insurance, burial societies (16 employees), contractors, building (17.3 employees), manufacturing cosmetics companies (37 employees), and taxicabs and taxicab companies (29.1 employees) also employed significant numbers of employees for small businesses. Most people working in this category were located in insurance companies (16.1 percent of total employees). Contractors and building firms employed 7.6 percent of all people who worked in the miscellaneous business category. Men's recreation places, beauty schools, hotels, insurance companies, and taxi companies reported more than ten unpaid employees.

These figures compared with those reported in studies which examine the activities of middleman groups. As with those groups, Afro-Americans reacted to hostility by developing enterprises to keep them from falling completely to the bottom of the economic structure.

The fact that the Afro-American business people had to survive under an economic detour, depending almost entirely on the Afro-American market, was also addressed by Pierce.

> Restricted patronage does not permit the enterprises owned and operated by Negroes to capitalize on the recognized advantages of normal commercial expansion. It tends to stifle business ingenuity and imagination, because it limits the variety of needs and demands to those of one racial group—a race that is kept in a lower bracket of purchasing power largely because of this limitation. The practice of Negro business in catering almost entirely to Negroes has contributed to the development of an attitude that the Negro consumer is obligated, as a matter of racial loyalty, to trade with enterprises owned and operated by Negroes.[28]

Pierce noted that Afro-American business people rely sometimes completely on racial pride rather than service as an incentive for patronage, but his data revealed that Afro-American consumers purchased most goods at white-owned stores. Table 4.9 shows the percentage of these consumers who purchased goods at Afro-American- and Euro-American-owned stores. Service

TABLE 4.6
Employees of Retail Stores in Twelve Cities, 1944

Line of Business	Number of Stores	Total Number of Employees	Percentage of Total Employees	Average Number of Employees per Business	Number of Paid Employees	Number of Unpaid Employees
Food	455	747	17.3	1.6	702	45
General Merchandise	22	27	0.6	2.1	27	—
Apparel	61	133	3.1	2.2	128	5
Furniture, household, radio	14	41	0.9	3.0	41	—
Automotive	1	1	0.1	1.0	1	—
Filling stations	70	181	4.2	2.5	179	2
Hardware	2	7	0.1	4.0	7	—
Eating places	603	1,867	43.2	3.1	1,823	44
Drinking places	86	712	16.5	8.3	687	25
Drug	65	306	7.1	4.7	305	1
Liquor	12	20	0.5	1.7	20	—
Other retail	153	263	6.1	1.7	249	14
Secondhand	12	13	0.3	1.1	13	—
Totals	1,556	4,318	100.0	2.8	4,182	136

Source: Joseph A. Pierce. Negro Business and Business Education. New York: Harper & Row, 1947. Appendix.

TABLE 4.7
Employees of Service Establishments in Twelve Cities, 1944.

Line of Business	Number of Stores	Total Number of Employees	Percentage of Total Employees	Average Number of Employees per Business	Number of Paid Employees	Number of Unpaid Employees
Personal services						
Barber shops	384	806	20.1	2.1	785	21
Barber, beauty shops	10	38	0.9	3.8	35	3
Beauty parlors	577	1,226	30.6	2.1	1,220	6
Beauty shops, schools	6	48	1.2	8.0	48	—
Cleaning, pressing shops	270	602	15.0	2.2	571	31
Funeral parlors	116	438	10.9	3.7	426	12
Laundries	15	183	4.6	12.2	183	—
Photographic studios	28	70	1.7	2.5	64	6
Shoe-repair shops	129	184	4.5	1.3	180	4
Shoe-shine parlors	46	58	4.4	1.2	57	1
Business services						
Booking agencies	2	4	0.1	2.0	4	—
Certified public accountants	1	7	0.2	7.0	7	—
Coin-operated machines	5	18	0.4	3.6	16	2
Employment agencies	3	3	0.1	1.0	3	—
Public stenographers	1	1	0.1	1.0	1	—
Sign-painting shops	7	10	0.2	1.4	10	—
Automotive repairs and services						
Automobile repair shops	62	104	2.6	1.7	87	17

Other repairs and services						
Blacksmith shops	5	0.1	3	0.6	3	—
Bicycle shops	2	0.2	5	2.5	5	—
Locksmith, gunsmith shops	4	0.1	3	0.7	3	—
Radio repair shops	36	0.8	33	0.5	31	2
Upholstery, furniture	8	0.2	10	1.1	7	3
Watch, clock, jewelry	3	—	—	—	—	—
Custom industries						
Bottling works	2	0.3	14	7.0	14	—
Printing, publishing shops	39	3.3	132	3.4	128	4
Miscellaneous services	4	0.3	12	3.0	12	—
Totals	1,766	100.0	4,012	2.3	3,900	114

Source: Joseph A. Pierce. *Negro Business Education.* New York: Harper & Row, 1947. Appendix.

TABLE 4.8

Number of Employees in 352 Miscellaneous Businesses by Line of Business, Twelve Cities, 1944

Line of Business	Number of Businesses Reporting	Total Number of Employees	Percent of Total Employees	Average Number of Employees	Number of Paid Employees	Number of Unpaid Employees
Amusements						
Bowling alleys	1	3	0.1	3.0	3	—
Carnival	1	8	0.2	8.0	8	—
Men's recreation places	48	92	2.9	1.9	75	17
Orchestras	2	11	0.3	5.5	11	—
Theaters	1	12	0.3	12.0	12	—
Financial Institutions						
Building, loan associations	1	2	0.1	2.0	2	—
Insurance, life, branch offices	21	513	16.1	24.4	502	11
Insurance, brokers	3	12	0.3	4.0	12	—
Insurance, burial societies	3	48	1.5	16.0	48	—
Insurance, other	2	4	0.1	2.0	4	—
Loan companies	7	5	0.1	0.7	5	—
Construction Businesses						
Contractors, building	14	243	7.6	17.3	238	5
Contractors, plumbing	9	34	1.1	4.0	32	3
Hotels	29	155	7.8	5.3	141	14
Institutions						
Clinics	3	9	0.3	3.0	9	—
Hospitals	4	56	1.7	14.0	56	—
Nurseries	2	9	0.3	4.5	9	—
Manufacturing						
Artificial flowers	1	—	—	—	—	—
Caskets	4	49	1.4	11.5	49	—
Cabinets	1	—	—	—	—	—

Chemicals	2	0.2	—	8	—
Cosmetics	8	9.2	37.0	295	1
Food	1	0.1	3.0	3	—
Hair	1	0.3	9.0	9	—
Newspapers	8	5.0	20.1	161	—
Real Estate Businesses					
Burial plot companies	6	1.0	5.2	25	6
Real estate agencies	60	5.7	3.1	175	8
Trade Schools					
Barber schools	1	—	—	—	—
Beauty schools	17	20.0	4.0	49	16
Business schools	3	0.5	4.6	14	—
Music schools	7	0.1	0.1	1	—
Transportation Businesses					
Moving, hauling	46	4.8	3.3	149	4
Taxicabs, taxicab companies	35	31.8	29.1	1,008	11
Total	352	100.00	9.1	3,112	96

TABLE 4.9

Percentage of Negro Consumers Who Purchased Goods at Black- and at White-Owned Stores

Percentage of Negro Consumers Who Buy at:

Types of Goods or Services Bought	Stores Owned by Negroes	Stores Owned by Whites	Total
Groceries	27.9	72.1	100.00
Drug-store purchases	41.1	58.9	100.00
Men's clothing	0.9	00.1	100.00
Women's clothing	1.1	98.9	100.00
Children's clothing	1.0	99.0	100.00
Men's shoes	0.6	99.4	100.00
Women's shoes	0.3	99.7	100.00
Children's shoes	1.0	99.0	100.00
Furniture	2.9	97.1	100.00
Hardware	4.3	95.7	100.00
Other household supplies	15.9	84.1	100.00
Flowers	47.0	53.0	100.00
Automobile repairs	41.8	58.2	100.00
Gasoline, oil, etc.	53.8	45.2	100.00
Shoe repairs	75.0	25.0	100.00
Cleaning and pressing	74.4	25.6	100.00
Tailoring	80.3	19.7	100.00
All types	27.6	72.4	100.00

Source: Joseph A. Pierce. *Negro Business and Business Education.* New York: Harper & Row, 1947. 52.

industries captured the highest percentage of Afro-American customers, thus reflecting less competition from white businesses. Negro consumers reported, for example, 80.3 percent of their tailoring patronage went to Afro-American businesses. Black-owned cleaning and pressing services captured 74.4 percent of Afro-American business, and shoe repairs by Afro-Americans captured 75 percent of black consumer business. On the other hand, only 0.9 percent of Afro-Americans patronized men's clothing stores owned by Afro-Americans. Similar low patronage by blacks is also true for Afro-American-owned women's and children's clothing stores; men's, women's and children's shoe stores; and furniture and hardware stores. The variation in purchasing was explained by quality of goods, proximity to home, good styles, courteous service, and low prices.[29]

The fact that Afro-American businesses followed the tradition of "bootstrap" achievement is reflected by the fact that Pierce reported that the number of employees with some type of business education was 91.2 percent. However, 59.4 percent stated that they would take part-time business education if they had the opportunity do so.

CONCLUSION

Pierce's excellent work has allowed us to look at the nature of Afro-American enterprise as it began to grow and flourish. His data follow the pattern of other research on minority groups which have been examined under the theory of middleman minorities. His work is also a testimony to the long tradition of examining the relationship between hostility received by a group in society and the development of business enterprises.

5

Durham, North Carolina

An Economic Enclave

Thus far, we have considered the development of Afro-American businesses as individual cases and in the aggregate, but all of the trends and data presented were developed from communities. This chapter chronicles the history of one of the most celebrated early Afro-American economic enclaves. The presentation of community-level data allows us to take advantage of the theoretical work of scholars such as Portes, Bach, and Wilson. As noted in the first chapter, they have advanced the concept of ethnic enclave as an explanatory tool to explain and explore the nature of entrepreneurship within ethnic communities. In order to move our analysis to the community level, we turn to Durham, North Carolina, as representative of one of the early old Southern city enclaves where extensive entrepreneurship developed among Afro-Americans. In this chapter and the next, we consider the historical settings of the cities selected as examples of entrepreneurial enclaves.

I

At the turn of the century, commentators and scholars were as excited about Durham, North Carolina, as they are today about the Cuban-American experience in Miami. The experience of Cuban-Americans in Miami has attracted not only the attention of scholars, but also has been brought to the attention of the general public by the popular media. The CBS-TV show *60 Minutes* dedicated an entire segment to the Cuban enclave. George Gilder referred to the Cuban-American experience as "The Cuban Miracle" with an excellent account of how different families turned a situation of despair into one of hope.[1] Around the turn of the century, commentators and scholars were just as excited about Afro-American enterprise in Durham, North Carolina, as they were most recently about the Cuban-American experience in Miami.

When the historian William Kenneth Boyd wrote *The Story of Durham*, he included a chapter on the significance of Afro-American enterprise and entrepreneurship within the city. Boyd stated, "The increase in wealth, the rise of institutions for public welfare, and the spirit of cooperation have not been confined to one race. The progress of whites has been accompanied by corresponding progress among the Negroes."[2]

In 1910, when the Afro-American business leadership of North Carolina was escorting Booker T. Washington through the hinterlands of the state, Washington was very impressed with "Farms, truck farms, grocery stores, thriving drugstores, insurance houses, and beautiful though modest homes."[3] Again and again Washington expressed to the businessmen in charge of his travels that here were excellent and encouraging signs of Negro business development; and again and again the men kept saying, "You haven't seen anything yet. Wait 'til you get to Durham."

During this period when news traveled slowly and there was no instant television to inform people of the progress in business enterprise, Durham, indeed, must have been a special place to visit. W. E. B. Du Bois, Washington's nemesis or personal rival of that day, noted after visiting the city that, "there is in this city a group of five thousand or more colored people, whose social and economic development is perhaps more striking than that of *any* [4] similar group in the nation."[5]

One of the leading sociologists of his day, E. Franklin Frazier, before he went sour on the black middle class, concluded:

> Durham offers none of the color and creative life we find among Negroes in New York City. It is a city of fine homes . . . and middle-class respectability. It is not the place where men write and dream; but a place where black men calculate and work. . . . As we read the lives of the men in Durham who have established the enterprises there, we find stories paralleling the most amazing accounts of the building of American Fortunes. We find them beginning their careers without much formal education and practicing the old-fashioned virtues of the old middle class. . . . These men have mastered the technique of modern business and acquired the spirit of modern enterprise.[6]

Durham was indeed special in its predisposition toward Afro-American enterprise. In many publications throughout America, it was called the "Wall Street of Negro America."[7] The story of Durham at the turn of the century is one of enterprise, sacrifice, and economic resilience. It is an excellent example of successful enterprise within the context of an economic detour.

If one were to enter North Carolina from the Atlantic Ocean and go straight west, three geographic divisions would become apparent; the Coastal Plain, the Piedmont Plateau and the Highlands.[8] Durham is located in the Piedmont region between Raleigh and Greensboro. As the largest of the three areas, the Piedmont region has gently rolling hills nestled within a plateau. It is the place in the state where major industries developed and, thus, became more highly urbanized than did the Coastal Plain or the Highlands.

At the turn of the century, the state of North Carolina was busy readjusting to the victory of the North in the Civil War. As did its other Southern counterparts, a big part of this adjustment involved redeeming the state from the hands of Northerners and Afro-Americans. Between 1895 and 1901, the Populist Movement had emerged and brought with it a high degree of political activity. In 1896, a coalition of Republicans, dissatisfied Democrats, and a solid Afro-American vote was strong enough to bring about a return to Republican rule. This political reality aroused Conservative Democrats and made them determined to regain control of government and establish a system of white supremacy under Democratic control.[9] During the campaign of 1898 the Democrats attacked the Populist coalition on the Afro-American question. As a result of this issue, the Democrats regained control of the legislature. Because they thought of their success as a mandate from the people to disenfranchise Afro-Americans, they prepared an amendment to the State Constitution designed to eliminate Afro-Americans from politics. By 1908, the Afro-Americans were completely disenfranchised.[10] Thus, even as other ethnic groups were arriving on American shores in search of freedom, Afro-Americans in Durham and elsewhere were being disenfranchised.

As was the case for Southern states in general, race relations within the state were at their lowest tide. In 1898, there was a major race riot in Wilmington. Between 1890 and 1899, twenty-two of the twenty-seven people lynched in the state were Afro-Americans. As a group, Afro-Americans were fearful, discouraged, and doubtful about their future. Some argued that migration was the answer to try and escape disenfranchisement and falling hope.

In a letter printed to the *Charlotte Observer*, the president of Slater Industrial School in Winston-Salem advised his people to stand "still and see the salvation of the Lord."[11] In addition, this influential educator urged the following:

> We will do well to turn our attention now especially to land-getting, to the work of education and to our improvement generally as individuals, relying—as I trust we may—on the purpose of all good men in the State, and upon those managing the administration of affairs, to give us an opportunity to shake off our doubts and fears, to win citizenship, and to have a permanent place in the future development of the state.[12]

The policies of the dominant whites in North Carolina affected more than 30 percent of the citizenry. In 1880, Afro-Americans made up 38 percent of the population of the state. In 1890, that percentage had dropped to 34.7 percent. As a matter of fact, between 1880 and 1950, the percentage of Afro-Americans in the state showed such a steady decline that, by 1950, the percentage was only 25.8. In addition to the obvious push factor of disenfranchisement, Afro-Americans were pulled to better opportunities in Northern states. Indeed, the census of 1900 reported that 136,468 or 18.6 percent of the State's native-born Afro-American population now lived in other states.[13] During the same time period there were only 26,347 Afro-American natives of other states living in North Carolina. This differential produced a net loss of 110,121 Afro-Americans for the state. From 1900 to 1910, the net loss, as a result of interstate migration, was 109,751, and, between 1910 and 1920, the northward movement grew even more intense. It was estimated that the state lost about 14,000 Afro-American males during this decade.[14] As Afro-Americans left the state for northern states, others from neighboring southern states migrated to North Carolina, but this movement still did not serve to replace the number of Afro-Americans who had left the state. Those who remained prepared for life under a system of complete governmental control—a control that manifested itself at every level of life. Those interested in going into business would have to operate under an economic detour.   •

TABLE 5.1
Selected Stores Operated by Negroes in North Carolina, 1929

Type of Business	Number of Stores	Number of Employees	Total Payroll	Net Sales Amount	Percentage of Total
Food Group	956	144	$91,256	$2,679,821	46.44
Candy	48	1	913	55,187	.96
Grocery	640	59	27,326	1,863,944	20.51
Grocery and meats	210	60	45,078	1,106,373	19.17
Meat markets	54	22	17,239	324,787	5.63
Other food stores	4	2	700	9,787	.17
General Stores	62	12	6,474	337,699	5.85
General Merchandise	10	6	7,842	98,226	1.70
Dry Goods	4	2	2,164	17,325	.30
Variety 5-and-10 to $1.00	2	—	—	—	—
Automotive	192	46	33,639	495,799	8.60
Filling stations	143	25	20,824	414,770	7.19
Garages	46	21	12,851	77,738	1.35
Apparel Group	22	11	11,088	70,650	1.22
Furniture, Household	3	9	12,910	95,200	1.65
Lumber-building	3	4	4,628	24,150	.42
Restaurant	478	206	89,781	911,935	15.00
Totals	1,907	577	$369,369	$5,770,830	100.00

Source: Bureau of the Census. Negroes in the United States, 1920–1932. 511–512.

As was the case in other states, the Afro-American citizens of North Carolina began to build a business enterprise community. Concentrating on small retail enterprises, by 1929, they operated 1,907 stores in which 2,077 firm members worked but were not on the payroll. There were, however, 577 full-time persons who were officially employed by these establishments (*see* Table 5.1). The total payroll then was $369,369, and the net sales from these establishments amounted to $5,770,830.[15] As Table 5.1 shows, the food group accounted for the largest amount of net sales, in excess of $2 million, with restaurants, automotive, general stores, and the apparel group following. Net sales from all stores averaged a little over $3,000 for 1929. It must be remembered that it was actually against the law and custom for non-Afro-Americans to visit these stores, and these enterprises, no matter how energetic their owners, had to be in the Afro-American community. Because of this situation, and in order to make ends meet, many businesses remained open for much longer hours than average. For example, in Wilmington some food stores operated from 6:00 A.M. until 11:00 P.M. for a seventeen-hour day.

Although there was economic activity throughout the state of North Carolina, the pride of the state—and indeed the South—was Durham. Even though it represented an example of a successful racial enclave, outside economic and racial hostility was such that it was impossible, on a large scale, to develop stores which catered to white clients. As emphasized throughout this essay, this is the critical difference between an ethnic enclave and the racial enclaves developed by Afro-Americans. Durham—which reacted much like its sister cities in North Carolina—was the city which Du Bois, Frazier, and Boyd all commented upon as a magnificent example of business enterprise. The development of this business activity is tied to the development of Durham as a center of enterprise in the south.

The history of Durham, North Carolina, is tied to tobacco growing. As early as 1852, people realized that the sandy siliceous soil of the area produced a lovely yellow tobacco leaf, excellent for smoking. Durham became the capital of what was called the "Bright Tobacco Belt" of North Carolina. By 1872, there were twelve companies which manufactured smoking and chewing tobacco and snuff. As competition increased and firms were consolidated, two of them—W. Duke Sons and Company, and Blackwell and Company—stood out as dominant. With the development of the cigarette machine in 1884, the Duke Company began an even more rapid expansion. Before this machine, cigarettes had been made entirely by hand, and most of the white laborers had been Jews.

After the Civil War, Afro-Americans started to migrate to Durham to work in this expanding tobacco industry. They settled in the Fayetteville Street area of Durham, in the vicinity of this industry. The land on which they settled was undeveloped and owned by wealthy whites of Durham. Most of it was owned by one merchant named M. A. Angier. As the Afro-American community expanded, these wealthy whites rented the land to them, and, as Afro-Americans began to develop their own business enterprises, they gradually began to purchase the land. The area became known as Hayti, and would become a major business district within the community.

The Afro-American community really began to take form, however, when religious institutions were established and served also as cultural and civic centers. The most prominent churches were St. Joseph's A.M.E. Church, founded in 1869, and White Rock Baptist Church, founded in 1875. St. Joseph's A.M.E. Church began on Fayetteville Street in a brush arbor shelter, but eventually became housed in a Gothic Revival Church. Booker T. Washington called it the finest structure in the South.[16] This structure was designed by architect Samuel Linton Leary, who had come to Durham to design buildings for Washington Duke.[17] The church featured a patterned slate roof, a square bell tower, and large stained glass windows. The interior was an unusual semi-elliptical radiating plan with a polychromed ceiling.[18]

The White Rock Baptist Church was also impressive. Constructed at the corner of Fayetteville Street and Mobile Street, the building featured three-storied towers on the main facade.[19] These two churches served the entire original community of Hayti, which was composed of mostly laborers and artisans, but the structures were funded almost totally by the increasingly successful businessmen of the community.

As businessmen, they were also the leaders of the community. They assumed responsibility, as the community grew, for improving the quality of life in Hayti. In fact, one of the reasons business activity flourished was due to the fact that Afro-Americans could find work in the developing industries as workers and skilled craftsmen, even though they had to fight racial problems as the overall community grew. A reconstruction of the general working community and class structure will give us a broader perspective on the nature of the overall community.

The Duke factory began to hire Afro-Americans in increasing numbers at the turn of the century. Their labor was used for the preparation of the tobacco while white workers operated the machines. The demand for cigarettes increased, and new factories were built. Eventually, the cigarette and general tobacco industry became a mainstay of the Durham economy.[20] The textile industry was also tied to the economic and social development of Durham. The Durham Cotton Manufacturing Company began operations in 1865, and, not surprisingly, the first product was a cotton cloth suitable for tobacco bags. This enterprise also employed whites to operate the machines and Afro-Americans to do the more preparatory work.

Still, other industries flourished in Durham. In 1894, the Durham Hosiery Mill began production. This became a major operation in the city and expanded rapidly. Then in 1904, when the number of white laborers proved to be insufficient because of the company's expansion, the first hosiery mill in

America to utilize an all-Afro-American labor force was established. In this year, fifty Afro-Americans started operating knitting machines, and, by 1919, the plant was employing four hundred people. Durham became a leading manufacturing center of the South in tobacco and textiles.[21] Thus, the tobacco factories and the hosiery mill provided the largest number of employment possibilities for Afro-Americans in Durham, but, correspondingly, domestic and personal service jobs remained secondary in contradiction to the pattern in many other Southern cities. Despite this truth, nearly one-third of Afro-American women still managed to make ends meet by engaging in domestic service. There were also a number of Afro-Americans engaged in the skilled trades, but as was the case for the entire South, the number of skilled workers among Afro-Americans decreased after slavery. Although slaves had been the skilled craftsmen of the South, the dawn of freedom brought them only limited opportunities to work in the open marketplace. Durham was no different. Whites formed labor unions and excluded Afro-Americans from occupations, regardless of their skills and abilities. Consider the following example taken from a study on Durham:

> At one time all carpenter work both for whites and colored was done by Negro carpenters. According to a Negro the beginning of the trouble came when "the whites saw that the Negroes were making good money. They entered the trade and formed unions which excluded the Negro." Still many were engaged as carpenters so the whites began a policy of running down the work of the Negroes, trying to make people believe that they lacked skill and could not be trusted to do the work of the better class of houses. When the Negro did get a job the whites tried all manner of underhand tactics to scare them off. One instance, given by a Negro carpenter, is as follows: "One morning I came to work and saw my men standing around with their coats on looking at a cloth sign stretched across the front of the house we were building. In the middle was a skull and crossbones and large red letters saying 'Run, Nigger, Run!' I told my men to tear it down and to work. I complained to the major and was no further molested on that job."[22]

Because of situations like the one just described, Afro-American skilled craftsmen were forced to resort to the economic detour—that is, they would eventually have to depend only on Afro-American clients for business. Among skilled trades such as painting, carpentry, and brick masonry, Afro-Americans clearly were replaced because whites refused to work side by side with them on the same job. For example, in 1903, there were 110 Afro-American brick masons as compared to 15 whites. By 1929, these numbers had changed from 85 to 150 respectively. The number of blacks in this occupation had dropped from 110 to 85 while the number of whites had increased from 15 to 150 during this time period.[23] Clearly, racial discrimination had a profound effect on the nature of Afro-American participation in the labor force.

Significantly, though, Afro-American brick masons in Durham did not automatically relinquish their trade to whites. In one of the most interesting labor issues in the history of race relations, the brick masons formed a union which was created and directed by Afro-Americans. When the organizational structure was in place, they agreed to ask whites to join, encouraging them to hold office and participate fully. Because their meeting place was located in the Afro-American neighborhood, whites refused to accept the invitation to participate in the union.

This was also during 1921 which was an era of general depression. When work became scarce, white contractors began hiring nonunion painters. The members of the Afro-American union went on strike. The whites—whom Afro-Americans referred to as *scabs* —were hired instead. The result of this situation was that Afro-Americans were forced to leave their union and join the scabs simply to find work. This is probably the only case in American history where white workers refused to join a black union and thus served as strike breakers.[24]

Table 5.2 gives the occupational classification of employed blacks ten years of age and older for the city of Durham. This census data, collected in 1930, allow us to step back and look at the overall nature of the work force. First, it can be seen that more than ten thousand Afro-Americans were engaged in gainful occupations in Durham when the U.S. Census was taken that year.

When one considers that this was during the Great Depression and that there was a total of only 18,717 Afro-Americans in the total population of the city, one can conclude, as E. F. Frazier noted, that this population was quite industrious. Although both male and female Afro-Americans were concentrated in the cigar and tobacco industries—as was also true for all others—the table reveals that there was occupational diversification within the labor force. Afro-American males were also concentrated in the building industry and, as was to be expected of an old Southern city, their female counterparts also worked in domestic and personal services.[25]

Having reviewed the situation of skilled labor in Durham, we must note that there was also a number of Afro-American professionals in Durham around the turn of the century. This group has been estimated to have been composed of one architect, two chiropractors, thirty-four clergymen, one college president, fourteen college professors, five dentists, eleven physicians, four lawyers, 103 teachers, nine trained nurses, and one newspaper editor. In this study, which was completed in 1930, it was also noted that it was impossible to obtain the names of all the professionals; those reported were those who lived and worked within the city limits. The numbers would have increased

TABLE 5.2

Occupational Classification of Gainfully Employed Negroes Ten Years of Age and Older, 1930

	All Groups		Negro Groups	
Industrial Group	Male	Female	Male	Female
All industries	15,300	9,512	5,508	5,013
Agriculture	238	16	132	8
Farmers (owners and tenants)	82	2	39	1
Farm managers and foremen	9	2	—	—
Farm laborers	139	9	89	7
Wage workers	135	8	89	6
Unpaid family workers	4	1	—	1
Forestry and fishing	11	—	9	—
Extraction of minerals	6	—	2	—
Building industry	2,413	33	1,018	10
Chemical and allied industries	109	38	61	2
Cigar and tobacco factories	2,373	2,824	1,298	1,941
Clothing industries	39	28	26	1
Food and allied industries	213	7	64	—
Automobile factories and repair shops	83	4	15	1
Iron and steel industries	71	3	14	1
Saw and planing mills	137	2	76	2
Other woodworking and furniture industries	33	1	3	—
Paper, printing, and allied industries	162	38	11	2
Cotton mills	1,012	473	45	6
Knitting mills	1,081	1,269	87	155
Silk mills	26	38	1	—
Other textile industries	89	73	9	5
Independent hand trades	60	99	25	38
Other manufacturing industries	562	339	328	295
Construction and maintenance of streets, etc.	145	—	88	—
Garage and greasing stations, etc.	185	—	57	—
Postal service	66	3	5	—
Steam and street railroads	481	16	250	2
Telegraph and telephone	60	48	13	1
Other transportation and communication	203	2	68	—
Banking and brokerage	140	58	20	3
Insurance and real estate	345	131	68	62
Automobile agencies and filling stations	258	8	63	—
Wholesale and retail trade, except automobiles	2,016	492	340	39
Other trade industries	60	5	16	—
Public service (not elsewhere classified)	377	35	159	4
Recreation and amusement	145	45	66	9
Other professional and semi-professional service	772	492	240	232
Hotels, restaurants, boarding houses, etc.	390	270	254	134
Laundries and cleaning and pressing shops	215	217	62	167
Other domestic and personal service	446	1,995	328	1,873
Industry not specified	278	41	137	15

Source: Thomas H. Houck, A Newspaper History of Race Relations In Durham, North Carolina, 30–33. Original source is U.S. Bureau of the Census, "Population," Fifteenth Census (1930) Vol. III, Part 2. (Washington: U.S. Government Printing Office, 1932).

significantly if those on the outskirts of the city or those who were recently retired had been counted as well.[26]

In a very real sense, the Afro-American community in Durham exemplified the sort of class stratification—based on education, occupation, and income—which was developing in Afro-American communities throughout the country. In addition to the separation by education and occupation, there was little social contact between professionals and the laboring classes. Understandably, this led to conflicts. The following quotation captures the essence of the schism which was developing in Durham and other Southern cities:

> On the one side of the chasm is a mass, not so much illiterate as underprivileged, that may conveniently be called unskilled labor. On the other side are the professional classes, the so-called intelligentsia. Between the two are very tenuous bonds of sympathy, little understanding of the problems of the other side, few friendly associations. The lower class resents being used as a stepping stone to help the doctor or lawyer or teacher to remove himself from their intellectual, social, and economic orbit; the upper classes condemned the lower for making it hard for us! The professional classes approach the masses with the typical twentieth-century "uplift" psychosis; the masses have the perfectly natural reaction of suspecting ulterior motives on the part of their self-professed friends. We are as a tree severed in twain: the broad base has its roots firmly planted in the ground; there are, however, no flourishing limbs; only a slim cord connects the base with the wavering flimsy pinnacle.[27]

The reality of class division in Durham meant that the Afro-American professional class, as was true in small towns and cities in the South, developed class-based neighborhoods, attended different churches, and developed a distinct set of aspirations for their children.

Although Durham was similar in this aspect, it was different when it came to business enterprise. For example, Charlotte, North Carolina, had a larger Afro-American population than did Durham, but it did not have a bank or loan association. Afro-Americans were aware of the limitations of Durham, and aware that it could not provide a job for every Afro-American. But they were also aware of the business and enterprise model that Afro-Americans were developing in that city.

> The Negro business group in Durham cannot give employment to a very large number of members of that race, but it can be a light to show the laboring class that they need not despair of rising. It serves as an inspiration to the common man demonstrating that ability will be rewarded. This power of giving self-confidence to the whole

Negro race is far more important than the individual wealth which is accumulated or the chances for office work which it offers. Negroes all over the country know of the success of the Durham group and it encourages the establishment of like businesses under the sound principles in other towns. Here are concentrated more Negro business firms both in size and variety than in any other small city and even many large cities do not have as much Negro enterprise.[28]

The central business section of the Afro-American community, Hayti, was fully developed by the turn of the century. Although most of the stores were simple frame buildings, development continued rapidly, and, by 1910, Hayti was taking on the appearance of a well-established business section. Simple frame buildings were replaced with attached brick buildings, and, all along Fayetteville Street, businesses were found. The St. Joseph's A.M.E. Church mentioned earlier stood as a landmark on the same street.[29]

By the late 1940s, more than one hundred and fifty business enterprises flourished in the city of Durham. Included in these businesses were traditional service industries such as cafes, movie houses, barber shops, boarding houses, pressing shops, grocery stores, and funeral parlors. Away from the central district of Hayti stood Parish Street, lined with Afro-American businesses. It was called *Negro Wall Street*. But what made the city special during that time period and with the Negro Wall Street, was the presence of large successful businesses.

Standing at the center was the North Carolina Mutual Life Insurance Company, one of the largest and most successful Afro-American enterprises in the nation. The most stable and financially sound bank—the Mechanics and Farmers Bank—was also located in Durham with a branch in Raleigh. Forming a circle around the North Carolina Mutual Life Insurance Company were The Bankers Fire Insurance Company, the Mutual Building and Loan Association, the Union Insurance and Realty Company, the Dunbar Realty and Insurance Company, the Southern Fidelity Mutual Insurance Company, the Home Modernization and Supply Company, the People's Building and Loan Association, the Royal Knights Savings and Loan Association, T. P. Parham and Associates (a brokerage corporation), and the Mortgage Company of Durham.[30] The businesses were personified by people who worked to develop Durham as a "City of Enterprise" for Afro-Americans.

All of the analyses done on the Durham group stress the significance of sound economic principles, thrift, savings, and hard work. As noted by Frazier, the lives of the Afro-Americans who had established enterprises in Durham paralleled the most amazing accounts of the building of non-Afro-American fortunes. They began their careers without much formal education and practiced the old-fashioned virtues of the old middle class while assuming the roles of organizers and promoters. Therefore, a second generation of Afro-American capitalists was to be found in Durham. These men mastered the techniques of modern business and had the spirit of enterprise.[31]

Again, we remind the reader of the exceptional impact that Durham, as an example, was to have on the national development of Afro-American enterprise. Throughout the South, Afro-American leaders pointed to Durham as the place to visit in order to learn the basics of business enterprise. One example is given by this excerpt from a weekly newspaper in Richmond, Virginia. The writer urged its business class to visit Durham rather than Europe.

> Go to Durham . . . you need the inspiration. Go to Durham and see the industrious Negro at his best. Go to Durham and see the cooperative spirit among Negroes at its best. Go to Durham and see Negro business with an aggregate capital of millions. Go to Durham and see twenty-two Negro men whose honesty and business sagacity are making modern history. Among your New Year's resolves, resolve to go to Durham.[32]

Indeed, Durham was both the center of entrepreneurship for Afro-Americans and the place where people went to observe and study the practice of business. Much as did the Cubans in Miami in the late 1970s and early 1980s, Afro-Americans in Durham were in the academic and practical spotlight during the turn-of-the-century time period.

The reasons for Durham developing into the "Negro Wall Street" continue to elicit speculation on the part of scholars. One of the first to pose such questions was William K. Boyd, in his work entitled, *The Story of Durham: City of the New South*.[33] Boyd first noted that the significant whites of Durham were very supportive of Afro-Americans as they began to become entrepreneurs.

> Live and let live, has characterized the attitude of the leading white men toward the colored race. This means that the Negro has been allowed to stand on his own merit; he has not been patronized as a dependent, neither has he met enmity and persecution because of his success or failure.[34]

Boyd notes that this attitude was indicated by the editorial policy of the *Morning Herald*, which was a reaction of racism criticism directed at Afro-Americans by the governor of the state. The newspaper noted that, "If the Negro is going down, for God's sake let it be because of his own fault, and not because of our pushing him."[35]

Of course, this attitude was applied only to business enterprise, and not to politics or any social activity. Indeed, it was simply a reiteration of Booker T.

Washington's Atlanta compromise, where he argued for white support of Afro-Americans in business affairs—or in those things which would lead to mutual progress—in exchange for the withdrawal of Afro-Americans from politics. Thus, in his analysis of Durham, Walter Weare identifies the support that whites gave blacks on the one hand, and their disdain for their participation in civil rights on the other.[36] Weare gives the example of Durham's Julian Shakespeare Carr, a cotton mill owner and financier, who loved the South and its history of slavery on the one hand, but supported black businesses in Durham on the other. He could not escape the historical fact that the South had lost the Civil War. Having seen his son die in "the cause," Carr believed that the wisest providence of a just God was enslaving blacks. He spoke of the rural South and of how it reflected off the waters of the Potomac, a place where birds sing so sweetly and where magnolia perfumes were in every passing breeze. In this view, the South was a paradise fit for the gods and, if it had not been for the Ku Klux Klan, would have turned into a Black Republic. This would, he noted, have spelled doom for white women of the South. Thus, they had been spared by the disenfranchisement of Afro-Americans.

He once told a black audience that "If we could but succeed in weaning the Negro from believing that politics is their calling by nature . . . and turn the bent of his mind into the development of manufacturing industries, what will the end be? But if the Negro is to continue to make politics his chief aim . . . there can be but one ending."[37] It was the Durham experience that convinced Carr that business enterprise among Afro-Americans could be developed systematically.

This same person, who had such a love for the old traditions of the South, supported Afro-Americans in all things which could lead to mutual progress. He established an all-black cotton mill to provide jobs in the segregated society, and he gave his support to a black-owned cotton mill which was established in 1898 in Concord, North Carolina. He also sent his white technicians to help the development of a mill which had been started by Afro-American entrepreneurs in Durham. In the black community, he was known as a philanthropist, who gave out cake and butter at the black county fair. Indeed, when Afro-Americans went to fight in the Spanish-American War, he insisted on supporting black families if they had a father who fought in that war. While he performed these deeds, the fear of Nat Turner, who had led a slave uprising, was still in the back of his mind.[38] Carr represented the developing schism in the minds of whites. It was an attitude which, on the one hand, invited Afro-Americans to help the South overtake the economy of the North by engaging in industry, but which, on the other hand, included an element of apprehension with respect to the political power of blacks.

Another influential white supporter of black enterprise in Durham was the multimillionaire Washington Duke. A frequent visitor to St. Joseph's

African Episcopal church, this tobacco baron—for whom Duke University is named—was famous for giving advice to Afro-Americans. His letter to an Afro-American education convention in 1890 summed up the tone of his advice, which emphasized the values which had contributed to his success:

> Five years more and I shall have lived three quarters of a century. Not long before I was born, Napoleon thundered at Waterloo, as the Old Guard melted itself before the hollow squares of the English army and England's Iron Duke conquered the world's most magnetic leader. Since then the destiny of nations has been changed. I have seen countries of Europe racked by terrible wars and here in our own land I have witnessed the greatest revolution of them all—the emancipation of your race. I have always had a friendly feeling toward you, and now address you in the spirit of a friend, wishing if I can to help you to overcome the hard conditions of your lot.
>
> I have no doubt that each of you would like to be a successful man. It is right that you should feel so, for a proper ambition is God's call to a higher life, but how shall that success be gained? . . . Be industrious, do not always be looking for an easy, soft place. I have made more furrows in God's earth than any man of forty years of age in North Carolina. And when you have made yourself industrious, you must be frugal. Establish it as a rule to always spend less than you make. I never closed a year's work in my life without being happy in the knowledge that I was better off than I was when it began. Be sure to put away every week part of your earnings in a Savings Bank. And when people begin to find out that you are industrious and reliable they will offer you positions of profit. Do honest work for your honest dollar, put it in your pocket, and at night it will sing you to sleep, because it knows you have earned it and can spend it properly.
>
> Be men of honest, upright lives; support your churches and your schools; regard your minister as your best friend and your school teacher as your next; work honestly for your money and give some of it to help support these institutions; cease to rely upon outside help, for you must work out your own salvation. Ever since I was twelve years old I have been trying to make the world better by having lived in it. Let this be the rule of your lives. I have regarded it as a part of my life. If I am anything, if my life has been successful, if from small beginnings I have brought myself to a successful point in life, then I say to you that it was by following these rules that I have gained it.[39]

The sources of an entrepreneurial spirit among Afro-Americans have also been traced to the quality of the Afro-Americans themselves. The first to speculate on this characteristic was William Boyd. He noted that:

Durham was fortunate in the early days in that it attracted a superior type of colored people. The first black man in the community on which tradition leaves any information was Lewis Pratt, the largest property owner of the neighborhood. His character was such that he was trusted by his master and commanded the respect of the public. . . . The period of prosperity and expansion which opened after 1865 drew to the town a new Negro population seeking work in the factories as well as in domestic service. Among these early immigrants were Dempsey Henderson, George and Cynthia Pearson, Monroe Jordan, Robert Justin, R. B. Fitzgerald, Charles Amey, and David Pointer. These proved to be industrious and thrifty citizens. Henderson bought one hundred acres of land . . . Monroe Jordan and Robert Justice purchased property on Elm Street, George Pearson an extensive tract in the Hayti region; and Fitzgerald, a native of Pennsylvania who came South in 1869, became the town's leading manufacturer of brick. The son of George and Cynthia Pearson was destined to be a pioneer teacher and a leader in Negro business; the descendants of Jordan became teachers, and the son of Charles Amey became a manufacturer and man of business. These and other individuals like them established a tradition of industry, reliability, and integrity which remains to this day.[40]

In a more recent analysis, Walter Weare noted that Durham was fertile ground for Afro-American enterprise because it was a "raw" city of the new South. This meant that it had neither a white aristocracy nor a "cream-of-colored" society as older Southern cities such as Charleston and New Orleans had. It was a city of upstarts without a strong economic lineage. The lack of a white aristocracy precluded the formation of a black aristocracy that would have derived its status from a symbolic attachment to the former. As noted earlier, a larger number of old South cities had developed a class of property owners among Afro-Americans. Durham was an exception. In Durham, the self-help tradition of Afro-American businessmen and professionals provided them with the opportunity to acquire a great deal of status, and they did not have to worry about an established class of Afro-Americans who would feel threatened by their success. Like all groups, internal social dynamics operated within the Afro-American community during the development of entrepreneurship throughout the country. As Weare points out, enterprise in Durham was fortunate in escaping some of those dynamics.

The invidious distinctions between "new issue" and "old issue," house servant and field hand, light and dark, had given the Negro society internal restraints to entrepreneurial activity based on racial solidarity. At the turn of the century increasing segregation, discrimination, and urbanization encouraged the rise of a black business class which threatened to reorder the Negro status system that had been determined by antebellum forces. Obviously the conflict would be less in cities without an entrenched antebellum social order. Durham thus escaped part of this institutional drag on its black economy. . . The kind of ideological conflict that found the colored gentry resisting the black capitalist had little meaning in Durham, where wealth and status coincided.[41]

It is certain that Durham represented something special at the turn of the century for Afro-American enterprise. Although we cannot examine all of those enterprises—as of 1949, more than three hundred were reported[42]—we can summarize a few. Durham was unique in that, in addition to businesses within the tradition of service, the Afro-American community also attempted to establish manufacturing firms. The largest firm in the city was the North Carolina Mutual Insurance Company. This company represented the "flagship" of all enterprises in Durham. In today's lingo, it represented the "Afro-American miracle."

II

When one begins to examine the literature in search of the sources of business excellence among Afro-Americans in Durham, one is struck by the fact that, at the turn of the century, a number of these enterprises were able to maintain a white clientele. One of the major theses of this work is that Afro-American business people were forced into an economic detour—that is, forced to do business only within their own group. It follows that, if they were allowed to enter the open-client market, they would have found business success which was independent of racial affiliations. One finds that in Durham, given its uniqueness vis-a-vis race relations, the most successful service and retail businesses were able to generate white clients.

In 1940, Smith's Fish Market—which was begun by a former postal clerk from Toledo, Freeman M. Smith—supplied Durham's largest white-operated hotel, The Washington Duke. Smith also was the major supplier for smaller white and Afro-American businesses. In 1940, Smith grossed more than $90,000 and was in the process of opening four more retail outlets throughout the city.

Another revealing example is that of Rowland and Mitchell who owned an outstanding tailor shop which had been established in 1930. They did high-class work for exclusive whites and alterations for the leading Durham department stores. Eighty percent of their customers were white.[43] These historical examples point to the fact that, when any business is allowed to compete in the open market for clients and is successful, then the enterprise will flourish. But it is also true that, in Durham, most of the Afro-American businesses had to follow the economic detour, thus restricted to serving a clientele which was only Afro-American.

Another successful business was that of Thomas Bailey & Sons, a meat market and grocery which opened in 1919 and which, by 1940, was grossing $80,000 a year. The Home Modernization and Supply Company, which was founded in 1938 by the brothers U. M. and R. S. George, constructed 500 homes in the Durham area. Employing 35 people, in 1948, it grossed more than $100,000. As in most Southern cities which had developed an entrepreneurial group, beautiful residential areas were built. In Durham, this area was called College Heights. Unlike their Northern counterparts, where excellent housing was associated with white residential areas, Afro-Americans in the South did not associate excellent homes with white exclusivity.

Many individuals came to Durham to learn the trade of beautician by attending the enterprise established by Jacquline DeShazor, who had moved to Durham in the late 1920s from Brooklyn, New York. From her beginning in three rooms, she expanded in 1945 to 36 rooms in a three-story building which she purchased for $42,500, reflecting the pattern of the ownership of one's building in which one's enterprise was located, a trademark of Durham. In the late 1940s, her building was worth $80,000.[44] One of the most interesting businesses in Durham was the Durham Textile Mill, the only hosiery mill in the world which was owned and operated by Afro-Americans. They operated 18 knitting machines and stood the test in the open market, again offering an example of a business which did not have to follow the economic detour.

But what made this business so interesting was that, given the reality of Jim Crow laws or segregation, their salesmen—who traveled mostly in North Carolina, Indiana, Georgia, South Carolina, and Alabama—were white. This manufacturing firm became perhaps the first large-scale black enterprise to hire whites, and the first firm owned by Afro-Americans where whites earned most of their income. As noted by a commentator of that day, "so far as I have heard, there has been no man to raise the color question when he put on a pair of those socks made by Negroes."[45]

Payton A. Smith, a general contractor, constructed some of the largest buildings in Durham, and R. E. Clegg was a manufacturer of bricks, producing about 2 million bricks per season. The pioneer in this industry was R.B. Fitzgerald who, around 1920, supplied the material for many of the brick structures in Durham.

Exemplifying the racial cooperation that existed among Afro-American and white entrepreneurs, Fitzgerald developed his business with the help of a white tobacco manufacturer named Blackwell. This person made the following statement: "Fitzgerald, get all the Negroes and mules you can and make brick. I will take all that you can make." By 1911, the entrepreneur Fitzgerald was producing 30,000 bricks a day from his plant and he owned 100 acres of land within the city limits of Durham worth about $50,000.[46]

In 1921, the Durham Commercial and Security Company was organized with the goal of financing Afro-American enterprises of all kinds. Afro-American enterprises were so stable and looked so promising for the future that, in 1924, Durham was chosen as the location of The National Negro Finance Corporation, which was capitalized at $1 million. The organization was started to provide working capital for firms, individuals, and corporations in all parts of the country. As with the Durham Commercial and Security Company, its major goal was to stimulate business among Afro-Americans.[47]

Actually Durham began as a financial district as early as 1907. In that year, Professor M. A. Johnson and Dr. M. T. Pope, both from Raleigh, went to Durham with the hope of establishing an Afro-American building and loan association. Afro-Americans in Durham were receptive to the idea. They also wanted to start a bank.

Through the initiative of the businessmen of that city—W. G. Pearson, R. B. Fitzgerald, J. A. Dodson, Dr. S. L. Warren, Dr. James E. Shepard, John Merrick, and W. O. Stevens—$10,000 was raised and one of the most successful banks ever known was born.

> House Bill 1342 and Senate Bill 673, outlined "An Action to Incorporate Mechanics and Farmers Bank of Durham, North Carolina" and "Ratified this 25th day of February, A.D. 1907," states that "The General Assembly of North Carolina do enact; section 1, that John Merrick, R. S. Fitzgerald, J. A. Dodson, James E. Shepard, A. W. Moore, S. L. Warren, W. G. Pearson, Jno. R. Hawkins, W. G. Stevens and their present and future associates, successors, and assigns, be, and they are hereby constituted a body politic and corporate under the name and style of Mechanics and Farmers Bank of Durham, North Carolina."[48]

With the backing of the major businessmen already mentioned, the first meeting of the incorporators and stockholders was held 29 July 1907. R. B. Fitzgerald was elected president; John Merrick, vice-president; and W. G. Pearson, cashier. In August of 1908, the bank began serving the public and was housed in the building of the North Carolina Mutual and Provident Association. As the years progressed, the two institutions became intertwined vis-a-vis financial matters. By 1915, the Mechanics and Farmers Bank had increased its capital from $10,000 to $50,000. By 1923, it boasted a capitalization of $113,000, by June 1940, the capital stock totaled $210,000. Of this amount,

$114,000 was common stock, and $96,000 was preferred. Total assets amounted to $1,398,311.71.[49]

The Mechanics and Farmers Bank had a tremendous effect on the Afro-American community in Durham. It not only encouraged thrift but also an awareness of the building of homes and the importance of educational achievement as a reason for borrowing. The result was that it helped the development of Afro-Americans in general and the middle class in particular. This bank had the distinction of being the only Afro-American bank in the nation to operate a branch office which was located in Raleigh. The effect was so tremendous, that it helped all if not most of the Afro-American businesses in Durham to survive the Great Depression, a feat which the great majority of American small businesses were unable to match.

> A common feature of the Negro business interests of Durham is the fact that not one of their group organizations failed during the period of depression. Such an achievement may well be considered a tribute to the spirit of cooperation that prevails, as well as a tribute to the sound advice and financial facilities that the Mechanics and Farmers Bank has been able to place at the disposal of its patrons. Subsequent to the bank holiday declared by President Roosevelt, the bank met all requirements fully and has been since operated without restrictions.[50]

The success of the bank drew observers from miles away to learn from Durham's example. In 1927, for example, the National Negro Bankers Association convention was held in the city. Participants from all parts of the country were in attendance, including whites. The mayor of Durham presented the welcome address. In part, he said:

> You visitors can go back home and tell your people that the whites and the blacks here are working shoulder to shoulder. Money is interesting and attractive, in a strong vault of a real bank. A bank is a measuring device. It gives the life and thrift of a people. Bankers are called upon to remedy many things which others cannot remedy. The achievements of the Negro in financial institutions are some of the outstanding features of Durham. If you maintain in the future the record you have made in the past, the future is indeed rosy. The man, or the institution, that contributes to an humble home, a hospital, such as the Lincoln, or plants in the bosom of a human inspiration and ambition, that institution will be deservedly blessed.[51]

In the Durham papers the next day, local editors filled the pages about racial understanding and its link to progress in business activity. The Durham *Morning Herald* noted that:

On the one hand was the delight of the Durham Negro community and business interest in having the national bankers convention to meet in this city, and witness the progress and developments made by the Durham Negro citizenry. On the other was the hearty appreciation of the members of the association of the cordial hospitality shown them, and the fine spirit exhibited by many of the white people in giving their presence to the meetings of the association, and cooperating with the Negro businessmen in entertaining their guests. It gave the visitors an idea of how the races live in Durham and do business.[52]

The respect and fairness with which the city of Durham treated the bank is reflected in the fact that, in 1936, when the city issued park bond notes, the Afro-American bank outbid other white banks in Durham. Because of its economic stability, it agreed to purchase $25,000 worth of park bond notes at an interest rate of .772 percent.[53]

It is impossible to reconstruct all of the business which appeared in Durham, but, as early as 1912, W. E. B. Du Bois, in his work on the city, listed "fifteen grocery stores, eight barber shops, seven meat and fish dealers, two drugstores, a shoe store, a haberdashery, and an undertaking establishment."[54] Du Bois also noted that Durham differed from other black enclaves in the sense that blacks had developed in this city "five manufacturing establishments which turned out mattresses, hosiery, brick, iron articles, and dressed lumber. Beyond this, the colored people have a building and loan association, a real estate company, a bank, and three industrial insurance companies."[55]

Although there were numerous successful enterprises in Durham, they pale when compared with the North Carolina Mutual Life Insurance Company. Without a doubt, this company is the most historically celebrated enterprise in the Afro-American tradition. This enterprise had its beginnings in October of 1898. Reflecting a characteristic of many businesses in Durham, most of the entrepreneurs were men of educational attainment. Present at the first meeting were John Merrick, Dr. Aaron McDuffie Moore (a physician), William G. Pearson (a teacher and a principal), Edward A. Johnson (a historian, attorney, and dean of the Law School at Shaw University), Pickney W. Dawkins (a Durham school teacher), and a local tinsmith by the name of Dock Watson. The meeting had been called by John Merrick, who was the least intellectual of the group but still the organizing force behind the venture.[56]

According to one historical account, James Duke, the tobacco tycoon, suggested that Merrick, a barber, start the enterprise. At the time, Merrick was cutting Duke's hair. The conversation went as follows:

MR. DUKE: John, you have too much sense to be a mere barber, why don't you make money among your own people?

MR. MERRICK: But how Mr. Duke?

"Well, for instance, why not establish an insurance company?" answered Mr. Duke.[57]

Another historical account stresses the relationship between the lower class blacks, Merrick and Duke. The story is that during the course of the business day in Merrick's barber shop, lower class blacks asked Merrick to "pass the hat" for collection so that a funeral could be financed. Mr. Duke, who was having his haircut, noticed and suggested that Afro-Americans should develop their own insurance company.[58] However the story goes, the fact of the matter is that the North Carolina Mutual Insurance Company became a reality.

The company began in earnest on 1 July 1900. With the exception of John Merrick and A. M. Moore, all of the original founders withdrew. The organizational chart found Merrick as president, A. M. Moore as vice-president, and C. C. Spaulding as general manager, agent, and janitor. It was around these men that the company would begin to grow. In a real sense, they were much like many Afro-Americans in the South who turned to business enterprise as a way of life. Let us look and see how the entrepreneurship spirit was developed.

The founder, John Merrick, began his career as a barber. Without an education, he was very successful in his trade. As noted before, Merrick counted as his clients wealthy white patrons. In addition to Duke, he was barber to the Carrs, Fullers, and many other wealthy men. When William Jennings Bryan visited Durham around 1895, he presented Merrick with a silver dollar and asked that he not spend it until the former became president.[59]

Merrick was born in 1859 in Clinton County, North Carolina. When slavery ended, he was about school age. When he was 12, and because he had to earn money to help support his family, he began to work in a brickyard at Chapel Hill. He managed to pick up enough understanding of mathematics and reading to be able to transact business affairs.

When he was eighteen, he went to Raleigh in search of a job, became a brick mason, and did most of his work at the developing Shaw University. He then landed a part-time job as a bootblack in the barbershop of W. G. Otey in Raleigh and was soon promoted to the position of barber. This promotion helped his understanding of enterpreneurship and the barbering trade. In 1880, he moved to the boomtown of Durham where he worked in a shop owned by a Mr. Wright. Within six months, he purchased a partnership in this business. In 1892, Mr. Wright left Durham, Merrick became the sole owner, and the shop became very prosperous. In a few years, Merrick was operating shops throughout the city—three of which served whites only and two which served Afro-Americans.[60]

In addition to his barbering business, Merrick began to buy real estate and developed products which related to the barbering trade. For example, in 1890 he decided that something should be done to stop dandruff, although history does not reveal much about the success of his product which was placed on the market. As he noted, "Hair when in a unhealthy condition needs treatment like sistum. Dandruff is a clear demonstration that it's unhealthy. Something ought to be done and must be if you are to save yourself from baldness."[61]

As Merrick began his ventures into commerce—which would eventually lead to the North Carolina Mutual Insurance Company—he continued to embrace the spirit of entrepreneurship. In an analysis on Merrick done in 1940, it was noted that college training could handicap some people by making them too cautious and less likely to attempt innovative change. Merrick was not college-educated which might explain why he so readily undertook several projects in different lines.[62] It was Merrick who was behind the Mechanics and Farmers Bank mentioned above. He served that bank as president and vice-president. In 1910, he organized the Merrick-Moore-Spaulding Real Estate Company. He was also successful in developing the Bull City Drug Company, a pharmaceutical business that provided a place for Afro-American pharmacists to practice. After he started two successful drug stores, he sold them to their managers who ran them as independent businesses.

The only business started by Merrick which did not do well was the Durham Textile Mill. In the long run, it did not live up to its founder's expectations.

Unlike Merrick, Dr. Aaron McDuffie Moore was a man of letters and a physician. Born in Rosindale, North Carolina, in 1863, he attended the country school there and entered Shaw University in 1885. Originally he had planned to be a college professor but was persuaded to study medicine. He completed medical school at Leonard Medical College. When he appeared before the Board of Medical Examiners of North Carolina, there were 46 other applicants, 30 of whom were white. Of those who passed, Moore was ranked second.[63]

In 1901, after having established his practice in Durham, Dr. Moore founded the Lincoln Hospital with the assistance of the wealthy Duke family. This hospital allowed the continued training of Afro-American doctors and nurses. The $150,000 that it took to complete the structure was secured almost entirely as a result of Moore's efforts.[64] Dr. Moore was also instrumental in the establishment of the Mechanics and Farmers Bank.

Given his intellectual background, it worried him that there was no decent library to serve the Afro-American community. After he failed to raise money from philanthropists or to secure funds from the city, he started a library in the basement of his church, the White Rock Baptist. Using his own funds, he supplied a significant number of books and other types of reading materials. But, because the library was in a Baptist Church, people of other denominations did not utilize it as expected. He then began to raise money from the public for a library where the entire community could gather in order to explore the wonders of the world. As president of the board of managers of the project, he worked to fulfill this dream until his death in 1923.

Also because of his intellectual background, Dr. Moore was concerned with the education of Afro-American youth in North Carolina. In order to improve the conditions and to measure change in Afro-American schools, he personally paid the salary of a State Public School Inspector for Afro-American schools, whose duty was to examine all rural schools, report their conditions, and make recommendations which would lead to improvements. During its first year, this task was so successful in improving the condition of these schools that the state took over the work and expense the following year. Dr. Moore was appointed secretary-treasurer of the Rural School Extension Department, which was North Carolina's Teachers Association.[65] He also served higher education when, for ten years, he was one of the largest individual donors in support of Shaw University, the institution which had given him his intellectual start.[66]

Dr. Moore was steeped in the tradition of self-help among Afro-Americans and was also exemplary of the true middle class of the Old South. People who remember him in Durham eulogize him as the physician-philosopher who worked very hard for the hospital which he founded. He is also remembered as a Messiah who walked among Afro-Americans and helped them whenever he could.[67] As the North Carolina Mutual Insurance Company became a reality, other persons became involved in entrepreneurship roles, but Merrick and Moore always stood out as the beacons in this business venture.

The North Carolina Mutual Life Insurance Company began operations in the medical office of Dr. Moore. He rented a small amount of space for $2.00 a month. Actually, the first name of the company was the North Carolina Mutual and Provident Association. In this "home office," the original founders began to feel the insecurity of beginning a new enterprise. Although the business grew rapidly, when the first claim of $40 became due, the stockholders found that there was not enough money in the treasury. Indeed, they had to dip into their own pockets in order to pay the claim. At the end of the first year in 1898, assets were $330.00, and insurance-in-force amounted to $247.92.[68] In 1900, the re-organization already mentioned took place. All of the original stockholders—except Merrick and Moore—ended their association with the company, and a new partner, Charles C. Spaulding, was added.[69] Spaulding attracted the attention of Merrick and Moore because of his "spirit of enterprise." After completing high school in Durham, Spualding turned immediately to business enterprise, and he became manager of a newly purchased grocery store. Because he felt that the owners were lacking in business foresight, he began to save his money so that, if the time arrived, he could purchase the store for himself. The time did come, and this man of thrift was able to become sole owner of a grocery business.

Although this business was successful, Spaulding saw that a small grocery store limited the possibilities of making large sums of money. He prepared himself to move on to enterprises which expanded more rapidly. In the grocery business, he became known for this strict honesty and reliability.

When Merrick and Moore approached Spaulding about a possible partnership, he had some reservations. He knew absolutely nothing about the insurance business and felt that these two men many have been placing too much confidence in him. He did agree, however, to join Moore and Merrick and thus formed perhaps the most successful business triangle within the Afro-American tradition.[70] Spaulding was the first and only agent of the new insurance enterprise. Although he was made general manager, he also filled the roles of clerk, office manager, office boy, and janitor. Soon he would begin to take an active part in the community of Durham, and, as time passed, he could count as his great civic and business accomplishments: (1) a member of the Durham Chamber of Commerce (the white chamber); (2) trustee and treasurer, Shaw University; (3) president, Mechanics and Farmers Bank; (4) president, Mutual Building and Loan Association of Durham; (5) president, mortgage company, Durham; (6) vice-president, Bankers Fire Insurance Company; (7) member, Board of Trustees of Southern Education Foundation; (8) trustee, Howard University; (9) treasurer, National Negro Bankers Association; (10) trustee, North Carolina College for Negroes, Durham; and (11) chairman, North Carolina Committee on Negro Affairs.[71]

With Spaulding safely aboard, the company decided, in 1903, to expand beyond the city of Durham and its vicinity. J. M. Avery was brought into the company as an agent to work in Morganton, North Carolina. In the following year, the company received a license to operate in South Carolina. By 1908, the company erected its own office building at a cost of $27,000. The following year, the company had its first examination by the Insurance Department of North Carolina. It voluntarily had its business evaluated and established reserves based on this evaluation. By then, it had assets of $93,000 and insurance-in-force had grown to $1,535,586.

In 1913, the company amended its charter and eliminated the assessment features of the enterprise. It placed its operation in the old-line legal-reserve tradition. That same year, a fire destroyed part of the home office, causing about $90,000 in damages. The records of the company were also destroyed. In 1915, the enterprise was licensed in Virginia, and, in 1916, it expanded to Washington, D.C. By 1918 it began operations in Tennessee and Maryland. The states of Arkansas, Florida, and Mississippi were added in 1919. Oklahoma and Alabama joined in 1920. By 1941, the company decided to concentrate only in North Carolina, South Carolina, Georgia, Virginia, Tennessee, Alabama, Maryland, Pennsylvania, and Washington, D.C. The executives made the decision to withdraw from Florida, Mississippi, Arkansas, and Oklahoma. As they were sensitive to the development of Afro-American insurance companies in those states, the directors transferred $10 million in insurance-in-force and $500,000 of the assets covering the reserves to Afro-American companies which operated in those states.[72]

In 1910, the name of the company was changed from the North Carolina Mutual and Provident Association to the North Carolina Mutual Life Insurance Company. By 1939, the company had the distinction of being the largest Afro-American insurance company in the world. It had about a thousand employees, serving more than a quarter of a million policyholders. There were district offices in Birmingham and Montgomery, Alabama, and in the state of Georgia there were offices in Atlanta, Americus, Savannah, Macon, and Augusta. In South Carolina, the company was active in Chester, Columbia, Darlington, Charleston, Greenville, and Spartanburg. In its home state of North Carolina, the company had district offices in Charlotte, Goldsboro, Greensboro, Raleigh, Wilmington, and Winston-Salem. The state of Virginia saw district offices in Danville, Newport News, Norfolk, Richmond, and Roanoke. In Maryland, offices were in East and West Baltimore, and there was also an office in the District of Columbia. Moving further north, there was an office in Philadelphia. Nashville, Memphis, Knoxville, and Chattanooga represented the state of Tennessee.[73]

By the same year, 1939, the company had paid $18,336,126 to policyholders and their beneficiaries.[74] In short, the North Carolina Mutual Insurance Company had become a major corporation. It had gone beyond the tradition of middleman groups and their small businesses, and it had done so by operating under an economic detour.

If America had welcomed Afro-Americans as businessmen on the basis of ability rather than race, then the expansion and success would have been more impressive. Despite the competence of this company, the reality of racism forced them to cater only to Afro-American clients. Again, few if any ethnic groups have been forced by law and custom to generate businesses only among their own group.

As noted in the theoretical chapter 1, early scholars who examined Afro-American business activity compared their efforts to totally white America. For example, as early as 1911, an audit was conducted of the North Carolina Mutual Insurance Company. It had a premium income of about $250,000 assets which amounted to $120,000, insurance-in-force of more than $2 million, and about 500 employees. For the same year, John Hancock, the smallest of the large white insurance companies, had assets totaling more than $90 million and insurance-in-force exceeding $500 million. New York Life, the largest company at the time, had assets of $735 million and more than $2 billion insurance-in-force.[75]

It does not, however, make sense to compare the development of "one-race" businesses, which could not enter the open market with businesses that had access to the total market. Furthermore, in the literature on ethnic businesses, this comparison is never made in a negative way. That is to say, receipts of Japanese eating establishments are not compared to those of major restaurant chains. Portes and Bach's analysis of Cubans in Miami does not downgrade their efforts by comparing them to successes in the larger market.

The point is that, when one-race businesses are successful, they must be seen in their own historical light. When compared to the efforts of other ethnic businesses that had the opportunity to draw other customers, the North Carolina Mutual Life Insurance Company certainly is an impressive case. As noted earlier, the fact that Durham had a successful working class contributed to the original success of the company. Of course, the overall success is related to the significant number of blacks in America.

The success enjoyed by North Carolina Mutual Life Insurance Company was the result of constant striving and working around problems of race. Although the white business class in Durham was quite supportive originally, the majority of whites in the city did not quite know what to make of the company. Although small businesses were accepted, the Mutual was an anomaly. After all, business enterprise among Afro-Americans was taking place in a South where theories of racial inferiority and racial violence against blacks were prevalent. In perhaps the most interesting analysis of the company, Weare sums up the situation as follows:

> Whites were never sure whether to consider the Mutual a novelty or an institution, whether to call it "nigger heaven" or the "big colored insurance company." Standing apart from black Hayti, up there on Parrish Street, so prominent, so proud, the Mutual violated what ought to be; yet it was so skillfully presented, so in tune with the white ethos, that it came to represent in the white mind a self-delusory promise of what the black community might be. Whites rationalized the success of the North Carolina Mutual as an exception to the rule of racial incapacity and at the same time proclaimed its success as general proof of the inevitable progress in store for the black man under the benign race policy of the white South. The black success was made over into a white success, even a sectional success. Durham offered three glittering examples of Southern achievement: Duke University, American Tobacco, and the North Carolina Mutual—three satisfying symbols of the New South.[76]

Because of its unique position in Afro-American life, the insurance company ended up being more than an insurance company in that it carried an awful burden for the race. Its community service was without precedent, and it served as a clearinghouse for Afro-American business, finance, and law; as a bureau of missing persons, an information center for federal legislation, and a complaint center. Requests for financial aid came from as far away as Africa and as close as Durham itself. The business was closely associated with the religious life of Durham and even served as a guardian of morality. Employees were encouraged to attend church on a regular basis. The company was the guardian of the values of the Afro-American middle class. It even built, next door to its headquarters, a dormitory for single female employees with no families or guardians in Durham. The company had a fight song—"Give me that Good Ol' Mutual Spirit"—and it established a sense of pride in its employees.[77]

Although we cannot examine the entire leadership of the company, this leadership was responsible for the original development and success of the company. The leadership also had long histories of service, thus assuring company continuity. As of 1939, the leadership was as follows:

President C. C. Spaulding, with service of 40 years; Vice-President and Treasurer M. R. Merrick, 39 years; Vice-President and Secretary W. J. Kennedy, Jr., 22 years; Vice-President and Medical Director Clyde Donnell, M.D., 22 years; Vice-President R. L. McDougald, 19 years; Assistant Secretary M. A. Goins, 22 years; Assistant Secretary-Controller W. D. Hill, 21 years; Assistant Secretary and Actuary Asa T. Spaulding, eight years and 11 summers; Vice-President and Director of Agents G. W. Cox, 19 years; Assistant Director of Agents J. L. Wheeler, 30 years; Assistant Director of Agents D. C. Deans, Jr., 18 years; District Manager A. J. Clemment, Sr., 32 years; Cashier Mrs. B. A. Whitted, 31 years; and Assistant to the Treasurer J. S. Hughson, eight years.[78]

Of all the names mentioned which have not been discussed thus far, perhaps Asa Spaulding had the greatest effect on the survival of the company, especially during the Great Depression. A second cousin of C. C. Spaulding, Asa Spaulding was born in the same county of Columbus. Always seeking outstanding talent, the Mutual invited Asa Spaulding to Durham in 1919. He enrolled in North Carolina College and worked summers for the Mutual. In 1923, he graduated as an outstanding student and left to study business at Howard University in 1924. After spending a summer at Howard, he returned to work for the Mutual. In 1927, he left Durham again and enrolled in New York University, where he graduated magna cum laude in 1930. One of his professors at New York University realized that he was interested in continuing to work in the Mutual. He recommended—and Asa Spaulding responded—that the young student study actuarial science at the University of Michigan where in 1932 he completed the M.A. degree in actuarial mathematics. The executive suite at the Mutual in Durham beamed with confidence and pride. The Afro-American press wrote articles about this outstanding student of academia and the Mutual.[79]

Asa Spaulding's travels introduced him to many things in New York City and Ann Arbor, home of the University of Michigan. He familiarized himself with Harlem, and white students sought him out in order to help them study while he was at Michigan. In the end, though, he returned to Durham because of the outstanding spirit of enterprise of that city. More importantly, he returned to the Mutual as the first Afro-American with a degree in actuarial science. With his scientific way of developing life charts, he took the Mutual through the Great Depression and became its guiding intellectual figure. Again, the insurance company continued its practice of hiring outstanding people.

It continued that tradition in 1934 when it hired Aaron Day, an economics professor and former Standard Life executive, as sales training supervisor with the task of developing an in-house curriculum of training.[80] True to its tradition of excellence, the company never looked back and continued to be the entrepreneurial example for Afro-Americans both in the city of Durham and within the nation as a whole.

III

One of the central concepts in the study of minority enterprises is that of the ethnic enclave. As noted in the first theoretical chapter, an ethnic enclave is defined as a distinctive economic formation, characterized by the spatial concentration of immigrants who organize a number of enterprises to serve their own ethnic market and the general population.[81] Given our concept of economic detour, we must modify this definition. As noted before, although Durham represented some exceptions, Afro-American business people were restricted to selling to members of their race. In the literature, the Cuban community in Miami has served as the prototype of an economic enclave, as is clearly the case in the works of Wilson and Portes, Portes and Bach, and Wilson and Martin.[82] In the latter analysis, the communities of Afro-Americans and Cubans were examined. The finding was, that while there was a great deal of entrepreneurship within the Cuban community, it was absent within the Afro-American community.

One of the problems with this type of comparison, which represents a major flaw in this sort of analysis, is that one is comparing two different groups at different times in their history in America. For example, one could not compare the entrepreneurship activities of Japanese communities today with the Cuban experience of today. The Japanese, as documented in Bonacich's work,[83] developed a strong ethnic enclave in California between 1900 and 1920. Thus, the comparison, if one is to be made, is the Afro-American experience within certain cities of the 1920s (for example, Durham) and the Cuban experience which began in the 1970s.

What we are suggesting is that there is a certain excitement about the development of grass roots entrepreneurship activities by groups who newly enter the economy of a country. The next generations, however, do not necessarily show an interest in developing small businesses. This was true of the Japanese, who, after they were educated, wanted to move into the large economy. There are, however, groups who never engaged in systematic entrepreneurship but who rather, became workers upon their arrival to America and remain as workers today. They became first-, second-, and third-generation steel or coal workers.

For groups who do engage in entrepreneurship, there is a decrease in the number of entrepreneurs as the years progress. But, more importantly, individuals from entrepreneurship groups look forward to moving into the larger economy. This was also true of Afro-Americans, except that, due to the presence of officially sanctioned discriminations, they were less likely to be launched into the larger economy. Thus, what has been called the black middle class, which was the product of business activity, could not launch their children into the larger economy. The creation of opportunities within the larger society was a struggle which took a complete civil rights movement to try and resolve.

IV

Present-day Durham is a "chip off of the old block." Although it would be difficult to repeat the excitement which was present in the early years, the city is alive with Afro-American enterprise. The "old ones" laid a foundation which has stood the test of time, and Durham is still a monument to the idea of entrepreneurship. If you happen to be in the city today, you will find that an expressway goes right through the center of what was called Hayti, the heart of the business section in the early years. This expressway is a testimony to the destructive program of urban renewal, brought in by politicians, that hit Durham during the decade of the 1960s. This program was successful in destroying, in a few months, a major section of the Hayti business section (over 100 enterprises and 600 homes) that had been developing for over fifty years in Durham.

As you exit from the Durham Expressway and go south onto Fayetteville Street, the old St. Joseph A.M.E. Church still stands like a soldier guarding history. This is truly a monument to enteprises that once occupied old Fayet-teville Street during the grand times of Hayti. In the old days, businesses lined this street with the church standing almost squarely in the middle. No one worships in the old majestic church that Booker T. Washington called the finest structure in the South. Fayetteville Street still is home to the surviving old majestic homes of the old entrepreneurs. The old Lincoln Hospital has been replaced with a modern medical structure. North Carolina College, now called North Carolina Central University, still stands square in the middle of the Fayetteville Street area. It has grown into a beautiful, well-manicured col-lege which continues its mission in the education of Afro-Americans. One can also see a number of white students on this traditional black campus.

Going back north on Fayetteville Street one crosses over the expressway and heads toward the other half of the once proud Hayti district. On the left is the remains of another historical monument, the Service Printing Company. Now overgrown with green ivy and having experienced a fire that destroyed its inside, the structure stands because its owner, Nathaniel P. White, Sr., refused to bow to politicians and their destructive program of urban renewal. Instead, he successfully operated his business for decades after the expressway cut through the Hayti section.

But despite the experience with urban renewal, the Hayti section of Durham is being revised by the children and grandchildren of the early entre-preneurs. They have picked up the spirit of enterprise and self-help that was synonymous with Durham in the early 1900s. This spirit can be found in Larry Hester, whose father owned a successful shoe repair enterprise and shoe repair school in old Hayti. Drawing on the lessons of his father, he has devel-oped two successful shoe repair shops at two white-owned shopping malls in Durham. But recently he returned to the heart of the old Hayti section and developed Phoenix Square Shopping Center, which contains 17 stores that gross between $100,000 and $250,000 annually. The mall is located right next to the historic St. Joseph A.M.E. Church that is the symbol of old Hayti. The efforts of Larry Hester sparked other development in the area, including the renovation of the old church. In addition to re-creating the majestic beauty of that church, an office building is being added to the structure that will make it useful for other black professionals who choose to locate in the old Hayti section of Durham.

The spirit of self-help and entrepreneurship of the old ones of Hayti also lives in Denise Weaver. Having worked successfully in corporate America, and with a Harvard degree in hand, she returned to Durham to take over Weaver's Cleaners and Laundromat that was founded by her aunt and uncle. The enter-prise, which is on Fayetteville Street, is experiencing the type of growth that is the result of her youthful energy. Like her relatives before her, she is active in making Hayti a successful place to live and work. Her dedication to creating better housing for the community, and making it an outstanding place to live, is indicative of her historical baptism in the spirit of self-help and entrepreneurship. This is also true of Eric Kelly, an artist who has captured the spirit of life on canvas and through photography.

Today, black entrepreneurs and professionals are still held together by the Durham Business and Professional chain, an organization founded 52 years ago. Contained in the chain is 150 or so of Durham's leading black business persons and professionals. New entrepreneurs such as Denise Weaver and Larry Hester have opportunities to interact with those who knew and learned their art of business sense from the early pioneers. These include F. V. Allison, Chairman, President & CEO of Mutual Savings and Loan, and F. Kelly Bryant, Jr., a distinguished business man in the community. A drive through the black community reveals enterprises of all types that are in the service tradition of middleman minorities in the United States and other parts of the world.

But the prize of the city are the two major institutions which were the key to the success during the old days, the North Carolina Mutual and the Mechanics and Farmers Bank. The former occupies a modern skyrise building in downtown Durham and the latter is located on Parrish Street in the old North Carolina Mutual building. There is also a branch of the bank located on old Fayetteville Street, near the old St. Joseph A.M.E. Church. Present business publications point to the fact that these two institutions are still hard at work. The North Carolina Mutual Life Insurance heads the top of the list of all Afro-American enterprises. Between 1985 and 1989 the number of employees increased from 88 to 220. During the same time period assets increased from $211.45 million to $215.70 million, and has over $7 million worth of insurance-in-force.

The Mechanics & Farmers Bank was chosen as *Black Enterprises'* bank of the year, and was featured because it had agreed to help nearby Shaw University with its financial difficulties by lending it $1 million. This is interesting and significant because one of the people present at the first meeting which formed the North Carolina Mutual in the late 1800s, which as noted earlier started the Mechanics and Farmers Bank, was Edward A. Johnson. He was an attorney and Dean of the Law School at Shaw University at the turn of the century. The present interim president of the university, said, "It made everyone around here realize how vital it is to have a black financial institution to which to turn."[85] Just as this bank capitalized many of the enterprises of old Hayti, it is active in the capitalization of enterprises in that area today. For example, the Phoenix Square Shipping Center mentioned above, became a reality because the Mechanics and Farmers Bank capitalized the project with a sum of $235,000. The present Chairperson, President & CEO is Julia W. Taylor, has deep family roots in the tradition of the bank. After working in the corporate world of America, she returned to Durham to take advantage of opportunities that were planted by the entrepreneurial activities of blacks in the city at the turn of the century.

The spirit of enterprise is much broader in Durham today that it was eighty years ago. Black business people compete head to head with business people in the white community. Their market is no longer limited by race. Thus Frank Anderson, president and chief executive officer of Custom Models, a plastics manufacturing firm, bid for a multi-million dollar contract by the Ford Motor Company and won.[86]

Thus the old Hayti area is experiencing a rebirth. If Booker T. Washington visited it today, he would again see signs of progress. He could also call the present day St. Joseph A.M.E. Church one of the finest structures of the South, because it is now a rambling modern building that the pioneers of Hayti would be proud to worship in; the White Rock Baptist Church also stands tall and beautiful. Present day Durham is a product of history and stands as the benefactor of early people who put their souls and hearts into entrepreneurship and left an outstanding legacy of achievement.

CONCLUSION

Thus, Durham represented one of the successful economic enterprises of early Afro-Americans. Operating under an economic detour, Afro-Americans were able to carve a mountain of economic stability out of an atmosphere of official racial oppression. Just as scholars today talk about the "Cuban Miracle" in Miami in the 1970s and 1980s, scholars around the turn of the century were excited about Durham, North Carolina. Just as the Japanese were able to develop economic success in California at the turn of the century, Afro-Americans were able to do the same. Like other groups, the Afro-Americans of Durham developed a strong Afro-American middle class and began a tradition of economic security which continues to the present. Although other cities throughout the country were not as strong as Durham, Afro-Americans in other cities also developed a strong middle class which was grounded in entrepreneurship and the professions. In cities throughout the country, entrepreneurship flourished within because of the structure of racial discrimination.

6

Tulsa, Oklahoma

Business Success and Tragedy

Much of the history of Afro-American entrepreneurship is locked in the minds of the elderly and in scattered magazines and journals. If Durham, North Carolina, stood as a show piece of successful entrepreneurship because of the solid application of certain business principles and the presence of inter-racial support and cooperation, Tulsa, Oklahoma, represented the analog of this success, which can be called entrepreneurship tragedy. Although this city was successful in the creation of Afro-American entrepreneurs who attained a degree of economic security, it met with a fate which must be explained not only by the theory of economic detour but also by certain other specific theories of race and economics as well. This chapter explores the economic community developed by Afro-Americans living in Tulsa at the turn of the century and attempts to offer an explanation for the tragic nature of its story.

I

Unlike North Carolina, which was immersed in the history of America and the Old South, Oklahoma was a new frontier for settlers and a passing homeland for Native Americans. Like North Carolina, though, the land which made up the boundaries of the state had an interesting typology. In the southeastern part of the state, the Red River, which divides Oklahoma from Texas, creates a vast fertile area which was, at one time, a Mecca for fields of cotton. Going east, one encounters the Wichita Mountains and the Arbuckle Mountains. The Ozark Plateau is a northern region which is very wooded and, at its southern end, are the Cookson Hills, an area of deep gullies, wild prairie, and oak-studded hills. Going west, there is a great open area where the primary product is wheat. The Oklahoma Panhandle is shortgrass country which freezes in the winter and burns in the summer.[1] Native Americans enjoyed this land for centuries, but like all land on the great frontier, it became the settling place for Europeans as the nation moved westward.

Europeans began to settle in an organized fashion in the Oklahoma Territory in 1889. The British—English, Scots, and Welsh—and the Irish were some of the first newcomers, and, by 1910, these two populations were spread all over the state, engaging mostly in agriculture. As more British and Irish came to Oklahoma, they began increasingly to settle in urban areas. The Irish were a key in this transition. By 1920, most Irishmen resided in urban areas. There was such a rapid wave of Scots, English, and Welsh that, by 1930, they also constituted an urban group. The British and Irish settled in Oklahoma City and Tulsa.[2]

The availability of cheap land also attracted German immigrants, who came by the thousands between 1880 and 1910. By 1910, a mere three years after Oklahoma became a state, the German-born population had doubled from its 1900 level to well over ten thousand with more than 77 percent of these individuals living in rural areas of the state.[3] The year 1910 also brought a wave of Italian immigrants to the state that peaked with 2,564 members of that ethnic group settling in Oklahoma.[4]

The Jewish group moved into small towns in the eastern half of the state and became an urban population.[5] The Poles and Czechs also made Oklahoma their home.[6] As these groups adjusted to each other, ethnic conflicts developed within the state. The Irish and Jews had to deal with anti-Catholicism and anti-Semitism. For example, the Ku Klux Klan in the state quickly turned against Catholics in the city of Tulsa. In 1923, anti-Catholic sentiment reached its peak when Catholic school teachers were fired as a result of the Klan's efforts.

Also in Tulsa, the engineer in charge of the construction of a water project was given a list of Catholic employees whom he had to fire. When he refused, the mayor and members of the city council called him and tried, unsuccessfully, to get him to comply with the wishes of the Klan. Catholics in Tulsa struck back when wealthy oil men of that religious faith hired an individual to attend KKK meetings and list the membership. The list was given to the Catholics of Tulsa, and they stopped doing business with individuals on the list.[7]

The community of Tulsa also tried to restrict the participation of the Jewish group. For example, the Tulsa City Club, which was founded in 1925, listed two Jews among its charter members and another who had joined shortly after it was chartered. Then, the club quickly closed its membership to Jews. The discrimination became so great that the three Jewish members resigned.[8]

Throughout all of this ethnic conflict, however, members of ethnic groups made significant contributions to the state of Oklahoma and the cities in which they resided. Although ethnic traditions were upheld, they learned to live together as "white people."

When Europeans arrived in Oklahoma, Afro-Americans had already begun to occupy the area called the Oklahoma Territory. Although Afro-Americans had come to that territory during early expeditions, their settlement really started in the 1830s, not as settlers in the traditional sense, but as slaves—the slaves of Native Americans.[9]

As Europeans began to populate the growing territory, an "Indian problem" developed. The problem was that, as Europeans wanted the land that Native Americans occupied, the latter kept being moved from place to place. As the 1700s turned into the 1800s, President Thomas Jefferson favored a policy which would move all Native Americans living east of the Mississippi River to the Upper Louisiana Territory. In 1803, a series of treaties was negotiated with the Shawnee, Delaware, Kickapoo, and other northern tribes that moved them westward in advance of the line of European settlement. Thomas Jefferson himself had issued an order to Indian agents living among the Cherokees to ask the chiefs and other influential people of that tribe what they thought of giving up their homes in Georgia and settling in new land west of the Mississippi. Under the next president, James Monroe, the push for removal of the Native Americans gained even more support.[10]

John C. Calhoun was Secretary of War during President James Monroe's administration. As such, Calhoun was concerned with Indian affairs. He recommended that all eastern Indians be removed. In 1825, the President recommended to Congress that these Indians should be moved to "The worthless great plains region where game was plentiful." In 1830, Congress passed a bill providing that the land west of the state of Missouri and the Territory of Arkansas should be set aside as a country in which the Indians east of the Mississippi could make their new home. This bill became the source of the solution to the Indian problem which had haunted Europeans since the end of the Revolutionary War. Although the bill was passed in 1830, ever since the 1790s, Native Americans had been removed—voluntarily or nonvoluntarily—into the Upper Louisiana Territory across the Mississippi River. Among the first tribes to enter this territory—which would later be called Oklahoma—were the Kickapoos, Delawares, Shawnees, Osages and Cherokees. In years to come, sixty-two tribes followed them.[11]

As eastern tribes moved westward from 1803 to 1830, they took their Afro-American slaves with them. Afro-Americans accompanied Native Americans on what has been called the "Trail of Tears." It was during this Trail of Tears that what was called the Five Civilized Tribes—the Cherokees, Choctaws, Chickasaws, Creeks, and Seminoles—were forced from Tennessee, Kentucky, North Carolina, Alabama, Georgia, Mississippi, and Florida. Over the years, these tribes especially had instituted slavery. Sometimes slaves were purchased; other times, they were acquired by the capture of runaways from white masters. History does not record the actual number of slaves that the civilized tribes held, but it is clear on the point that slavery was introduced to the new territory west of the Mississippi which became known as Indian Territory.

> Slavery did not become established as an institution in Indian Terri-
> tory until the Indian tribes from the Southern states brought slaves
> with them that they might be useful in the work of opening up farm-
> lands and plantations. Slavery as it existed in the Indian Territory was
> not materially different from slavery in some of the most advanced
> Southern states. The owners were mainly humane, and the brutal
> type was the exception to the rule. Slavery took various forms among
> the different tribes and also with individuals within the tribe.[12]

But, as did slave owners in the Old South, the native tribes were careful to draw the line dividing slave, master, and privilege. They passed laws that prohibited the movement of slaves. Consider the following quotation about the Choctaw:

> Since the economic welfare of the Choctaw Nation depended largely
> upon its agricultural interests which were fostered by slave labor, its
> Council passed in reference to slavery a number of laws which
> reflected how completely the Choctaws had become allied with the
> institution as it existed in the South. In 1838, the Choctaw National
> Council passed a law prohibiting the co-habitation of any member of
> the nation with a Negro slave. Intermarriage with Negro slaves was
> prohibited by a law passed in the beginning of the Choctaw consti-
> tutional form of government. Slaves were also prohibited by law from
> owning property or arms except a good honest slave, and only then
> with the written permission of his owner. To keep their slaves in the
> position of peaceful servitude in spite of the rising wave of abolition-
> ism the council passed a law prohibiting teaching of slaves to read,
> write and sing or gather without the consent of the owner. In 1858 a
> law was enacted to the effect: The General Council shall have no
> power to pass laws for the emancipation of slaves without the consent
> of their owner, unless the slaves shall have rendered to the Nation
> some distinguished service—in which case the owner shall be paid a
> full equivalent for the slave so emancipated. Other laws passed pro-
> vided that slaves brought to the Indian Territory would continue as
> slaves: that owners treat their slaves with humanity: and that no

person of Negro blood would be eligible to office under the Choctaw government.[13]

Thus, as Europeans began to settle the Indian Lands, they ran into Native Americans who owned slaves and who had reestablished a way of life. For, when the Trail of Tears was completed, the federal government declared that Indian Territory could not be settled by whites. The policy was that only a handful of whites—preachers, teachers, governmental agents, and attachés to the Army—were allowed in this territory. Any citizen of the United States who ventured into Indian Territory possessed few rights. They could not legally occupy or own land. They were subject to be ejected at any time because of complaints made to authorities, and heavy penalties were brought against them if they returned to the territory. All trade and interactions with Native Americans were regulated by law and were confined to traders who were bonded.

The government did everything possible, at first, to keep Europeans out. The government noted that Indian Territory was on the extreme western frontier of America. This territory was the ultimate place for Native Americans. It was thought that many decades would pass before whites again bothered Native Americans so that they could settle. It was assumed that by the time this happened, Native Americans would be so advanced in the arts of civilization, the ways of peace, and the techniques of government that they would be able to take care of themselves and live forever in an excellent homogeneous Indian state of the American Union.

There was, thus, no government land in Indian Territory. Native Americans owned it lock, stock, and barrel. The United States granted and patented the territory to the tribes and the titles were vested to the different nations. Thus, the Cherokee Nation, as a nation and municipal corporation, owned the legal title to all lands of the Cherokee Nation.

But Western European migration was on the move. Arkansas was filling up fast, and the migration to Texas was on. Small numbers of Europeans began to infiltrate Indian Territory. Soon, their numbers were so large that they spilled over into the Native American Territory. Promises and treaties were broken, and Indian Territory soon became the land of Europeans and, again, Native Americans were pushed further into wastelands and reservations.

One can say that Indian settlement lasted from 1820 to the 1880s. As noted earlier, white settlement began in 1889. Thus, for sixty years—from 1820 to 1880—Indian Territory existed in a vacuum of governmental protection with the white settlement constantly surging against it. The barrier eroded first, then collapsed.[14]

Nestled within the history of Indian Territory is an almost invisible history of Afro-American experiences. Although we know little about them, we do know that they were introduced to what is now called Oklahoma by Native Americans who were forced to participate in the Trail of Tears which began in the eastern part of the United States.

By the Civil War, the Five Civilized Tribes numbered about 62,500, and they owned about 7,603 slaves by 1860.[15]

As members of the Kansas First Colored Volunteers Infantry Regiment, Afro-American Union troops participated in battles in Indian Territory.[16] They were instrumental in the defeat of the Confederate troops at the Battle of Honey Springs or Elk Creek and the Battle of Cabin Creek.[17]

The Five Civilized Tribes chose their alignments in the Civil War based on their investment in slaves. Thus, the Choctaw, who owned about three thousand slaves, joined the Confederate troops. The Seminoles and Creeks, on the other hand, fought on the side of the Union.[18] Although slavery was abolished with the defeat of the Confederacy and the Emancipation Proclamation of 1863, it continued to exist in Indian Territory until 1866. It was in this year that the United States government signed formal treaties with the Five Civilized Tribes. From 1866 to 1886, central Oklahoma was under consideration as a permanent home for the former slaves of the Indian Tribes. This option was entertained because the government was uncertain as to what extent the tribes would extend rights to their former slaves. But Chickasaw and Choctaw leaders asked the leaders in Washington to allow their former slaves to be settled in Oklahoma territory. By 1879, because of the agitation for opening the territory to white homesteaders, the government's concept for colonizing Native Americans and former slaves into the Oklahoma District was soon overshadowed.[19]

But the idea of an Afro-American settlement in Oklahoma did not die. It was taken over by black leaders who argued that the Oklahoma District be set aside as a resettlement zone for Afro-Americans from the entire nation, but especially those from the South. The personification of this idea was Hannibal C. Carter, who helped establish the Freedmen's Oklahoma Immigration Association in Chicago in 1881. Carter noted that he could colonize at least thirty thousand former slaves in the Creek portion of the Oklahoma Territory and have them become self-sufficient within a year. Carter's association sent out a circular from St. Louis in 1881 to all new freedman; it declared that the federal government had secured—by virtue of treaties with the Creek, Seminole, and Chickasaw Indians—fourteen million acres of land in the Oklahoma Territory on which Afro-Americans could settle.

When the government learned of this circular, Carter was informed that the land referred to in the treaties was available only to blacks who had been slaves under the Indians. Although this put an official end to parts of Oklahoma as exclusive Afro-American settlements, groups sprang up over the state which continued the dream.[20] But as their white counterparts did, Afro-Americans migrated to Oklahoma and began to establish themselves without the sanctioning of the government or any organization. They settled several all-black towns as an expression of racial solidarity and to escape negative racial experiences with whites.[21]

By 1900, the total black population of Oklahoma was 18,719.[22] Seeking to establish a life of economic security, freedmen from the Old South and the nations of the Five Civilized Tribes looked to the Oklahoma Territory as a new state.

Afro-American business in Oklahoma never reached the plateau of the Durham experience. Perhaps because of the relatively small number of Afro-Americans in the developing territory as compared with the Old South, a strong business tradition did not flourish, although, through enterprise and professional training, a middle class did evolve. As did their counterparts in other sections of the country, these blacks were forced to try to develop economic security by way of the economic detour. There are few instances, however, when they were able to market their business among blacks and whites. The following analysis, however, of Oklahoma could be applied to the Afro-American experience as a whole:

> Segregation [and an economic detour] gave to the black professional a virtually protected market, but that represented a mixed blessing. If they profited economically by avoiding intense competition from their white counterparts, which was not always the case, they also suffered from being unable to practice their professions in the best institutions and in the best atmosphere. Doctors, for example, could not take advantage of the modern equipment and facilities at white hospitals. A few of them established small hospitals of their own, but they could not provide the service or the expensive equipment of larger institutions. Black lawyers had to endure prejudiced juries and harsh judges who could always threaten them with contempt of court. Faced with segregation and discrimination black professional groups such as teachers, lawyers, doctors, dentists, and undertakers very early organized their own state associations.[23]

As was the case in developing cities in the new territory, each ethnic group was not required to establish its own hospitals and other community service organizations. If they did do so, others were allowed to participate, provided they were Euro-Americans. Again, however, racial hostility forced Afro-Americans in Oklahoma into economic development strictly on their own. Of course, this was especially true where labor was concerned. Occupationally, Afro-Americans who arrived in cities were concentrated in domestic or laboring jobs. Their occupations required little training and were the least profitable. Only within the Afro-American business community did they find work in other than unskilled occupations.[24]

The business which developed among Afro-Americans in Oklahoma were small and service-oriented. They established dry cleaners, hotels, theaters, shoe shops, barbershops, restaurants, and nightclubs. As in Durham, Oklahoma produced business people who were able to develop beyond the small business enterprise, albeit not with the same amount of success.

Mr. and Mrs. P. H. James developed a company in Oklahoma City which bottled a soft drink called Jay Cola. They were able to sell their product to both the black and white communities, and earned a reputation as excellent business people. W. C. Reed developed a successful telephone system shortly after Oklahoma became a state and made a small fortune. T. J. Elliott of Muskogee developed a men's clothing store and employed almost thirty people. Sydney Lyons began his career as a proprietor of a grocery store in the small town of Guthrie. Later he moved to Oklahoma City where he founded the East India Toilet Goods and Manufacturing Company. Because of this enterprise, he gained an international reputation for the quality of products produced. Lyons also received income from the discovery of oil in Oklahoma. He built a major park for blacks in Oklahoma City and was a philanthropist.[25]

In 1915, Walter Edwards moved to Oklahoma City and began work for nine dollars a week. After saving some money, he purchased a carpet cleaning enterprise and acquired a drugstore. Then, because of the Great Depression, he lost everything that he had acquired. But he was able to acquire a small junkyard which did not pay off until the outbreak of World War II. Because of the demand created during the war, Edwards Scrap Iron and Junk Yard bought and sold millions of pounds of junk. He became one of the richest citizens in the state, and was very good to the Afro-American community. In 1948, he constructed a hospital in Oklahoma City at a cost of $430,000. The 105-bed Edwards Memorial Hospital had a black staff and remained open until 1966.[26] Throughout the state, Afro-American business people developed enterprises which provide a degree of economic security and a great deal of wealth.[27]

II

Tulsa represented one of the towns where enterprise developed into a strong sense of security in Oklahoma. In 1828, when the Creek Indians arrived from Alabama, they settled in Tulsa Town. This is a tribal name and a settlement in the original land of Alabama. When the first post office was established in the area, Tulsa Town was moved closer to the railroad and was renamed simply Tulsa. In 1866, two Native American policemen were appointed to the new city by Robert Owen, United States Indian agent for the Five Civilized Tribes. By an Act of Congress in 1898, the Creek and Cherokee nations surveyed for the creation of town sites. When European settlers began to overflow, Tulsa became a settlement of prime importance. In 1905, the great Glen Oil Pool was discovered, and Tulsa became a boom town.[28]

Because Afro-Americans had been slaves of Native Americans in Indian Territory, they came to be a significant population in Tulsa. In 1900, they made up 5 percent of the population. By 1910, they comprised 10 percent of the population. This percentage increase was also due to immigration to the state.[29] As Tulsa was growing from a population of 1,390 in 1900 to 98,878 in 1921, Euro-American immigrants developed their businesses on numbered streets which intersected with Main Street. A popular magazine of the day described the city as follows:

> Tulsa is a thriving, bustling, enormously wealthy town of between 90,000 and 100,000. In 1910 it was the home of 18,182 souls, a dead and hopeless outlook ahead. Then oil was discovered. The town grew amazingly. On December 29, 1920, it had bank deposits totaling $6,549,985.90, almost $1,000 per capita when compared with the Federal Census figures of 1920, which gave Tulsa 72,075. The town lies in the center of the oil region, and many are the stories told of the making of fabulous fortunes by men who were operating on a shoe-string. Some of the stories rival those of the "forty-niners" in California. The town has a number of modern office buildings, many beautiful homes, miles of clean, well-paved streets, and aggressive and progressive business men who well exemplify Tulsa's motto "The City with a Personality."[30]

Of course, Afro-Americans were not allowed to try their luck at business enterprise in the major enterprise district of the city. As a matter of fact, they were not even welcomed as customers in the white business district. They were, however, allowed to work at common labor, domestic, and service jobs in all parts of the city. Thus, as was the case with Afro-Americans in other cities, they had to develop their own business district under an economic detour. However, unlike the racial cooperation which took place in a segregated Durham, North Carolina, the development of enterprise in Tulsa by Afro-Americans took place within a completely negative racial situation.

It was in the face of this hostility that the Greenwood section of Tulsa—sometimes called Little Africa or Negro Wall Street—was born. As Tulsa boomed, there was a concomitant expansion of Afro-American enterprises.

History has left us scattered accounts of the Greenwood business district which developed in Tulsa. In the most scholarly account, Scott Ellsworth uncovered the beginning of this district. John Williams and his wife, Loula, ventured to Tulsa in search of a promised land during the first years of the twentieth century. Both had left the Old South with its rigid racial laws and codes which made it difficult simply to make it through the day. John was from Mississippi and Loula from Tennessee.

When they first arrived, Tulsa was still within Indian Territory. John worked at the ice cream company and managed to become the first

Afro-American in the town to own an automobile. John began to work on his car and soon developed the skills of a true auto mechanic. Gradually, other Tulsans took their cars to John so that he could work on them when he was not working at the ice cream factory. This trade became so lucrative that he stopped working at the ice cream factory and opened a full-time auto garage on Greenwood Avenue.

The first structure, built in about 1912, was a three-story brick building. In 1914, because of the growth of the business, John built a larger garage. The second story of the 1914 structure was a twenty-one room boarding house. John had planned to have his garage on the first floor, but the city did not allow such a business arrangement. He moved back to the old garage and created the first black silent movie theater.[31]

After 1914, the number of enterprises increased in the Greenwood area of Tulsa. Edward Goodwin and his family began publication of the Oklahoma *Eagle,* one of the most successful of newspaper enterprises. By 1921, the business enclave had developed into an impressive array of enterprises. Given encouragement by Booker T. Washington's National Negro Business League, some Afro-Americans exhibited the spirit of entrepreneurship. When one of Washington's organizers from the League's national office visited Tulsa in 1913, he referred to it as "a regular Monte Carlo."[32]

Although this section of Tulsa may not have been a Monte Carlo, it was certainly an impressive array of business enterprises. Although historical accounts of this vicinity are very rare, Scott Ellsworth describes it best.

> The first two blocks of Greenwood Avenue North of Archer were known as "Deep Greenwood." It comprised the heart of Tulsa's black business community, and was known by some . . . as the "Negro Wall Street" . . . Two- and three-story brick buildings lined the avenue, housing a variety of commercial establishments, including a dry goods store, two theaters, groceries, confectionaries, restaurants, and billiard halls. A number of black Tulsa's eleven rooming houses and four hotels were located here. "Deep Greenwood" was also a favorite place for the offices of Tulsa's unusually large number of black lawyers, doctors and other professionals.[33]

Because of the tragic experience of this short-lived business district, it is difficult to reconstruct the history of this section of Tulsa. The limited literature on the Greenwood District presents conflicting evidence as to the number of businesses, namely because it concentrates on the destruction of the district.[34] Table 6.1 presents a reconstruction of enterprises in the Greenwood section by Ellsworth. It shows the growth of the community by year and by category.

TABLE 6.1

Black Business Establishments and Business Persons in Tulsa as Listed in City Directories, 1907, 1909–1914, and 1916–1923

Establishments	'07	'09	'10	'11	'12	'13	'14	'16	'17	'18	'19	'20	'21	'22	'23
Bath parlors								1							
Billiard halls			2	1	3	3	3	6	5	4	5	6	9	4	6
Cigars and tobacco							1	2				2			
Clothing, dry goods, racket, second-hand, music, furniture, paints and oils, shoes												1	1		1
Confectionary, soft drinks			1	1	3	1	3	4	2	2	2	1	2	2	2
Feed and grain			1	2	1	1			5	7	5	2	4	6	6
Furnished rooms, boarding and rooming houses	3		2	3	2	1	4	3	1	6	16	9	11	1	3
Garages, auto repair and filling stations							1	1	1		1	1	2		3
Grocers, meat markets	3	3	2	5	8	10	9	7	18	11	21	23	41	34	31
Hotels			1	1	2	1	1	1	1	2	2	4	5	4	9
Restaurants	1	1		5	3	13	17	15	11	17	21	20	30	29	19
Theaters						1		1	1	1	1	1	2	1	
Undertakers' parlors								1	2	2	2	2	1	2	1
Total	7	4	9	18	22	31	39	42	47	52	76	72	108	83	81
Professionals	'07	'09	'10	'11	'12	'13	'14	'16	'17	'18	'19	'20	'21	'22	'23
Dentists				1		1	1	1	1	1	1	3	2	2	2
Druggists and medicine manufacturers		1			1	2	1	1	4	3	3	1	4	3	3
Jewelers										1	1	1	1		3

TABLE 6.1—*Continued*

Professionals	'07	'09	'10	'11	'12	'13	'14	'16	'17	'18	'19	'20	'21	'22	'23
Lawyers	1	1	3	4	2	1	5	6	4	4	5	4	3	4	6
Nurses												2		1	
Photographers											1	1	2	1	2
Physicians and surgeons	2	2	2	3	4	7	5	3	4	10	12	13	15	10	10
Real estate, loans, and insurance agents	2						1	2	4	4	3	6	6	4	5
Private detectives															
Total	5	4	5	8	8	11	13	13	17	23	26	30	33	25	29

Skilled Crafts Persons	'07	'09	'10	'11	'12	'13	'14	'16	'17	'18	'19	'20	'21	'22	'23
Bakers												1			
Blacksmiths	1	1				1	1	1	1	1	1			3	2
Contractors, carpenters, builders, house and sign painters								1		2	7	3	5	6	2
Dressmakers					1			1	1	3	4		2	1	1
Milliners															1
Plumbers										2			11		
Printers							1			1	1	1	1	1	
Shoemakers and shoe repairers			2	2		1	2	1	1	1	3	2	4	6	3
Tailors				1		1	2	3	2	5	6	7	10	6	9
Upholsterers													1	1	
Total		1	2	3	1	3	6	7	5	15	22	14	24	24	18

Service Workers	'07	'09	'10	'11	'12	'13	'14	'16	'17	'18	'19	'20	'21	'22	'23
Barbers	1	2	2	4	3	3	5	7	6	10	11	9	12	11	13
Cleaners, hatters, dyers, and pressers			2	2	1	6	4	4	7	10	7	5	5	5	6
Hairdressers										3	3		3		1
Launderers							1	1	1	4		1		2	1
Shoe shiners							2	2	5		6	4	6	6	1
Total	1	2	4	6	4	9	12	14	19	27	27	19	26	24	22

Semi-Skilled Workers	'07	'09	'10	'11	'12	'13	'14	'16	'17	'18	'19	'20	'21	'22	'23
Expressmen and Messengers							2	1							
Housemovers					1										
News dealers											1	1		1	
Total					1		2	1			1	1		1	

Source: Scott Ellsworth. *Death In A Promised Land*. Baton Rouge: Louisiana State University Press, 1982. 115–117.

[1] There is evidence in the Record of Commission Proceedings, City of Tulsa, *Vol. XV*, that there were a number more black plumbers in Tulsa in 1921.

Between 1907 and 1921, the year of the destruction of the district, the number of establishments increased significantly. As expected, the largest category under establishments was service industries.

For example, the number of grocers and meat markets increased from three in 1907 to forty-one in 1921. Restaurants increased from one to thirty for the same time period. Among professionals, the number of physicians and surgeons increased from two to fifteen between 1907 and 1921. The number of skilled craft persons remained small over that time period. Shoemakers and shoe repair enterprises increased from two to four, and, by 1921, there were two dressmakers. Service workers such as barbers and hairdressers also showed small increases during this time period. As noted by Ellsworth, there is evidence that other enterprises existed, and his reconstruction is only an estimation. Another source estimates that more than "860 stores and homes existed in the Greenwood section." The problem is that one cannot partition homes from enterprises in this estimation.[35]

Nevertheless, we do know that entrepreneurs who developed the enterprise section known as Greenwood made up the Afro-American economically well-off group of that city. On Detroit Avenue and other streets around Greenwood were found the lovely homes of these entrepreneurs augmented by homes of professionals. But as in all cities, Afro-Tulsa had its poor section. In addition, some Afro-Americans lived in white neighborhoods as housekeepers for the rich white citizens of Tulsa. They resided in living quarters or garage apartments on the property of these citizens. Greenwood's service and professional businesses catered to this wage-earning class.[36] Taken together they made up the Afro-American community of the city.

There were also a number of wealthy men in the Afro-American community. Some had shared in the investment in land on which oil was found. Tragically, it was this wealth, along with the economic success of the Afro-American entrepreneurs, which led to what Ellsworth so vividly calls "death in a promised land."

III

The events which took place in Tulsa in 1921 have been overlooked by scholars of race, economics, and violence, as were other events relating to race and enterprise. There is evidence that people who grew up in the state of Oklahoma have little or any knowledge of those events. R. Halliburton, Jr. a former Oklahoma state senator who served on President Lyndon Johnson's National Advisory Commission on Civil Disorders following the riots of the 1960s, notes how surprised he was that such an event had taken place in his native Oklahoma. He was so taken aback by the events and the absence of scholarly treatment that he wrote what is perhaps the first narrative treatment of the riot. As he notes in his preface, "This small volume owes its genesis to a seminar in which the author found that the Tulsa race riot was the only major American racial disturbance that has been ignored by scholars. Textbooks and monographs treating Oklahoma history are silent about the event. General works treating racial disturbances omit the Tulsa riot and there are no journal articles directly concerning the event.[37] But what happened in Tulsa was more than a riot. It was also the destruction of the efforts of entrepreneurs and the end of the Greenwood business district.

On May 30, a Monday morning in 1921, nineteen-year-old Richard Rowland arrived at the Drexel Building in downtown Tulsa to deliver a package. When he entered the elevator, he stumbled and brushed against Sara Page, a white female elevator operator. The elevator operator became excited and screamed for help. Her scream influenced Rowland to run from the department store.

For reasons unknown, Sara Page claimed that a black man, Rowland, had tried to assault her. The crowd grew rapidly and the police were summoned. After an investigation, two black policemen arrested Rowland on Greenwood Avenue and took him to jail.

Rowland explained that when the elevator operator screamed, he became frightened and ran.[38] He also noted that many blacks had been hung or burned to death for alleged rape of white females. He argued that his fleeing was not an indicator of guilt, especially since the incident had taken place on a public elevator, where people were constantly coming and going.[39] His hearing was set for June 7 in Tulsa Municipal Court.

In the meantime, rumors began to circulate in the Afro-and Euro-American communities. The flames were fanned when the Tulsa *Tribune* published an article with a headline which read: "Nab Negro for Attacking Girl in an Elevator."

A negro delivery boy . . . was arrested on South Greenwood Avenue this morning . . . and charged with attempting to assault the 17-year-old white elevator girl in the Drexel Building early yesterday. He will be tried in Municipal Court this afternoon on a state charge. The girl said she noticed the negro a few minutes before the attempted assault looking up and down the hallway on the third floor of the Drexel building to see if there was anyone in sight but thought nothing of it at the time. A few minutes later he entered the elevator she claimed, and attacked her, scratching her hands and face and tearing her clothes. Her screams brought a clerk from Renberg's store to her assistance and the negro fled. He was captured and identified this morning by both the girl and the clerk, police say. Rowland denied that he tried to harm the girl, but admitted he put his hand on her arm in the elevator when she was alone. Tenants of the Drexel

Building said the girl is an orphan who works as an elevator operator to pay her way through business college.[40]

The *Tribune* article proved to be inaccurate. Rowland had not torn Page's dress, scratched her face, nor had he touched her hand.[41] People became interested, as is always true in these types of cases for better or worse, in the background of the woman involved. Page had been in Tulsa for only a very short period of time. She and her husband, who was in Kansas City, had separated. The sheriff's office of Tulsa had served divorce papers to her on behalf of her husband about sixty days prior to the incident on the elevator. For whatever reasons, during this time he described her as a "notorious character."[42] Nevertheless, after the newspaper article, the situation intensified.

The Afro-American community in Tulsa was not passive when it came to race relations. W. E. B. Du Bois had spoken there, and a great deal of interest was generated for the development of an NAACP branch in 1917. A chapter of the African Blood Brothers, who argued not only for business development but also for para-military organizations to protect their community, was also active in Tulsa. There were also a significant number of World War I veterans who had fought overseas. While religious leaders of the community spoke against the use of violence, they did argue that blacks should use arms if it became necessary to protect their homes. As Ellsworth noted, there were certainly black Tulsans who did not seek trouble, but who were not about to dodge it if it came their way.[43]

Based on rumors and the newspaper article, a white lynch mob began to gather at the jail. When this news spread to the Greenwood District, blacks armed themselves and proceeded to the jail in order to protect the prisoner. In July of the preceding year, Roy Belton, a white accused of murdering a taxicab driver, had been taken from the jail and lynched. During the lynching, local police officers had directed traffic so that everyone could view the incident.[44] The Afro-American community feared the same would happen to Rowland.

A group of about thirty armed blacks converged on the courthouse. A black officer met with them and persuaded them to leave. The white crowd, however, refused to disperse after repeated orders from the sheriff's office. This crowd grew to more than two thousand people and was developing into a mob. The officers barricaded themselves in the jail, disabled the elevator to the prisoner's cell, and prepared to protect him. Then blacks, mostly those armed at this time, returned and began to circle the jail in their cars. They then left their cars, crossed the street to the jail, and began to mingle with the whites. There were about seventy-five blacks, and although the officers made an unsuccessful attempt to disarm them, they offered their "service" to the officers.[45]

Just as the blacks were about to leave, a white man approached one of them and said to a tall veteran who possessed an army issue 45-caliber weapon, "Nigger, what are you doing with that pistol?" The veteran noted that he would use it if necessary. The white man said, "No, you give it to me." The reply came back, "Like hell I will." The white man tried to disarm the veteran, a shot was fired, and the riot or more accurately, war, started.[46] This happened at about 9:30 P.M.

After the first shot was fired, an exchange of fire between the two groups took place. A black man was wounded in the stomach. A white man in an auto was killed by a stray bullet. Afro-Americans began to retreat to the Greenwood section.

Whites began to plan their strategy and to search for more weapons. They broke the doors and windows of sporting goods and hardware stores in order to secure weapons and ammunition. They looted these stores and also took other items such as tools, tires, watches, and bathing suits. One hardware store reported more than $10,000 in losses. The whites consisted of a diverse group of people dressed in clothes which ranged from overalls to Palm Beach suits.[47]

The entire police force of the city was alerted by 10:00 P.M. They were stationed in a line and ordered to separate Little Africa from the rest of the city. They had heard a report that Afro-Americans were planning an invasion of the city. White citizens started to volunteer their services to control the situation. People were deputized on the scene. Even a very light-skinned Afro-American, a journalist from New York City, was unknowingly deputized by the authorities and told, "Now you go out and shoot any nigger you see and the law'll protect you." Later, when they discovered he was black and an officer of the NAACP, he received letters from Tulsa while in New York threatening his life.[48]

As blacks retreated to the Greenwood district, the fighting intensified. It became apparent that some blacks were well-armed and fortified in selected parts of the district. Although they were outnumbered, they were determined to fight back. Cars filled with whites firing indiscriminately cruised down the avenues of the Afro-American community. The most active fighting occurred along the Frisco railroad tracks, an important dividing line between black and white Tulsa.[49]

As conditions continued to deteriorate, the mayor of Tulsa, Bryon Kirkpatrick, sent a Western Union telegram to Governor J. Robertson which noted that "Race riot developed here. Several killed. Unable to handle situation. Request that National Guard forces be sent by special train. Situation serious."[50] By 11 P.M. blacks began to surrender and were taken as prisoners.

Around 4:30 A.M., the riot changed from the taking of lives to the taking of property. The police inspector of the city had stationed guards around the Frisco railroad station where the previous fighting had been furious.

The inspector arrived to find that his guards were surrounded by a white mob who were preparing to enter the Greenwood section. Immediately, he called for reinforcements. Because of the intensity of the situation, all his officers were busy arresting blacks, and the mob could not be stopped. The burning of property began.

Not only were stores burned, but also churches, schools and other institutions which had been constructed by blacks. Consider the following account:

> For unexplained reasons, probably sheer mob psychology, the white attack became more aggressive. Many in the mob now wanted to "invade" the black community to "burn the nigger out." And they did! Black people did not yield submissively, and fought back to defend their homes from lawless white mobs. [Afterward] many of Tulsa's most noted black institutions lay in ruins. A. J. Smitherman's Tulsa *Star*, champion of black manhood and equality, met the torch, and so did the Oklahoma *Sun*. The Howard Cavers, business leaders in the community, lost all they had worked to attain. White arsonists reduced elaborate and beautiful Mount Zion Church to ashes. A $84,000 building, one of the most beautiful in the Southwest, had literally gone up in smoke.[51]

At first, the looting and burning by whites was centered on the poorer southernmost section of the Greenwood district. This included some businesses. Around 6:40 A.M., fires were started in "Deep Greenwood," the heart of the more impressive district.[52]

When the destruction was over, the statistics told the story; 18,000 homes and enterprises burned to the ground; 304 homes looted by whites but not burned; 4,241 blacks left homeless; between $2 and $3 million in damage, and 300 people dead. There were 304 people admitted to surgery in Tulsa hospitals, and 531 people were treated for multiple injuries. These figures do not include the refugees who staggered into the nearby towns of Sapulpa, Muskogee, and Bartlesville, Oklahoma. Wounded were also reported as far north as Kansas City, Kansas.

As the businesses burned, white mobs threatened to shoot any person from the fire department who attempted to lay hose and extinguish the fire.[53] Horror stories about the "war" started to surface immediately. A rope was tied around the neck of a slain black, attached to an automobile, and he was then dragged down the avenues of the Greenwood district.[54] A white man was mistakenly identified as being black and killed by whites. An elderly black couple was murdered on their way home after church service. Dr. A. C. Jackson, called by some the most able black surgeon in America, was killed by whites after they had convinced him to surrender under a promise to protect him from other whites. A white woman was killed by blacks as she sat on her porch, and a black man was killed in front of Convention Hall after he had surrendered.

Perhaps the situation was best described by General Barrett, commander of the Oklahoma National Guard. He said:

The troop train arrived in Tulsa and halted in the midst of fifteen or twenty thousand blood-maddened rioters. All of the colored section appeared to be on fire and desultory firing kept on between snipers on both sides while the Guard marched through the crowded streets ... Trucks, loaded with scared and partially clothed negro men and women were parading the streets under heavily armed guards. In all my experience I have never witnessed such scenes as prevailed in this city when I arrived at the height of the rioting. Twenty-five thousand whites, armed to the teeth, were ranging the city in utter and ruthless defiance of every concept of law and righteousness. Motor cars, bristling with guns, swept through [Greenwood], their occupants firing at will.[55]

In addition to motor cars, a private plane was used to bomb Greenwood from the air.[56] The Chicago *Defender* noted that this was the case. More importantly, eyewitness accounts reveal that bombs were dropped on the area. A survivor of the riot describes events as follows:

After watching the men unload on First Street where we could see them from our windows, we heard such a buzzing noise that on running to the door to get a better view of what was going on, the sights our eyes beheld made our poor hearts stand still for a moment. There was a great shadow in the sky and upon a second look we discerned that this cloud was caused by fast approaching enemy aeroplanes. It then dawned upon us that the enemy had organized in the night and was invading our district the same as the Germans invaded France and Belgium. The firing of guns was renewed in quick succession. People were seen to flee from their burning homes, some with babes in their arms and leading crying and excited children by the hand; others, old and feeble, all fleeing to safety. Yet, seemingly, I could not leave. I walked as one in a horrible dream. By this time my little girl was up and dressed, but I made her lie on the dufold in order that bullets must penetrate it before reaching her. By this time a machine gun had been installed in the granary and was raining bullets down on our section.[57]

When the National Guard arrived early the next day, the restoration of order was already underway. In the process, more than 6,000 Afro-Americans were placed in temporary camps which were located at the Tulsa County Fair Grounds, McNulty Ball Park, and Convention Hall. They were marched through downtown Tulsa with their hands raised high in the air over their heads. When they arrived at the three temporary detention camps, they were searched and given identification tags. These tags were important because they defined black Tulsans' relationship with the white community in months to come. On the tags blacks had to give their 1. name, 2. gender, 3. home address, 4. place and type of employment and, 5. date of detention.

Perhaps the most important blank on the identification tag was a place where whites had to sign in order for them to leave one of the detention centers. Many white employers signed the tags so that blacks could return to work. As blacks moved around the city of Tulsa, they had to make sure that the tag was prominently displayed.

On Wednesday, June 1, two days after the conflict began, martial law was proclaimed in Tulsa. The National Guard was removed from Greenwood where they had been stationed since their arrival, and whites throughout the city were disarmed.[58]

The Tulsa riots resulted in a unique phenomenon in the history of America's refugees. Before Tulsa, Americans were accustomed to refugees coming from other parts of the world in search of freedom from political and economic chaos. Perhaps for the first time in American history, refugees came from an American city, Tulsa. They staggered to other cities in Oklahoma, to the countryside, and to the big cities of the North. In New York, the NAACP established a relief and refugee fund for the Oklahoma riot victims. In doing so, it noted that "Already refugees have come to this office in New York City, possessing little or nothing except the clothes they were wearing, and it was necessary for their immediate relief to ask for contributions from the association's staff."[59]

The national office in New York asked churches and fraternal organizations to make donations to the fund. These organizations responded with contributions.[60]

Throughout the nation, the print media tried to explain how the events of Tulsa could possibly have taken place. Although there had been other race riots in the country, none matched the almost total destruction which took place in Oklahoma. Some explanations concentrated on the overall political climate of the city. One writer noted that:

A vice ring was in control of the city, allowing open operation of houses of ill fame, of gambling joints, the illegal sale of whiskey, the robbing of banks and stores, with hardly a slight possibility of the arrest of the criminals, and even less of their conviction. For fourteen years Tulsa has been in the absolute control of this element. Most of the better element, and there is a large percentage of Tulsans who can properly be classed as such, are interested solely in making money and getting away. They have taken little or no interest in the election of city or county officials, leaving it to those whose interest it was to secure officials who would protect them in their vice operations. About two months ago, the State Legislature assigned two additional judges to Tulsa County to aid the present two in clearing the badly clogged dockets. These judges found more than six thousand cases awaiting trial. Thus, in a county of approximately 100,000 population, six out of every one hundred citizens were under indictment for some sort of crime, with little likelihood of trial in any of them.[61]

Another explanation centered around the radical nature of Afro-Americans in Tulsa. When a correspondent questioned Tulsans after the conflict, he found that radicalism meant that Negroes were uncompromisingly denouncing 'Jim-Crow' cars, lynching, peonage, in short, were asking that the federal Constitution guarantees of "life, liberty, and the pursuit of happiness" be given regardless of color.[62]

Some commentators placed the blame of the riot on the development of the Greenwood district as a separate entity. Within this area, the "bad niggers" were allowed to exist.

It was in the sordid and neglected "Nigger town" that the crooks found their best hiding place. It was a cesspool of crime. There were the low brothels where the low whites mixed with the low blacks. There were the dope venders and the dope consumers. These crimes were plotted and loot hidden. . . . There, for months past, the bad "niggers," the silk-shirted parasites of society, had been collecting guns and munitions. Tulsa was living on a Vesuvius that was ready to vomit fire at any time. Officials admit they knew of it but hoped it would not come off.[63]

The view that "bad niggers" were responsible for the riot was adopted by the majority of Oklahoma newspapers. Out-of-state newspapers tended to blame the existence of white racism and the unwillingness to solve the race problem. For example, the St. Louis *Post Dispatch* noted that "We have in this country a race problem, and to ignore it is only to postpone the reckoning."[64] This source has an excellent collection of the responses to the riot in newspapers across the country.

Tulsa reacted to the riot by establishing a grand jury to determine the leaders of the black and white mobs, who initiated the first shots, who started the fire, the performance of the police force and the ultimate cause of the riot. They asked citizens who had knowledge of the riot to step forward and testify. As the inquiry was taking place, leading citizens stirred emotions by speculating on the cause of the riot.

Bishop E. Mouzon, in a speech given in Boston, argued that the words of W. E. B. Du Bois had initiated attitudes which caused Afro-Americans to become sinister. He called him the most dangerous Negro alive.

General Barrett, who was in charge of the National Guard during the riot, blamed it all on a hysterical girl, an impudent black, and a yellow journal. The Tulsa Ministerial Alliance argued that the riot was caused by a total disregard for morality, by the fact that the Bible had been outlawed in public schools and by the fact that there were uncensored motion pictures.[65] Public officials blamed Afro-Americans for the riot, and on 25 June the Grand Jury issued its report:

> We find that the recent race riot was the direct result of an effort on the part of a certain group of colored men who appeared at the courthouse on the night of May 31, 1921, for the purpose of protecting one Dick Rowland then and now in the custody of the sheriff of Tulsa County for an alleged assault upon a young white woman. We have not been able to find any evidence either from white or colored citizens that any organized attempt was made or planned to take from the sheriff's custody any prisoner; the crowd assembled about the courthouse being purely spectators and curiosity seekers resulting from rumors circulated about the city. There was no mob spirit among the whites, no talk of lynching and no arms. The Assembly was quiet until the arrival of the armed negroes, which precipitated and was the direct cause of the entire affair. . . . We further find that there existed indirect causes more vital to the public than the direct cause. Among them were agitation among the negroes of social equality, and the laxity of law enforcement . . . of the city and county.[66]

The City Fathers of Tulsa wanted the nation to understand that the invasion of Greenwood City was not supported by the "best" of white Tulsans, and that strong outstanding citizens did not sanction the violence. The president of the Chamber of Commerce released the following statement to the press:

> A bad psychological condition, occasioned by a spirit of unrest, and some unemployment, dovetailed into the lawlessness which grew like a snowball and rapidly got beyond control of officials. The situation was quickly taken advantage of by some of the lawless element among the whites. Stores were broken open. People with no authority were quickly armed and the situation became desperate in the extreme and wholly out of control. The deplorable event is the greatest wound Tulsa's civic pride has ever received and every right thinking man and woman in the city, white and black, is now doing everything possible to heal the wound as quickly as may be. Leading businessmen are in hourly conference and a movement is now being organized, not only for the succor, protection and alleviation of the suffering of the

negroes, but to formulate a plan of reparation in order that homes may be rebuilt and families as nearly as possible rehabilitated. The sympathy of the citizenship of Tulsa in a great wave has gone out to the unfortunate law-abiding negroes who became victims of the action and bad advice of some of the lawless leaders and as quickly as possible rehabilitation will take place and reparation be made. . . .[67]

Although good intentions were expressed, the creative entrepreneurial activities of Afro-Tulsans, along with the dream of homes and "good living," died in the ashes of the riot.

IV

Although most historical accounts blame the "death in a promised land" on a single event which got out of control, we must see the events in the sociological tradition of entrepreneurs who have faced hostility because of race and ethnicity. Put differently, we must look at the relationship between the economic activities of Afro-Americans and the riot which took place.

One of the interesting things about economic success in given situations is that there is always the threat that the host group will react to excluded groups in a negative way. This was demonstrated by Bonacich and Modell's data on the Japanese, when California passed laws against them because they were so economically successful.

Even in Durham, where Afro-Americans had been successful in enterprise, they were constantly on guard as to the reaction of whites to that success. For example, when the successful North Carolina Mutual Company constructed its high-rise building, the president of the company made sure that it was not as tall as any other building in the white community.[68]

Throughout the history of expanding America, when land which Native Americans occupied became valuable they were removed from that land. To the extent that something became valuable, minorities were not expected—or allowed—to benefit from it. Thus, we have the example of Native Americans who did not become wealthy as a result of oil found on their land.

The determinant theoretical argument here is, if money is to be made, then the host group should benefit the most. In a very real sense, the occupations which middleman groups have occupied throughout history have been accommodations to the host group. They engage in enterprises which the majority group of the nation neglects, and they do not compete with them for major business enterprise activities.

But what happens when a minority begins to threaten the majority group? What happens when the minority group owns valuable resources from which the majority group would benefit? How do majority members justify the "take-over" of resources which minority groups possess in a given society? Everett Hughes offered a very interesting essay regarding this particular theoretical problem. His major theoretical problem was how horrors in race relations took place; his substantive issue was the treatment of Jews during the Nazi reign of terror in Germany. His ideas appear in an article entitled "Good People and Dirty Work."[69]

Hughes begins his essay by noting that his examination of the Nazi final solution is not designed to condemn Germans, nor to make them look worse than other people. Rather, his purpose is to call to our attention the danger which always lurks in our midst. Under the Nazi regime, several million people were delivered to concentration camps. They were subjected to perverse cruelty. Prisoners were ordered to climb trees as guards whipped them to move faster. Once they reached the top of the tree, other prisoners were told to shake the trees. When the victims fell, they were kicked to see if they could stand. Those injured badly were shot to death. Many victims were drowned in pits full of human excrement. Soon a policy of mass liquidation was added as a final solution to the Jewish problem.[70]

Hughes' work is unique because he does not seek to answer the usual question of race relations research—questions such as, "How could racial hatred increase to such a high level?" Or "What motivated the S.S. guards to engage in such cruelty?" Rather, his focus is on the "good" German people. He asked:

> How could such dirty work be done among, and, in a sense, by the millions of ordinary, civilized German people? . . . How could these millions of ordinary people live in the midst of such cruelty and murder without a general uprising against it and against the people who did it? How, once freed from the regime that did it, could they be apparently so little concerned about it, so toughly silent about it, not only in talking with outsiders—which is easy to understand—but among themselves? How and where could there be found in a modern civilized country the several hundred thousand men and women capable of such work? How were these people so far released from the inhibitions of civilized life as to be able to imagine, let alone perform, the ferocious, obscene and perverse actions which they did imagine and perform? How could they be kept at such a height of fury through years of having to see, daily, at close range, the human wrecks they made and being often literally spattered with the filth produced and accumulated by their own actions?[71]

Nested within Hughes' thoughts are two types of questions. The first is related to the good people who did not themselves engage in atrocities. The second series of questions revolve around those who actually carried out the atrocities and the dirty work. For Hughes, the two sets of questions are inter-related and cannot be separated. As he noted, "The crucial question concerning the good people is their relation to the people who did the dirty work, with a related one which asks under what circumstances good people let the others get away with such actions?"[72]

Hughes goes to great lengths to show that Germans were no different from other people. On matters of racial sentiments and decent behavior, they were similar to others. But how did the ordinary Germans react? Did they really consider the Jews to be a problem? The following quotation, taken from Hughes' conversation with an architect is revealing:

I am ashamed for my people whenever I think of it. But we didn't know it. We only learned about all that later. You must remember the pressure we were under; we had to join the party. We had to keep our mouths shut and do as we were told. It was a terrible pressure. Still, I am ashamed. But you see, we had lost our colonies, and our national honor was hurt. And these Nazis exploited that feeling. And the Jews, they *were* a problem. They came from the east. You should see them in Poland; the lowest class of people, full of lice, dirty and poor, running about in their Ghettos in filthy caftans. They came here, and got rich by unbelievable methods after the first war. They occupied all the good places. Why they were in proportion of ten to one in medicine and law and government posts! [Emphasis added].[73]

From these types of reactions by "ordinary good German people," Hughes concludes that they did believe that Jews presented a problem. Jews had taken positions which "good Germans" did not occupy. Although the architect himself would never take Jews to concentration camps, he was willing to allow others to do the dirty work that he himself would not do. Furthermore, his data reveal that the good people were unwilling to talk about the Jewish experience in Germany:

Somewhere in consideration of this problem of discussion versus silence we must ask what the good (that is, ordinary) people in Germany did know about these things. It is clear that the S.S. kept the more gory details of the concentration camps a close secret. Even high officials of the government, the army and the Nazi party itself were in some measure held in ignorance, although, of course, they kept the camps supplied with victims. The common people of Germany knew that the camps existed; most knew people who disappeared into them; some saw the victims, walking skeletons in rags, being transported in trucks and trains or being herded on the road from station to camp or to work in fields or factories near the camps.

Many knew people who had been released from concentration camps; such released persons kept their counsel on pain of death. But secrecy was cultivated and supported by fear and terror.[74]

The general point is that the Jewish group, which had been successful in Germany partly as a result of hard academic work and entrepreneurship, were viewed as a problem. Ordinary Germans felt that the Jewish group had received an unfair share of accomplishments in their country. Thus, they wanted some of the very things that the Jews had achieved. In a real sense, racial and economic jealousy on the part of the majority group generates a great deal of hostility.

Throughout the literature, there are accounts of racial hostility revolving around the material goods of middleman groups or minority groups. As noted previously, this was particularly true of Native Americans as a minority group. They were moved constantly when the nation was developing because they happened to live on valuable land. Anti-Semitism stems partly from the successes of the Jewish group in Europe and America.

Can this process be related to the events of Tulsa? Could Afro-Americans in that city possess something which would add to racial hostility and trigger the massive destruction of the Greenwood district?

One of the interesting things about reading reports concerning the riot is that blacks who lived in Tulsa did not concentrate on the elevator incident—or the accused sexual assault, when explaining the riot. When refugees from Tulsa arrived in New York and contacted the NAACP, they noted that warnings had been distributed weeks and months before the riot informing blacks to leave Oklahoma by June 1 or suffer the consequences. Cards had been posted outside their homes warning them to get out of the state. A white newspaper in Okmulgee had even published a similar warning. The warnings were connected to the economic prosperity of some blacks. In an editorial entitled "Blood and Oil," the events of Tulsa were squarely connected to this Afro-American prosperity:

No explanation was given for this anonymous warning, which was repeated on unsigned cards and pasted on the doors of Negro homes. But it was not needed, since the attitude of certain circles of whites and the reason for the warning were well-known. Along with white men, many Negroes from Southern states had bought small parcels of oil land in Oklahoma, originally owned by Indians, and since they were held to be a good investment, some five hundred colored owners had in the last decade resisted all offers, often accompanied by threats, to part with these lands to whites at prices which the Negroes deemed insufficient. Every increase in the price of oil made the strife more bitter. With the depression of the labor market, white employ-

ers of labor at last thought they had the whip hand and ordered
Negro employees to sell out or quit. Even housewives refused to continue colored women in their employ. Petty persecutions, the refugees
say, were common, though there had been no physical violence during
the last few years.[75]

Accounts of the riot even note that specific stores within the Greenwood
district had been targeted. That charge is nested within the following
comments:

What are the causes of the race riot that occurred in such a place?
First, the Negro in Oklahoma has shared in the sudden prosperity
that has come to many of his white brothers, and there are some colored men there who are wealthy. This fact has caused a bitter resent-
ment on the part of the lower order of whites, who feel that these
colored men, members of an "inferior race," are exceedingly pre-
sumptuous in achieving greater economic prosperity than they who
are members of a divinely ordered superior race. . . In one case where
a colored man owned and operated a printing plant with $25,000
worth of printing machinery in it, the leader of the mob that set fire
to and destroyed the plant was a Linotype operator employed for
years by the colored owner at $48 per week. The white man was killed
while attacking the plant.[76]

Without a doubt, the evidence allows one to apply the theoretical work
developed by Hughes. Afro-Americans in Tulsa were victims because of their
own economic success. When reports of the alleged sexual assault by a black
man on a white women reached the white community, blacks had already been
warned to leave. There existed in the white community a certain attitude about
the wealth in the black community as evidenced by the cooperation of white
housewives not to hire blacks as domestics in order to pressure them to sell oil
land. This attitude was pervasive throughout the community. In short, blacks
were considered to be an economic problem. This helps to explain the fact
that, when the riot started, white men and boys from every part of the city
armed themselves, raided hardware stores for more arms and ammunition, and
burned the Greenwood section to the ground.

After the riot, whites of Tulsa and officials of the state as a whole refused
to speak of the events. As a matter of fact, the events were buried.

But in the tradition of middleman groups that experience hostility in societies, blacks in Tulsa made a remarkable recovery. During a slow and painful
process, a bigger and better Greenwood section was constructed. Symbolic of
this massive self-help effort was the dedication of the members of Mount Zion
Baptist Church, the beautiful structure that was burned to the ground during

the riot. A special riot clause in the insurance policy meant that members had to pay the balance owed on the burned church, which was $50,000. After this balance was paid off, efforts were started to rebuild a new church and other people of the Greenwood section of Tulsa started to create a new black business section of Tulsa.

The efforts to rebuild Greenwood were not welcomed by the white city fathers of Tulsa. The burned-out section of what was once called Little Africa was located very close to the downtown section of Tulsa; the section had the potential to be a real estate boom for white business people. Thus when black business people and others went to white banks, whites refused to lend money to them. When blacks began to build temporary enterprises themselves, the Tulsa City Council passed an ordinance making it mandatory that all buildings be constructed with fire-proof materials. In the days and months following the conflict, the Greenwood section was mostly army tents that were furnished by the Red Cross, and shacks.

Like many other black business areas at the turn of the century, Greenwood had an outstanding group of professionals. B. C. Franklin was a lawyer and stepped forward to encourage blacks to ignore the city ordinance regarding fire proof building codes, and build any type of structure on their property. When blacks were arrested for violating the Tulsa building code, Lawyer Franklin came to their defense. At the same time, white businessmen were roaming the area offering blacks ten cents on a dollar for their property. Largely as the results of Lawyer Franklin, the city ordinance was overturned by the Supreme Court and the people looked forward to rebuilding a business section for black Tulsans.

By 1923 the business district, mostly because of self-help and the pooling of money for the capitalization of business enterprises, the Greenwood section was on its way to becoming bigger and better than the old days before the riot. By 1925 the ingenuity of Tulsa's blacks was recognized when the annual convention of the Negro Business League was held in the Greenwood section. By 1938 the black Wall Street of America had been completely rebuilt, along with important community institutions.

Table 6.2 shows that over 300 service and professional enterprises made up the rebuilt Greenwood section. This table does not include enterprises that were not registered in the directory of the Negro Business League. Again, one can see that the enterprises are in the tradition of middleman minorities. The Greenwood district remained a viable business district until the outcomes of the civil rights movement, and urban renewal, transformed the community.

In the late 1950s and early 1960s the enterprises of the once proud district began to suffer because blacks won the right to spend their money freely anywhere in Tulsa. But the community suffered its destruction at the hands of urban renewal. By the early 1970s, the area had fallen into decay; gone were all

TABLE 6.2
Enterprises (Service and Professional) of the Rebuilt Greenwood District as of 1942

Service	Number
Auto Repair	6
Bakeries	2
Barbecue Establishments	8
Beauty Salons	28
Barber Shops	11
Cafes	34
Chili Parlors	12
Coal and Ice Dealers	5
Confectionaries	2
Drug Stores	8
Electrical Services	1
Furniture Repair Ships	3
Florists	2
Funeral Parlors	3
Furriers	8
Grocers	38
Hotels	16
Insurance Agencies	3
Jewelers	1
Laundries	7
Photographers	5
Printers	3
Radio Repair Shops	5
Realtors	6
Service Stations	7
Shoe Repair Shops	9
Stores, Clothing	6
Tailors and Cleaning Shops	15
Taxicabs	2
Theatres	3
Total	242

Professionals	
Attorneys	5
Librarians	1
Dentists	4
Physicians	9
Pharmacists	8
Ministers	38
Social Workers	8
Nurses	12
Teachers	9
Total	94

Source: Negro City Directory—Tulsa, Oklahoma. This table was taken from a frame that is on the wall of the present office of the Oklahoma Eagle in the Greenwood Section of Tulsa.

of the bustling business activities and life that had once dominated this area of Tulsa.

But if you ever go to Tulsa, it is worth going to the northern part of the city and finding the intersection of Greenwood and Archer. This intersection is very important to the self-help tradition of black America and should become a national monument. At the intersection you will be met by modern enterprises that are only symbolic of the old black Wall Street of America. As you drive down Greenwood Avenue, you will go under an overpass which is symbolic of urban renewal programs; thus the Greenwood neighborhood shares with the old Hayti area of Durham an expressway that cuts through the center of its neighborhood. But further down Greenwood you are met with clean green pasture land that at one time was full of enterprises. Interesting enough, the churches of old Greenwood still stand, sometimes in fields all by themselves. The Mount Zion Baptist Church, like the old church in Durham, North Carolina, stands as majestic as it did before it was burned by whites during the riot. It appears that the interstate highway, which comes very close to the church, was designed so that it would not disturb this monument.

Also where enterprises once flourished is a university consortium made up of Oklahoma State University, The University of Oklahoma and Langston University. At the gates of the intersection of Archer and Greenwood stands the building of the Oklahoma *Eagle*, Greenwood's black newspaper that published so many of the business ads and community news of the old community. It is the only enterprise that has remained within the Greenwood section continuously since the tragic race riot. As a matter of fact, during the days of decay, it was the only enterprise that remained in the business sector of Greenwood.

The rebuilding of the present abbreviated Greenwood section began in 1979 when black businessmen of Tulsa put together a private financing and public funding money package to breathe new life into the historic district. They visualized a new business district that would be an open market shopping area, with quaint shops and other types of service enterprises. They presented a series of developmental plans to the city of Tulsa, only to have each plan rejected. Some black Tulsans drew parallels between the city's treatment of blacks after the race war, when they tried to rebuild the district, and the redevelopment efforts of the late 1970s. After all, the closeness of Greenwood to the downtown area still makes it valuable property. As black businessmen tried to get their developmental plan through city hall, the city took over the project and gave it to the Urban Renewal Authority. Thus an interesting historical catch to the present redevelopment of Greenwood is that blacks as a group did not finance, nor do they own, the first three blocks of the old Greenwood section.

But like Durham, North Carolina, the children and grandchildren of the old business people can be found in the Greenwood section. These include

Lloyd H. Williams, Jr., who operates the Greenwood Pharmacy in the same area where his father operated his pharmacy during the 1940s. Gary R. Davis, a family medical doctor, has his practice in the building right on the corner of Greenwood and Archer. During the destruction of Greenwood, black citizens set up a perimeter around this building to protect it from the rioters. James Goodwin is still producing outstanding issues of the Oklahoma *Eagle*, a paper that his father once owned. Rosalyn Williams operates a Gift Shop and she remembers when the area was alive with joy and business activity. The older people of the Greenwood section speak proudly of other sons and daughters who left Tulsa and who are making outstanding contributions to their professional fields. Perhaps the one mentioned the most is John Hope Franklin, a prominent historian, and the son of the lawyer, B. C. Franklin, who was instrumental in the rebuilding of the Greenwood section after its destruction.[77]

Every year, the Greenwood Chamber of Commerce sponsors a Jazz Festival in the area, and the lights and people once again return to the district to enjoy themselves and have a joyful time. Most of the younger ones in the crowds who come from other cities and towns have no idea of the drastic events that happened in the early 1920s, nor of the self-help spirit that flourished in the face of discrimination and racism. But in a very real sense, Tulsa Oklahoma, and the Greenwood section are just as important to black Americans as the cities of Birmingham and Montgomery, Alabama. Like these Alabama cities, where the modern civil rights movement witnessed significant events, Tulsa holds the forgotten historical light of self-help in the tradition of black America.

CONCLUSION

The city of Tulsa, Oklahoma, developed on the rugged frontier as an oil boom town. As the town developed, Afro-Americans looked forward to economic security through business enterprise. They developed a section known as the Greenwood District, which was the hub of the social and business life of the community. As a middle class developed, they constructed lovely homes, churches, and other community centers. The politics of race, gender, and economics set the spark which saw all of their dreams vanish in clouds of smoke. The lesson has to do with the relationship between being an "out" group with a degree of economic security which the majority group feels is theirs by right. In Tulsa, Afro-Americans refused to sell valuable land to Euro-Americans; the spark was set, and their dreams died in a "Promised Land."

7

The Reconstruction of
Race, Ethnicity, and Economics

Toward a Theory of the Afro-American Middleman

As has been shown thus far, tucked within the battered Afro-American experience is an interesting record of business activity. Although we have presented only a small portion of this experience, the historical record clearly contradicts the treatment of Afro-American enterprise by sociologists studying the relationship between ethnicity and entrepreneurship. Indeed, within this literature, the Afro-American experience itself is rarely mentioned, except in a negative sense; this, despite the fact that praise is systematically accorded to the development of any small enterprise by ethnic groups.[1] In this chapter, we reconstruct race, ethnicity, and economics by giving a consideration to the reality of Afro-American enterprise.

In order to begin this reconstruction, we must reiterate the significance of ideas developed by Weber in *The Protestant Ethic and the Spirit of Capitalism*. As we noted in chapter 1, Weber's major concern was to explain the variability in the business activities of differing religious groups. Despite this fact, the sociological literature on ethnicity and enterprise has not drawn heavily on Weber's work. Instead, middleman theory has anchored the theoretical approach to ethnic enterprise. This tradition—along with race relations theory in general—has neither incorporated the history of Afro-American enterprise nor treated it in a viable way. Three of the most significant reasons for this omission include: 1. the failure to compare and contrast different theoretical frameworks when studying race and economic enterprise; 2. the treatment of the entire Afro-American experience as though it were completely congruent with the experience of most European ethnic groups who, for the most part, immigrated to the industrial north in search of economic security; and 3. the utilization of the Marxist theoretical framework which, when applied to Afro-Americans, is more religious than predictive.

In this chapter we present an alternative framework which allows a better understanding of racial and economic patterns. More specifically, the major argument is that, among Afro-Americans, there was a subgroup of entrepreneurs—although not limited completely to entrepreneurs—which developed in a fashion very similar to that of ethnic middleman groups. I refer to them as a *truncated middleman group*, however, because their experience is distinguished by the presence of segregation and because they were forced to use the economic detour.

As noted in chapter 1, middleman groups are so named because they occupy the center of an economic structure, serving, for example, groups whose status lies between those of the elite and those of the masses. As far as this analysis is concerned, it is critical to recognize that a group of Afro-Americans also played this role in America, especially among those who were free prior to the Civil War. Indeed, as confirmed by data presented in this manuscript, Afro-Americans controlled small service enterprises in northern cities long before the massive waves of European immigrant groups arrived in America.

Nevertheless, after the Civil War, these individuals were truncated or cut off from occupying a position within the mainstream economic market. Discrimination, prejudice, and laws of the state (or governmental interference in business) combined to force them to develop enterprises that were limited to serving only members of their own group. Despite these limitations, our analysis will reveal that these entrepreneurs were middleman both in their spirit and in their approach to American life, and that this approach was passed on to future generations, much as were the patterns followed by other middleman groups.

Because of their socialization, and the experience of their parents, they were—and their offspring are—different from middle class blacks today in their approach to life in America. Thus, today, we must make a distinction between what we call the descendants of the truncated Afro-American middleman and descendants of Afro-Americans who adjusted to America in the tradition of ethnic groups.

This must be done because, although offspring of both groups may enjoy a degree of economic stability, their history influences how they continue to adjust to American society. These categories are heuristic and should not be taken to mean that there is absolutely no overlap between them.

The specification of such a theory will explain many of the variations in the Afro-American community, both now and in the past. It will also help us to develop a better understanding of the economic differences between European ethnic groups. Finally, this section attempts to explain why there was a general decline in emphasis on the importance of enterprise within the Afro-American culture.

I

Our discussion of race and economics must begin with the work of E. Franklin Frazier. Since the publication of his work on the rise of a new black middle class in America, there has been general intellectual antagonism toward the class.[2] It must be specified that Frazier's work was written about what he termed the "so-called new middle class," which he distinguished from the old black aristocracy. The latter emerged following the Civil War and was partially grounded in business activity. Unlike outstanding works by Frazier, such as *Negro Youth at the Crossroads*, *The Negro Family in the United States*, and *The Negro Church in America*, his *Black Bourgeoisie* reads as a quick polemic study of what he calls the new "black middle class." Written in France as part of a collection of studies which appeared in an edited book entitled *Recherches en Sciences Humanines*, Frazier himself thought that his work would be relegated to the shelves of university libraries, buried in an insignificant book. But, when his contribution to the edited work was published in Paris as *Bourgeoisie Noire* in 1955 and then translated to English in 1957, the popularity of his work grew rapidly.

This fact itself surprised Frazier, as indicated by his comments in the preface to the second edition of the work. He noted that "It came as a pleasant surprise, therefore, to learn that it attracted sufficient attention in the academic world for it to be made the basis of the MacIver Lectureship Award by the American Sociological Society by 1956. When the English edition was published . . . I was even more surprised by the controversy which it aroused among Negroes and by unfavorable reactions of many whites.[3] "

Despite the many criticisms, *Black Bourgeoisie* has remained the starting block for scholars interested in the black middle-class.[4]

The academic criticisms of Frazier's work revolve around issues of method. Oliver Cox noted that, in Frazier's *Black Bourgeoisie*, "There is hardly a consequential assertion regarding traits of the Negro Middle Class that does not prove to be unreliable or egregiously misleading. Its critical evidence is a composite of personal anecdotes, hearsay, erratic news items, and distorted social science information."[5] Cox also noted that the work is methodologically flawed because Frazier operates with two definitions of the black middle class.

One definition is operationalized by income, with blacks making more than $2,000 a year being defined as middle class. The other definition utilizes occupation as a measure of middle-class status.

Based on the former definition, Cox noted that at least 40 percent of blacks in the North during the time of the study would be classified as middle class. He argues that this two-pronged definitional approach creates a picture of the black middle class which "does not constitute a sociological group but rather statistical categories of unstable dimensions."[6] Cox then argues that Frazier's definitions are a poor basis for examining the social characteristics of any class.

A similar criticism of Frazier is found in the work of Muraskin.[7] He observes that:

> The most obvious flaw in Frazier's study is his attempt to delimit the boundaries of the black bourgeoisie. Frazier's black middle class is primarily a white-collar group with most of its recent growth in the clerical and kindred occupations, though it also includes professional and technical workers, managers and proprietors, craftsmen and foremen. This group is estimated at 16 percent of the male black population. The book itself, however, is not about this group, most of which is ignored in the text. Rather, the study focuses on the small elite at the top of the black bourgeoisie—the professionals, businessmen, and to a lesser extent college graduates generally. Most of the important examples he provides of the new middle class's ethics, or lack of them, involves doctors, college professors, or other successful professionals. . . Frazier's formal definition and his actual discussion do not cover the same people.[8]

Despite methodological and other types of criticisms of Frazier's work,[9] one can say that the book has weathered the literature and created a situation, especially among intellectuals, in which middle class status, and its accompanying value system, is viewed as a negative phenomenon within the Afro-American tradition. All of the entrepreneurial trials and tribulations, since they are tied to middle-class status, are rejected in a body of literature. But this rejection is based on faulty theoretical understanding and a failure to compare historically oppressed groups within capitalist societies. When the Afro-American business experience is placed within a comparative theoretical framework, the accomplishments of this group emerge in a positive light.

Although Frazier criticized the entire black middle-class experience, for our purposes it is important to commence with his view of Afro-American business, which he called a myth. Indeed, he devoted an entire chapter to developing a thesis on the myth of black business. Despite acknowledging the history of Afro-American business since the Civil War, he concluded that Afro-American enterprise was a myth because capital investment represented by Negro business was insignificant from the standpoint of the American economy and because it provided an exceedingly small amount of employment and income for Negro workers.[10] In fact, he discusses how the Negro Business League, as organized by Booker T. Washington, perpetuated the myth with stories of success.

Frazier's basic reasoning has served as the fundamental basis for the criticism of entrepreneurial efforts by Afro-Americans. His reasoning can be found throughout works on Afro-American enterprise, but a recent publication exemplies this approach especially well. *The New Black Middle Class* by

Bart Landry presents data on the total sales of the top one hundred black businesses between 1973 and 1983. These sales increased from what Landry termed a "modest," $601.1 million to $2.3 billion between these years. He further noted that Johnson Publishing led the pack with more than $100 million in sales for 1983, compared to $27.8 million in 1973, and that Motown Industries topped $100 million in 1983 with total sales of $108.2 million, up from $46 million in 1973. Although the number of employees increased dramatically at Johnson Publishing—from 245 to 1,690—Motown employed 375 people in 1973, and 231 in 1983.[11] Landry then proceeds to evaluate these top Afro-American businesses in the tradition of Frazier.

> These figures represent impressive growth over a ten-year period, yet neither Johnson Publishing nor Motown made the Fortune 500 list or even came close. The last company on the Fortune 500 list, Tandem Computers with sales of $418.3 million, grossed almost four times as much as Johnson Publishing in 1983 and had 4,396 employees. Exxon, which had gross sales of $88.5 billion in 1983 and employed 156,000 people, was number one on the list. . . . There is no hope for the emergence of enough qualifying individuals to create a black upper class in the foreseeable future.[12]

Landry insists that it is not his intention to diminish the performance of black enterprises between 1973 and 1983, but to point out that the facts serve as evidence that they simply cannot compete with larger businesses.

The problem with Landry's reasoning, which is grounded in the work of Frazier, is that it has no theoretical basis. It seems evident that small businesses cannot compete with the big companies. In fact, the author might be surprised to learn that none of the enterprises established by the Cubans in Miami in the 1970s or the Japanese in California could compete with these big companies. Nevertheless, the theory which examines the relationship between oppressed groups and business activities makes the entire Afro-American business tradition, both past and present, quite predictable.

Let us return to the theoretical source of Max Weber which was introduced in chapter 1. If one were to follow the reasoning of Frazier and that of the already cited example, all entrepreneurial activities of ethnic and racial groups would have to be mythic. Because these writers did not take a comparative approach, they completely missed the significance and importance of the Afro-American enterprises, no matter how small, that developed within a hostile racial environment.

What Frazier and many other researchers such as Landry have failed to understand is that Afro-Americans who adjusted to and continue to adjust to America through successful business enterprise are really a variation of a middleman group. Although, because of the realities of discrimination, racism, and the economic detour, they represent a truncated sort of middleman. What is important, however, is that their outlook and approach to life and their patterns of adjustment to hostility in America are in the same mode as the Japanese in California and the Jews in Europe. Let us recall that middleman groups, especially in the first generation, become economically stable through nontraditional approaches to economic mobility. They achieve despite the hostility directed against them. It is their offspring who, because of the importance of education and expanding opportunities, enter the professional labor market. This differentiates them from other groups which become economically stable by conforming to the extant opportunity structure of the society. As we attempt to specify the theory of the Afro-American middleman, the distinction between the Afro-American middle-class and the Afro-American middleman will become crucial.

In order to understand the logic of our argument, we must return to Max Weber. One of the major contributions of his *The Protestant Ethic and The Spirit of Capitalism* is his focus on the relationship between the development of business activity and the presence of group oppression. His most important comment, which was quoted in chapter 1 and is worth repeating, is as follows:

> National or religious minorities which are in a position of subordination to a group of rulers are likely, through their voluntary or involuntary exclusion from positions of political influence, to be driven with peculiar force into economic activity. Their ablest members seek to satisfy the desire for recognition of their abilities in this field, since there is no opportunity in the service of the State.[13]

Weber continues by noting that this goal of attaining recognition has been true of the Poles of Russia and Eastern Prussia, two groups which, at that time in history, developed economic advancement at a rapid pace. He observes that, in earlier times, the same was true of the Huguenots in France under Louis XIV, the Nonconformists and Quakers in England, and the Jewish group for thousands of years.[14] We can conclude that, when Weber refers to oppressed groups' ablest members, he is speaking of individuals within these groups who were willing to become entrepreneurs.

As noted in our theoretical chapter, the study of racial and ethnic business in America is a natural extension of Weber's ideas. These ideas were given theoretical strength with the development of middleman minorities. One characteristic of these groups is that their lines of business are not immediately productive. Unlike groups who mobilize the productive labor of many others, middleman minorities concentrate their efforts on the circulation of goods and services. The businesses in which they concentrate are usually quite marginal. Because of hostility and general discrimination, they engage in fields that others reject as unacceptable.

Thus, medieval Jews operated in the area of money lending because Christians did not like that trade. Chinese and Indians engaged in trade activities because it was despised and hated in the colonial territories in which they operated. Generally speaking, middleman groups also serve as shopkeepers and cater to other subordinated groups. Again, the typifying feature of these groups is that they serve as go-betweens for the elites and masses because the former reject contact with the latter.[15]

As the present historical overview confirms in terms of the form of enterprise, middleman minorities are typically found in small business. They are more likely to be self-employed or on track to be self-employed. They are tailors, barbers, or launderers who engage in their trade in small shop settings. The capitalization of the business is usually small as well. For example, Bonacich and Modell noted that, in 1909, the capital invested in Japanese business was very small (68.7 percent) of the firms having a capital investment of less than $1,000.

Members of these groups also tend to enter professions which have a degree of independence—including medicine, law, and dentistry—professions which can be successfully run as small businesses.[16] We must conclude—and it is obvious from the application of an historical comparative framework—that the nature of the enterprises which have been specified as characteristically middleman is extremely similar to enterprises developed by portions of the Afro-American community since the 1700s.

This point prompts us to reexamine our idea of the historical economic structure that affected Afro-Americans from a comparative perspective. It means taking a fresh new look at the interaction of race and economics. It means we must question established ideas which have guided research in this area for the last seventy to eighty years.

We begin with the fact that—already noted within the history of America and, indeed, the world—oppressed groups have adapted in different ways. For example, in *Latin Journey*, Portes and Bach note that, although the Jews and Japanese have different cultural and religious backgrounds, they adapted to America in a way which was different from other ethnic groups.

> Both groups were non-Christian, but they were different in religion, language, and race. They disembarked at opposite ends of the continent and never met in sizeable numbers at any point. Yet, Jews and Japanese developed patterns of economic and social adaptation that were remarkably similar. What both groups had in common was their collective resistance to serving as a mere source of labor power. From the start, their economic conduct was oriented toward two goals: (1) the acquisition of property; and (2) the search for entrepreneurial opportunities that would give them an "edge" in the American market.[17]

My major argument is that there has always been an element within the Afro-American group which adapted to racism and discrimination in the same kind of way as did middleman groups. As this analysis has shown, since the 1700s, there has always been a group of Afro-Americans who were concerned with the acquisition of property and the search for entrepreneurial opportunities which allowed them to survive economically in America. Their history in America is similar, vis-a-vis economic approach, to the examples of middleman groups as presented in chapter 1. This historical fact has interesting implications for both the study of the Afro-American community in history and the study of the "black middle class."

The major implication is that, among this group today (those who have attained a degree of economic security), we really have two groups which trace their success to different patterns of adjustment to America by their foreparents. Because of this, the two groups continue to adjust to racism and discrimination in similar but significantly different ways. Thus, it is a theoretical and methodological mistake to lump all Afro-Americans with economic stability into one group called the "middle class."

As a matter of fact, class analysis—which is dependent on classifying people based on prestige of occupation or census categories—is misleading. The first group, I call the "truncated Afro-American middleman." Following conventional categories, I refer to the second group as the Afro-American "new middle class." Such a distinction is based on the two groups' historical adjustment to American society. Let us explore the differences between the two groups.

The truncated Afro-American middleman is grounded in the tradition of self-help and entrepreneurship within the Afro-American community. They were responsible for the creation of business enterprises, educational institutions, certain values, and general outlook on life in America. Put another way, they created opportunities from despair at a time when Afro-Americans were legally excluded from the opportunity structure in the nation.

Their values were almost identical to middleman groups discussed in the literature, such as Jews in Germany and the United States, Japanese in America, and Vietnamese in America. More specifically, they: (1) adjusted to hostility by turning inward and developing economic and community institutions; (2) developed a strong tradition of family stability and excellent quality of life through housing, health care, and other means; and, perhaps the most important similarity, (3) began a very strong emphasis on the importance of higher education for their offspring.

These values, which in some places began as early as the late 1700s but can more broadly be traced to the dawn of freedom, were passed down through generations by the truncated Afro-American middlemen and their offspring. Thus, today, descendants of this group have middleman ideas about the adjustment to American life, especially where racism and discrimination is concerned.

Because a great deal of institutional building took place in the segregated South, they are more likely (but not always) to be Southern in origin. Their outlook on life is influenced by the fact that they can be first-, second-, or third-generation college graduates. Because of their parents, grandparents, or great-grandparents, they have a history of economic stability and stable family ties. Despite the heavy effects of discrimination and racism as Afro-Americans, they have never lived in substandard housing or ghettos.

In the South, because of the availability of land, they were able to build housing areas which reflected their success. Because they are grounded in a unique tradition of self-help, their role models, funding for education, and aspirations are grounded in their communities rather than white communities; they support historically black organizations and institutions, even when they live today in integrated communities.

No matter their achievements in life, they never refer to Afro-American institutions, which were established by Afro-Americans as inferior. Their positions in life today—which are, for the most part, related to business, the professions (such as doctors, lawyers, professors, dentists, and the like), are the result of the self-help values of their parents which were passed down through the generations.

It is important to point out that, long before desegregation and the expansion of racial opportunities, these were the occupations specified by parents in the tradition of the truncated Afro-American middleman. Thus, this group shares with all Afro-Americans the problems of racism and discrimination, but because of historical circumstances, they continue to adjust, as their parents, grandparents and great-grandparents before them, in a different way to these American realities.

The group that I call the truncated Afro-American middleman has, over the years, been documented in scholarly studies of communities throughout the United States. Without a firm theoretical framework, however, most scholars did not know what do with them and simply considered them to be an anomaly. For example, in the classic work of John Dollard entitled *Caste and Class in a Southern Town*, he described a group of Afro-Americans of that Southern city who were quite different. They stressed education for their children and believed that mobility could be achieved, even with the hostility of racism. He also noted that he did not know much about this small group of Afro-Americans in this Southern town.[18] In an analysis which was done outside of the Old South, Stephen Birmingham described this segment of the Afro-American population of Washington, D.C.

Then there is the Old Guard, Washington's black "cave-dwellers," people whose roots in Washington go back three, four, even five generations. These families, who have had money, social position, and—most important—education, since the turn of the century and earlier, live in three- or four-story town houses in quiet, tree-shaded streets. . . . Quiet, conservative, devoted to thrift, . . . these families generally have not, though they could have, moved to glossier, newer neighborhoods. They stayed where they are because their friends and relatives are there, just as their grandmothers' and great-grandmothers' friends were there.[19]

This author refers to this historical type of Afro-American as the "Old Guard" or "cave-dwellers." They have also been called the *black bourgeoisie*, *black Brahmans*, *black elite*, and the *black upper class*. Whatever they are called, their adjustments to America bears a striking resemblance to middleman minorities throughout history.

We formally define the Afro-American middleman group as consisting of those individuals who were entrepreneurs and professionals of the old segregated economy. Both of these groups, significantly, were service-oriented. Entrepreneurs, of course, refer to those who started business enterprises, including the owners of small independent farms. Professionals consisted of doctors, teachers, professors, ministers, and lawyers.

It is important to point out that, in order to be included in the group, it was not important as to *what* one did, but rather that one did *something* in the tradition of self-help. Thus, the small shop owner, the owner of a small farm, the pushcart owner, the owner of the shoeshine stand, the founder of a church, lawyers, and doctors are all interacted together because of the importance of a common experience vis-a-vis discrimination and other hostile acts from the larger society.

These people come together in the institutions of the community—such as religious institutions and fraternal institutions—and view their interests and mission of economic stability in the same light. Census class categories, which are so often utilized to categorize people, become useless when describing any type of middleman group because of the common hostility—in this case, racial and received from the larger society. This Afro-American group has been in America since the 1700s, but picked up steam at the turn of the century. This definition is similar to that developed by Munford and Staples, although they simply called it the "Service Stratum."[20]

We should also point out that the boundaries of the Afro-American middleman were not rigid, but were always in the becoming. People were constantly entering its ranks. Indeed, sacrifices made by poor working parents to send their children to college (mostly Afro-American colleges and universities) became success stories within Afro-American communities.

Success was measured by the fact that their children could work in one of the institutions of the segregated economy, especially in the South, as opposed to working for wealthy whites as a domestic or some other kind of occupation. But this fact can be traced as far back as the early 1800s, not just to the more recent segregated South. Consider the following analysis of free heads of Afro-American families in the 1830s:

> Many a Negro leader today, with a fine education obtained from Oberlin, Yale, [or] Harvard [owe] their start [to] hard-working mothers or fathers who literally "bore the burden in the heat of the day." These mothers and fathers worked without any hope that they personally would ever "lay down their heavy load" of unrecompensed toil but they saw the triumph of their children from afar and they toiled unceasingly that their posterity might have a better, fuller, and freer life. They were the real "unsung heroes." . . .[21]

Thus, as early as the 1800s, entrance into this group depended on attitudes of self-help, such as the importance of education, sacrifice, and hard work. An example of the importance of building strong educational institutions and instilling in their offspring the importance of education is captured in the following analyses of, again, the "Old Guard" of Washington, D.C.

> The creation of Dunbar appeared to black educators as a kind of salvation, and the best black teachers from all over the country competed for posts at Dunbar. With the best faculty available, and the best students that could be found, Dunbar was indeed a school for the upwardly mobile elite. Generations of black achievers attended Dunbar, and went on to shine in the best colleges of the Ivy League. . . Its alumni today . . . consider themselves a special breed, and hold regular reunions once a year and sing the old school song.[22]

The same kind of statement could have been made in schools in the South such as St. Augustine in New Orleans, Louisiana, and Southern University High in Baton Rouge, Louisiana.

Table 7.1 allows us to document empirically the fact that, in the face of hostility at the turn of the century, there was a culture which stressed the importance of education among parents who, in fact, created the Afro-American truncated middleman. In 1920, Frazier first collected data on the relationship between the occupation of the father and college attendance from two sources: *Who's Who in Colored America* and graduates of a black American college.[23] These data are presented in Table 7.1, with some modifications. Frazier's original table showed independent effects for the occupation of children (in Table 7.1 called simply "persons"). We have collapsed these two categories into one professional and business category.

First, look at offspring who were graduates of a black college for the year 1931. Notice that, although there is variation, all categories of father's occupation—with the exception of public office—contributed to offspring who were

TABLE 7.1

Occupations of the Fathers of Selected Groups of Afro-Americans in the Professions, Business, Who's Who in Colored America, and Those Who Graduated from a Black College (1931)

Occupation of Persons	Agriculture	Common Labor	Domestic and Personal Service	Skilled Occupation	Clerical	Business	Professional Service	Public Office	Total
			Occupation of Father						
			Who's Who in Colored America						
Professional and business*	.23% N=72	.13% N=40	.08% N=26	.16% N=51	.04% N=13	.07% N=24	.25% N=76	00% N=3	T=305
			Graduates of a Black College						
Professional* and business	.18 N=23	.13 N=17	.05 N=7	.20 N=25	.13 N=7	.10 N=13	.25 N=31	N=0	T=125

Source: E. Franklin Frazier. "The Changing Status of the Negro Family." *Social Forces* 9: March 1931. 386–393.

*In original tables, the categories Professional and Business were not collapsed, but analyzed separately. The data are for a community in Chicago.

in the professional and business category. The highest contribution of 25 percent was from fathers who were in professional service, such as dentists and medical doctors. Fathers who worked in skilled occupations produced 20 percent of black college graduates in the professional and business category. This is followed by fathers in agriculture, who owned their own small farms, who contributed 18 percent of those who graduated from a black college. Those fathers who worked as domestics had the smallest percentage of offspring completing college (5 percent).

Now, let us examine the sample of people in Table 7.1 who were listed in *Who's Who in Colored America* for the year 1931. It is not at all clear whether or not these individuals finished college. But it is clear that those who made the *Who's Who* list—or those selected as making a significant contribution in the professional and business enterprises—had fathers who also had a range of occupations. There were, of course, variations: 23 percent of the professional and businesspersons' fathers had an occupation related to agriculture (owners of small farms); 16 percent had fathers who worked in the skilled trades; 25 percent had fathers who were engaged in professional service; 13 percent had fathers who were common laborers; and .08 percent came from homes where the father worked in domestic and personal service. Although all fathers' backgrounds contributed to the professional and business class in both samples (*Who's Who* sample and graduates of a black college) in these data, the percentages are much more dramatic when we recode these data to produce an entrepreneurial self-help category.

This is done in Table 7.2. People who owned their own farms (agriculture); who were doctors, dentists, lawyers (professional service); and those in business were collapsed to comprise an entrepreneur category. One can see from the table that these categories, which are fairly good measures of the entrepreneurs in the segregated economy, reveal that fathers who were entrepreneurs produced 56 percent of the next generation's professionals and businessmen who were listed in *Who's Who in Colored America*. More importantly, this entrepreneurial sector produced slightly more than half (54 percent) of the college graduates from this community. Those parents who worked in skilled occupations produced the next highest number of college graduates, with 20 percent. This is followed by the common labor category, which produced 13 percent of the college graduates in the community. Although Frazier limited his analysis to only a selected city, his data testify to the fact that just after the turn of the century, the impact of fathers' occupation did have a significant effect on their children's futures.

This effect of fathers' education and occupation on the education of the offspring is also present in a study of more than twenty-five thousand Afro-American college graduates in 1938. It was found that, taken as a whole, 27 percent of college graduates in 1938 had fathers who were in professional service occupations. The next largest groups which contributed to the college

TABLE 7.2

Occupations of Afro-Americans Whose Fathers Were in the Entrepreneurial Sector, as Compared with Other Occupations, 1931

Occupation of Person	Entrepreneurs (Service)	Common Labor	Domestic and Personal Service	Skilled Labor	Clerical	Public Office	Total
			Who's Who in Colored America				
Professional and business*	.56% N=172	.13% N=40	.08% N=26	.16% N=501	N=13	N=3	T=305
			Graduates of Black Colleges				
Professional and business*	54% N=67	.13 N=17	.05 N=7	.20 N=25	.03 N=7	N=0	T=123

Source: E. Franklin Frazier. "The Changing Status of the Negro Family." Social Forces 9: March 1931. 386–393.

*In original tables, the categories Professional and Business were not collapsed, but analyzed separately. The data are for a community in Chicago.

graduate population were manufacturing and mechanical industries, agricultural, and domestic and personal service with 8.3 percent, 6.3 percent, and 5.2 percent of the fathers, respectively.[24]

As noted by the author of that work, the relatively high proportion of college graduates whose fathers were professionals is even more striking when comparisons were made with the proportion of persons in professional occupations in the general Afro-American population. Of the total Afro-American male population that was working, 2 percent were in professions as compared to 27 percent of the employed fathers of college graduates.[25] This work also gives a consideration to the importance of gender when considering who attended college during this time period.

The great preponderance of professional occupations among the parents of college graduates is even more strikingly seen when the mothers of these graduates are considered. Forty-nine and nine-tenths percent . . . are in professional service, as compared with 3.4 percent of all employed Negro women in professional service. The percentage in domestic and personal service is relatively low, only 20.6 percent of the mothers of college graduates being in this field, as against 62.6 percent in the general population.[26]

From the above data, it is obvious that knowing how Afro-Americans adjusted to America allows us to predict where their offspring ended up. This type of analysis means that we must reconsider some of the conclusions in the literature about race and mobility. For example, Otis Dudley Duncan's study of mobility patterns reveal that the relationship between a son's occupational prestige to his father's educational prestige was weaker among blacks than whites as of 1962.[27] Featherman and Hauser found that the differences between blacks and whites decreased between 1972 and 1973. They report that the pattern of intergenerational mobility of blacks began to converge with those of whites. They measured intergenerational transmission of status by educational attainment, occupational prestige, and earnings.[28]

In this work we argue that, when the Afro-Americans who adjusted to America in the tradition of middleman were controlled, then it has always been true that, overall, intergenerational mobility took place. We must be careful to point out, however, that the data that we have examined look only at destination vis-a-vis occupations rather than occupational prestige scores. But it is clear that the tradition of launching one's children into a better occupational and educational path can be historically documented among the truncated Afro-American middleman. This is a middleman effect, and can be seen in other data which examined, for example, the Japanese-American experience on the West Coast.[29]

The majority of the Afro-American population adjusted to America in the same manner as did most ethnic groups. They migrated to northern cities in search of economic stability in the expanding industrial sector. If they remained in the South, they worked in the open hostile white economy in the midst of racism and discrimination. Those who moved North went directly into low-paying, unskilled, or semiskilled occupations in steel mills, packing houses, foundries, construction, and automobile plants.[30] Within these industries they were located in jobs which most European ethnic groups rejected as dirty and demeaning. In northern cities, as they moved into neighborhoods, white European ethnic groups fled as rapidly as possible. Consider the following quotation which describes this process in New York City, as Afro-Americans began to move into that area:

> The whole movement, in the eyes of whites, took on the aspect of an "invasion"; they became panic-stricken, and began fleeing as from a plague. The presence of one colored family in a block, no matter how well-bred and orderly, was sufficient to precipitate a flight. House after house and block after block was actually deserted.[31]

As Afro-Americans moved into previously all-white neighborhoods, they also purchased religious buildings which had been originally built by the ethnic group that went before them. More often than not, however, business enterprises were maintained by the businessmen of the fleeing ethnic group. In some cities, such as Philadelphia and New York, when the newcomers arrived from the South, there was already an established truncated Afro-American middleman group which had adjusted to America through self-help and business activity.

The new arrivals to the Northern Industrial Belt worked very hard to establish economic stability. In the early years, the most important thing for them and their offspring was an excellent job in industry and the benefit of union wages. They entered schools that were once inhabited by ethnic groups from Europe. Although we know very little about the educational process of Afro-Americans who moved North, we do know that their teachers and role models were less likely to be of Afro-American descent. We also know that tracking, or the killing of aspirations, took place in those schools. The classic literature on this process is found in the experience of Malcolm X. When Malcolm X informed his white teacher that he was thinking about being a lawyer, the teacher responded as follows: "Malcolm, one of life's first needs is for us to be realistic... We all here like you ... but you've got to be realistic about being a nigger. A lawyer—that's no realistic goal for a nigger. You need to think about something you can be. You're good with your hands... Why don't you plan on carpentry?" This experience is in contrast to the experience of blacks in southern schools who had black teachers, who encouraged them to aspire to all kinds of professional occupations. Indeed, it is these teachers who should be seen as the prime catalyst for educational aspirations in the South for black Americans.[32]

Unlike the Afro-American middleman group, which established an early dogmatic emphasis on education for their children and who were mostly Southern in origin, it wasn't until the late 1960s that offspring of this group (mostly Northern in origin) began to enter college.[33]

Indeed, those individuals who adjusted to America actually created what is called "Afro-American new middle class." Also, unlike the descendants of the truncated Afro-American middleman, which is grounded in self-help, members of the so-called "new middle class" today trace their origins to individuals who are quite different. Bart Landry describes the background of this class.

> One of the results of this increased mobility into the middle class was that the Black Middle Class in the mid-1970s was "recruited" from the sons and daughters of garbage collectors, assembly line workers, domestics, waiters, taxicab drivers and farmers. Even with the increased rate of inheritance within the middle class, around 80 percent of the black middle class is today first generation. This is true no less of the upper than the lower middle-class stratum. Thus, with 40 and 23 percent of the black middle class having moved up from the skilled and unskilled strata of the working class, respectively, most of its members continue to have roots stretching far down into the neighborhoods and homes of truck drivers, assembly line workers, and waiters.[34]

Because of strict segregation in the urban North, Afro-Americans who are historically tied to the new middle class occupied one area of the city. This is in marked contrast to the South, where Afro-Americans with economic stability built and maintained their own housing areas, thus creating housing patterns within race and based on economic stability. As can be seen in the following quotation, the Afro-American experience in the North was different.

> The concentration of Negroes in the central cities of our metropolitan areas and whites in the outlying cores of these central cities is too well documented to warrant elaboration here. Our concern is with the fact that the areas inhabited by Negroes are inferior in terms of housing quality, recreational facilities, schools, and general welfare services, and that all of these deficiencies contribute to crime, delinquency, school dropouts, dependency, broken families, excessive deaths, and other conditions which represent the "pathology of the ghetto." In 1960, for example, 44 percent of all dwelling units occupied by Negroes were substandard. Though nonwhites occupied only

10 percent of all dwelling units, they occupied 27 percent of those classed as substandard. Thirteen percent of nonwhites lived in units which were seriously overcrowded, and there was an increase of 85,000 such units occupied by Negroes between 1950 and 1960.[35]

Afro-Americans who migrated to the North worked hard to get out of their condition and began to send the first generation of their children to college in the late 1960s.

The distinction between Afro-Americans based on their historical adjustment to America is important because patterns of historical adjustments still influence the offspring of the two groups today, especially in regard to historical Afro-American organizations and institutions. The significance of this point will become increasingly obvious as we proceed to make our point stronger by grounding the concept of an Afro-American middleman into the overall middleman literature. As we do so, we will return to the work of Frazier, reanalyzing his observations in a middleman framework. We then turn to a more thorough discussion of Afro-Americans who did not adjust to America in the tradition of middleman minorities.

II

In the preceding discussion, one of the most important variables in distinguishing the Afro-American middleman is the degree of economic stability of the individual's ancestors. A key element in middleman theory is that parents work long hours in business enterprise so that their children can do better. This is an important justification for working in small enterprises. The emphasis is always on the success of future generations. Also, we must recall that service industries and professions are hallmark professions of middleman communities. In the same way, this fact frames our definition of the Afro-American middleman, a definition that builds on the evidence presented in earlier chapters.

When we move to historical comparative data, it really justifies describing a portion of the Afro-American experience as a type of a middleman experience. Even old scholarly manuscripts which describes the entrepreneurial tradition of Afro-Americans are similar to those recent ones which describe middleman groups. For example, contrast the following paragraphs which were written sixty-seven years apart. The first is from Bonacich and Modell's excellent work on Japanese-Americans:

The movement into farm proprietorship occurred in a series of stages: first came labor contracting (providing workers to other farmers), then contract farming (contracting to produce a crop for a fixed fee), share tenancy (sharecropping), leasing the land, and finally, owner-ship of the land. Hindered by the enactment in several states of Alien Land Laws, which tried to prevent the process . . . Japanese still moved rapidly into self-employment in farming.[36]

The second quotation is from Henry M. Minton's work on business activity of blacks in Philadelphia in the late 1700s.

After the Act of 1780, the freemen started their new life by hiring themselves out to others, or working as day laborers. Presumably, after having accumulated small savings, they began to go into business. . . In 1789 . . . they were keeping small shops and doing moderately well, though handicapped on account of their inability to borrow money.[37]

If Frazier had utilized a comparative theoretical framework, he would never have come to the many conclusions found in *Black Bourgeoisie*. Without an adequate comparative framework, one of the greatest sociologists of all time was unable to adequately evaluate the relationship between the forms of Afro-American business and their experiences living in an oppressive society. One can say, without a doubt, that the great majority of scholars who examine Afro-American business also do so without this comparative theoretical framework.

For example, Earl Ofari in *The Myth of Black Capitalism* attempts to show why there is no black capitalism.[38] without an adequate theoretical framework, he, as others who write on this topic, have been unable to come to grips with racial enterprise in an oppressive society.[39] As a result, the hard work of Afro-American businessmen, beginning as early as the 1700s, has been simultaneously undervalued and devalued, and treated as insignificant. The fact that Afro-Americans responded to oppression in the same way as did other groups in the middleman tradition has been systematically overlooked. Viewing the Afro-American business experience in a middleman framework, as presented in this work, sheds a new light on the nature of their activities. As with other oppressed groups, portions of the group responded to racism and oppression by developing business activity. They took disappointments and tried to create appointments. They took an oppressive situation and tried to extract from it a situation of successful economic development.

It is important at this time to consider how ethnic middleman groups have been treated in the literature in comparison with what I called the truncated Afro-American middleman. My goal is to show how a comparative perspective could have informed the scholarly sociological treatment of the Afro-American business experience.

Let us begin with Portes' and Bach's treatment of middleman minorities, more specifically the Jewish and Japanese experiences. When we see how the literature on ethnic enterprise treats community development and then juxtapose that to the treatment of Afro-American community formation, the non-comparative approach is fully revealed as inadequate. It was pointed out previously, that one reason why middleman groups adjusted differently was because their neighborhoods were not only residential but also economic in character. As noted in chapter 1, these communities were called *economic enclaves*: a segment of the group engaged in enterprise. These entrepreneurs were also able to hire some members of the community. In the tradition of middleman groups and because of hostility, Jewish and Japanese business people, nevertheless, utilized the resources of the community. For those who wanted to engage in business enterprise, cheap labor and creative types of financing—such as the rotating credit system—were used to enhance business profits. Portes and Bach pointed out that this type of community cooperation represents a positive mode of adaptation to American society.[40]

Contrast this analysis with that of Allan H. Spear's treatment of the reaction of Afro-American leaders and businessmen to hostilities experienced by blacks in Chicago. Unable to place the Afro-American experience in a broad historical perspective, Spear gives an analysis which is typical of this group's treatment by academic scholars.

> The rise of the new middle-class leadership was closely interrelated with the development of Chicago's black ghetto. White hostility and population growth combined to create the physical ghetto on the South Side. The response of Negro leadership, on the other hand, created the institutional ghetto. Between 1900 and 1915, Chicago's Negro leaders built a complex of community organizations, institutions, and enterprises that made the South Side not simply an area of Negro concentration but a city within a city. Chicago's tightening color bar encouraged the development of a new economic and political leadership with its primary loyalty to a segregated Negro community. By meeting discrimination with self-help rather than militant protest, this leadership converted the dream of an integrated city into the vision of a "black metropolis."[41]

Spear was unable to give credit to Afro-Americans in Chicago who turned to enterprise in order to develop economic stability. Thus, he failed to understand that, throughout world history, hostility has served as a driving force encouraging economic solidarity among oppressed groups. Thus, Afro-American leadership's reaction to hostility in Chicago between 1900 and 1915 accorded with what Weber's proposition predicted and parallels the experiences of other oppressed groups.

Spear's analysis presupposes that militant protest would have created a better world than the self-help activities within the black community. Indeed, this militant protest is seen as leading to an integrated Chicago.

While there is nothing wrong with the process of integration, historical data show that oppressed groups create solidarity in order to turn hostility into a positive force. Thus, a normal reaction by Afro-Americans is analyzed as the causes of the creation of the ghetto. Of course, this author does not give a blueprint for what an integrated Chicago would have looked like at the turn of the century— a difficult task then and now—since it remains as one of the most segregated cities in America today. But instead of seeing the creative efforts of black leadership in the economic area as positive, Spear turned it into a negative.

The limitations of the application of a noncomparative method are also revealed when one examines the literature on the capitalization of Afro-American enterprise. Because of the small amounts of money needed for capitalization, these enterprises have been written off by scholars as insignificant. Let us again compare and contrast two treatments of ethnic middleman enterprises and Afro-American enterprises. The first type is exemplified in research on Japanese-Americans and the second is by way of a comment of Afro-American business. Bonacich and Modell noted that:

> The most common Japanese businesses as of 1909 were lodgings . . . and restaurants, with about 300 concerns of each kind in California. Their average capitalization was $680 and $585, respectively; their work force was made up of 1.36 and 1.7 owners or partners and 0.38 and 0.73 employees, on the average. Running a boarding-house meant little more than renting a large house, and most restaurants involved mainly an outlay for rent. Even laundries, a long-standing type of business that served non-Japanese customers and employed on the average 7.5 workers . . . had an average net capitalization of only $1,652.[42]

These authors show that, in addition to employees, Japanese businesses utilized unpaid family members as a means of generating economic stability. In the following quotation, it is quite apparent that the researcher, Eugene Foley, is unaware that one of the trademarks of the businesses of groups which are experiencing group hostility is that they draw upon the presence of their own family members as an independent and internal economic resource. Foley showed no appreciation for or understanding of the nature of Afro-American enterprise, especially to the extent that he failed to appreciate the significance of the use of family labor. Consider this comment:

> Nearly all were retail and service trades, and most were single proprietorships. Personal services were the more numerous, hair-dressing

and barbering comprising 24 percent and 11 percent, respectively, of the total number of Negroes in business. Luncheonettes and restaurants comprised 11.5 percent of the total. Many of the businesses would be submarginal if free family labor were not available.[43]

Without a knowledge of middleman theory, the author simply described some of the enterprises which are synonymous with middleman groups across history. It is worth repeating that hostility by the larger society, coupled with the group's desire to excel economically, drives them into these types of enterprises.

One of the hallmarks of middleman groups is the importance of the organizations that they create in order to maintain a sense of community and guidance. Nevertheless, even a casual review of the literature reveals that, in the tradition of Frazier, scholars have mounted an all-out attack on the institutions and organizations developed by Afro-American middlemen. Although other ethnic groups created community and other types of organizations which helped in their adjustment to hostility and discrimination, the ones created by Afro-Americans have been "raked over the coals" in the literature.

In the ethnic literature, class differentiation based on entrepreneurship is seen as a natural consequence of capitalist society. The institutions which the middleman group creates are also seen as a positive force in the development of the middleman community. These statements are also true for the general literature on ethnic groups.

These organizations include benevolent associations, lodges, and other secret societies. Indeed, as has been pointed out in the literature, fraternal groups, lodges, and even vigilance committees have been part of the order of ethnic neighborhoods. At a time when government was seen as a last resort for community help, the ordering of society was considered to be a matter of scrutiny by one's colleagues.[44]

Within ethnic communities, elite social groups developed because they were often excluded from the broader community organizations because of religion or belief. This is especially true of those groups which we consider to be middleman in their adjustment to a community. Examine the following analysis from *The Making of an Ethnic Middle Class* in Portland Oregon:

Lodge 416 provided the capstone to the formation of a Jewish elite similar to those coalescing in many other middle-sized American cities at the time. Many of the men who joined Lodge 416 . . . had in the 1880s helped organize the convivial Concordia Club, one of only four social clubs whose membership lists were published in the first Portland "400" Directory in 1891. Concordia Clubs were being formed throughout the United States by Jews of German descent in emulation of exclusive city clubs being formed by gentiles. . . But

Jews never expressed displeasure at such exclusion, because they met
gentile merchants as equals in Masonic lodges. . . . Wealthy Jews
retained sociability for themselves through the Concordia Club and
the B'rith.[45]

This author further shows how stratification was simply part and parcel of
the ethnic community. Such social differentiation is documented throughout
the literature on ethnic enterprises and is always related to the development of
more successful business enterprises.

The treatment of the institutions formed by Afro-Americans is in sharp
contrast to the treatment of others found throughout the ethnic literature. In
Black Bourgeoisie, Frazier criticized every organization created in the history of
the Afro-American experience on the grounds that they were created by the
black middle class to serve its own interests and to structure their world of
make-believe. Of course, the "myth of business enterprise" constituted the
chief element in Frazier's world of make-believe. As Frazier said, "Faith in the
myth of Negro business, which symbolizes the power and status of white
America, has been the main element in the world of make-believe that the
black bourgeoisie has created."[46]

Indeed, Frazier is equally critical of all organizations developed as a result
of self-help and which added a sense of stability to the community. Despite
the tremendous efforts of organizations such as the Masons, who organized
in 1775, and the Odd Fellows, dating from 1843, Frazier displayed a clear
contempt for them. This is true for fraternal organizations, social clubs, religious institutions, and even the efforts of Afro-Americans to educate their
children. Consider the following quotations, the first relating to fraternal
organizations and the second to the relationship between business development and education:

It is in the Greek letter fraternities that the so-called intellectual
members of the black bourgeoisie often gain recognition and
power. . . These Greek letter societies are especially important in
molding the outlook of the black bourgeoisie. In the Negro colleges,
membership in these organizations indicates that the student has
escaped from his working-class background and achieved middle-
class status. In their social activities these societies foster all the
middle-class values, especially conspicuous consumption. Moreover,
they tend to divert the students from a serious interest in education. . . The fraternities represent very often the widest social and
intellectual orientations of the leaders as well as their deepest loyal-
ties. One college professor, what a "great fraternity man," stated that
the three things which he loved most were his God, his wife and his
fraternity. All of the fraternities and sororities attempt to justify their

existence on the grounds that they render service to the Negro masses. . . But the real spirit of these societies is best represented by the Greek letter fraternity which conducts a campaign for "Better and Bigger Negro Business."[47]

And:

Thus it turned out that Negro higher education has become devoted chiefly to the task of educating the black bourgeoisie. The United Negro College Fund, which was started in 1944, provides the small sum of about two million dollars for thirty-two Negro colleges. This is a gesture on the part of white America, expressing its approval of middle-class education for Negroes behind the walls of segregation. . . the present generation of Negro college students (who are not the children but the great-grandchildren of slaves) do not wish to recall the past. As they ride to school in their automobiles, they prefer to think of the money which they will earn as professional and business men. For they have been taught that money will bring them justice and equality in American life, and they propose to get money.[48]

As will be shown later, education within historically black colleges of what Frazier called black middle class youth served more than an economic purpose. The values and skills learned there became the backbone for not only the black community but also for leadership in the Civil Rights Movement and present-day corporate America. Frazier also does a devastating job on the presentation of black role models in the press, especially as it relates to entrepreneurship or any type of relative success.[49] He criticizes this middle class for shielding itself and its children from the harsh economic and social realities of American life, racism, and discrimination. He termed this process the creation of a world of "make-believe."

Although economic stability brought about a differentiation in life-style, Frazier accused them of buying nice homes, overspending on clothes and being extravagant. The same kind of analysis appears in Drake's and Clayton's study of the middle class in Chicago.[50]

As if cultural is biological rather than learned, these authors harp on the idea that Afro-Americans' pattern of behavior was simply mimicking those of the white middle class or even the white upper class. But, if Frazier, Drake, and Clayton had had any sense of comparative history, they would have understood that this pattern of behavior was set by Afro-American entrepreneurs as early as the 1700s in cities such as Philadelphia and Cincinnati, and that their pattern of economic development parallels other oppressed groups in capitalist societies. Indeed, a reading of the middleman literature reveals that they, too, created worlds of make-believe in hostile societies.

Of course, this entire pattern of differentiation along economic lines was occurring in America, since the hallmark of the nation has been the idea of upward mobility. Indeed, in the preface to a later edition of *Black Bourgeoisie*, Frazier noted that:

[A] criticism which deserves attention was that this study did not reveal anything peculiar to Negroes. This was a criticism offered not only by Negroes who are sensitive about being different from other people, but by white people as well. . . Other whites pointed out what is undoubtedly true: that this book deals with behavior which is characteristic of middle-class people—white, black or brown. Some of my Jewish friends, including some young sociologists, went so far as to say that the book was the best account that they had ever read concerning middle-class Jews. Here I might repeat what I stated in the book: The behavior of middle-class Negroes was an American phenomenon.[51]

Again, if Frazier had understood, as Weber did, the importance of the relationship between being excluded from a society, hostility, and business activity, he would have understood that the behavior of what he called "middle-class" Negroes was not an exclusively American phenomenon, but rather one that has been seen for hundreds of years. Indeed, Frazier was not describing a black middle class at all, but rather a group quite similar in its adjustment to America as did other groups which are called "middleman." While middle-class groups usually depend upon the larger host society for upward mobility, middleman groups create their own opportunities. While there is an Afro-American middle-class tradition in America, it is quite different from the truncated Afro-American middleman. This is exactly why we made the earlier distinction between the two groups of Afro-Americans who possess a degree of economic stability today.

Frazier's *Black Bourgeoisie* stands as the starting point for a rejection of the basic institutions and values of Afro-Americans who developed self-help institutions and organizations and managed a degree of economic stability. Even today, to be called a black *bourgeois*, or "Bourge," in the Afro-American culture are negative connotations. In an interesting kind of way, despite the struggle of Afro-Americans, economic success is suspect within the black community. Despite the excellent quality of the sociology of Frazier, his work on the black middle class lacked a comparative theoretical guide which would have allowed him to make sense of what was happening as Afro-Americans developed within an oppressive society.

In order to make the present thesis clearer, let us briefly reconstruct the Afro-American experience and give consideration to the concept of the Afro-American middleman. As always, we want to be comparative, especially in terms of traditional middleman theory and the difference between the Afro-American middlemen and middle-class blacks today. Keep in the mind that the difference between the two groups lies in the adjustment of their predecessors to America.

In the late 1700s, there were free Afro-Americans in Philadelphia who developed small businesses in order to survive economically. Although they also developed large-scale enterprises, the majority of their businesses were small and served white clients. Obviously these individuals were neither sojourners or birds of passage. Unlike many others, they did not come to America voluntarily from other parts of the world in order to engage in business activity.

Nevertheless, in accord with the specifications of Bonacich's middleman theory, they were not slaves but free people. They could be found in Philadelphia and in other cities throughout the country, actively engaging in enterprise. Cincinnati was a major city for this type of activity. Free blacks in the South showed a keen interest in business activities. Even slaves engaged in entrepreneurship to some degree, but they obviously did not have the same type of independence as did the free blacks. During the period before the Civil War, these free entrepreneurs faced systematic hostility from the larger society. Thus, in the Weberian theoretical tradition, they found economic rewards in this kind of environment.

After the Civil War, hostile race relations developed in the South. In order to survive economically, Afro-Americans developed institutions of business enterprise. Although Booker T. Washington was soft on civil rights, he stressed an economic program which concentrated on business enterprise. Between the 1890s and the Great Depression, Afro-Americans engaged in a tremendous amount of business activity. As did middleman groups, they placed a great deal of emphasis on the education of their children. This was true even before Frazier criticized their most recent efforts.

We find that, in 1869 entrepreneurial or thrifty blacks considered it a stigma to send their children to the "free schools" that had been established for them. They felt that, if they took advantage of these schools, the number of seats for poor children who were less fortunate than they were would decrease. Instead, they sent their children to private institutions managed by friendly white teachers or by black teachers.

In this same year of 1869, recently emancipated freedmen raised more than $200,000 for the construction of a schoolhouse and support of teachers.[52] As noted in chapter 2, although philanthropists helped to develop educational institutions, private schools were established by blacks in a systematic way. Middleman theory specifies that education is important to the group because it cannot be taken away despite the hostility of the society in which they find themselves.

Thus, the Jews in Germany and the Japanese in California built schools in order to educate their children. Similarly, education became one of the most important experiences for the Afro-Americans who developed in ways similar to other middleman groups. Returning to our earlier comparison, we noted how this concern with education developed as a "middle-class" phenomenon among Afro-Americans. In both the North and the South, we find that, in the face of hostility, what Frazier calls the Black Bourgeoisie began a tradition of higher education.

Middleman theory posits that certain stereotypes develop about middleman groups. They are considered to be clannish, pushy, and anxious to enter a social order in which they are not welcome. They are also considered to be disloyal to the country in which they live and to possess a split loyalty between their original homeland and the nation to which they have migrated.[53]

Although the split loyalty concept does not fit Afro-American entrepreneurs, it is obvious that the bulk of what Frazier said about his subjects does fit.

He noted that they were excluded from interaction with the white middle class despite their desire for open relations. In fact, a reading of Frazier's comments square with the readings of some, if not most, of the stereotypes of middleman groups. For like these groups, his black bourgeoisie developed their own institutions and ways of doing things.

As did the Japanese and the Jews, they protected their children from the hostility that surrounded them by giving them a future in the best jobs of the segregated economy and by developing entrepreneurial skills which kept them from falling to the bottom of the economic ladder. Bonacich and Modell calls this the importance of ethnic solidarity for ethnic groups.

Despite the lack of opportunities in the larger society, they developed opportunities within their own communities. Thus, in the early 1930s, the second generation of Japanese-Americans, or Nisei, were refused opportunities in the larger society by the developing corporate sector because of racism and discrimination. This is indicated by the fact that placement officials at Stanford University during that time period stated, "It is almost impossible to place a Chinese or Japanese of either the first or second generation in any kind of position, engineering, manufacturing or business. Many firms have general regulations against employing them; others object to them on the ground that the other men employed by the firms do not care to work with them."[54]

Bonacich and Modell show that the educated Nisei were forced back into the ethnic economy and into the small firms of their mothers and fathers in order to maintain economic stability. In some cases, frustration developed among the second generation Japanese to the point that they questioned the need to attend college, and instead accepted the path to the economic stability of their parents.

Bonacich and Modell noted that, for example, in 1926 a Japanese teenager became self-employed with a small business rather than go to college and continue his education. His attitude was:

> What's the use of going to college? I have a little fruit-stand, and I give the American customers the kind of service they want. I have a comfortable income. I am happy. But you go on to college and get a lot of theories that make you dissatisfied with the conditions of the Japanese here. You want to change things. But just the same, after graduation . . . fellows come around to my fruit store begging for a job.[55]

Thus, while Bonacich and Modell see the importance of an alternative opportunity structure for an ethnic group faced with hostility in the larger society, Frazier refers to the efforts of Afro-Americans to do the same thing as the creation of "a world of make-believe."

How other middleman groups in America really differ from the experience of Afro-Americans is in the speed with which their children were provided opportunities in the larger society. For instance, despite the anti-Japanese sentiment in California before World War II and the relocation camp experience, postwar attitudes in California toward the Japanese were less racist. As a result, the Japanese community became increasingly integrated into the larger society. They were able to work in corporate America, especially in professional areas, which was a reflection of the education that they received and valued over the years. The change in attitudes by members of the larger society had to do with the defeat of the Japanese in World War II, guilt feelings about the parallel between Hitler's treatment of the Jews in Germany and the treatment of the Japanese in America, and the less threatening economic position of the Japanese because their economic hold on agriculture in California had been destroyed by the war.[56]

For children of Afro-Americans who struggled to educate their children, generations and generations were excluded from taking advantage of opportunities in the larger society. Indeed, it took a massive Civil Rights Movement so that Afro-Americans could simply drink from unsegregated water fountains and use public bathrooms. Thus, although the education of their children began as early as the late 1700s, it was not until the late 1900s that they began to go into the integrated workplace.

To reiterate an earlier point, however, the group developed a value in education because it could not be taken away from them. Life chances were also better in the segregated marketplace. Thus, the content of their values were the same as middleman groups, but, because of discrimination and racism, the manifestation of their values took a different form.

III

Let us now return to Afro-Americans who did not follow the middleman model in terms of adjustment to America. As noted earlier, the great majority of individuals who were not connected to one race economy migrated and looked for work in the hostile larger society. Thus, they adjusted to America—or tried to adjust to America—in the model of most immigrant groups. It is important to point out that we are not evaluating the "rightness" or "wrongness" of the two modes of adaptation to America. Nevertheless, they represent two different types of adaptations to the country and have produced different values which were passed down through generations.

After the Civil War, both Afro-Americans and white Euro-Americans began to move to urban areas in the North and South. However, it wasn't until World War I that the "Great Migration" of the former to the North began.

This migration began in 1915 and reached its peak between 1916 and 1917. It has been estimated that up to 400,000 blacks migrated in the time frame of just three years. In addition to a lack of opportunities in the South, the migration was fueled by racism in the South.[57]

With World War II, another great period of migration began. Between 1940 and 1950, the number of nonwhites in 168 statistical metropolitan areas increased from 5.72 to 8.25 million. In major industrial cities, the racial composition began to change.

For example, Chicago gained more than 200,000 nonwhites during this period and lost 3,000 whites. Cleveland, Ohio, had an increase of about 65,000 nonwhites and lost 28,000 whites. The nonwhite population of St. Louis increased by 45,000 and the white population decreased by 4,000. In Newark, New Jersey, nonwhites increased by 29,000 and whites decreased by 20,000. The same patterns were found in Pittsburgh, Buffalo, Jersey City, Youngstown, and Trenton.[58] And, more than 95 percent of these nonwhites were blacks. Gradually, American cities became systematically segregated on the basis of color, and, interestingly, the scholarly literature mirrored this phenomenon as it shifted from migration issues to those having to do with the development of the ghetto.[59]

As did their European counterparts, blacks migrated to northern cities in search of what Stanley Lieberson calls "A Piece of the Pie." Lieberson's work on black and white immigrants since the 1880s show the similarities and differences between these two groups.

Although both Afro-Americans and European ethnic groups faced similar situations, issues such as the lack of universal suffrage and racial visibility prevented or hampered the former group's ability to achieve at rates similar to those of the new European groups.[60] Although Lieberson is quite aware of the differences between Afro-Americans and Euro-Americans, the total Afro-

American experience is placed in the model of the Euro-American experience, with the quest for economic stability beginning for blacks when they migrated to northern cities.

While this approach is interesting, it fails to take into consideration the tradition of self-help and the establishment of economic security by blacks through entrepreneurship in both the North and South. But more importantly, while blacks who migrated to the North received better jobs and pay, they never developed the institutions and attitudes toward life as did blacks who remained in the South and developed economic security within the segregated marketplace under the economic detour.

Of course, the development of this attitude toward life—which is similar to middleman groups—was not restricted to the South, but was forced to flourish there more abundantly. Cities such as Philadelphia and New York City have a history of black economically stable self-help groups which developed those ideas. But more to the point, Afro-American migration to the central cities represented an adaptation similar to nonmiddleman ethnic groups.

This adaptation is very different from the adaptation of the Afro-American middleman. Because of racism and discrimination in the larger society, the rewards and benefits received by white ethnic groups were not enjoyed by blacks. There were no indications of assimilation for Afro-Americans.

This point is developed by Karl and Alma Taeuber, who asked the question "Is the Negro an immigrant group?" They noted that, historically, the economic status of European immigrant groups was related to decreasing residential segregation. Writing in 1963, they argued that many of the first generation black immigrants to northern cities had been present for at least twenty years. Thus, enough time had elapsed to make adjustments to urban life. But the systematic presence of segregation and poor educational preparation caused segregation of blacks to continue at a rapid rate. This trend was in marked contrast to the fact that other ethnic colonies were rapidly disappearing. This was true even for the racially different Japanese who were located in northern cities.[61]

Despite research findings from the work by Taeuber and Taeuber, the idea that Afro-Americans simply represented an example of the European ethnic experience became the prime model for the study of the group. Put another way, the model was that Afro-Americans, as with other groups, really began to enter into American society when they moved to northern cities. Like their ethnic counterparts, they were expected to begin a tradition of education, acquire excellent occupations, and move away from the central cities. As already noted by Taeuber and Taeuber, the question as to whether or not the central cities would be a way station or a permanent home became a legitimate question.

As other ethnic groups moved up economically in America, research began to document the living conditions of Afro-Americans in the cities. As conditions worsened, Afro-American families living in cities were placed under a critical and all-encompassing microscope by the popular media and scholars. They have been conceptualized as the very poor ghetto blacks, the underclass, or inner cities. The social disorganization of this family structure received national attention with the publication of the Moynihan Report.[62] Senator Moynihan's findings stirred a national debate which further centered research on the Afro-American family.[63]

As some scholars wrote about the deterioration of black family structure and problems associated with it,[64] others examined the strengths of black families.[65] This research is some of the most divided in the discipline of sociology and is worth examining because of the relationship between adjustment to racism and discrimination in America and family structure among Afro-Americans.

In a major review of the literature on Afro-American families, Walter R. Allen divided the literature along three dimensions. The first dimension stresses the Afro-American family as culturally deviant. In this sense, the family structure is viewed as abnormal. The second dimension stressed the similarities of the Afro-American family to the white family—usually without regard to ethnicity—which he calls the culturally equivalent perspective. The final category is the cultural variant dimension, which examines the differences between black and white families but does not view the former as deviant.[66]

In yet another major effort to understand the nature of research on the Afro-American Family, Robert Staples suggests five periods for research on the family. They are: (1) the Poverty and Acculturation Period (before 1950); (2) the Pathology Period (1950–1960); (3) the Apology Period (the late 1960s); (4) the Black Nationalist Period (middle 1960s to early 1970s); and (5) Proactive Revisionism Period (late 1970s).[67] Not since the now classic works of W. E. B. Du Bois and E. F. Frazier had so much attention been given to this area of research.[68]

More recently, the work of William Julius Wilson concentrates on the problem of the "truly disadvantaged." He argues that since the mid-1960s, the condition of poor urban blacks has deteriorated. There are out-of-wedlock births, welfare dependency, high crime rates, and large numbers of female-headed households. Wilson noted that the exodus of the middle- and working-class families from many ghetto neighborhoods takes away role models in terms of work and general accomplishments. They served as a "social buffer" that could "deflect the full impact of the kind of the prolonged and increasing joblessness that plagued inner-city neighborhoods in the 1970s and 1980s."[69]

This family literature has neglected the relationship between adjustment to America through self-help and family structure. As in other literature, it has treated the Afro-American experience as being in the total tradition of an immigrant group, full of social problems as it struggled with racism and discrimination and as its members tried desperately to make a living in a hostile society. As noted earlier, when Afro-Americans who had established a degree of economic stability were considered, the literature, because of the absence of a theoretical framework, did not know what to do with them.

IV

The distinction between Afro-Americans themselves which is based on adjustment to hostility in America leads us to an interesting question: Are there any differences between how descendants of the truncated Afro-American middleman and descendants of Afro-Americans who adjusted to America in the tradition of ethnic groups deal with their racial status today? Put differently, do the children, grandchildren, and great-grandchildren of today face racial problems differently because of the adjustment of America of their predecessors? Based on ongoing research and some published work, we must answer these types of questions in the affirmative. In this effort, we argue that knowing the historical adjustment of parents of present-day Afro-Americans helps us to significantly predict how they deal with living in America as a member of a minority group which has had to battle for inclusion into the society.[70]

As can be seen from earlier discussions, in addition to the importance of business enterprise for middleman groups, they also develop an outlook on life based on their experiences. In some instances, the business enterprise is passed down to the next generation. In other instances, it is not. What is passed down, however, is a philosophy of life in a hostile society.

This is also true of the truncated Afro-American middleman. If Frazier thought that their parents and grandparents were a "total mess" as they built institutions and their "world of make-believe," he should see their offspring. In the turmoil of social changes which accompanied the Civil Rights Movement years, their offspring have adjusted, rather than changed, their approach to American life. The lessons, values, and attitudes toward America which sustained their foreparents still influence their actions in America today.

What are the lessons and values passed on from former generations? They are interesting, and weigh on descendants of the Afro-American middleman group like a historical boulder. These lessons and values are a challenge and burden which constantly remind them of their success or failure in American society. The questions are always, "Will I be the generation to fail to adjust to the hostility?" "Will I fail to pass on to my children the lessons of the past?" Specifically, what are the lessons or values which guide the offspring of the truncated Afro-American middleman and color their outlooks on life as they operate in society?

Perhaps the most important value is that, despite the presence of racism and discrimination, economic security is possible in America. Because whites will be given advantages purely because they are white, education is very important if the individual is to compete in the larger society.[71] As was noted in our specification of this group's characteristics, this factor is perhaps of the most important value. Remember that this value emerged in the segregated economy among Afro-Americans who did not necessarily have education themselves.

Another value passed down from the truncated Afro-American middleman group to descendants is a respect for Afro-American institutions. Although others—Afro-Americans who are not descendants of the truncated middleman and whites—may question the importance of Afro-American institutions, descendants of the truncated Afro-American middlemen maintain a praise for such institutions. These institutions and organizations are mainly those which Frazier critized so thoroughly in *Black Bourgeoisie* and include educational, religious, fraternal, and other community-based organizations. It must be remembered that these institutions represent their historical nurturing and served as launching pads for their participation today in American society. Because of the historical importance of education among the truncated middleman, let us look at how they view historical Afro-American educational institutions.

Among the descendants of the truncated Afro-American middleman, there is a great appreciation for historically black educational institutions. There is a general feeling that these schools prepare them well for participation in society.[72] Their aspirations are high and professors at those schools fuel those aspirations and expect great things. They recognize that all institutions of higher education were not created equal. But they also recognize that, simply because a school is attended and operated by whites, it is not automatically superior, and that there were historically "good" and "bad" one-race schools—whether they were all-white or all-black—in the old segregated South.

These themes are constantly present in my ongoing research, and I maintain that they are representative of the middleman tradition of adjustment to America which can be distinguished from other patterns of adjustment to the country.

The middleman effect on these issues is supported in a recent work by Daniel C. Thompson entitled *A Black Elite*.[73] Although Thompson placed a more conventional class analysis on his work, his sample fits almost perfectly the conceptualization of the truncated Afro-American middleman.

The median age of his sample is forty-three, which means that the great majority of them went to public school during the late 1940s and 1950s during the heyday of segregation. A total of 81 percent of the sample was southern in origin, and 8 percent of their fathers had college degrees as compared with 12 percent of their mothers. Seven percent of their fathers had graduate or professional degrees, and 6 percent of their mothers had obtained these high degrees. Most, however, were sent to college by parents who worked hard in the old segregated South and had an intense desire to send their children to college.

The individuals in Thompson's sample also have the same attitude toward the importance of education. Most of their children represent the second generation of their family which attended college. But some—because their parents completed college and some of them held advanced degrees—are sending the third generation of children to college. It is almost as if Professor Thompson had in mind the idea of a truncated Afro-American middleman when the sample was taken.[74] Indeed, when this theoretical idea is applied to his work, his findings which, at first, appeared to be anomalies are easily explained.

Thompson found that occupational aspirations and achievements of his sample were in sharp contradiction to those studies which had looked at ethnic groups in America. For example, in an extensive study, Thompson concluded that very few children of working-class parents ever rose very far up the occupational and social scale, even when there was rapid industrial expansion in the United States.[75] To Thompson, his findings appeared to be a collection of interesting anomalies.

> . . . The parents of approximately 80 percent of our respondents a generation ago were much too poor and too academically limited to be expected to encourage their children to place high value on formal education and sufficiently motivate them to make almost any sacrifice to do well in school. Certainly they would not be expected to prepare their children to go on to graduate or professional schools and finally to compete successfully for some high-status occupation with challenging career opportunities. Yet . . . this is precisely the academic and career scenario characteristic of the graduates of UNCF colleges.[76]

This is a classic example of what is expected of middleman groups in the history of the world. It is the reason why children of traditional middleman groups—such as Jews and Japanese in the United States, and more recently the Vietnamese—excel in the academic and professional world. It would be difficult to trace this type of pattern among both ethnic groups and Afro-Americans who adjusted to America in what I have referred to as the traditional ethnic group pattern of adaptation. When seen from a middleman theoretical perspective, the conclusions of Thompson are not as hard to find as he thinks—especially the findings that this group does just as well as whites who are from affluent backgrounds.

> The central, most significant finding of this study is quite clear: the socioeconomic status achieved by the college-educated blacks in our

sample, on the whole, is far beyond the level that may have been rationally expected of them. The fact is, the considerable academic and occupational success attained by the representative respondents in our sample is a diametrical contradiction to the basic findings of sound social research that children are not likely to move far from the academic or occupational level of their parents. Nevertheless, not only have most of the black college graduates in this study moved fairly beyond their parents, but . . . their overall success is indeed comparable to that of their white peers from much more affluent socioeconomic backgrounds.[77]

This middleman effect is really apparent when studies concentrate on Afro-Americans who had been economically secure for more than three generations. Because of the academic and occupational achievements of members of families in early years, present-day offspring find it difficult to move beyond their grandmothers or grandfathers. The early generations were grounded in self-help in the old segregated economy. Consider the following quotation which addresses mobility within the Afro-American group. As you read it, think about the conceptualization of the Afro-American middleman presented in this work. Substitute "middleman" for "middle class."

An interesting finding for this small group was that the subjects who had been born into families which had been middle class for at least two generations had the lowest percentage (42) of advanced professional degrees of all the mobility groups. The parent generation had the same level of achievement as the subjects (father, 42 percent; mother, 25 percent). They had maintained their accomplishments but had not moved beyond their parents. However, grandfathers on both sides were very well-educated, even by today's standards, *with 60 percent of the paternal grandfathers and 20 percent of the maternal grandfathers having college and advanced degrees.* [Emphasis added.][78]

Although it is plausible to note that children of the Afro-Americans in the middleman tradition attend historically "white" universities, it is also plausible to expect that their children will continue to attend historically Afro-American institutions. Indeed, based on the work of Thompson, graduates of traditional Afro-American colleges and universities (from about one half to three-fourths) are convinced that the institutions from which they graduated at one time served the best purposes for them and would be the best choice for their children. He found that 69 percent of the males who graduated from United Negro College Fund institutions would return there for their undergraduate degrees, if they had to go to college again. Among females the percentage was 65 percent. Sixteen percent of the males were uncertain that they would return, and 20 percent of the females were uncertain. Fifteen percent of both males and females would not return to their alma mater.[79]

These data show the respect that Thompson's sample had for their experiences at Afro-American colleges. Even when Thompson's sample did not want their children to return to their alma maters, 39 percent would choose another United Negro College Fund college, 16 percent would choose some public black college, and the remaining 46 percent would choose among a variety of colleges ranging from local community colleges (7 percent) to Ivy League colleges (46 percent).[80]

From this data, it is obvious that Thompson's respondents were sending—or would send—their children to some type of education beyond high school. Thompson's research confirms a point which we have stressed in this chapter: the values of the old segregated economy are passed from generation to generation with a high respect for the college experience.

> Another consideration is that college-educated black parents are, without doubt, among the most ambitious parents in regards to the academic and occupational success of their children. This fact is reflected in many statements made by our respondents, whose parents made great sacrifices to send them to school. Like their ancestors, they seem willing to make almost any sacrifice to see that their own children receive the very best education available to them.[81]

Available data show that traditional Afro-American schools continue to play a significant role in the lives of Afro-Americans. Recent studies show, for example, that Afro-American students attending traditional black colleges and universities were more likely to have fathers who had attained a baccalaureate degree or higher than the fathers of Afro-American students who are now attending traditional white schools.[82] Also, the leading sources of Afro-Americans who received Ph.D.s in 1984 were all traditional Afro-American schools: Howard University, Morgan State College, Tennessee State University, and Hampton University.[83]

When we select a major as an example, the first four top granters of bachelor degrees in engineering to Afro-Americans were black schools. Based on the research of Thompson, one would expect that these students in years to come will make important contributions to their professions, live decent lives in America, and be very dogmatic about the continued education of their children.

Findings such as these contradict research reports which say that if blacks go to black schools they will not be successful.

Within sociological research, education is one of the major predictors of success. There are so many essays which begin with the importance of a college degree in order to attain success in America that we need not review them.[84] This, of course, has been picked up by the popular media and has melded into our culture.

But a quick glance of the statistics shows that, while only 11 percent of Afro-Americans completed college as late as 1986, only 19 percent of whites completed four years of college. Given our discussion of middleman minorities and education, it is plausible to predict that groups defined as *middleman* in America would show the highest propensity to complete college.

Likewise, it is logical to suggest that, if we examine closely the percentage of blacks who come from the Afro-American middleman group, they would account for the greatest majority of blacks who completed four years of college. Indeed, throughout the literature on race and education, the effect of what we call the Afro-American middleman can be seen. Some of the literature can be viewed as reflecting the idea that Afro-Americans in this lineage have a better attendance college record than do whites in general. As noted earlier, these many findings are generally placed in a class analysis. Consider the following analysis:

> Here it can be seen that the previous finding . . . of a higher education of whites in postsecondary institutions does not hold when blacks and whites are compared within family status and test performance categories. Instead, when controlling for these background variables, a higher percentage of blacks enter college than whites. . . Among students who are high on [status and test performance], racial differences in college enrollment are far less significant. Sixty-four percent of the high family-status, high test-performing blacks attend college versus 54 percent of the whites in these categories. However, 17 percent of the low family-status, low-achieving blacks attend college versus only 6 percent of the whites of comparable status. . . Among low family-status, high-achieving students, the black-white percentages are 44 and 25 respectively.[85]

The tradition of the importance of education which can be traced back through generations continues for truncated Afro-American middleman.

Thus, among whites and blacks, it is plausible that the middleman experience is an accurate predictor of college completion. Based on ongoing research, one can predict that as high as 95 percent of Afro-Americans who are in the tradition of the middleman group and are between the ages of 18 and 22 are in college.[86] More importantly, they would have gone to college even if civil rights laws had not changed the structure of racial participation in colleges and universities.

If these institutions had remained segregated, their children would have continued to populate, in increasing numbers, traditional Afro-American colleges and universities. If there were no college scholarships or other types of aid, their children would have been in college. Without Affirmative Action and college recruitment programs, their children would still complete college.

While these programs broaden the base of possible choices, they had no direct impact on the educational aspirations of their children. This was set historically by their ancestors. If segregation still existed in the South, they would work in that restricted job market. Indeed, one of the major differences between the children of today and their professional parents is not what they *do*, but rather *where they do it*.

In some cases, their professional service hasn't changed that much. Thus, physicians of today whose fathers were physicians, still serve the Afro-American community although they may also have a racially mixed clientele. The same is true for dentists. Professors of today whose parents were professors at Afro-American schools may or may not be employed in traditional black universities. In most cases, the quality of lives—housing, health care, friends, and the like—hasn't changed between generations. Especially for the professionals, the children of today have a difficult time matching the type of house in which they grew up and the things to which they were accustomed during their childhood.

For groups in America who have experienced hostility, education becomes very important. Statistics already cited show that almost 81 percent of whites do not finish college but obviously are able to make their economic way in America.

We really do not know much about it, and it appears that scholars are uninterested in examining the type of schools which non—Afro-Americans attend. Most of the racial and ethnic literature reads as if there was no variability in the performance of traditional white schools. The literature assumes that all whites had the "Harvard and Northwestern" experience in college. But there were thousands of small colleges created by ethnic and religious European groups in America that produced graduates who have entered the work force of America. There is no literature which calls these schools "inferior." But, in an interesting manner, schools within the Afro-American tradition are called "inferior."

This is interesting because, in the South, some traditional Afro-American colleges had faculty members who came from more prestigious schools than did faculty members at traditionally white universities. While southern white schools drew their doctoral faculty from schools of the South—University of Alabama, University of Georgia, Louisiana State University, and the University of Mississippi—traditionally black schools drew their doctoral faculty from northern schools, such as Indiana University, Michigan, Michigan State, Harvard, and the like. Since southern schools were segregated, they had to attend these schools in the North. It is interesting to ask whether the faculty at some traditional black colleges were just as prestigious—or more prestigious—than those at some of the major white colleges of the South. Did Afro-

American faculty publish more scholarly works? Were they more oriented toward research? Indeed, W. E. B. Du Bois, a scholar in the tradition of scholars, at one time served on the faculty of Atlanta University, and it would be difficult to find anyone who published at a higher rate. Tuskegee Institute in Alabama, through George Washington Carver's work with the peanut, was known as a significant research institution in the South long before any of the white southern colleges or universities became known. Carver's research had a very significant impact on the development of industry in the South.

These questions are interesting and should be developed in further research. The major point is that Afro-American educational institutions should not be labeled as *inferior* simply because of their tradition. They should be compared with similar small white colleges on the American scene. The major point is that there is a great respect for traditionally black colleges and universities among the Afro-American middleman.

Another value which has been passed through generations among the Afro-American middleman group is the importance of participating in community organizations. In the tradition of middleman groups, the organizations in which they participate are those which were given birth to during the height of self-help and segregation in America—organizations which Afro-Americans formed in order to help structure their lives in a hostile society. Today, they still include church organizations, sports clubs, veterans groups, women's rights groups, work-related professional associations, and fraternities and sororities.[87] Although Frazier, in *Black Bourgeoisie*, criticized these types of organizations, even a cursory historical analysis reveals that these organizations have had an impact on Afro-American leadership and accomplishments. For example, Martin Luther King, Jr., received his background from church, and he was a member of many fraternal organizations, including Alpha Phi Alpha, a college social fraternity; and Sigma Phi Pi, organized by Du Bois as a way of getting college-educated men together to exchange intellectual ideas. Jesse Jackson is a member of Omega Psi Phi, a college social fraternity, and was also grounded in religious institutions.

Put simply, Afro-Americans in the middleman tradition have nurtured organizations founded by their forefathers. This is in stark contrast, by the way, to the predictions made by Frazier in *Black Bourgeoisie*, who argued that the black bourgeoisie wanted to be included into the organizations of the white middle class. In fact, as a middleman group, these Afro-Americans would have most likely created their own organizations even if there were no segregation during those years. Even today, it is these organizations which continue to occupy the time of the truncated Afro-American middleman.

In Thompson's *A Black Elite*, which as already noted comes very close to fitting my conceptualization of the truncated Afro-American middleman, he characterized graduates of traditional black colleges as "joiners." Fifty-eight percent belonged to two to four organizations, 16 percent belonged to just one organization, and only 10 percent did not belong to any organization. In terms of religious participation, 69 percent attended church once a week or more, 15 percent attended church about once a month, 14 percent attended church occasionally, and only 7 percent seldom or never attended church. Also, 41 percent of Thompson's black elite were active members of the church.[88]

There is also support in the literature for the idea that there is a strong regional effect for participation in organizations during the post-Civil Rights era, and that being from the South—the region where most of the truncated Afro-American middlemen developed—increases the probability of community participation today. For example, in an analysis of Chicago, a northern city, it was found that members of community organizations—including church and civil rights groups—are more likely to be women from the rural South with at least twelve years of education.[89]

Some also continue as active members of Greek-letter organizations. Thus, in Thompson's analysis, 19 percent were active leaders in alumni chapters of fraternities and sororities, 18 percent were simply active members, 31 percent were inactive members, and only 32 percent of his sample had never been a member of this type of organization.[90]

Frazier noted that these organizations were created, in part, to help Afro-Americans develop "better and bigger" enterprises.[91] Of course, as noted previously, organizations among middleman groups are geared toward business activity. Today, these organizations are carrying on the tradition which Frazier criticized so well. This is indicated by the national networking in which those organizations engage. Of course, all organizations—whether service, religious, professional or social—engage in networking for opportunities. The fraternities and sororities, however, appear to be better organized because of their structure for communication.

At the present time, there are more than 5,000 chapters of Afro-American fraternities and sororities in the United States. This is inclusive of the four major social college fraternities and sororities. Their membership is almost two million and is growing by leaps and bounds. And they are growing today for the same reason that Frazier criticized them—business activity. Students are drawn to a fraternity or sorority by their friendship systems, the help they provide with studies, their feeling of belonging and the possible future business contacts it provides. Of course, this is "old hat" and is being rediscovered today. Old tried wine in new energized bottles. But, today's fraternities and sororities have taken their activities to a high-tech level of networking:

> Like many other professional groups, the black fraternities and sororities have established data on resource banks. For example, Kappa Alpha Psi . . . has stored this information [matching job opportunities to its national membership], as well as names and addresses of all members, in computers, and others plan to follow suit. . . Such com-

munications capabilities must have seemed as remote as space travel to the founder of the black fraternities and sororities. . . Membership often meant having the inside track on better jobs and educational opportunities. Clearly, these college groups were "networking" before the term was even invented.[92]

As noted earlier, these types of organizations, albeit in different forms, emerge among middleman groups during periods of hostility. This is where these groups get their "stick-together" reputations. With Afro-Americans, fraternities and sororities simply became a way of developing certain networking skills in college, in addition to the obvious social arrangements.

Without a doubt, as with all organizations which develop standards for selection, Greek-letter organizations historically had—and will probably always have—a degree of snobbishness associated with them. As noted by Thompson, "while the black church provides the most effective network whereby blacks in all walks of life, representing all socioeconomic classes, may identify, communicate, and cooperate, black Greek-letter organizations proved to be the most effective means whereby black college students and graduates can preserve a common identity and cooperate in the pursuit of common goals. They are essentially middle-class oriented."[93]

Of course, I argue that when placed in the tradition of middleman groups, these kinds of organizations are to be expected. It is this type of "stick-together" attitude which has become so much a part of stereotypes of middleman groups in America.

There is also no doubt that it is the children of what I refer to as the truncated Afro-American middleman who are responsible for the continuation of the sororities and fraternities. It is not uncommon to find that significant numbers of members today are second and third generations of these organizations. Thus, the tradition that Frazier criticized is alive and well, and his "world of make-believe" is just as strong today as it was when he first examined it.

This is to be expected since racial hostility and exclusion remains a part of the American scene. As noted by Frazier, albeit in a critical way, black fraternities and sororities have always had more than a social agenda. This is unlike white sororities and fraternities which tend to demise in influence after their membership has left college. But the significant thing is that the children and grandchildren of black fraternity and sorority members are now populating colleges and universities. They are just as proud to "make these societies" in 1989 as they were in 1920, 1940, and 1960. Mainly because of family background, they represent some of the best students on college campuses. On recently integrated campuses, they represent the reconstruction of the experience of their mothers and fathers who viewed participation in such organizations as a positive force in one's future life.

When first generation Afro-Americans join these organizations, they are introduced to some of the values of the truncated Afro-American middleman. As noted by Thompson, many Afro-American students today come from humble socioeconomic backgrounds, and joining a fraternity or sorority provides them with an opportunity to associate with fellow students from more affluent backgrounds. It also allows them to identify with renowned members, past and present, who also serve as their role models.[94] Also, in terms of things that are social, they are perhaps more interesting than when Frazier wrote about them thirty years ago. Their peculiar traditions and habits have been passed from generation to generation. But people continue to join them for the same reasons that people joined them eighty years ago. This is just one of the many organizations that the truncated Afro-American middleman continues to maintain what was created by predecessors.

In summary, descendants of the truncated Afro-American middleman continue to cherish and keep alive the ideas and institutions which helped to sustain their successors during the years of intensive racial segregation and hostility. It is important to point out that, even with desegregation, descendants of this group are more likely to instill in their offspring a respect for and the need to participate in historically black institutions.

It is also important to understand that descendants of this group do not equate a good quality of life in America with integration, although the latter is certainly accepted as a fact of life. Because of a degree of economic stability, especially in the South, living in excellent housing has never been problematic because of Afro-American suburbia. Role models of family stability, professional occupations, and aspirations do not evolve from white America but from their immediate families. It is also important to understand that this middleman tradition of Afro-Americans must be distinguished from others who adjusted to America in the non-middleman tradition. When this is not done, faulty conclusions are drawn, such as the one which follows:

> Living in a segregated world, the old black middle class pursued a social life behind the closed doors of their homes or of black social clubs—a practice that earned them the nickname "cave dwellers." Frazier also criticized them for their frivolous lifestyle, especially their frequent card games, lavish home entertainment, cotillions, and dances. Drake and Clayton, in their study of blacks in Chicago, documented the accuracy of such charges up to the early sixties. As the new middle class emerged in the late sixties and early seventies, with most of its members rising from the humble origins of working-class families, what happened to the insular and pretentious lifestyle of the [old] black middle class? Did they take advantage of their hard-won access to the recreational facilities of the larger community, or did they, too, remain homebound?[95]

This passage is misinformed because descendants of what Landry calls *the old black middle class*—or what I would call the truncated Afro-American middleman—are "cave dwellers" in the same tradition as their offspring which were criticized by Frazier, and Drake and Clayton. Home entertainment is alive and well, even more so than when Frazier, Drake and Clayton brought their charges. Their cotillions, dances, fraternity parties, and lavish homes still exist and represent showcases of their success. What Landry does not realize is that values do not die, but are passed from generation to generation. We can say, however, that the descendants of the truncated Afro-American middleman have taken their lifestyle underground because of the fear of being called *bourgeoisie*, a negative connotation in the Afro-American culture.

The just cited passage brings us to Afro-Americans who migrated to northern cities and adjusted to America as did other European ethnic groups, albeit with more struggle and problems. They represent, as the above quotation notes, a new middle class which evolved from the late 1960s and early 1970s. Although some of their parents and grandparents established enterprises and engaged in professional services in communities, they never developed the range of enterprises as did their counterparts in the South because of the absence of official segregation in the North. Most of their predecessors worked in the hostile racial environment of industry in the North, and, as noted earlier, struggled very hard for a degree of economic success.

What distinguishes this group is, given their adjustment to America, they were neither socialized nor exposed to the many institutions and organizations which were created by the truncated Afro-American middleman of the South. Because of this, everything they accomplished was in the face of extensive hostility from white America. Unless they went to school in the South,[96] future generations of this group had to attend previously white schools—which traditionally were for upper and middle class whites—in the North and interact with administrators who treated them as foreigners, new to the shores of America. One researcher called them "Guest in a Strange House."[97]

The offspring of Afro-Americans who did not adjust to America in a middleman way did not begin attending colleges and universities in significant numbers until the very late 1960s and early 1970s, thus becoming the first generation in their families to do so. As noted earlier, white high school teachers to whom they were exposed provided them with little encouragement. Earlier in this section we noted the classic example in the literature of Malcolm X, whose teacher informed him that, since he was black, he should not aspire to do certain things. Actually, these types of examples are found throughout the literature on race and education for northern blacks who were beginning to populate central cities. Consider the following example:

> As soon as I entered the classroom Mrs. X told me in front of the
> class that the parents of these children are not professional and

therefore they do not have much background or interest in going to college . . . She discussed each child openly in front of the entire class and myself . . . She spoke about each child in a belittling manner . . . She told me in private that "heredity is what really counts," and since they don't have a high culture in Africa and have not yet built one in New York, they are intellectually inferior from birth.[98]

As noted by Charles Silberman in *Crisis in Black and White*, every school system in the black inner city has teachers who wear gloves so as not to be contaminated by anything. This attitude represents a terrible barrier to learning, since young children tend to fulfill the expectations which their elders hold out for them.[99] This experience was in sharp contrast to Afro-American students who were taught by Afro-American teachers and who are in the tradition of the truncated Afro-American middleman.

It is interesting to note, in passing, that ongoing research on the descendants of the truncated Afro-American middleman considers the influence of white teachers in integrated America on the aspirations of their children as their number one concern. This is a concern because all of their role models, teachers, and generators of aspirations were all Afro-Americans.[100] But Afro-Americans who adjusted to America in the model of European ethnic groups faced this situation early in life.

Their college experience was in stark contrast to Afro-Americans who had been attending traditional Afro-American colleges in the South—an experience that included academics, social life, participation in organizations, and the development of lifetime friends, a process which was started at the turn of the century. As noted earlier, some parents paid to send their children to school as a result of owning small enterprises, and others paid their children's tuition by engaging in menial labor. As for the generation of Afro-Americans who started the process in the late 1960s, they were recruited by schools which, because of social programs, had to engage in minority recruitment. Instead of being welcomed, they sometimes found that they were "guests in a strange house."

I am part of a new and growing group of black students for whom Harvard is a new experience. In fact, until I was a sophomore in high school, I had never heard of Harvard College. When I graduate . . . I will be the first member of my family to receive a college degree. . . I still find it extremely difficult—even impossible—to think of myself as a "Harvard man." Instead, I feel more like a guest in a strange house where my welcome has all but run out. . . Wherever they could be found—in the graduating classes of inner-city high schools or on ghetto street corners—young black kids who had never even heard of the Ivy League were brought to Harvard "to make it" in the white

world. Unquestionably, it was a bold and—in one sense—even
admirable venture; yet it also was blind. For, in essence, Harvard was
bringing black students to a swimming hole and telling them to
swim.[101]

Throughout the country in the late 1960s, northern universities began to
recruit students in significant numbers from inner city ghettos. These were
often students who were the first members of their families to attend college.
Unlike segregated schools of the South, some northern universities always
welcomed a small number of Afro-Americans, mostly those whose parents fit
the truncated Afro-American middleman model. Thus, while there were
always Afro-Americans at Harvard—as late as 1965, there were less than
twenty-four Afro-Americans in the entire college—it wasn't until 1968 that,
for the first time, there were almost 100 black students in Harvard's freshman
class. By 1972, there were about 520 black students in a total undergraduate
population of about 6,000 students.[102] Given their socioeconomic backgrounds, in addition to feeling like "a guest in a strange house," students had
to confront a feeling of guilt because of their educational pursuits.

I remember well the guilt my roommate and I felt as sophomores
living in a plush apartment-like dormitory suite equipped with such
luxuries as a refrigerator, private bath, private bedrooms, and a living
room with a large plate-glass picture window looking out over the
banks of the Charles River. To this day it still seems terribly incon-
sistent that we are actually living better as students in a college dormitory than we have ever lived in our own homes in two of the many
overcrowded, dirty housing projects of Chicago and New York
City.[103]

It must be remembered that the great majority of students, starting in the
late 1960s, brought into college life in large numbers by universities were not
descendants of what I call the truncated Afro-American middleman. Thus, it
has been pointed out that many white universities overlooked black middle-
class youth, and, instead, concentrated on those from inner city ghettos. Thus,
they did not reward these youth who were, for the most part, more likely to
have high academic achievements in high school. Because they overlooked
these youth, these institutions found it more difficult to make black students
successful because they originally chose those who were poorly trained, and
perhaps should not have been admitted to a university.[104] But conclusions such
as this reflect problems that first generation Afro-American students
encounter in college—problems which are different from those whose parents
have attended college. This problem has been addressed in the literature, and
the conclusions give support to the difference between what I call the offspring

of the truncated Afro-American middleman and the offspring of those who struggled in the hostile economy for economic security.

In a major research effort, Will Scott identified four important attributes necessary to negotiate through the college environment. They are: (1) interpersonal skills appropriate for the academic environment; (2) internalization and translation of educational beliefs and values into appropriate behavioral expressions; (3) participation in and development of functional peer and reference groups that are congruent with future personal, academic, and professional expectations; and (4) possession of a clear understanding of one's self as a responsible person.[105] Scott goes on to point out that, for the students who come from economically secure homes, these attributes are developed and learned within the immediate family during adolescent and childhood socializations.[106] After all, these students grow up with college-educated parents who have developed certain expectations. For them, going to college is like the next automatic step from high school, just as from eighth to ninth grade is viewed as automatic. These traits are indicative of the truncated Afro-American middleman group.

On the other hand, a different perspective emerges for the first-generation college student. As noted by Scott, while the already cited attributes are generated in the home for the second and third generation, this is not so for most first-generation black college students. Instead of learning these skills in the home, they are often learned from a relative or a friend. Put differently, role models for college do not come from immediate family members, but rather from someone whom they have touched along the way. Unlike Afro-Americans who adjusted to America in the tradition of middlemen and whose parents sacrificed in order to send their children to college at the turn of the century, Afro-Americans from the central city who were recruited by colleges and universities utilized a host of governmental programs in order to attend college.

In a real sense, their struggle for education was much more difficult than it was for the children of the truncated Afro-American middleman, especially those who started college in the late 1940s and 1950s. Afro-Americans who were recruited from the central cities had to face charges that they were in college simply because of Affirmative Action Programs. They had to face professors in class who had previously tried to keep them out of their universities and colleges. In an interesting manner, in order to make their college experiences enriching, they had to re-create organizations which were present in traditional black colleges and universities. They included sororities, fraternities, social clubs, black unions, and black houses. They even went further and were successful in creating Afro-American studies departments and programs, programs which did not exist in an organized fashion even at traditionally black colleges and universities. But through all the hostility, by the mid-1970s, they were emerging as college graduates and entered the society with an increased sense of pride and security.

It is this group which now constitutes what Landry called *The New Black Middle Class*.[107] This class is described in William Julius Wilson's works, *The Declining Significance of Race* and *The Truly Disadvantaged*.[108] Because they were not historically baptized in the tradition of segregated institutions and the old segregated market, for analytical and predictive purposes they must be distinguished from the truncated Afro-American middleman. For example, because they had little experience with traditional Afro-American institutions and organizations, they are less likely to appreciate and respect them as much as Afro-Americans who have been attending them for years, or whose parents and grandparents attended those schools.

The new black middle class is also less likely to be involved in traditional Afro-American organizations, again because of how they adjusted to America. Earlier, it was noted that Thompson found that graduates who completed college at traditionally black colleges and universities in the 1950s could be classified as "joiners." They were quite active in church, with 69 percent attending at least once a week.[109] They were also active in campus Greek-letter organizations and other community organizations. This finding is in sharp contrast with the data presented in Landry's work on the new black middle class.

> Only 10 percent said they regularly participated in more social recreational activities such as parties, card games, socials, clubs, and visiting friends. Another eight percent placed church activities as their regular . . . outing. Of those who belong to any organization (about one-half), only 14 percent held membership in organizations devoted to socializing, such as fraternal, athletic, or hobby groups. . . The highest number of black middle class joiners belonged to job-related associations, mutual benefit, or service groups. Only ten percent were in church-related groups or political organizations.[110]

It is these types of findings which makes it important to understand the importance of controlling for the historical adjustment of past generations of Afro-Americans to the nation. When this is done, there are important differences between the offspring of Afro-Americans who can be grounded in the middleman tradition and those who adjusted to America in the tradition of ethnic groups. A very important question is the extent to which that group called the "new black middle class" will have the same dogmatic attitude toward the education of their children as those who represent the Afro-American middleman.

Will they send their children to college even in the face of declining federal aid to college students? While there is no doubt that offspring of the

Afro-American middleman have done so for generations and will continue to do so in the future, data are not yet available which would allow us to say the same thing about the new black middle class, although one would expect that they would develop the same type of tradition.

V

Given the massive literature on race relations in America, one must ask why scholars have not taken a comparative approach which includes the significance of business enterprise when the Afro-American experience is discussed. Put differently, why does the literature offer considerable praise to ethnic enterprise in America while, at the same time, dismissing the significance of Afro-American enterprise? The answers to such questions are very complicated, but we must begin to find those answers if we are to continue to reconstruct the sociology of entrepreneurship and the research area of race relations.

It is plausible to say that part of the reason for the noncomparative treatment of Afro-American businesses lies in the integration-versus-assimilation issues which have been so much a part of analyses of Afro-American history. Unlike other groups, which did not have to contend with constitutional efforts to completely exclude them from participating in life in America, Afro-Americans had to expend large amounts of time, money, and talent in order to change constitutional laws which excluded them. Thus, any support of Afro-American business activity was seen by some scholars as supporting segregation. Nestled within the segregation has been the issue of nationalism, which stresses solving the problem of racial inequality without an emphasis on racial integration. Thus, any intellectual support of Afro-American business constitutes to be a threat to the overall goal of integration.

The fact that debates revolving around segregation and integration have colored the treatment of Afro-American business is well-documented in the literature.[111] To even admit that Afro-Americans have a business tradition was congruent with interfering with the process of integration. No one has understood this better than Harold Cruse.

> The integrationists have always said that a separate Negro economy in the United States is a myth. But is it really? The reason that the debate on the black economy has gone on back and forth for years, with no conclusions reached, is because the idea is closely linked with nationalism, and the integrationists would rather be tarred and feathered than suspected of the nationalist taint. This was the great weakness of W. E. B. Du Bois—the only real flaw in the man's intellectual equipment. Du Bois upheld the idea of a separate black economy as "not so easily dismissed" because "in the first place we have already

got a partially separate economy in the United States." He remarked in 1940 that his economic program for Negro advancement "can easily be mistaken for a program of complete racial segregation and even nationalism among Negroes . . . this is a misapprehension."[112]

Other ethnic groups generated business activity in order to become economically secure and looked forward to moving up in the next generation. As has been noted in this work, one of the hallmarks of the sociology of entrepreneurship is that children of entrepreneurs utilized the economic framework of their parents in order to integrate into the larger society. Thus, integration—or participation in American society without regard to ethnicity—is what the American dream has been all about for ethnic America.

Certainly there have always been variations in the degrees of assimilation for ethnic groups. Warner and Srole have analyzed this process for ethnic America.[113] The fact that the children of Afro-American business people had trouble taking this path because of racially motivated discrimination and hostility does not detract from the successful entrepreneurial activities of their parents. There is an abundant literature on this process of ethnic assimilation and adjustment to American life.[114] The topic of integration and assimilation is something to be observed rather than debated, and, indeed the same holds true when one considers the literature on ethnic pluralism.[115]

Despite the above considerations, the massive literature on racial and ethnic assimilation has failed to explain the position of Afro-Americans. This is because it leaves out the entrepreneurial or economic variable, or alternatively stated, the variable of self-help. The assimilationist perspective that has guided a great deal of research on this topic was developed by Milton Gordon.[116] He enumerated and defined several different dimensions of the assimilation process which ultimately led to the ethnic groups' full participation in American society. Cultural assimilation is defined as the change in a group's prior cultural patterns to those of the host or core society. Structural assimilation is when the newcomers finally penetrate cliques and other associations which produce primary types of relationships. Marital assimilation is when ethnicity is not important in mate selection, and attitudinal-receptional assimilation is the agent of prejudice and stereotyping. Behavioral-receptional assimilation is the absence of discrimination, and civil assimilation is the absence of value and power conflict.

Economic assimilation, from a marketplace point of view, should also be added. The reason why some ethnic groups were able to develop a middle class was because of entrepreneurial activities. They were able to sell their goods, not only to members of their own group, but to anyone in the larger society. In this sense, economic stability was achieved because these individuals were able to participate economically in the larger society. This observation does not include the marketplace advantage vis-a-vis the hiring of ethnic groups by developing industrial firms. For this reason, ethnics could find economic stability even when ethnic discrimination was strong. However, with Afro-Americans, this process of economic assimilation was quite different. This group was never able to assimilate from a marketplace point of view. As noted in earlier chapters, this was especially true after the Civil War when Afro-Americans were forced to develop enterprises which served only their communities or to operate in an economic detour. Without economic assimilation, the dimensions of assimilation enumerated by Gordon simply mean that groups are accepted into American society.

Even if one accepts the idea of cultural pluralism along certain dimensions for ethnic groups, one has to say that there was no pluralism when it came to the marketplace. Although ethnic groups found niches in the market in which to engage in enterprise—or they really accommodated themselves to certain areas—they still operated in the same general market. From an entrepreneurial, middleman self-help perspective, Gordon's dimensions of assimilation cannot explain economic stability of ethnic groups. They do, however, have an impact on obtaining a job in the open marketplace because, as has been shown in the literature, the more individuals resemble members of the core host society, the higher the probability of their finding a job.[117]

This explains why some ethnic group members changed their names, dyed their hair, and so on in order to become fully assimilated into American society. As noted by Stanley Lieberson, "The New European groups are physically distinguishable on the aggregate from each other and from the Northwestern Europeans, but there is sufficient overlap and variation that such criteria do not operate very adequately."[118] Unlike these European ethnic groups, Afro-Americans developed a sense of economic stability under an economic detour wherein those members who developed business enterprises simultaneously acquired a sense of economic stability. Despite the fact that Afro-Americans developed economic stability in the most hostile of environments, scholars such as Frazier and others after him, misinterpreted the process because they had no theoretical foundation on which to base a comparison of the experiences of Afro-Americans with those of other groups.

Yet, another example of a misapplied theoretical framework that has resulted in the Afro-American business tradition being viewed as insignificant relates to the application of a Marxist framework to race and economics. As will be seen, this is also connected to the issues of integration and separatism already noted. Indeed, it is interesting to observe how Marxist scholars handle the fact that Afro-Americans do have a business tradition. For example, in *How Capitalism Underdeveloped Black America*, Manning Marable wrote: "In Northern cities, some Blacks own *surprisingly* large amounts of real estate." [Emphasis added.][119]

This type of historical data is always surprising to researchers who apply a Marxist framework to race and economics. For reasons of exposition, let us very briefly review the fundamental premises of Marx.

The work of Karl Marx centers around an analysis of capitalism as an economic system. Capitalism depends on the exploitation of the working class or proletariat by the owners of capital, or the bourgeoisie. The profits of the latter are developed as a result of the difference between the wages of labor and the value of the products produced. The value of a product, or commodity, is determined by the labor time necessary to produce it. Wages, which are paid to workers, are reduced constantly to the level of subsistence by an ever increasing population and held there by the reserve army of the unemployed. This reserve army can always be called upon to undermine the wage-laborers' job security. The capitalist is interested in keeping the wage level down so that the value of the product is reduced. The difference between wage level and the product is surplus value, which the capitalist takes as profit.

Marx's overall theory of society, or historical materialism, concentrates on the influence of economics on all aspects of life. He argues that the technological conditions of the forces of production—that of producing and changing goods—combined with the relations of production—or the system of property ownership—are causal factors which determine the worker-and-owner relationship. These economic forces also determined the nature of cultural and religious institutions at any given time in history.

In the final analysis, Marx argues that the contradiction between the social nature of industry and capitalism, or the continued concentration of private property, will ultimately paralyze and destroy the economic system.

Marx's thesis is grounded in the method of dialectics. In this view, a given situation or thesis generates opposing forces which represent the antithesis. This dynamic breaks up the original situation and produces a new social situation or thesis. Thus, capitalism contained the seeds of its opposite—communism. The working class is seen as the driving revolutionary force that will ultimately triumph over capitalism.[120]

Nestled within the overall theoretical Marxist framework are ideas about equality and cooperation among people, a situation which improves after the destruction of capitalism. Thus, according to Marx, communism is, in reality, the essence of the emergence of humanism. People react to each other, not as the result of their place in the economic system, but as *people*.[121] It is on this level that Marxism has been applied to race relations in America and other countries. In Marxist terms, as long as capitalism exists, racism will always exist. The following quotation summarizes an analysis of the different historical segments of the Afro-American community experience, and concludes by calling for a coalition among all oppressed people:

As we have seen, the basic social division within the Black community, the Black worker majority vs. the Black elite, was an essential by-product of primitive accumulation in slave societies. This class division became more pronounced in the twentieth century, and represented a tendency among many "middle class" Blacks in electoral politics, the church, small business and education to articulate a capitalist road to black liberation. . . I have argued the thesis that Black economic, political and social development is possible only on the basis of a radical break with the capitalist system, which has been the principal agency of underdevelopment. . . What remains to be developed, however, is the formulation of a strategy and tactics implied within the historical evaluation, which will uproot the hegemony of American capitalism. By necessity, such a strategy cannot be limited to Black Americans and their conditions, because the symbiotic processes of institutional racism and capital accumulation affect all America working and poor people.[122]

Marable does not accept the accomplishments of Afro-Americans in business, politics, religion, and education because, historically, they had to be accomplished under racial solidarity. Marxist writers also have trouble grounding their thesis in the different movements which have been generated on the basis of some kind of racial solidarity. For Marxism, the basic social divisions should be class-based, rather than racial.

Despite the contribution of Marx's original work, the application of his theory has become more of a religious dogma, based on what will or should be, rather than on what the data actually reveal to be true. As Irving Louis Horowitz argues, what has happened in sociology is a split between methodologists and ideologists, between those with a neo-Kantian belief in the purity of the research process and those with a neo-Marxian belief in the purity of revolutionary goals apart from empirical considerations.[123]

The empirical evidence, throughout history, is that race has been much more important than class in determining all types of economic outcomes in America. Marxist scholars have never been able to accept this, especially where business development within the Afro-American is concerned. Harold Cruse understood this when he noted that, although the overwhelming majority of blacks have always supported the development of Afro-American business, the Marxist-Communists, both black and white, could never support this idea because they are obsessed with the idea that capitalism will ultimately radicalize the working class and bring about a proletarian revolution. Although Cruse missed the historical significance of middlemen in oppressed situations throughout the world, he came close when he noted that the Afro-American question, contrary to Marxist dogma, is more a question of group or race than one of class.[124]

Of course, this has been true for years, since it is ethnic solidarity which helps to create economic stability, especially among groups which experience hostility from core societies. But Marxist scholars of race and ethnic relations have never been able to see this. Indeed, when Marxism is applied to race relations, its radical ideological tenets are anything but a radical ideology. Rather, Marxism appears to be just another brand of integrationist ideology. As Cruse noted:

> The great dichotomy, the underlying ideological schism that dominates the Negro social outlook in America, is that of integrationism vs. all trends that reflect nationalism, separatism or ethnic group identity. Negro Integrationists become pro-Marxist-Communists, and Negro Marxist-Communists become prointegrationist because, for Negro Integrationists, Marxism lends a radical flavor to integrationism which in itself is not revolutionary in essence. On the other hand, Marxist-Communist becomes prointegrationist because of its essentially opportunistic pro-Negro policies. Pronationalist Negro trends must reject Marxist-Communist, and vice versa, because the latter, being theoretically opposed to independent black political power on internationalist premises, must seek to control nationalist trends by directing them into integrationist channels. This has been historically demonstrated.[125]

Thus, it would be difficult for Marxist scholars to accept any type of racial solidarity in the United States because the underlying philosophy is basically integrationist.[126] As noted again by Cruse, Marxists cannot let go of the idea that the white working class will save the world's humanity. Rooted in their preconceived propositions and their undialectical ideas is the ingrained white nation ideal.

Socialism becomes similar to capitalism—a white nation's conception which is basically the white working-class prerogative. Thus, the white man's burden shifts from the capitalist missionaries to the working class revolutionaries, whose mission is to lift backward peoples into civilization and into a socialist state.

But Marxists—especially the Afro-American Marxists—cannot let go of the idea of a socialist revolution in conjunction with the white working class, even though there is no historical data to even begin to support such an idea.[127] White labor, whether factory or professional, has made it very hard for Afro-Americans to receive a piece of the pie. Despite Karl Marx's most frequently quoted comment among Afro-American scholars that, "Labor cannot emancipate itself in the white skin where in the black it is branded," white labor has shown little concern for Afro-Americans.[128] As a matter of fact, it is quite easy to say that white workers in America identify more with whites in the Soviet Union, South Africa, Poland, and other parts of the world than they do with Afro-Americans.

It must be pointed out that the application of the Marxist framework to race relations is critiqued here as a failure in applied methods rather than as a failure in the ability of Marx's work in general. Far more salient than the content of his work and his predictions—for example, the failure of the social revolution to develop in advanced capitalist nations—the value of his work lies in his dialectical method. Marx developed his ideas during a time period when revolution appeared to be the ultimate conclusion of political and social conflict in Europe. The fact that such conflicts have not developed is a failure in content rather than method. But what is a failure is the application of Marxist method in the twentieth century, especially in terms of race relations.

A fundamental idea of dialectics is that everything is always changing, especially social life. This should also apply to the historical role given to the working class by Marx. It should not be excluded from the process of dialectical change. Thus, if the working class changes from politically radical to politically conservative, then this represents a change which is dialectic. When Marxist scholars fail to recognize this change, and write it off as "false consciousness," then the method becomes mechanistic rather than dialectic.

> But if this dialectical premise is "true," why then is it assumed that everything in society is subject to the processes of change (except the historical role of the working class in advanced capitalist nations)? Why is this white European, North American labor movement itself exempt from dialectical change in terms of class position, ideology, consciousness, etc., and in terms of what other groups or classes this labor movement fights, supports, or compromises with in the "class struggle?" Has it not become abundantly clear that the white labor movement in the advanced capitalist countries has, indeed, abandoned the Marxian historical role assigned to it? And do we not, therefore, have the right to claim that European and American Marxists who still hew to this white working class line are practicing mechanistic materialism rather than dialectical materialism?[129]

The failure of Afro-American Marxists to cling to the content rather than the methods of Marx has led to a distortion in race relations theory. Add to this fact that the great majority of the literature on Marxism does not even consider race effects. European and Euro-American Marxists, as they search for the new working class, are concerned with white workers being the ultimate revolutionary source.[130]

Nevertheless, between the search for the new working class and the liberation of Afro-Americans from capitalism, lies the historical fact of real data. Again, as noted by Cruse:

> White Labor (as differentiated from black labor) went conservative, pro-capitalist and strongly anti-Negro. This creates a serious . . . insoluble dilemma for the Marxist . . . because the theory and practice of revolutionary Marxism in America is based on the assumption that white labor, both organized and unorganized, must be a radical, anticapitalist force in America and must form an alliance with Negroes for the liberation of both labor and the Negro from capitalist exploitation.[131]

Historical data from around the world show that revolutions are based more on ethnic, religious, racial or nationalist solidarity rather than economic solidarity.

Although there are many other issues related to Marxism, race, and economics, the emphasis here is that the attempted application of Marxist theory to race relations is one of the major reasons for the failure of scholars not to come to grips with the reality of the Afro-American experience in relation to entrepreneurship. Actual historical data have been ignored in favor of a fantasy dream world of the future.[132] If we are going to explain the Afro-American experience in America—and indeed make policy recommendations for the future—it is imperative that we consider theoretical frameworks which are able to handle the diversity of that experience. A theory of the truncated Afro-American middleman moves us in this important theoretical direction. In future research, it is important to collect intergenerational data that will allow one to track the development of the self-help entrepreneurial tradition in America. I think that we will find that such data will support the theoretical approach presented in this chapter. More importantly, Marxism and its application has been a failure around the globe. The former Soviet Union is a failed experiment in nation building and economic security.

CONCLUSION

The purpose of this chapter has been to develop the theory of the truncated Afro-American middleman. The major point is that, grounded within the Afro-American tradition, is a group which developed in the form of what is referred to as middleman groups. In addition to business activity, this group of

Afro-Americans developed ideas about life which were passed from generation to generation. As a result, offspring of this group differ in their ideas about adjustment to America from Afro-Americans who are offspring of those who adjusted to America as did other ethnic groups who are not middlemen in origin. In order to fully understand the tradition of Afro-Americans in the middleman tradition, it is necessary to engage in a comparative analysis which utilizes research on other middleman groups in America. In order to fully understand this tradition, it is also necessary to reject theoretical frameworks, such as the Marxist approach to race relations.

8

The Present Status of
Afro-American Business

The Resurrection of Past Solutions

Since the original publication of *Entrepreneurship and Self-Help Among Black Americans*, there have been a number of works that address the issue of putting business enterprise at the center of community. Robert L. Wallace, in *Black Wealth through Black Entrepreneurship*, notes that while the right to vote and other political rewards of the civil rights movement were great, they did little to add to the overall wealth of the community. Wallace asks, "Why, with all the great victories won during the 1960s has the African-American community's economic prosperity, on all fronts, been so delayed? Can Racism be used to justify all of the economic and social problems that still confront this community in such a big way?[1] Wallace then puts a plan together for wealth development and entrepreneurial success, a plan that draws on the strong history of new ventures.

Perhaps the most powerful statement about putting new ventures at the center of community was done by T.M. Pryor in a work entitled *Wealth Building: Lessons of Booker T. Washington For a New Black America*.[2] Pryor argues that Washington's teachings and lessons moved the black community to new heights of economic wealth building in the early years and could have a tremendous impact today. But the "talking heads" of Washington's era, or those who criticized him, did not understand the importance of economics and entrepreneurship. He also notes that "talking heads" today must be separated into those who understand wealth building and future generations from those who do not understand these dynamics. In an interesting twist on the criticism of Washington's speech given at the Atlanta Exposition at the turn of the century, which was reviewed in an earlier chapter of this book, Pryor argues that "White publishers would not publish Washington's Atlanta Speech if it were

295

given today. Why not? It is a blue-print for black upward mobility."³ He notes that the solution of the problems of black America, in a broad sense, can be found in the economic writings of Booker T. Washington, the most significant figure in the history of the race and economics. Other books such as T.M. Alexander's *Beyond the Timberline*, Jonathan Greenberg's *Staking a Claim: Jake Simmons, Jr. and the Making of an African-American Oil Dynasty* and Robert C. Kenzer's *Enterprising Southerners* clearly pointed to the importance of entrepreneurship for black Americans.⁴ Thomas D. Boston, in *Affirmative Action and Black Entrepreneurship*,⁵ compares the strong historical business district of Atlanta, when there were no city contracts presented to that community, with the impact of set aside programs on the development of "new" black enterprises in Atlanta. This goes well with the excellent research of Karen Starks, who examined the contributions of urban entrepreneurs in that same city.⁶ Michael Porter has an initiative on the competitive advantage of the inner city.⁷ There is no doubt that there is more of a consciousness about the importance of entrepreneurship as we move toward a new century. Returning from the wilderness, at least for a large percentage of the black population, took a journey that lasted almost forty years.

I

Between the 1950s and late 1960s, Afro-Americans engaged in what has been simply called "The Civil Rights Movement." It is difficult to place dates around activities of protest, for protest has been so much a part of Afro-American history. But this time period saw the application of a variety of programs designed to deal with the social and economic problems of Afro-Americans. Although these programs differed in methods, they all had basically the same goal: the full participation of the group in American society. The major emphasis was on upward mobility through the accessibility of occupations from which they had been previously excluded.

Standing at the center of the movement was the Southern Christian Leadership Conference. Under the direction of Martin Luther King, Jr., the organization's goal was full "integration" into American society to be achieved through a deliberate program of nonviolent protest. Nonviolent direct protest was aimed very specifically against the presence of discriminatory "white only" signs and other such symbols of racial segregation. It captured the conscience of the nation as protestors were brutalized in the street and sent to jail, and the churches and homes of leaders were bombed. The black power movement, as personified by Stokely Carmichael, also had integration as its main goal, but argued that integration should be delayed until Afro-Americans developed a strong political base. With the Student Non-Violent Coordinating Committee as an organizational base, this movement questioned long-standing assumptions about the need for integration and the goals of the integrationists. The Black Muslims took the economic philosophy of Booker T. Washington and added a religious dimension wherein the teachings of Elijah Mohammed were mixed with the development of independent business enterprises. The Black Panthers saw themselves as defenders of the Afro-American community, substituting self-defense for nonviolence. This was also true of the Deacons for Defense, an organization founded in Southeastern Louisiana. In addition, the NAACP continued its historical role of dealing with issues in the legal arena. In 1964 the Civil Rights Bill was passed, and in 1968 it was followed by passage of the Voting Rights Bill. Within twenty years, many people gave their lives to achieve changes in laws which were designed to simply make America a better place to live. In a real sense, this period of history was the product of ideas that had begun with early thinkers such as Martin Delaney, Frederick Douglass, Marcus Garvey, Booker T. Washington, and Malcolm X.[8] As major legislative programs were put in place, the nation began to look forward to "progress" in race relations.

As changes began to take place in American society, racial issues dominated the social science literature. Changes in the status of Afro-Americans vis-a-vis "whites" (as opposed to ethnicity) were examined on every conceivable dimension, the most attention revolving around education, occupation, income, housing, and racial attitudes. In terms of education, as measured by years of school completed, present research shows that the overall gap between blacks and whites has converged. By 1983, the median number of years completed for whites was 12.6 and for blacks 12.2.[9] Although the differences in degree of educational attainment between the two races have almost converged, this is not true for occupational categories. There is still a very large gap between the occupational distribution of Afro-Americans and whites. For example, in 1982 about three out of ten employed nonwhite men were in white-collar occupations, just as was the case in 1940. Afro-Americans, on the other hand, are still found at the lowest categories of the occupational distribution. In the early 1980s, for example, about one employed nonwhite woman in sixteen worked as a domestic servant. This is compared to about one white woman in fifty; also, one employed nonwhite man in eight was an unskilled laborer compared to about one white man in fifteen.[10] Although this is true, there was some progress in the occupational sphere because the number of Afro-Americans who worked in prestigious occupations increased more quickly than the number of whites. Thus, during the 1970s, the number of nonwhite men who worked as professionals or managers increased by five percent each year. At the same time, the number of white men increased by about two percent. Additionally, during this same decade, the number of men who worked in the most highly paid manual occupations, namely craft workers, increased more rapidly for nonwhites than for whites. The average increase in this occupational category for nonwhites increased by three percent while for whites the average increase was one percent.[11]

In terms of residential housing, research began to show that, although the residential areas of America are highly segregated by race and ethnicity, integration definitely exists on a significant scale. The number of one-race neighborhoods was shown to be, in part, the result of income differentials and the individual preferences of home owners, but primarily a function of political, economic, and social constraints.[12] At the same time, scholars reported a decrease in negative attitudes on the part of whites towards Afro-Americans. For example, the proportion of whites favoring separate schools for the two races dropped from 33 percent to 17 percent between 1958 and 1971. Also, during the same time period significant changes were found in response to the question "Would you be at all disturbed or unhappy if a Negro with the same income and education as you moved into your block?" The proportion responding "NOT" increased from 40 to 68 percent.[13] Overall, survey data showed a significant decline in "race prejudice," especially as related to the legal and social equality of the two groups. Although segregationist attitudes are still prevalent in America, these sentiments have also declined.[14]

Since the 1950s, Afro-American income has remained at about 55 to 60 percent of white income, an indication that Afro-Americans have not made systematic gains in income relative to whites. Their income, as a percent of white family income fluctuated during the 1950s, increased in the late 1960s, and then dropped again in the 1970s. In terms of the dollar gap, by 1980, the median family income for whites was $24,904, while for Afro-American families it was $12,600, or about 58 percent of white income. Between 1970 and 1980 the real income (adjusted for inflation) for black families declined while for white families it increased.

In 1959, the number of Afro-American families below the poverty line was 1.9 million; in 1981 over two million fell below the line.[15] The income of workers, however, shows that in 1959, Afro-American men earned only 61 percent as much per hour as their white counterparts. By 1979 they earned 74 percent as much. When gender is considered, in 1959 black females earned about 61 percent as much per hour as white females. By 1979 they earned 98 percent as much. Thus, for women, the racial income gap almost closed completely.[16] In short, there has been progress in some areas, and no progress in other areas. Areas of progress include educational attainment, employment in better occupations, and earnings of employed workers. Areas showing no progress include family income, poverty, and despite the positive research, residential segregation.[17]

In addition to descriptive comparative work, the sociological literature has shown a major concern with the problem of differential access of Afro-

Americans and whites to positions in the opportunity structure of America. This literature documents racial inequalities in the attainment process while controlling for major factors that should serve to decrease or even negate the differences between blacks and whites on a given dimension. For example, it has been shown that, for both groups, education is the most important factor in determining occupational and income attainment, but the influence of education is about half as large for blacks as for whites.[18] Research has systematically shown that, despite controls, overall racial differences continue to be a staple of the American scene.[19]

In the areas where advancements have been made, it is obvious that this progress is not evenly distributed even within the Afro-American population itself. Put differently, in a country where money distinguishes the life-styles of people, Afro-Americans with money were able to take advantages of "benefits" that developed after the passage of civil rights laws. These Afro-Americans could now live in expensive hotels, buy expensive houses, eat in expensive restaurants, and send their children to previously segregated schools. This is one of the phenomenons that Carmichael and Hamilton objected to in *Black Power: The Politics of Liberation*. In that work they noted that "Integration" as a goal today speaks to the problem of blackness not only in an unrealistic way but also in a despicable way. It is based on complete acceptance of the fact that in order to have a decent house or education, black people must move into white neighborhoods or send their children to a white school. . . It allows the nation to focus on a handful of Southern black children who get into white schools at a great price, and to ignore the ninety-four percent who are left in unimproved all-black schools.[20] Reacting to the "class" split within the Afro-American community, Carmichael and Hamilton also made an assessment of the relationship between economic security and the goals of Afro-Americans:

> The goals of integrationists are middle-class goals, articulated primarily by a small group of Negroes with middle-class aspirations or status. This kind of integration has meant that a few blacks "make it," leaving the black community, sapping it of leadership potential and know-how . . . those token Negroes—absorbed into a white mass-are of no value to the remaining black masses. They become meaningless show-pieces for a conscience—soothed white society.[21]

Carmichael and Hamilton were writing at a time when black secondary and high schools were closing throughout the South. The most experienced black teachers and students who showed the most academic promise were transferred to previously all-white schools.[22] In terms of integrated America, Afro-Americans with economic stability, or credentials in place, were able to take advantage of newly created opportunities.

This theme became more prevalent in the literature as years passed. For "highly qualified" Afro-Americans, there appeared to be a decrease in traditional patterns of discrimination. Both Richard Freeman and Nathan Glazer wrote about this phenomenon.[23] William Julius Wilson went a step further and argued that the significance of race was declining. He argued that class has become more important than race in determining life-chances in the present modern industrial period.[24] Of course, all of these theses, especially the declining significance of race, approached race relations from the "northern ethnic perspective" discussed in the previous chapter. Let us say that in terms of class, the Civil Rights Movement overall brought the truncated Afro-American middleman and the masses of blacks closer together. In the days of segregation, economic lines were well-defined between the truncated middleman and other Afro-Americans. The Civil Rights Movement actually brought them closer, and created a consciousness between them that was not present before the movement. Although the Afro-American truncated middleman has always lived in economic comfort, albeit in a sea of discrimination and racism, there was a large gap in terms of quality of life between that of this group and that of other blacks. Thus, members of the truncated middleman group suffered, but like other middleman groups who had experienced hostility, they suffered in a degree of relative comfort.

As "well-qualified" Afro-Americans began to move into corporate America, mainly due to the expanding economy of the 1970s, their life-styles began to improve. In fact, their quality of life began to resemble that of the traditional truncated Afro-American middleman. As they pushed forward, the research tradition of "reverse discrimination" began to emerge. Before the period of expanded opportunities, Afro-Americans as a group had competed with working class whites. When they began to compete with the white middle class, charges of reverse discrimination rang out across the land. Although most of the research which compared Afro-Americans utilized the variables "black" and "white," ethnicity re-emerged as a major variable in data analysis. The argument was, that if Afro-Americans had bonded together as a group for "special treatment," one must remember that all Americans belong to an ethnic group. Groups that had given up large amounts of cultural baggage (language, customs, names. etc.), tried to recapture the essence of their roots or origins. Much like research on Afro-Americans that employed the terms Negro and Black, whites were broken out into "ethnics" and "whites."[25] Of course, Jewish-Americans always had a special place for their customs and heritage, and were one of the few European ethnic groups that did not give up everything in order to reap the economic benefits of a developing America. This fact also helped to account for the continued persistence of anti-Semitism. During this period, other ethnic groups began to try to relate to their ethnicity in much the same way. As governmental programs were developed to increase Afro-American participation in the larger economy around

company coffee machines and other informal places, one could hear the following: "So he is Black, I'm Scandinavian and Scottish, why should his group
have special treatment?" In an interesting kind of way, the first generation of
some European groups which had denied its ethnic heritage and given up a
great deal in order to be considered white for better opportunities in America, now was denying being simply a "White American" and tried to re-dis-
cover its ethnic roots and to rally around those roots. The new emphasis on
ethnicity (at least in scholarship if not in the everyday affairs of people) was
fueled by the experience of Afro-Americans vis-a-vis the development of
group consciousness.

In a major research effort by Kluegel and Smith, it was found that over 60
percent of whites felt that, compared to the average person in America, the
chance of getting ahead for blacks and other racial minorities is much better
than average.[26] Research began to show some parity along racial lines when
age cohorts were controlled. For example, in 1969 black males earned 77 percent as much as white males when both graduated from high school. In 1977,
for the age category twenty-five to twenty-nine, Afro-American males who
had a high school diploma earned 75 percent as much as their white counterparts. Blacks who finished college earned 93 percent as much as their white
counterparts who finished college.[27] Even if the "highly educated" were "well-
qualified," the complaints about reverse discrimination continued. Affirmative
Action Programs were viewed as an intrusion on the rights and privileges of
White America, especially for men. As noted by Lester Thurow, ". . . any government program to aid economic minorities must hurt economic majorities.
This is the most direct of all of our zero-sum conflicts. If women and minorities have more of the best jobs, white males must have fewer. Here the gains
and losses are precisely one for one." Affirmative Action is thus taking place in
a zero-sum society, according to Thurow.[28] Nathan Glazer called it Affirmative Discrimination against whites.[29]

For those Afro-Americans who did make it to corporate America, previously segregated universities, public office, and other uncharted waters, they
lived, and continue to live, under a cloud of Affirmative Action. No matter
what their level of skill, they perceive that their colleagues view them as an
Affirmative Action case. When they speak with their black colleagues (if
others are around), this is a major area of concern. They are quite aware of the
relationship between their opportunities and the Civil Rights Movement. In a
survey concerned with the Afro-American experience in large business, it was
found that 67 percent of the participants felt that they were hired due to Civil
Rights Legislation. Over 72 percent felt that they would not have had the
same opportunity without this legislation, but over ninety percent felt that
they were qualified for their first position in the corporation. Over 68 percent
felt that if Civil Rights Legislation was rescinded, their opportunities would
not remain the same. Fifty-one percent felt that during their careers they have

been treated differently from other workers, and 86 percent of those who felt that way said it was because of their race.[30]

It is an interesting racial soap opera that is being played in corporate America. Where cooperation should be the watchword, there is often divisiveness. The following quotation is indicative of this situation:

> The racial situation has changed very little. The implementation of Affirmative Action Programs has created bitterness in some situations worse than what was there previously. Most of the Black persons in management positions are overqualified for the positions they hold in comparison with the ability of their White peers. However, the White workers constantly cry out that Blacks are not qualified. I wonder. Where are we headed? Whites have bad attitudes about the programs. Upper management is not really listening to the people to find more effective ways of implementing the programs so that they might be more acceptable and thereby create better employee attitudes toward Affirmative Action. . . There is a lot of work to be done. We all have to *hang in there* and do what we can until we create a situation of harmony that we want so badly. It is sad to see Blacks treated like welfare cases because this society is festering in its self-created diseased bed. . . Whites don't respect us as citizens, but treat us like a sore that won't heal.[31]

Repeatedly, research on Afro-Americans in the corporate world affirms similar sentiments:

> . . . Any promotion of a Black is greeted with the spoken or unspoken thought that it is only because (s)he is a minority. The degree of acceptance of Blacks progressed only to the point where Whites can tolerate working with but not for them. To me, there has been little or no progress in the last three years. Because of and under the protest of Affirmative Action, Whites have (in a subtle manner) vented their anger against Blacks and closed many doors that were open.[32]

Significantly, the above themes are appearing more and more in the literature of race and corporate America. Writing in the *Harvard Business Review*, Edward W. Jones, Jr., describes his experience as a black manager. His most telling comment was "I didn't know which way to turn, whom to trust, or who would be willing to listen. The personnel executive had told me to expect prejudice, but when he saw that I was being treated unfairly, he sent me off on my own. . . I tossed my work problems around in my mind, trying to find the right approach. The only answer I came up with was to stand fast, do my best, ask for no special favors, and refuse to quit voluntary."[33]

The fact that Afro-Americans are having a tough time behind the walls of corporate America does not mean that they don't struggle to stay there. In the same survey, it was found that 91 percent would like to go higher in business, and over 90 of those surveyed noted that they enjoyed working in the corporate sector. Nevertheless, over 48 percent felt that their white peers think that they are better than they are and over 48 percent felt that they are watched more closely by supervisors than their white peers are watched.

In short, it is difficult to function simply as a worker in corporate America. But for Afro-Americans, this has been true throughout their American history. The situations change, the opportunities change, but the basic problem remains the same. Like other Americans, college-age Afro-Americans look forward to reaping the benefits of working for major corporations. Despite the perceived drawbacks, they look forward to climbing the corporate ladder and performing well. They make the adjustment to racial discrimination, fight the battle, run the course, and have an excellent economic life-style. After all, this is what the civil rights struggles were all about. The debate will continue, racial situations will become tense, blacks will asked to be considered for promotions and other opportunities, whites will react, the soap opera will continue. This, after all, is the essence of the American dream: the culmination of the occupational assimilation process. For the great majority of Afro-Americans, like other Americans, working for someone in the larger society will be the route to a degree of economic stability.

Between the 1950s and 1970s, during the heyday of the civil rights struggle, Afro-Americans joined with other Americans in fighting the major battles of the country. With racism and discrimination facing them at home, they went to Korea in the early 1950s and served as though they had all of the rights and privileges of the Constitution. They died in Vietnam in the 1960s at a rate that was much higher than their percentage in the American population. After those conflicts, they returned to a country that was still struggling to provide them basic economic rights and privileges. As in other wars, Vietnam and Korea stimulated a flow of immigrants from the country where the battle had taken place. After America defeated Germany in World War II, German Americans migrated here and simply continued their lives. Ex-Nazi soldiers and others did not have to utilize their energy in order to fight for basic rights. When they became citizens, they simply exercised their privileges as Americans. The same was true for Koreans and Vietnamese. For Afro-Americans, the struggle for better jobs and acceptance into the overall economic structure of the country remained problematic.

As the 1970s turned into the 1980s, the most debated theme was the idea of the division of Afro-Americans into two sectors: those with education who were achieving and those who had no skills who were falling farther and farther behind. As noted in the previous chapter, the first part of this statement has always been true. For the historically privileged blacks, the Civil Rights

Legislation broadened their opportunities, but did not change their lifestyle or quality of life which had been developed in early years. The greatest change was the emergence of a new black middle class.

In 1985, a very interesting interview with Bayard Rustin was published in the major magazine of the NAACP, *The Crisis*. Rustin was one of the key organizers of the famous 1963 March on Washington. *The Crisis* was interested in analyzing exactly why Afro-Americans as a group were still at the bottom of the economic ladder in 1985. In the midst of central city poverty, where the "underclass" resides, immigrants were busy developing business enterprises. In Houston, Dallas, Chicago, New York, and other cities, previous areas of poverty were turned into centers for small business enterprises. The obvious question became, where is the spirit of Afro-American entrepreneurship? After showing how the Federal Government handed out free land and other "goodies" to European ethnic groups which blacks historically were denied, Rustin commented on the recent development of business enterprise by recent immigrant groups:

> If you want to raise the question about Koreans coming in, I want you to note something. Those Koreans open those shops at five o'-clock in the morning, close them at 11 o'clock at night, the whole family works in the shop. And there was a time when we [Afro-Americans] had extended families of that type. But there is not that kind of extended families in [black] America any longer. In other words, when people have been acculturated to a certain point you cannot expect the same kind of behavior out of them that you can expect out of people who came yesterday. For an example, that is one of the reasons that not only Black but White and Hispanic poor Americans, having been Americanized enough simply will not leave the cities and go to Florida to pick grapes and vegetables. That's the reason we have to have the Mexican-Americans come in to do it. Because you can't expect people who have lived in a culture, who have been affected by the norms of that culture to behave as if that isn't the case.[34]

Although Rustin missed the significance of Afro-American entrepreneurship at the turn of the century, he makes the point that the time of "economic hunger" for an ethnic group is during the time when the group first arrives in a new country. As noted in the previous chapter, parents of the first generation find that economic entrepreneurial gap and develop some kind of economic stability. They then look forward to making professionals out of their children; they don't necessarily want their children to labor in a small business sixteen hours a day. The second generation wants major medical programs, paid Social Security, paid vacations, and other benefits associated with "good" jobs. Put another way, entrepreneurial activities of newly arrived groups decline with successive generations. As a matter of fact, it is these groups that re-light the flame of "struggling entrepreneurship" and remind us of its historical past. It has been noted, to take one example from the American experience, that "The Cubans are just another in the long line of immigrant swarms on the ever-changing American frontier, and their upsurge differs only in speed and number from any other in the continuing saga of American revival. Viet-namese, Central Americans, Lebanese, and even the much abused Haitians are making similar breakthroughs. . . It has always been immigrants who have revitalized America's faith. As long as the United States is open to these flows from afar, it is open to its own revival: a continuing rebirth from the well-springs of its own historic mission in the world."[35]

Let us note in passing, that because of the relationship between the economic activity of groups and recent arrival, it is theoretically unsound to compare economic entrepreneurial activities by race and ethnicity without controlling for time. For example, Cuban-American and Afro-American entrepreneurship was compared for the city of Miami. It was found that Cuban-Americans had higher degrees of entrepreneurial activity.[36] The proper comparison would have been Cuban-Americans in the 1970's and Afro-Americans at the turn of the century. The time of entry variable is too important to be ignored. Thus, studies which do not control for time are theoretically and methodologically troublesome.

Entry into major occupations, or any occupation at all, in the larger economy presupposes a decline in discrimination against a group that has recently arrived. In cases where discrimination and hostility against the group remain somewhat constant, the entrepreneurship of the group also remains somewhat constant. This accounts for the long tradition of Jewish entrepreneurship in Europe, where anti-Semitism has historical roots. In America, Afro-Americans face a similar historical hostility. During the early days of entrepreneurship among Afro-Americans, even when they had achieved economic stability, it was impossible for them to reap the benefits of living in the larger society. Because of laws and customs due to race, their assimilation was cut off or truncated. Thus, they have, like other ethnic groups, had their day of economic hunger, when the spirit of entrepreneurship burns in the hearts of some members of a group that is trying to enter the society. But today, the Afro-American group as a whole is still on the bottom of the economic ladder. Since racism and discrimination are still parts of the American scene, one would expect a re-emergence of the idea of business enterprise for economic stability. There is no doubt that this is the case, but current entrepreneurship is quite different from the bootstrap entrepreneurship that took place at the turn of the century. After all, times have changed, and expectations of people have changed. And, given the passage of time, it is very difficult to re-light that spirit.

Afro-American entrepreneurship, whether in the 1700's or at the turn of this century, was forced because of hostility in the form of discrimination and racism. This, of course, is true of entrepreneurial groups such as the Japanese in America as well. Weber[37] accounted for the development of business activity by positing a relationship between the oppression of a group and business enterprise. The fact that Catholics in Germany were an oppressed group but did not develop a history of enterprise was an anomaly which sparked his work entitled *The Protestant Ethnic and the Spirit of Capitalism*. Today, the Afro-American experience presents a challenge to the ideas of Weber. On the one hand, a massive Civil Rights Movement has made it possible for members of this group to enter "good jobs" in their quest for economic stability. But still, significant numbers of the group remain in an economically unstable category today. Historically, when poverty, discrimination, and racism were greatest, Afro-American business activity was also greatest. They developed the spirit of enterprise and tried to carve economic stability out of a hostile sea of racism and discrimination. Their choices were limited, and they had few, if any, options. These entrepreneurs were considered the leaders of their communities, people of affairs, people to whom other Afro-Americans turned. They were responsible for producing what others calls a middle class and what this work calls the truncated Afro-American middleman. In the economically depressed areas of cities, is it possible to re-kindle that kind of spirit? Is it possible to develop the kind of "bootstrap" capitalization of small enterprises that took place before the Civil War and at the turn of the century? Will a new economically stable class that is in poverty at this point, who make up the celebrated "underclass," emerge based on entrepreneurship? Is Afro-American business enterprise still subjected to the economic detour, where they are forced to sell only to members of their own group? More specifically, what is the nature of Afro-American entrepreneurship today?

As we begin this analysis, we must note that the spirit of entrepreneurship in general has been problematic in America. A reading of the history of entrepreneurship reveals a simple fact. Unlike the first generation, following generations who come to America are less likely to engage in self-help economic activities. This is even true of what we have called middleman groups, although their offspring may have more of a cultural awareness of entrepreneurship. But overall, Americans are less likely to start small business enterprises. Afro-Americans are stamped in the same mold. The quotation below compares the historical reality of self-help during an earlier period with the decline in self-help of today:

> The story of black America as a winner, not a whiner, has been lost. Its historical zest for free enterprise, self-assertion, and open debate within its ranks is a peculiarly American story of trial, tribulation, and triumph. In the past, the black community had to rely on its own resources to survive. Black advancement was inextricably linked with black self-determination. With a sassy and fearless newspaper pub-

lished during the height of slavery, with entrepreneurs ready and willing to purchase a slave's freedom or guarantee his safety after escape, with the formation of all-black towns and the building of a self-sustaining support apparatus, black Americans exhibited backbone, resolve, energy, vitality, creativity, innovation, and intellect at a time when the country, was generally either indifferent or hostile to black interests. . . Black America would eventually become derailed, however, but not before the evidence was in that slavery, Jim Crow laws, lynching and race-baiting politicians could not kill the community's collective will and determination to leap over barriers to accomplish its goals. Seemingly, the more restrictive the political, social, and economic barriers, the more determined black America became in its resolve to overcome them. And progress, for the most part, came about because it took its matters into its own hands. Rather than accept solutions parachuted in by middle-class, professional service providers, black America must recognize and expand on indigenous, self-help neighborhood efforts. The originators of these self-help programs have unique, first-hand knowledge concerning the problems and resources to be found within their communities. They have established track records for effectively solving social problems by motivating their communities to develop innovative solutions to the problems of unemployment, substandard education, teenage pregnancy, gang violence, day-care, and other sources of community travail.[38]

The above quotation is reflective of a more recent "movement" which sees self-help activities, especially business enterprise, as one of the major programs that could revive the Afro-American communities of the inner city. The call for business enterprise as a way of breathing life into economically depressed areas, of course, is not new; it emerged from a revival of the economic ideas of Booker T. Washington and W. E. B. Du Bois. Although the former has been identified with this approach, the latter also developed a platform. More recently, such ideas can be found in the writings of Durham, Cross, and Bailey.[39] This regeneration of an old idea occurs, of course, in a new historical environment. Whereas the Afro-Entrepreneurs before the Civil War and at the turn of the century were "self-starters" with no form of governmental help, entrepreneurship today in the community, and America in general, has the support of governmental programs. This is simply a historical fact and should not be viewed as a negative or positive point when comparisons are made across time. Perhaps the most important point is that programs had to be established in order to generate business activity within the community. Such activity had to have a "jump start." Contrast this with the fact, for example, that Booker T. Washington's Negro Business League was organized to support business enterprises established before the inception of the league. When Washington himself saw Durham, North Carolina, it was already a center of "booming" business enterprise. To recreate the spirit of enterprise today, the support system for business activity that was so evident around the turn of the century is being reactivated. When one reads the literature today, one takes a journey back through time; the ideas and systems which supported entrepreneurship in the old days are alive and well in the 1980s, albeit in a form which is not quite as strong because of alternative opportunities and choices in the larger society. What is most significant, however, is that the interest in Afro-American entrepreneurship parallels a similar interest in the larger society. According to researchers, a bottom-up small business entrepreneurial revolution is occurring. It is so significant that it is being called the American Revolution. Over 7 million of the 21 million new jobs were created in between 1983 and 1985, an average of 300,000 jobs a month. Over 90 percent of these were created by small companies.[40] Thus, although the corporate dimension is important and desired in the world of work, entrepreneurship in the form of enterprise ownership has seen a re-awakening in this country. Afro-Americans have been a part of this trend.

In 1956, fifty-six years after Washington founded the National Negro Business League and nearly four and a half decades since it was a force in Afro-American affairs, the organization was quietly resurrected. There was little, if any, fanfare during this resurrection. Just as quietly as it re-emerged, the name of the organization was changed from the National Negro Business League to The National Business League. In a racial climate charged with needed protest vis-a-vis the right to vote and hold better job occupations, the organization almost silently argued that blacks do not possess the economic base which is required for assimilation; without such an economic base, it was argued, the elimination of economic disparities between blacks and whites would be quite difficult. Because of these facts, the organization dedicated itself "to the development of this required economic base and the entrepreneurial leadership essential for the achievement of economic, political and social equality."[41] In order to achieve this goal, the organization posited a program which consisted of (1) outreach, (2) uplift, and (3) mainstream; the purpose of Project Outreach is to identify those things such as technical assistance, profit potential, training needs, and other necessities of small business development. Project Mainstream developed as a program designed to foster economic growth within the Afro-American community with the help of Federal programs. Like the companies which developed in Durham, North Carolina, and discussed in a previous chapter, a major goal of this program was the creation of small business investment companies to provide equity capital resources for neighborhood enterprises. Following the original aims of the organization laid out in 1900, the present National Business League assumes that if Afro-Americans are to generate influence and a degree of economic stability and satisfy their needs, they must develop the tools of influence. These tools include land, capital, labor and business enterprise.[42]

In American cities, which were quickly becoming the turf of the "underclass," other kinds of self-help organizations silently developed. In the Boston area, Freedom Enterprises, Inc., with an emphasis on food, electronics, engineering, and advertising was born. In Harlem, the Ghetto Economic Development and Industrialization Plan was initiated. Chicago saw the development of The Chicago Economic Development Corporation. In a small kind of way, the idea of entrepreneurship for the development of economic security was creeping back into the consciousness of some Afro-Americans.

One could even find the historical debate between education and economic stability which Booker T. Washington and W. E. B. Du Bois had made famous, sneaking back into the public consciousness. It will be recalled that the former stressed industrial education which increased the ability to make a living with one's hands while the latter advocated higher education. Higher education stressed the importance of "classical" ideas and philosophy. In 1973, at the third and fourth symposiums on the state of the black economy, Margaret Simms examined the relationship between the Afro-American community, education, and economic stability. In doing so, an old skeleton was revived which indicates a renewed concern with the importance of business activity.

> If education is the vehicle for economic and social change in the black community, there will have to be some drastic changes. . . It has not provided the black community with economic leaders. It has not even been successful at teaching the majority of blacks the cognitive skills that are needed to perform well in many dependent occupations. . . The decade of the sixties saw a great push for economic equality through integration, but the results were disappointing. Where blacks increased their percentage share of family income relative to whites . . . the dollar gap between the groups grew. College graduates made the greatest strides toward eliminating the gap between themselves and white graduates; they did so however at the cost of increasing the income gap *within* the black population.[43]

Thus, beginning in the early 1970s, questions were raised about the effect of education on the economic stability of the total Afro-American community. But such concerns and ideas never captured the Afro-American community as they did at the turn of the century. They were rather confined to interest groups and selected professional meetings.

In 1969 President Nixon established the Office of Minority Business Enterprise in the Department of Commerce. The major goal of the office is to show that Americans, regardless of color, can participate in the economy on an equal basis. According to official reports, the establishment of the office "is also an act of faith in individual initiative in the competitive free enterprise system. And most important of all, it is an expression of faith in recognition of their eagerness to become profit-making participants in our competitive system."[44] The Federal government created more than 130 programs designed to enhance minority enterprise directly or indirectly. It should also be pointed out that these programs were established ten years after programs directed to benefit non-minority small business people. In 1959 the Small Business Investment Act was signed and placed under the Small Business Administration. Under this Act, small business investment companies were established in order to provide long-term equity-type financing for small business. These programs did not address the needs of minority business enterprises.[45] Between the Great Depression and the decades of the 1950s and 1960s Afro-American businesses, like all small businesses, struggled to survive. Small enterprises could not compete with the expansion of large retail chains, shopping malls, and franchises that developed. During this time period, the sizes and types of Afro-American enterprises resembled those that developed in the 1880s. In the theoretical tradition of middleman groups, they were small and service-oriented. They were also, of course, forced on the economic detour path wherein they served only Afro-Americans. Unique to Afro-American business was the impact of urban renewal. By the 1950s, urban ghettoes were well-established. One of the solutions provided by the government was to rebuild them and provide better housing for its residents. This program, sometimes called black removal, also affected businesses. As noted by Blaustein and Faux, "like black residents of the inner cities, black businesses were among the prime victims of federally sponsored urban renewal programs. . . . Of all businesses which were "urban removed' out of their present locations, over 30 percent do not open up again, and of those that do, half fail within the first five years."[46] The segregated wall that had forced the community together also began to fall. Add to this the fact that many offspring did not take over the enterprises of their parents, instead accepting opportunities in the larger society.[47] Thus the re-emergence of Afro-American business really represented a new phenomenon.

The present status of Afro-American enterprise, however, must be seen in light of the overall self-employment explosion in America. Recent years have seen the development of a global economy, downsizing or re-engineering by American corporations, and the development of what scholars have called the entrepreneurial age. Entrepreneurs have and are creating new and emerging enterprises in biotechnology and those related to the use of the Internet or the World Wide Web. Service enterprises have emerged as the largest portion of the entrepreneurial economy.[48]

The power of new firms created by entrepreneurs was given notice when an article appeared in *The Wall Street Journal* by David Birch which noted that in the immediate preceding four years, eighty-seven percent of all new jobs in

America had come from just five percent of the companies, and that two-thirds of these companies had less than twenty employees.[49] Thus from 1990 to 1994, small, growing companies with one hundred or less employees generated seven to eight million new jobs in the U.S. economy, whereas firms with more than 100 employees destroyed over three million jobs.[50] In an interesting kind of way the American economy is starting to resemble what we have called middle man firms throughout this work. Small, lean, with the ability to move on a dime because of societal hostility, black firms are also in this tradition, with over two thirds being classified as sole proprietorships. Also emerging black enterprises are no longer truncated, or cut off from doing business with "white" America. All entrepreneurs responded to the downsizing of the American economy in the 1970s with an entrepreneurial boom and black Americans were and are part of this entrepreneurial boom.

Afro-Americans emerged from traditional enterprises, which characterized enclave communities from the 1700s to the segregated 1960s, to the emerging enterprises of this and future decades. Indeed, the most significant trend is that black enterprises are moving back on "mainstreet," with location being determined by their own resources and where they can place their enterprises rather than race. Indeed, the use of the internet and E-Commerce is making "place" of enterprise almost obsolete. E-Commerce, driven by the continued improvement of the Internet, is changing the face of American enterprises. Present day black entrepreneurs are adding their own experiences to the long history of entrepreneurship in America.

II

After more than thirty years of putting civil rights at the head of its agenda, data sets started to show that black entrepreneurs are returning to the tradition of business enterprises. When business enterprise was at the very center of communities during the days of segregation and the economic detour, the collection of business data was also a focus of scholars and others in the black community. From W.E.B. Dubois' 1898 work, *The Negro in Business,* to Henry Minton's *Early History of Negroes in Business in Philadelphia* (1901) to Joseph Pierce' *Negro Business and Business Education* (1947), there was always a reality that business enterprise (which produced money for the education of children) was the shoulders on which to build for future generations. Indeed, 1929 black Americans were the only people of color, or ethnic group in America, to ask that the Bureau of the Census to conduct a separate survey of their enterprises. In a rare document stacked in the archives in Washington, it is noted that "In this chapter are presented data collected at the first Nation-wide census of retail stores conducted by Negro proprietors in the United States. At the request of a number of organizations of colored people, stores operated by

Negro proprietors are classified separately, and in all States in which there are enough such stores to justify analysis, the stores are classified by kinds of business.[51] In recent years, as the concern for civil rights replaced enterprise at the center of the black community, there was also a decrease in the interest of collecting business data on black America.

The present data workhorse for blacks in business is The Survey of Minority-owned Business Enterprises (SMOBE). Although this data set is not perfect, it has helped to shape conclusions about black enterprise in America. Another data set, though not widely used because of privacy issues, is the Characteristics of Business Owners. This set is very expansive, and adds a lot to our understanding of Afro-American enterprise. The magazine *Black Enterprise* provides snap shoots of entrepreneurs and also ranks the top 100 businesses everyday. These data sets will be utilized to highlight the present status of black entrepreneurship.

Data from the Survey of Minority-Owned Business Enterprises for black Americans for the year 1997, shows that black owned enterprises totaled 823,500, employed 718,300 people and generated $71.2 billion in revenues. These enterprises made up 4 percent of the 20.8 million nonfarm enterprises in America and 0.4 percent of the $18.6 trillion in receipts for all enterprises. The great majority (90 percent) were sole proprietorships (unincorporated enterprises with individual ownership). Legally incorporated C corporations ranked first in receipts among all black enterprises and reported receipts of $28.5 billion.[52]

Perhaps the greatest increase in the number of black firms happened between 1987 and 1992. In a standard release by the Census Bureau, it was noted that "The number of African-American-owned businesses in the United States increased 46 percent from 424,165 to 620,912 between 1987 and 1992. . . . Receipts from these firms increased by 63 percent during the five-year span, from $19.8 billion to $32.2 billion. While the total number of black firms increased 46 percent, firms in America overall increased 26 percent from 13.7 million in 1987 to 17.3 million in 1992. For this category receipts grew from $2 trillion to $3 trillion." As noted above, the entrepreneurial boom in America has created an entrepreneurial economy. Getting back on main street is clearly the most distinctive trend of enterprises owned by Afro-Americans over the past two decades.

Let us make sense out of this given the history of Black entrepreneurship in America. One of the things we noted in this work was that the workhorse for Black entrepreneurship prior to the Civil War was in the North. After the Civil War, Blacks responded to segregation with building business communities. Table 8.1 is designed to capture the nature of Black enterprises at the height of these economic enclaves or business communities, thus the year 1929 is used. So that the older census data could be matched, only retail stores are uses. The table is divided into those states that formed the original Confeder-

TABLE 8.1
Percentage of Black-Owned Firms (Retail Only) by Civil War Affiliation, 1929 and 1992

	1929		1992	
	Number of Firms	*Percentage of All Black Firms*	*Number of Firms*	*Percentage of All Black Firms*
Original Confederate States	10834	42.12%	28566	32.98%
Seceeded After the War to Join Confederacy	5689	22.12%	11285	13.03%
Slave States Pro Union	2144	8.34%	6856	7.92%
Free States	6096	23.70%	35715	41.24%
Territories	712	2.77%	3222	3.72%
District of Columbia	244	2.25%	960	1.11%
Total	25719	101.30%	86604	100%

Source: U.S. Department of Commerce, Bureau of the Census

Confederate States: South Carolina, Georgia, Florida, Alabama, Mississippi, Louisiana, and Texas.

States Seceeded after War: Virginia, North Carolina, Tennessee, and Arkansas.

Slave States Pro-Union: Maryland, West Virginia, Kentucky, Delaware, and Missouri.

Free States: Maine, New Hampshire, Massachusetts, Kansas, Rhode Island, Connecticut, New Jersey, Pennsylvania, New York, Vermont, Ohio, Indiana, Illinois, Michigan, Wisconsin, Iowa, Minnesota, Oregon, and California.

Territories: North Dakota, South Dakota, Nebraska, Colorado, New Mexico, Utah, Nevada, Washington, Montana, Wyoming, Arizona, Oklahoma, and Idaho.

ate States, those that succeed after the start of the war to join the Confederacy, slaves states that were pro-union, free states, and territories.

The patterns for 1929 that emerge are expected, given our theory of the truncated middleman and hostility and the fact that the great majority of the population was located in the South. But population alone does not account for business development. One must understand the importance of business for the development of communities and the education of children. It can be seen that those states which withdrew from the union to form the original confederate states sixty years earlier (South Carolina, Georgia, Florida, Alabama, Mississippi, Louisiana and Texas), accounted for 42 percent of all black firms in America. The next highest percentage, 22 percent, is found in states that withdrew from the Union and joined the Confederacy after the conflict had begun (Virginia, North Carolina, Tennessee, Arkansas). When these two categories are combined, 62 percent of all black enterprises were found in states that finally formed the old Confederate states.

Slave states that were pro-union (Maryland, West Virginia, Kentucky, Delaware and Missouri) accounted for 8.34 percent of all black enterprises in 1929. Those states that were considered free states (Maine, New Hampshire, Massachusetts, Kansas, Rhode Island, Connecticut, New Jersey, Pennsylvania

New York, Vermont, Ohio, Indiana, Illinois, Michigan, Wisconsin, Iowa, Minnesota, Oregon, California) during the Civil War period accounted for 23 percent of black enterprise during this time period.

At the time of the Civil War, areas that had not as yet become states were called territories. By 1929 territories became North Dakota, South Dakota, Nebraska, Colorado, New Mexico, Utah, Nevada, Washington, Montana, Wyoming, Arizona, Oklahoma and Idaho. This category accounted for 2.2 percent of all black enterprises in 1929.

The left column of table 8.1 shows the same Civil War affiliations for black enterprises for 1992. Despite the passage of decades, the states of the old Confederacy (combining original Confederate states with those that joined after the war started) house 45 percent of all black enterprises. This is compared to 62 percent in 1929. The free states moved from 23 percent in 1929 to 41 percent in 1992, reflecting the movement in the black population away from the old South, and carrying the legacy of self-help with them and combined it with the old legacy in the North. The 41 percent is four percentage points behind the old South when it comes to business start-ups. The District of Columbia dropped from 2 percent in 1929 to 1 percent in 1992.

When the same analysis is done for all black enterprises using the survey of minority owned enterprises for 1997 data (which are inclusive of all types of enterprises, not just retail trade), a similar pattern emerges. States that made up the old Confederacy account for 32 percent of black enterprises, and those that succeeded after the Civil War account for 12 percent of black enterprises. When combined, the old Confederate States make up 42 percent of all black enterprises in America. The pro-union slave states account for 8 percent of all black enterprises, followed by the free states (43 percent), territories (1 percent), and the District of Columbia (1 percent).[53]

When this analysis does not consider the historical categories for the 1997 data, states with the highest percentages of black enterprises are New York (10.5), California (9.6), Texas (7.3), Florida (7.2), Georgia (6.8), Maryland (5.8), Illinois (5.0) North Carolina (4.8) Virginia (4.1), and Ohio (3.3). The lessons of history during segregation, and the continued ethos of self-help which was so much a part of the post Civil War South and the pre-Civil War North, is seeing an emergence of entrepreneurial behavior.

One of the primary theses of this work is how the truncated middleman, or those blacks that were self-employed, placed a great deal of emphasis on the education of children. Since Dubois' landmark study, *The College Bred Negro*, research has shown that black college graduates are more likely to be Southern. Another excellent research example is Loren Schweninger's *Black Owners in the South 1790–1915*. In his book, he was surprised to find that free blacks placed a strong value on the education of their children, a value that whites as a whole had not developed. After careful analysis, he concluded that among

TABLE 8.2a
States Where Blacks Made Up the Largest Percentage of Total Enrollment
in Higher Education in 1992

Mississipi	27.9%
Louisiana	24.6
Georgia	22.3
South Carolina	21.2
Alabama	20.1
Maryland	19
North Carolina	18.7
Virginia	14.9
Tennessee	14.6
Arkansas	14.4
Illinois	12.5
Delaware	12.1
New York	12

TABLE 8.2b
States Where Blacks Made Up the Largest Percentage of the Total Bachelor's Degrees
Awarded in 1991

Mississippi	20.50%
Louisiana	19.3
North Carolina	14.4
Alabama	13.6
South Carolina	13.4
Maryland	12
Georgia	11.8
Virginia	10.5
Arkansas	9.5
Tennessee	8.7

Source: U.S. Department of Education.

200 black families in one Louisiana parish, only 1 percent was illiterate. In the same parish, 20-25 percent of the white families were illiterate.

Table 8.2a reveals that the areas of the country where blacks make up the largest percentage of total enrollment in higher education, or college matriculation, are also the old Confederate States. In Mississippi, 27.9 percent of students enrolled in college are black. This is followed by Louisiana (24.6 percent), Georgia (22.3 percent), South Carolina (21.2 percent), Alabama (20.1 percent), Maryland (19 percent), North Carolina (18.7 percent), Virginia (14.9 percent), Tennessee (14.6 percent) and Arkansas (14.9 percent). Illinois, Delaware and New York are the only states outside of the old south on the list.

Table 8.2b shows states where blacks make up the largest percentage of the total Bachelor's Degrees awarded in 1991. Again, Southern states not only lead, but completely dominate the list. It should be pointed out that although historical black colleges and universities carry a great load, southern traditional historical white schools have a high percentage of black students. These data point to the value structure of the South that was put in place when racial hostility was highest. In an interesting, but expected pattern of middleman minorities, blacks are involved in higher education wherever racial hostility and legal segregation was the worst.

Returning to the entrepreneurship, while the Survey of Minority-Owned Business enterprises is the public workhorse for data on black entrepreneurship, early data significantly underestimate the performance of these enterprises because it does not include subchapter C corporations (or larger firms with shareholders) and concentrates only smaller, or S, corporations. Research by Thomas Boston informs us that when this is done, the survey understates total employment in black-owned businesses by at least 27 percent and financial capacity by 23 percent. Significant growth that took place among C corporations was not recorded by the earlier census, and therefore the performance of enterprises is underestimated. As noted earlier, this has been corrected since we now can report data on C corporations.

When all enterprises are taken into consideration, the picture of entrepreneurship among black Americans is very different from the era of the segregated racial enclaves. Independent research done by Thomas Boston[54] and Timothy Bates,[55] and others, points to the trend that successful black business owners are highly educated, with lots of talent, and can be found in what is called emerging enterprises. Indeed, the last five years has seen a strong debate within the academic literature as black enterprises, with the rest of the country, increased in numbers and significance.

The present day debate was fueled when Timothy Bates published an article entitled "Why are Firms Owned by Asian Immigrants Lagging Behind Black-Owned Businesses?" in the *National Journal of Sociology*.[56] Using firms operated by their present owner for less than ten years, Bates added a consideration of receipts when assessing the performance of firms. Using receipts, he placed the performance of black enterprises in a different light:

> Widely held perceptions about minority-owned enterprises are poorly grounded in facts. Paucity of empirical underpinnings coexists with numerous stylized facts about self-employment patterns, particularly regarding the experiences of Asian immigrants creating small businesses in the U.S. Asian immigrants, according to popular imagination, are successful; black Americans, in contrast, are unsuccessful in the self-employment realm. This study relies upon comprehensive small business data compiled by the U.S. Bureau of the Census: conventional financial measures of small business profitability are calculated for three owner groups—blacks, whites, and Asian immigrants. Using financial returns to owners investments of time and money

into the applicable businesses as the success criterion, the Asian immigrants rank last, nonminority firms produce the highest returns, and black Americans are in the middle. Profitability criteria suggest that Asian immigrant owners collectively lag behind the black business community.[57]

Bates's analysis is concerned strictly with the business side of receipts, debt equity, and the death of firms. As a matter of fact, although he gives a consideration of race and ethnicity as a factor in business enterprise in his analysis, he concludes that those lacking the requisite skills and capital, whether immigrant or not, are less likely to start small enterprises. Among those who choose self-employment without appropriate education, financial resources, and skills, business failure and the exit form self-employment are high. These patterns, notes Bates, can be related to black, Asian, and white Americans, men and women, immigrants and the native born.[58]

Bates's data shows, as other research notes that the present state of black enterprise is more in the tradition of getting "back on mainstreet" and that education levels for entrepreneurs are very high. Getting back on main street means doing business where it is profitable; where one can get the highest rate of return, and not just in the traditional black enclave. In terms of the emergence of immigrant Asian enterprises in some inner-city communities, Bates argues that black entrepreneurs tend to avoid such enterprise. In his words, "College-educated African Americans tend to avoid such businesses because they can earn higher returns elsewhere. Running a small retail store in the ghetto, bluntly, is a waste of their time."[59]

Bates's analysis is more about black Americans being Americans than immigrants. Certainly the old black enclaves that started after the Civil War and ended in about the middle of the 1960s possess attributes of the present day ethnic immigrant enclaves. Some of these enclaves, of course, are also changing and dying as immigration patterns decline and immigrants assimilate into American society. As noted by Min Zhou, it is immigrants who foster and maintain ethnic enterprises through the generations. Her work shows that New York City's Chinatown prosperity during this time in history is due to the increasing number of immigrants who revived the economic structure of that community.[60]

Bates's analysis brings a business side to the study of entrepreneurship, with special emphasis on successful self-employment. In terms of the absolute number of enterprises started by Afro-Americans, he notes that they start fewer enterprises because they have less household wealth. Also, Asians start more enterprises than whites or blacks because they have more household wealth. Bates's data lead to the conclusion that the variation in ethnic racial enterprises is influenced greatly by household wealth. His analysis is an interesting and intriguing look into racial and ethnic enterprise in America.

Thomas Boston uses Atlanta as a case study to assess the present state of black enterprise. Like Bates, he found that business owners were highly educated. Because black enterprises are located in the greater Atlanta area, rather than being confined due to an economic detour of segregation, he compared the educational rates in different areas of the city. He found that "The owners of business located in the city have a much higher educational attainment than do suburban owners. . . 74.8 percent of owners with businesses located in the city have a college degree or better, as compared to 61.5 percent of owners in non-city locations." It is interesting to note that these educational levels are higher than white males who are business owners. As reported by *The Characteristics of Business Owners*, which is produced by the Bureau of the Census, only 35.1 percent of non-minority male business owners have a college education. Wherever they are located, education appears as a major variable in both Bates and Boston's analysis.

Boston's analysis is historically rich because he takes Atlanta from its oldest business tradition of separate enclaves to the state of enterprises today. As noted earlier in this work, it is very important to understand that black entrepreneurship did not start in the 1970s. Boston shows that "By 1911 Atlanta had some two thousand black-owned establishments representing over a hundred types of businesses, including one bank, three insurance companies, 12 drugstores, 60 tailor shops, 83 barber shops, 85 groceries, 80 hack line, and 125 drayage places."[61] In the "old" Atlanta, before the passage of historical laws aimed at driving black contractors out of the local marketplace and the institution of what we called the economic detour, blacks were as competitive as whites in many areas of enterprise.[62]

While the old black enclave enriched the black community, Boston notes that 126 years passed before Atlanta offered a business contract to a black-owned enterprise. New opportunities in contracting with the city of Atlanta, coupled with strong educational private black institutions and the cultural value of just going to college at any institution, helped to launch a new prosperity for black entrepreneurs. The new opportunities were related to the development of laws, under the Secretary of Commerce, to develop and coordinate activities aimed at promoting minority business development.[63]

Once opportunities were granted, enterprises that these entrepreneurs created were impressive, and while the trends were similar to other cities, there appears to be an "Atlanta" effect because of comparative figures.[64] For example, in the entire country, four percent of all black-owned business are corporations, standing alone as separate entities from one's own personal wealth or other property. In Atlanta, however, 57.9 percent of the black-owned enterprises were listed as corporations. Also, while the average revenue of all black-owned enterprises in the Atlanta area, for 1992, was $44,668, the average revenue of firms registered with the city of Atlanta was $606, 208.[65] Boston's study points out how difficult it is to estimate the actual performance of black owned enterprises in America because his data shows a performance standard, as measured by income, which outperforms national data sets. While this is an issue for all business data, the important point is that black owned enterprises in Atlanta has re-kindled the tradition that was started at the turn of the century.

Over the last twenty-five years or so *Black Enterprise* has published a list of the top 100 enterprises. Like Booker T. Washington's publications at the turn of the century, this magazine re-creates the success and triumphs of black business. It also discusses the failures and gives examples of how to succeed in business. From a historical comparative perspective, the magazine is a re-creation of the positive aspects of business activity that were so prevalent in the writings of the "Tuskegee Machine." The performance of a company is measured by total sales for the year.

The enterprises ranked by *Black Enterprise* are done by categories which include the industrial sector, advertising agencies, asset managers, auto dealers, insurance companies, investment banks, and banks. The categories allow us to compare historical data with new enterprise categories that developed since the early days of black entrepreneurship.[66] For example, a visit to their web site (www.blackenterprise.com) revealed that among insurance companies, every top ten company was started during the heyday of black enterprise, or prior to the 1960s. The North Carolina Mutual Life Insurance Company, founded in Durham, North Carolina in 1898, is the top insurance company on the list. This is followed by Atlanta Life (founded in 1905), Golden State Mutual Life Insurance (1925, Los Angles) and Booker T. Washington Insurance Company of Birmingham, Alabama (1932).

When one looks at the banking category, twelve out of the twenty-five banks on *Black Enterprises Top 100* were founded between 1895 and 1956, or during the days of official segregation. For those in the Industrial and Service sector, two are from the segregated era. All of the companies in the categories of Investment Banking, Auto Dealers, Asset Managers, and Advertising Agencies were founded after the 1960s. Let us take a closer look at banking and insurance companies.

As noted in chapter 3, one of the major institutions that Afro-Americans tried to organize during the days of forced self-help was that of banking. Between 1888 and 1934, there were no less than 134 banks developed by the group. In 1926, the total resources of all these banks reached a high of $12,831,348.05.[67] In 1986, there were thirty-nine Afro-American-owned banks with total assets of $1,608,668.[68] A year later this number decreased to thirty-six and assets were $1,612,916.[69] As was true for their forerunners, developed by Afro-Americans at the turn of the century, banking is small and the going is tough today. But banking in general has been tough. A 1988 study by the Office of the Comptroller of the U.S. Currency found that the overwhelming majority of all bank failures are related to incompetent management. The study looked at 162 bank failures since 1979 and found that seven percent failed due specifically to depressed economic conditions, but that 89 percent of those that failed were found to have incompetent officers and/or boards of directors who were essentially ignorant of banking industry regulations. This situation led to poor loan policies and failure to supervise bank officers and employees.[70] But perhaps due to the fact that Afro-American banks are forced out of the large risk areas of banking such as real estate, a kind of natural insulation from economic hard times has occurred. Thus, according to the Sheshunoff Competitive Analysis for 1986, black banks outperformed the industry when their return on assets were compared to all banks. For that year, Afro-American banks had a 0.71 percent return on assets as compared with a 0.63 percent for the total industry in general. Also, when the Federal Reserve Board compared selected assets and liabilities of banks that were at least three years old in 1987, and with assets of between 50 and 300 million dollars, the return on assets and equities recorded by the top ten Afro-American banks surpasses those owned by whites. The very top banks achieved a return on assets average of 1.05 percent compared with 0.06 percent for others in the industry. The gap between Afro-American banks and majority-owned banks was even greater when one looked only at return of equities. The former posted a 14.34 percent return and the latter an 8.14 percent return. While majority banks were being destroyed by bad foreign and agricultural loans, Afro-American banks showed strong measures of profitability serving disadvantaged communities with long-term economic difficulties.[71] The latter is the re-establishment of an old relationship between banks that had paid dividends in the community, in some cases, seventy years ago.

The most recent ranking of the important institution of banking[72] allows us to see which Afro-American banks are survivors from the early years when their numbers were more than 120. They are ranked according to their assets, which are in millions of dollars to the nearest thousand. Of the twenty-five banks, seven were formed between 1895 and 1930, four in the decade of the 1940s, eight between 1950 and 1970, and six in the decades of the 1980s and 90s. The banks formed between 1895 and 1970 trace their spirit to early beneficial societies, and are testimony to a period that is forgotten by most and appreciated by few. The oldest bank on the list is the First Tuskegee Bank, founded in 1895 in the city that Booker T. Washington made famous.

In 1932 there had developed over sixty insurance companies that catered to the Afro-American market. As noted in earlier chapters, this was one of the most "successful" industries during the period of the forced economic detour. By 1937 this industry employed 9,010 people (see table 3.6 in Chapter 3). Let us return to the rankings in the category by *Black Enterprise* to see how the insurance companies founded during the period of self-help and the economic detour still dominate the industry. All of those listed in the top ten (not all insurance companies are shown) were founded during the age of Booker T. Washington and the era of business self-help, or prior to the 1950s. So dominant have these companies been within portions of the Afro-American community that the youngest company on the list was founded in 1950. One was founded in the late 1800s, one in 1900, two in 1920 and 1930, three in the 1940s. A company from the old Durham, North Carolina, economic enclave, the North Carolina Mutual, stands at the top of the list.

The digital economy, or the ability to do perform all transactions of an enterprise on the Internet, is changing all business models and creating different forms of organizations. The idea of "place" of enterprise is quickly becoming obsolete. The new model is that one can develop an enterprise on-line and interact with individuals on-line. This economy merges computing, communications, and content, and is growing rapidly. As noted by Don Tapscott in *The Digital Economy: Promise and Peril in the Age of Networked Intelligence*, this type of economy is narrowly defined as about 10 percent of the U.S. GDP. At the end of 1996, the industry was almost one trillion dollars. By 2005 the industry will have jumped to 1.47 trillion dollars.[73] This type of economy means that issues such as race should become less important. Enterprises are launched on the internet and payment is made through the internet. Although research is just starting, black Americans are also taking advantage of this new model for business and wealth creation.

The explosion of enterprises among black American also has meant more problems in the capitalization of new ventures. This is nothing new for Afro-American businesses, or businesses operated by people who have excluded from society. Indeed, finding capital to start an enterprise is the problem of the great majority of new start-ups, regardless of group membership. A 1992 Roper Organization Pool puts the numbers behind the everyday observation that lack of access to credit and capital remains the major barrier to new ventures start-ups. Although this article argued that this is why there is a lag in black entrepreneurship, as we shall see below this is not the whole story.[74] As this work has pointed out, an historical trademark of excluded minority entrepreneurs is that they take racial discrimination as a given; this discrimination forces them to become creative in the capitalization of business enterprise. This was certainly true of Afro-American entrepreneurs in Philadelphia in the 1700s and in Durham during the early 1900s, the Japanese at the turn of the century, and the Vietnamese of today. As a member of a group which has been traditionally discriminated against, or as newcomers to society, it is difficult to expect to be treated equally vis-à-vis the acquisition of loans. Especially for Afro-Americans, living in America has always been tough and full of disappointments. Economic discrimination and racism are nothing new to the Afro-American experience.

III

Traditional sources of capitalization for Afro-American enterprises are the minority enterprise small business investment corporations. These corporations are endorsed by the Small Business Administration, which combines with firms who participate in the program to finance enterprises. For every dollar that private firms provide for capitalization of business, the Small Business Administration can provide up to four dollars. From an historical view, in 1983 alone, 150 public venture firms put more than $55.9 million into 677 business ventures. About 44 percent of this capital went to start-up firms. The Small Business Administration supplied these venture firms with more than $30 million in 1983 for participating in the program. All participating firms must invest in small enterprises which are 50 percent owned by women and minorities. The government defines a small business as one that has assets of less than $9 million and a net worth which does not exceed $4 million.[75]

As noted by Thomas Boston in his analysis of venture capital for black enterprise, recent policies of the Small Business Administration are helping to lay the groundwork for additional new ventures. He reports that in 1998 a $1.5 billion loan guarantee fund was announced for black entrepreneurs. The Government will increase SBA loan guarantees from $286 million in 1997 to $588 million for year 2000. Indeed, over the next three years the Small Business Administration will have a guarantee program that reaches 1.4 billion dollars.[76]

Although loans augmented by the Small Business Administration have been the capitalization backbone of Afro-American enterprise, private venture capital funds have also been employed. Since these funds emerge completely from the private sector, they are unregulated by the Federal government. It has been estimated that these institutions invest about $1.8 billion a year in new business adventures. For example, in 1983, venture companies attracted $4.1 billion from investors, an increase from $1.7 billion in 1982. There exists more than ten venture capital "megafunds" which contain 100 million dollars. Overall, it has been estimated that $11.5 billion exists for investment from venture capital pools. These private enterprises financed about 1,500 of the 60,000 new enterprises incorporated in 1983.[77]

Like those firms which participate in the programs of the Small Business Administration, private venture enterprises provide services to start-up companies such as marketing, consulting, management audits, and negotiated contracts with customers.[78] Unlike governmental funds, private venture capital concerns expect returns of 45 percent to 60 percent.[79] They also like for a small company to "go public" within five years. Put simply, there are financial restrictions on these funds which are not placed on funds generated from Federal concerns.

Research on the financial performance of Afro-American firms can be divided into two categories. The first is composed of those studies that examine firms that were financed by Federal funds. They tend to be noncomparative in nature and to utilize data from the Small Business Administration. Other studies are comparative along funding and racial lines. These studies utilize a much more broader data base for analysis.

Studies that concentrate on enterprises that utilize Federal funds for capitalization, and are non-comparative, show that these enterprises do not have an overall strong performance record; they have a poor repayment record, lack cash, overall profitability, and liquidity. They are also strongly in debt.[80] On the other hand, comparative studies show that minority firms that do not receive assistance from the Small Business Administration have the same performance characteristics as non-minority enterprises with regard to profit, debt and liquidity. Thus, funding source, as chronicled by the literature, emerges as a predictor of enterprise performance. Thus, ethnic background is not equated with economic stability of firms.[81]

Although governmental and private funding have played an important part in the development of Afro-American enterprise, it is also true that significant numbers of Afro-Americans start their enterprises without borrowing money.[82] Thus, in 1982, 69 percent of Afro-American owners started their enterprises without borrowing money. Thirty-one percent of Afro-American owners did not borrow because capital was not required. Indeed, about seventy percent of these enterprises were capitalized with less than $5,000 dollars. In order to place these percentages in a comparative perspective, research shows that 75 percent of women, 67 percent of Hispanics, 66 percent of white males, and 62 percent of Asians (and of their racial minority owners) started their enterprises without borrowing capital.[83] One of the best documentation of private funding for venture start-ups in found in Michael D. Woodard's *Black Entrepreneurs in America: Stories of Struggle and Success*.[84] Timothy Bates, in *Race, Self-Employment & Upward Mobility* argues that household wealth is the key to understanding those who start enterprises. Asians have more household wealth than whites, thus start more enterprises. Also, blacks start fewer enterprises than Asians or Whites because overall they have less household wealth.[85]

Although there are thousands of "success" stories in the literature on Afro-American enterprises, it is obvious that entrepreneurship and success continues to be problematic. But it is also obvious that there is a growing tendency to think about entrepreneurship among Afro-Americans. For example, while rates of self-employment are lower among Afro-Americans when compared with whites and the foreign-born, initiation rates of self-employment activities among Afro-American men and women are nearly three times that of white men and women and twice that of white women.[86] The problems encountered by these business people are well-documented in the historical literature.[87]

There is, however, a new line of research that compares new venture start-ups by ethnicity rather than race. Instead of dividing the data by black/white, ethnicity is given a strong consideration. This research shows that individuals from the Jewish "white" group are significantly more likely to be self-employed than other whites. As noted by the authors, the data are picking up many of the cultural attributes associated with middleman theory and the hostility that goes along with that experience in host societies. It is thus important to understand that we need to look closely within "white" groups instead of lumping them all together when self-employment is studied.[88]

Afro-American entrepreneurship, as it has been since the 1700s in Philadelphia, continues to represent a specific adjustment to differential treatment in American society. As has been argued from a theoretical point of view, this adjustment is squarely in the tradition of groups that have been discriminated against throughout history. The need for creativity in the face of oppression held true for the Jews in Europe and America, the Japanese on the West Coast at the turn of the century, and present day Vietnamese and Koreans. The Afro-American situation is surely unique when viewed from an historical perspective. The natural flow of assimilation and equal opportunity continues to escape them on a broad basis because of the reality of race. Each generation has to be creative in the quest for economic stability in America. Entrepreneurship represents only one kind of adjustment. The other most prominent adjustment has been protest for civil rights and equal opportunity. Both traditions have nurtured and gain a degree of hope for members of the group throughout history.

The development of entrepreneurship is difficult to predict. In the case of Afro-Americans, some run small stores in the inner-city and have no education, while some are fresh from the corporate sector with college degrees and MBA's in hand. Frustrated over white colleagues insisting that they hold position because of Affirmative Action Programs rather than because of their education and other human capital traits, frustrated as a result of being passed over for promotions, they leave corporate America and branch out on their own.[89] As this process continues and grows, one should expect researchers to continue to call efforts of entrepreneurs insignificant and a myth. Without a theoretical tradition to guide them, researchers and writers in the field of race and economics will continue to downgrade this effect because of substantial disadvantages which they bring to the marketplace, such as limited access to capital and managerial experience.[90] While this is happening in the literature on Afro-Americans, the literature on other ethnic group is at the same time guided by middleman theory, and researchers and writers will continue to praise and give encouragement to the development of small Asian enterprises, even if the entrepreneurs are first generation and can only say the price of the product which is being sold. It is certainly true that Asian enterprises, like Afro-American enterprises, cannot hire all members of their community, a comment which has never been true, and will never be true. Ultimately, most Americans will survive economically by joining the national workforce. But Afro-American entrepreneurs, like their counterparts at the turn of the century and their ethnic colleagues of today, will today become the truly advantaged of the disadvantaged. They are in the self-help tradition of the Afro-American truncated middleman and their offspring will reap the economic and educational benefits that their parents will be able to afford.

CONCLUSION

The 1950s saw the development of the Civil Rights Movement. The purpose of the movement was to include Afro-Americans in every aspect of American life. Formal laws designed to maintain racial separation were removed from Federal and State Constitutions. There was "progress" made as a result of the movement, especially for those individual Afro-Americans who were prepared educationally to take advantage of developing opportunities. In the middle of this movement, a "silent revolution" in entrepreneurship began to take place. While some members of the group settled into corporate America and other jobs from which they had been historically excluded, others turned to the development of business enterprise. From 1987 to 1992, the census data, which underestimates the number of black owned firms, shows that these firms increased 46 percent (from 424,165 to 620,912). Comparable data for all enterprises show a 26 percent increase. Like their historical counterparts, Afro-Americans found that starting a firm and keeping it afloat is tough, although some have done extremely well. Although these firms will never be able to hire all Afro-Americans, or create an Afro-American economy, they are in the tradition of enterprises developed by members of a group that has been historically oppressed. As Weber noted in *The Protestant Ethnic and the Spirit of Capitalism*, throughout history selected members of oppressed groups have always turned to business enterprise as a way of adapting to oppressive conditions. Like the entrepreneurial Jews of Europe, the entrepreneurial Huguenots of France, and the entrepreneurial Chinese of Mississippi, Afro-American entrepreneurs of today will represent the truly advantaged of the disadvantaged. The development of the digital economy, or business on the internet, can have a profound effect on black enterprise in the future.

9

Conclusion and Policy Implications

The major purpose of this manuscript has been to reconstruct the sociology of entrepreneurship by giving a special consideration to the Afro-American experience. The sociology of entrepreneurship, which is concerned with the relationship between ethnicity and business activity, has almost completely ignored the Afro-American experience. Thus, the sociohistorical examples which interact with theoretical ideas have stressed the ethnic experience.

Although this is certainly fine, it is quite ironic that most of the major ideas developed in theories—such as middleman, ethnic enclave, and collectivism—were already prevalent in old books and manuscripts written about the Afro-American experience. Thus, not only is the Afro-American experience overlooked in the sociology of entrepreneurship, but scholarship—mostly by Afro-Americans—has also been overlooked. This, in itself, is an interesting comment on American society, race, and scholarship.

This manuscript has also argued that, although all Afro-Americans have had to face racism, prejudice, and discrimination, those of today who can trace their roots back to entrepreneurship and the self-help experience possess a set of values which are similar—if not identical—to middleman ethnic groups. Such an approach means that we must reconstruct how we think about race and economics in America, and about policy which relates to that experience.

I

In order to show the reality and significance of the Afro-American business tradition, old data, manuscripts, and ideas were taken from the historical shelf in order to enumerate the reality of self-help and business activity of this group. Although the presentation of this data could fill volumes of manuscripts, we presented only a very small portion of the data.

We have shown that business activity, in the form of economic enclaves, was part of the Afro-American experience as early as the 1700s. Mainly because of scholarship done on Afro-American entrepreneurs *before* the Civil War, we were able to show the development of economic enclaves during that time period in such cities as Philadelphia and Cincinnati. In Philadelphia, Afro-Americans were instrumental in the development of service enterprises. This was also true in Cincinnati, which was actually one of the stronger cities for enterprise before the Civil War. In New York City, one of the best restaurants in the Wall Street area was owned by Afro-Americans. Even in the South, the pattern of small business activity, for the generation of economic activity, was very prevalent among free Afro-Americans before the Civil War. Their clients were not limited to Afro-Americans, but included people of European descent, as well. One can say without a doubt and based on available data, that they controlled service enterprises during this time period. As with other middleman groups who have played this role throughout history, they operated under racial hostility. This pattern of business activity, especially as regards clientele, changed due to the immigration of other ethnic groups in large numbers to the northeastern part of the United States and the influences of increased racial discrimination.

Also discussed was the rich and interesting data on Afro-American entrepreneurship under the institution of slavery. Even while in bondage, some Afro-Americans showed a propensity to enter enterprise in order to generate income. Sometimes this income was used for the purchase of their loved ones' freedom from slave masters, while at other times it was used to enhance their own plantations. In addition, Afro-Americans were quite active in inventing new products which were—and still are—important in this country. This activity in itself was a significant entrepreneurial one, representing adjustment under severe conditions of racism and discrimination.

After the Civil War, Afro-Americans were faced with the problem of adjusting to hostility in both the North and the South. In the South, those who had fought so strongly against America during the Civil War developed laws to exclude Afro-Americans from full participation in that society, although the latter clearly fought on the side of the Union. The systematic conscious program of Jim Crow segregation was designed to re-create the analog of slavery.

The program applied exclusively to Afro-Americans. There were no "Irish Only," "Italian Only," or "Jewish Only" signs found in public places with the sanctioning of laws. The members of European ethnic groups all thought of themselves and lived as "whites," and they knowingly went along with the subordination of Afro-Americans. Indeed, during the period of white redemption in the South, Afro-Americans were lynched and generally killed in unprecedented numbers. They had no rights that whites—whether they were German, Irish, Italian, English, Polish, white ethnic male, or white ethnic female—had to respect.[1]

Faced with this situation, the group responded as free Afro-Americans had done before the Civil War. Although Booker T. Washington organized the Negro Business League at the turn of the century, business activity had been underway long before his call for a unified business effort. Because of the laws of segregation and Jim Crow, or because of complete governmental interference into the everyday lives of people, Afro-Americans were forced to operate under an economic detour.

After the passage of *Plessey v. Ferguson* in 1899, which sanctioned separate but equal facilities, Afro-American enterprises were forced to operate only in their own communities. This was in sharp contrast to European and non-European groups, who were welcomed on the business Broadway of America. At this time, Afro-American business leadership complained that any foreigners, who had no military or other type of service to America, were allowed to operate in the broader economic arena, whereas Afro-Americans were denied similar opportunities. Afro-Americans had served in all military conflicts of the country, and Afro-American leadership could not understand why this service to country was not taken into consideration in relationship to citizenship rights.

Indeed, by 1900, a complete program of racial segregation was in place, and the economic detour became a fundamental reality of Afro-American enterpreneurship. In addition to responding with the development of business activity, one of the strongest traditions of self-help ever to be developed in America was established by Afro-Americans.

They developed private educational institutions that ranged from the elementary levels to college. They built churches, developed financial institutions to finance the building of homes, established self-help fraternal societies, and started their own insurance companies. No other group in the history of America has had to go to "go-it-alone" as did Afro-Americans at the turn of the century. The institutions which they built are a testimony to sheer entrepreneurship effort and the indomitability of the human spirit.

In order to highlight the nature of the economic struggles experienced by Afro-Americans during this period, this discussion considered the two communities of Durham, North Carolina, and Tulsa, Oklahoma. Both were similar in their fostering of a spirit of entrepreneurship, but they ultimately met with very different fates. At the turn of the century, Durham, North Carolina, was written about in newspapers and popular magazines in much the same way that the Cuban-American phenomenon in Miami is today. Anchored by the presence of the North Carolina Mutual Life Insurance Company, Durham served as a model for Afro-American enterprise. With some help from the

330 Entrepreneurship and Self-Help among Black Americans

white business community, Afro-American entrepreneurs developed service and manufacturing enterprises. Although the majority of these firms had to operate under the economic detour, there were some firms that had white clients. Today, sections of Durham still exhibit the same entrepreneurial spirit in the Afro-American community that was planted in the late 1800s.

On the other hand, Afro-Americans in Tulsa, Oklahoma, had their spirit of entrepreneurship killed in a supposed "city of opportunity." The Greenwood section housed the service and business enterprises which were developed by Afro-Americans as Tulsa was becoming a rugged frontier town with oil as its major drawing card. When some Afro-Americans refused to sell portions of their oil holdings, bulletins were posted in their community informing them to leave the city or meet a tragic fate. Although there was concern within the Afro-American community, few could have imagined, let alone believed, the fate which was in store for this community.

With racial tensions increasing daily, an incident involving an Afro-American male and a white female set off a "war" within the city. When it was over, the entire business section, along with religious institutions and the homes of Afro-American business people and professionals had been destroyed.

Refugees from the smoking ruins scattered throughout cities in America informing people of the almost unbelievable events. Tulsa, Oklahoma, represented an example of success and disappointment within the Afro-American business tradition.

From a theoretical point of view, the experience of Afro-Americans in Tulsa makes us conscious of the fact that, throughout history, middleman groups who are also viewed as minorities can face severe consequences if they find a degree of economic success within hostile environments. Other historical examples of this phenomenon include—albeit with different degrees of hostility—Arab business people in England today, and Jews in Hitler's Germany.

Another key result which evolved from the struggle for self-help and business activity among Afro-Americans was that this group obtained a degree of economic success. One of the major arguments of this work is that, through the years, scholars have not been guided by theory adequate to the purpose of explaining this reality. Indeed, scholarship has not been kind to this group. It has neglected its building and maintaining of institutions, its values, and its adaptation to extreme racist circumstances.

E. Franklin Frazier, one of the greatest of all sociologists, called them the *black bourgeoisie* and so started an intellectual tradition that downplayed Afro-American institution building and accomplishments, especially in the area of business enterprise. Frazier argued that, because the profits of these enterprises did not compare to those of large-scale corporations in America, the history of Afro-American enterprise was simply a myth.

This theme has continued to influence and bias the work of researchers and can be seen in such recent works as Bart Landry's *The New Black Middle Class*.[2] The continued destruction of institution building by this economically stable group can also be seen in the recent work of Thomas Sowell. Despite the fact that Afro-American colleges traditionally were involved in self-help programs in the community and reached out to all, Sowell noted that "Negro colleges were geared to serving the social elite and had none of the adult-education, job-preparation, acculturation-of-the-masses, service-to-the-community orientation of other colleges serving low-income populations, such as the Catholic colleges and some urban colleges.[3]

One wonders how such a conclusion could be reached, especially since the classic debate between Booker T. Washington and W. E. B. Du Bois revolved around the point that Du Bois considered Washington's idea of education to be practically devoid of intellectual training. Certainly these colleges and universities reached out to masses, for it was from the masses that they drew their students. What Frazier called the *black bourgeoisie* was not a group that materialized from nowhere, but rather one which was established over the years as a result of hard entrepreneurial and other self-help activities in the face of severe conditions. Analyses such as those of Landry and Sowell appear throughout the literature on those Afro-Americans who were able to achieve economic security by way of their own adaptability and tenaciousness.

One of the major arguments of this work is that scholars have misunderstood the experience of Afro-Americans who developed economically because they have had no comparative theoretical framework to guide them. In other words, when this Afro-American experience is compared to those of other groups which have experienced hostility throughout history, it is revealed as a case consistent with the special types of adjustments to society that other groups have had to make.

This special adjustment has interested scholars for years, as is apparent in Max Weber's *Protestant Ethic and the Spirit of Capitalism*.[4] He argues that religious or national minorities who are in positions of subordination to rulers are more likely to be driven into economic activity. Because of exclusion from participation in service to the state, the group's best members seek to satisfy the desire for recognition of their abilities in this field, and, we might add, to keep from falling to the bottom of the economic ladder. Weber wrote that this has been true for centuries, as noted by the Poles in Russia and Eastern Prussia, the Huguenots in France under Louis XIV, the Nonconformists and Quakers in England, and the Jews for two thousand years. Middleman theory can be grounded in Weber's ideas, especially since it stresses the relationship that exists between hostility, ethnic solidarity, and business activity. Thus, this work argues that the development of Afro-American enterprise since the 1700s, can best be understood through a reapplication of Weber's principles. Doing so throws a positive, and expected light on the self-help tradition of Afro-

Americans. It also makes all of the criticisms by scholars in the Frazier tradition both obsolete and irrelevant. With an appropriate theoretical tradition to guide us, it becomes clear that there have always been Afro-Americans who adjusted to America by way of self-help and entrepreneurial activities. In the theoretical tradition of sociology of entrepreneurship, I called this group the *truncated Afro-American middleman.*

As with other middleman groups—such as Jewish and Japanese who are so central in sociological studies today—members of the truncated Afro-American middleman group adjusted to America in the tradition of self-help. Significantly, this group developed not only business enterprises but also held strong educational and achievement expectations for their children. They built institutions, especially under the hostile atmosphere of segregation, which served their interests and the interests of their children. Today, these values continue to influence the descendants of the original Afro-American middleman. Like their parents, this group has a great respect for the Afro-American institutions that were founded under slavery. They are still active in those organizations which enhanced the development of their grandparents and parents. They are more likely to continue to be active, sometimes representing the third generation of active participants in these organizations which allowed their parents and grandparents to adapt to a hostile America.

The values passed down from their parents are very similar, if not identical, to those found in the literature on middleman minorities. Without a doubt, my ongoing research convinces me that the descendants of the truncated Afro-American middleman, because of the adjustment of their parents, continue to live an economically stable life that is in sharp contrast to most Afro-Americans, and that for generations *they* have been the truly advantaged of the disadvantaged in America.

It is important to understand that—although scholars throughout the years have tried to document a class structure based on occupational types in the Afro-American community—this is inappropriate. Historically, in order to be included in what I call the Afro-American middleman group, one simply had to show evidence of self-help and achievement. It didn't matter if one owned a grocery store, a pushcart business, or worked as railway porter. There was a great deal of variation in *what* people did, but the key point was that they all came together in community organizations—such as the Masons, fraternities, sororities, churches, and the like—as one solid group.

In the early years and under extreme segregation, one of the most important things families could do was to educate their children. No matter what the individual's occupation, respect within a community was also based on the achievement of offspring.

Such a picture of the Afro-American community moves the unit of analysis away from a simple statistical category to the analyses of a sociological group. This approach is especially true for groups which have historically been refused opportunities in different societies. In other words, although members of a group achieve differentially, they are held together by the common variable that places them in a subordinate status within society. Most often, the source of this status is either religious or racial.

On the other hand, most Afro-Americans adjusted to America by following the ethnic pattern of inclusion. Mostly northern in tradition but not exclusively, they were drawn to that part of the country in order to take advantage of the excellent work opportunities provided by the industrial sector. As with most other ethnic groups, they did not, early on, develop an aggressive attitude toward the education of their children. Because of opportunities in industry, success was measured by having an excellent job. They worked hard in industry, moved from the central city, and now represent what scholars call the new black middle class.

In the late 1960s, with the advent of the Civil Rights Movement, their children became the first in their families to attend college and were more likely to attend the integrated schools of the North which started a series of minority recruitment programs. Unlike the truncated Afro-American middleman, they know little about, or have the same type of respect for the institutions which developed under segregation. Often, they view Afro-American schools as inferior and alien. On the other hand, the Afro-American middleman, both old and young, has a more positive attitude toward the historical role of these institutions. Thus, like ethnic America, we have within the Afro-American tradition two groups whose ancestors adjusted to racism and hostility in America differently. Although the truncated Afro-American middleman and the Afro-American middle class are both economically secure groups, they are the products of two different adjustment patterns. As noted earlier, the pattern of achievement for the two groups has been different over the years. The important point is that, within the Afro-American experience, a clear variation of middleman group behavior and adaptability has been documented and is empirically grounded in this work.

II

As we start the twenty-first century, it is clear that a bifurcation of experience has taken place within the Afro-American community. On the one hand, there are members of the group who are able to take advantage of new opportunities due to their own hard work and the passage of Civil Rights laws within this century. On the other hand, there are members of the group who remain in a state of poverty and despair. The most recent literature on race and economics has tried to capture and understand this bifurcation in the Afro-American experience.

The literature on new opportunities for this group stresses the importance of credentials—such as education and other human capital variables—and job opportunities. In *The Declining Significance of Race*, Wilson noted that members of the Afro-American group who have completed a college degree have enjoyed unprecedented opportunities in the corporate world, especially during the expansion of the economy during the 1970s.[5] It is also clear from this literature that there is no middle ground vis-a-vis the importance of credentials, and that there is little room for Afro-Americans who cannot meet the high credential demands of this marketplace. This point is clearly driven home in a work entitled *The Black Elite: The New Market for Highly Educated Black Americans*.[6]

The theme that there is a portion of the Afro-American community which continues to be in a state of despair can be found in writings as early as Sidney Wilhiem and Edwin Powell's work entitled *Who Needs the Negro?* Wilhiem argued that, within the black community, there were populations of Afro-Americans who were becoming obsolete because they lacked the skills and education to function in a competitive society and thus were not needed.[7] In a book entitled *The Choice*, Sammuel Yette followed this theme by noting that, not only was there a large population of Afro-Americans who had become obsolete, but that the country faced a choice in dealing with this population. In a radical conclusion, Yette argued that one of these choices was the possibility of genocide.[8]

More recently, William Julius Wilson has followed in the tradition of Wilhiem and Yette. He has analyzed the relationship between education, new opportunites, and the changing structure of the Afro-American community. He calls the population of Afro-Americans who are without opportunities in the central cities of America the *underclass*. While this population was falling behind economically, the opportunities for what he calls the *middle class* became unprecedented. This led Wilson to the conclusion that class is more important than race in determining one's life chances in America.[9]

In *The Truly Disadvantaged*, Wilson extends his analysis of the plight of the underclass. He notes that the inner-city ghettos, between the 1960s and the present, underwent a great transformation. The middle class and the working class left those cities, taking with them important values and role models of success. As a result, those people who today make up the core of the central cities are the really poor in America, or the truly disadvantaged, the underclass. Wilson does an outstanding job of showing the struggle and devastating conditions of these Afro-Americans in the "rust belt" cities of the North.

In the final analysis, we must come to the core of the problem—poverty and inequality in American society. The basic question is how will this massive problem be solved? What can be done with the decaying inner-city neighborhoods of Afro-Americans, where hope seems to have died?

Although the problem is great, it is insignificant compared to the problems which Afro-Americans faced at the dawn of their freedom.

From nothing, they created role models, great people, and an economically stable class. Their stability was based on the type of economic foundation which has been peculiar to oppressed people in various societies—namely small enterprise. They carved an economic niche out of nothing. Despite the barriers thrown up by white America, they produced the great men and women who made their marks in history. Their ideas, deeds, institutions, and way of life served as the launching pad for many of today's successful blacks, especially those who are descendants from the *truncated Afro-American middleman.*

Indeed, it is my thesis that their values and deeds—albeit with some augmentation due to historical changes—should serve as the blueprints for Afro-Americans today who find themselves locked into poverty and despair in the core central cities. In addition, researchers in the discipline of race and economics must adjust their approach to the basic problems of poverty and discrimination.

It is quite apparent, given the research on the relationship between human capital and economic stability in America, that those who possess this type of capital in America are more likely to work in what sociologists and economists refer to as the primary sector. In addition to employment, this sector provides important "perks" or advantages which are important in the labor force. These include excellent pay, opportunities for advancement, health care, and adequate employment opportunities. Thus, Afro-Americans who possess these credentials are more likely to work in this labor force.

On the other hand, those with less human capital occupy the secondary labor market, a market composed of bad jobs that do not have the "perks" of the primary sector. Research has documented that Afro-Americans, along with other groups which have experienced discrimination, are more likely to be in this sector. Although different requirements are necessary, both sectors do provide occupations.

But the problem has been that those without credentials fall to the bottom of the economic ladder. This population has been called the "lost generation," the "human junk heap," the "underclass"—a hopeless people because they do not have the skills to operate in American society. However, the interesting thing about research on middleman groups throughout the history of the world—including the Afro-American experience presented here—is that entrepreneurial activities, or small-scale enterprises within communities and throughout communities, help to keep a group from falling to the bottom despite the human capital that members of a group possess.[10] More importantly, in addition to business activity, a set of values about adjusting to America in the face of racial hostility is acquired. More to the point, self-help activities in the form of community enterprises can be accomplished by those without the required human capital—especially if one is a member of a minority group—in order to work in the larger economic sector.

Thus, the first thing that scholars must understand is that the blueprint for the rebuilding of Afro-American communities and a degree of economic security already exists. This is, of course, the model of the Afro-American middleman presented in this work. But because of the theoretical hostility toward the group and this method of adjusting to racism and discrimination, this blueprint for success has been scandalized and rejected as being in the bourgeoisie tradition. In actuality, and as noted in the previous chapter, this adjustment to America is similar, if not identical, to that of other groups which adjusted as middleman minorities.

The major difference is that, while other middleman groups such as the Jews and Japanese maintained their identity, they were not excluded by governmental laws from operating their enterprises in the American marketplace. If they had had to make money only among their own groups, then their offspring would simply become additional groups struggling with poverty in America. In a real sense, given the reality of racial discrimination, and the economic detour, the fact that Afro-Americans were forced to operate enterprises only within their own communities, the adjustment by Afro-Americans is even more impressive. The first thing which scholars must do is redefine their research priorities, placing a great deal of emphasis on the historical role of Afro-Americans as business people using the theoretical framework of middleman minorities. How can this be done?

A moratorium, or at least a partial moratorium, on research on what is called the underclass has to be called. Excellent research has documented the reality of poverty and its consequences. As a result of years and years of research, we know more about the poverty population than about any other problem in the United States. We know about high crime rates, high illegitimacy rates among unmarried mothers, high unemployment rates, and aberrant behavioral patterns.

It is time to develop another research agenda which informs policy, not only because of the abundance of past research on this topic, but also because we can learn nothing about adjusting successfully to racism and discrimination from studying this population. It is obvious that they have not been successful in the face of racial hostility and racism. It is also clear that, when they are successful, they follow the pattern of what I call the truncated Afro-American middleman.

For example, in New Jersey, poor people were faced with a commuting problem because desired occupations were not in the inner city. They were faced with long bus rides, with many transfers, in order to get to work. They started their own commuting service with vans and now own the van company and solved their problem.[11] Continued emphasis of research exclusively on underclass problems provides no blueprint for successful adjustment to America. The major research question should be, given the reality and staying power of racial discrimination—albeit with variations throughout the years—how have some Afro-Americans managed to adjust successfully to American racial hostility? More to the point, if there is an economic cure for the underclass, it will not be found by studying that group alone, but rather by studying the Afro-Americans who have followed successful paths to economic stability for generations in America. We must study how their foreparents were able to lift themselves up in the face of extreme racial hostility since the 1700s. Only then, will we begin to learn about adjusting to America in the face of racial hostility.

Such an approach means, as was our goal in this work, searching for evidence of positive adjustments to racism and discrimination. From a historical perspective, this means rediscovering the positive role models which are buried so deeply in Afro-American culture, showing an appreciation for their economic efforts, and emphasizing the presence of the historical fact of a middleman business tradition. Although overlooked by both scholars and Afro-Americans, the group provides some of the best economic role models of any group that has ever occupied the land of America.

The fact that they were cut off from their mission of complete economic stability for all Afro-Americans is due more to the programs and presence of racism and racial discrimination than to their work, wishes, and desires. The barriers that they overcame were tremendous, for they started with absolutely nothing. Indeed, if Wilson refers to the underclass as the truly disadvantaged, Afro-Americans at the turn of the century were the only helpless disadvantaged.

From a theoretical point of view, it should also be understood that the blueprint for economic advancement—which is that of the truncated Afro-American middleman group—should not be debated in terms of liberal versus conservative orientation. The blueprint is neither conservative nor liberal, but draws its strength from the adjustment of oppressed groups throughout history.

Centuries before Booker T. Washington was born, minority groups in Europe and America utilized the blueprint of self-help and business activity. Part of the reason people have not been able to place the economic ideas of Booker T. Washington in a broader context is because race-relations theory has been noncomparative and somewhat nontheoretical.

As has been shown in this manuscript, the ideas of Booker T. Washington which emerged around the turn of the century were not new when seen in the light of middleman minority theory. To be sure, Washington's ideas on politics were absolutely weak and not nearly as strong as his ideas on race and economics. To "re-baptize" Afro-Americans in the role models and solutions which their forefathers developed under oppressive situations is not to baptize them in the conservative theories of Booker T. Washington, but rather to encourage a path which has been followed for centuries by oppressed and out-cast groups.

This point is very important because there has developed a conservative literature on race and economics which is as theoretically misinformed as Franklin's work, *Black Bourgeoisie*. This literature attempts to account for inequality without giving a considerable weight to the importance of racial discrimination.[12] Instead, it is argued that racial difference in earnings, for example, cannot be explained by discrimination but, instead, reflects the inability of researchers to control for age, geographic location, family size, occupational distribution, educational attainment, and other important background variables.[13] By trying to deny the importance of discrimination, this research tradition denies the very reason that pushed middleman minorities to carve out an economic niche in order to survive, and the reason why their offspring are successful today. It was because of racism and discrimination that groups utilized their ethnic solidarity in order to develop business activity which produced stability. This is inclusive of the truncated Afro-American middleman.

Indeed, one can even argue that, if it were not for the realities of history such as anti-Semitism in Europe and America and racism against Asians in the United States, the descendants of these groups would simply be individuals looking for a job in America. It is because parents, over generations, did not want their children coming face to face with the reality of racial discrimination and anti-Semitism that they stressed the importance of education and small business enterprises, including those which are entrepreneurial in nature such as doctors, lawyers and to an extent educators.

Thus, it is not surprising that Japanese Americans today are less concentrated in semi-skilled occupations than are whites. They are also just as likely to be concentrated in high-status administrative, professional, and technical occupations as are whites. In an interesting way and because of the type of adjustment to middleman made by ancestors due to racial discrimination, Japanese Americans are not concentrated in jobs that are vulnerable to the decline of America's heavy industrial base,[14] a situation which is true for most white Americans, especially in the Northeast. Generations of some European ethnic groups placed their future and the future of their children in the hands of large industries because they were welcomed and not discriminated against, and in the power of the industrial union for their economic security. Thus, they were and are the first to be hurt during times of economic instability.

Because these jobs were so available and had been good for generations, there was and is less of an emphasis on the importance of higher education among these Euro-American groups. Thus, the absence of discrimination and economic hostility actually had a negative effect on the importance of education for future generations of working-class white immigrants in America.

The opposite is true, as has been stressed in this manuscript, for ethnic groups and the truncated Afro-American middleman who experienced hostility based on race or religion. Thus, discrimination and racism must be recognized and acknowledged when one explains the economic success of middleman ethnic groups.[15]

We return, then, to the problem of the underclass in American cities. The spirit of enterprise must be re-created. Unlike Afro-Americans who were forced, after the Civil War, to limit their business efforts to the black community, there must be a concentration on expanding enterprises within and outside of the community.

The first task is to re-create the importance of business activity and economic stability within the central cities. It is obvious from American history that racial discrimination and racism will continue to be a feature of American society for generations to come. Although progress is made within this area, it is clear that each new generation of Euro-Americans contains the seeds of racism and discrimination. It is also obvious from this research that the excellent quality of life which some Afro-Americans enjoy, especially over the generations, is a function not only of the gains of the Civil Rights Movement which began in the 1950s, but also of how their ancestors adjusted to racism and discrimination. Therefore, one must concentrate on methods of adjustments to American society with all its hostile forces.

The task must begin by essentially re-creating the importance of community organizations which, at one time, were so much a part of the self-help tradition in Afro-American communities. These include religious, fraternal, mass media (radio and television), and financial institutions. The National Business League, as was the case during the early part of the century, must become one of the major institutions of Afro-American communities. In short, all of the institutions and self-help attitudes, which E. Franklin Frazier criticized, must be re-created within Afro-American communities.

This task will be difficult, but it can be done. There are so many things which have changed since Afro-Americans were forced to "go-it-alone" during the days of legal segregation and exclusion. But, as noted in the previous chapter, one of the major arguments of this manuscript is that the sons and daughters of the truncated Afro-American middleman continue to be successful because they continue to keep alive those institutions which their foreparents created in order to guide them through very troublesome times. These organizations still include religious, fraternal, and other types of community-based organizations. The approach to America which this group continues to take must be generated throughout the Afro-American community. After the Civil Rights Movement era, the influence of self-help organizations declined in the Afro-American communities. At any rate, these community-based organizations must become active and must be created where they do not exist in order to begin to solve the problems of the underclass in American cities.

It should also be understood that all American cities are not the same. Atlanta is not Detroit, and New York City is not Chicago. Although there are differences between the problems of Afro-Americans in central cities, there is also a major similarity. One of the major differences is the presence and influence of major institutions which are historically significant to the Afro-American experience. Atlanta has always produced a strong college-educated business community among Afro-Americans. This is because, even during segregation, it developed an outstanding reputation as a center of higher learning. Atlanta University, Morehouse College, and Spelman College all developed a certain educational element which, for years, has nurtured the Afro-American community. Detroit has none of these institutions, thus, problems within the Afro-American community have been great. These differences must be considered when we call for a rebuilding of the spirit of enterprise within Afro-American communities.

There are also differences in the movement of the middle class away from traditional Afro-American communities, a theme which has occupied the ethnic literature for years and has just begun to appear in the literature on Afro-Americans.[16] But "moving up" or "moving away" has been a feature of *all* American communities for years, although among Afro-Americans in the South it was more prevalent than with their counterparts in the North. In the South, as noted in the previous chapter, Afro-Americans who were able to afford housing banded together and developed neighborhoods which would be called "suburbs" today. But the fact that the middle class or working class leaves a community does not mean that a community cannot continue to produce working class or middle class people, maintaining itself as a self-respecting community. Consider the following quotation:

> Nationwide, nothing could so strikingly emphasize this point as emergence of public housing resident management corporations. In Washington, Boston, New Orleans, St. Louis, Louisville, Jersey City, Minneapolis, Chicago, Denver, Tulsa, Los Angeles, Kansas City, Baltimore, Pittsburgh, Houston, and wherever public housing authorities have allowed residents to manage public housing units, dramatic changes have taken place—scores of small businesses and hundreds of jobs have been created, crime and vandalism have decreased, teenage pregnancy statistics have been reversed, and fathers and husbands have returned to abandoned families. At the same time, administrative costs have been drastically reduced, vacant apartments repaired, and rent collections doubled and tripled. Before the wave of resident management corporations swept the land, these same residents were looked upon as government wards who could not be trusted to think for themselves. Now operating multi-million dollar budgets, resident managers have turned crime-ridden hell-holes into healthy communities that place a premium on education, family, and self-motivation.[17]

One of the interesting points about this quotation is that, after the people develop a sense of self-help, then values pertaining to education, family and self-motivation follow almost automatically. This is not unlike what took place after slavery and into the beginning of the century. Let us remember that many Afro-Americans who became business people, religious leaders, and educational leaders were born as slaves. One of the fallacies evolving from research on the nature of the inner-city Afro-American community is that the people are not capable of creating or re-creating organizations which can help to bring a sense of stability to their community.

Because of the expansion of opportunities over the last twenty or so years, Afro-Americans certainly will continue to show diversity in terms of where they live and where they work. Those with credentials which are competitive in the larger society will be more likely to work in the open corporate marketplace, and some with credentials will also turn to an entrepreneurship as a way to adjust to America. But it is very important for those people without the credentials which are needed to operate in the larger society—especially if they are from an oppressed minority group—to develop means so they will not fall to the bottom of the economic ladder. Community and broad-based entrepreneurship, which includes enterprises stationed inside and outside of the traditional Afro-American community, must be developed. In other words, entrepreneurship by Afro-Americans today must go beyond the economic detour which was forced upon their ancestors after the Civil War. They must feel free, and they must be welcomed by others to place enterprises throughout the city. They must be accepted as individual business people in the economic marketplace of America.

The blueprint for the development of economic stability is clear and, indeed, was followed by Afro-Americans in earlier years. Certainly the task is difficult, but America has been a difficult place for Afro-Americans ever since they arrived on its shores. At this time, new immigrant groups inhabit once decaying areas of Afro-American communities and turning them into bustling areas of small enterprises. There, the spirit of enterprise, through a conscious community effort, has been or can be reconstructed.

In America today, we have a situation which is almost unprecedented. Our theoretical framework, which comes from the work of Weber, is that oppressed groups throughout history are driven into business activity in order to survive economically. Afro-Americans today seem to have lost the spirit of enterprise which was so prevalent during the early part of this century despite—and because of—the fact that racial oppression is so much a part of their lives. But there are positive signs throughout the country, and occasionally these signs appear in the national media. In Tunica, Mississippi, Peggie Henderson cofounded two clothing stores in 1979. In that same year, her family started the Southern Group, Inc. This company began by providing the service of duplicating videocassettes and distributing chemical cleaners.

Recently, production was augmented when the corporation began to manufacture all-purpose dishwashing liquid at the rate of about 50 bottles a minute. At present, the enterprise employs about twelve people, and expectations are that the number will increase to about 150 at the end of 1989.

Combining the old-fashioned ideas of the Afro-American entrepreneurs with the frustrations of Afro-Americans in the corporate world today, Peggie Henderson notes that, "The only way the conditions of black people will improve is for us to provide jobs for ourselves. I think it's going to get worse as far as white people hiring blacks, unless we are super, super people."[18] Certainly, Afro-American entrepreneurs will not be able to hire the entire Afro-American population of a city, but community enterprises will help people to stay afloat economically and provide alternative sectors for employment. Another example is in the hard-core central city of Miami, Florida. Otis Pitts, a former police officer, has been busy trying to re-create neighborhood stores operated by Afro-American entrepreneurs in the troubled section of Liberty City which experienced a major riot in 1989. Meanwhile, Robert Woodson has created the National Center for Neighborhood Enterprise, which is working to create the spirit of entrepreneurship and self-help in inner cities. This center's focus is the same as that of the organizations which were founded in North Carolina at the turn of the century and which provided the spark for cities such as Durham.

In the South there are scholars who are concerned with redeveloping, on a large scale, the importance of entrepreneurship within agriculture. As pointed out by those individuals who are developing entrepreneurial spirit within this field, blacks are fleeing in droves the profession that their ancestors mastered. Most have done so because of the stigma that slavery cast on farming or because they were forced out of the enterprise due to high taxes levied against their land. One must also consider the historical national trend away from farming as an enterprise. But this does not mean that Afro-Americans cannot re-create the spirit of enterprise within this field.[19]

Our purpose in this work is not to enumerate all of these enterprises, but rather to show the importance of business activity in Afro-American culture. The new research agenda should study enterprises everywhere as they struggle to emerge in American cities. Of course, this is already being done for ethnic groups such as the Chinese, Koreans, and Arabs. But when Afro-Americans engage in business activity, their enterprises are called a myth by scholars—a myth not worth studying. By concentrating on Afro-American enterprise as an area of study, the blueprint for adjustment to American society will be constantly revealed to the Afro-American community, and a new agenda for economic stability will reemerge.

More importantly, this economic stability will launch new generations into the higher educational arena of America. As has been shown in this work, there is no doubt that there is a relationship between the tradition of self-help and the education of offspring. Entrepreneurship within communities means the creation of new launching pads for Afro-American youth. As federal programs cut back on funds for education, these self-help launching pads will become more important.

Such an agenda does not mean a return to the importance of segregation in the inner city. Indeed, one of the characteristics of major American cities is that they are segregated by race. It simply means that people who live in that part of the city should be encouraged to build and maintain community institutions. The fact that Little League baseball returned to Harlem in 1989 after being dormant for more than ten years was due to people who had a spirit of self-help in that community.

Such an agenda also means that any outside programs should be focused in the tradition of self-help and entrepreneurship. There is absolutely no reason why people—even people who are called the underclass—cannot change their focus to this tradition. There is nothing permanent, as can be seen in the presentation of data in this work, about underclass status. Indeed, the most recent research which concentrates on the adjustment of a minority as a middleman group shows how they combine thrift, family cooperation, and governmental resources for the development of business enterprise and the self-help.[20] Such an agenda simply means that, within the constant attempt to develop opportunities within American society, there will be a deliberate return to self-help in order to augment the overall attempt to create opportunities in American society.

It should also be noted that, throughout America, this process is already underway. People are constantly using the tradition of self-help and entrepreneurship to make their lives better. Although the national and local media are less likely to concentrate on this process, people are still running small enterprises in order to send children to college and develop a sense of economic stability. In many communities, there is tutoring of elementary and high-school students so that they can perform better in classrooms. In many communities business people are reemerging as leaders of the community, a position which they occupied when the tradition of self-help was strongest in the Afro-American tradition. This process should be studied and the lessons scattered throughout the land. In a real sense this is also a return to the presentation of early scholarship on Afro-Americans, when during this research, it was very difficult to find systematic research on the success of Afro-Americans in scholarly journals and publications after the late 1950s.

In closing, it is worth noting that a recent *Fortune* magazine article examined the gains made by blacks in America over the last twenty years in business and called it dismal.[21] This article did, however, state that there is an increasing black middle class in the country that consists of lawyers, physicians, other professionals, military officers, entrepreneurs, and state and city officials. One should note that with the exception of the latter—state and city officials—the occupations enumerated by *Fortune* are the same ones that anchored the Afro-American community during segregation. Most are the same lawyers, physicians, entrepreneurs, and others who achieved a degree of success within that segregated economy that were produced by the truncated Afro-American middleman.

Notes

NOTES TO CHAPTER ONE

1. The term entrepreneurship was chosen for this work after much thought and deliberation. This is because some works make a distinction between being engaged in entrepreneurship and self-employment. Those engaged in the former are considered to be bold and imaginative, concentrating on opportunities missed by others, and always in search of profits. People who are self-employed are thought of as primarily interested in simply providing themselves with a job and not interested in enhanced profits and the growth of an enterprise. Although this distinction has merit, it is also true that the types of experiences that we will examine in this book, calls for imagination, the creation of opportunities, or, indeed entrepreneurship. (For a theoretical discussion of the distinction between self-employment and entrepreneurship, *see* Balkin, 1989).

2. See, for example, Lois B. Moreland, *White Racism and the Law* (Columbus, Ohio: A Bell & Howell Company, 1970); Richard Kluger, *Simple Justice* (New York: Alfred A. Knopf, 1975); Joe R. Feagin, *Racial and Ethnic Relations* (New Jersey: Prentice-Hall, 1984).

3. Max Weber, *The Protestant Ethic and the Spirit of Capitalism* (New York: Charles Scribner's Sons, 1930), 35.

4. *Ibid.*, 43. Although Weber recognized the fact that the religious minorities are driven into economic activity or entrepreneurship, it must be pointed out that he drew a distinction between small scale enterprises and large enterprises that were at the center of the capitalist system. For example, in *The Protestant Ethic and the Spirit of Capitalism* (pp. 614–615), he argues that although the Jewish group has a strong history of business activity, they cannot engage in large scale capitalism because they represented a minority that was discriminated against in Europe.

5. Werner Sombart, *The Jews and Modern Capitalism* (New Jersey: Transaction, Inc. Original material copyright by The Free Press, 1951), selections in quotation taken from 11–21.

6. Ivan Light, "Asian Enterprise in America, Chinese, Japanese, and Koreans in Small Business," in *Self-Help in Urban America: Patterns of Minority Economic Development*, Scott Cummings ed. (Port Washington, N.Y.: Kennikat Press, 1980), 33.

7. See, for example, William Toll, *The Making of an Ethnic Middle Class*. New York: State University of New York Press. 1982.

8. Jonathan H. Turner and Edna Bonacich, "Toward a Composite Theory of Middleman Minorities," *Ethnicity*, 7:144–158.

9. Edna Bonacich, "A Theory of Middleman Minorities," *America Sociological Review*, 38 October 1972:583–594.

10. See, for example, *Howard Becker, Man in Reciprocity* (New York: Praeger, 1956); Hubert M. Blalock, Jr., *Toward a Theory of Minority Group Relations* (New York: John Wiley & Sons, 1967); R. A. Schermerhorn, *Comparative and Ethnic Relations* (New York: Random House, 1970); and Sheldon Stryker, "Social Structure and Prejudice," *Social Problems* 6 Spring 1959:340–54.

11. Bonacich, "A Theory of Middleman Minorities," 583.

12. For an exposition on this point see Walter P. Zenner, "Middleman Minorities in The Syrian Mosaic," *Sociological Perspectives* 30 (October, 1987): 400–421.

13. *Op. cit.* Bonacich 584.

14. *Ibid.*, 584.

15. *Ibid.*, 584.

16. *Ibid.*, 590.

17. *Ibid.*, 591. The nested comment is from John Modell, "Class or Ethnic Solidarity: The Japanese American Company Union," *Pacific Historical Review* 38 (May, 1969): 193–206.

18. William Peterson, *Japanese Americans* (New York: Random House, 1971), 9–10.

19. For the reader interested in the Japanese in Hawaii, see Hilary Conroy, *The Japanese Frontier in Hawaii, 1868–1898*, (Berkeley: University of California Press, 1953).

20. Joe R. Feagin, *Racial and Ethnic Relations* (New York: Prentice Hall, 1978), pp. 109 and 140.

21. Vincent N. Parrillo, *Strangers to These Shores* (New York: John Wiley and Sons, 1985), 252.

22. William Peterson, *Japanese Americans* (New York: Random House, 1971), 13–14.

23. *Sacramento Union*, June 18, 1869, 2. Quoted from H. Brett Melendy, *The Oriental Americans* (New York: Hippocrene Books, Inc., 1972), 99.

24. H. Brett Melendy, The Oriental Americans (New York: Hippocrene Books, Inc., 1972).

25. Harry H. L. Kitano, *Japanese Americans* (New York: Prentice Hall, 1969), 7–9.

26. Parillo, *Strangers to These Shores*, 252–253.

27. Feagin, *Racial and Ethnic Relations*, 322–323.

28. Peterson, *Japanese Americans*, 75.

29. Esther B. Rhoads, "My Experience with the Wartime Relocation of Japanese," in *East Across the Pacific: Historical and Sociological Studies of Japanese Immigration and Assimilation*, ed. Hilary Conroy and T. Scott Miyakawa 131–132. Reprinted in Parrillo, *Strangers To These Shores*, 254–255.

30. William Peterson, *The New York Times Magazine*, 9 January 1966.

31. Edna Bonacich and John Modell, *The Economic Basis of Ethnic Solidarity* (Berkeley: University of California Press, 1980), 38.

32. *Ibid.*, 41.

33. *Ibid.*, 41.

34. Bonacich and Modell, *Economic Basis*, 84–85.

35. *Ibid.*, 96.

36. *Ibid.*, 250.

37. Chaim Bermant, *The Jews* (New York: Times Books, 1977), 18–21.

38. *Ibid.*, 24–25.

39. *Ibid.*, 1.

40. There are numerous works of the experience of Jews in European history. For example, *see* Israel Abrams, *Jewish Life in the Middle Ages* (New York: Meridan Books, 1958); Louis Finkelstein, ed., *The Jews: Their History, Culture and Religion* (New York: Harper & Brothers, 1960); Heinrich Graetz, *The History of the Jews* (Philadelphia: The Jewish Publication Society of America, 1956); Max Dimont, *The Indestructible Jews* (New York: The World Publishing Company, 1971); Ellis Rivkin, *The Shaping of Jewish History* (New York: Charles Scribner's Sons, 1971); and Abram Leon Sachar, *A History of The Jews* (New York: Alfred A. Knopf, 1930).

41. As will be seen from further discussion, the Jewish experience cannot be separated from the expansion of Europe nor from the development of capitalism. Thus, in a real sense, the experience deviates significantly from that of the Japanese, although the same theoretical framework has been applied by Max Dimont, *The Jews in America* (New York: Simon and Schuster, 1980), 11.

42. Within the Jewish religious group, different traditions revolve around the nation of origin. Sephardic Jews are from Spain and Portugal. Marranos are Spanish and Portuguese people who converted to Christianity at one time in their history, but later returned to the Jewish faith. Ashkenazi Jews are of European descent, and Oriental Jews hail from North African countries, Egypt, Syria, the Balkans, the former Ottoman Empire and Palestine before 1900. This becomes important as one examines the *Jewish* experience in America. This classification comes from Dimont, *The Jews in America*, 17.

43. Priscilla Fishman, ed., *The Jews of the United States* (New York: Quadrangle, 1973), 5.

44. *Ibid.*

45. Fishman, *Jews of the United States*.

46. *Ibid.*, 39–40.

47. Fishman, 8.

48. Dimont, *Jews in America*, 12–13.

49. Dimont, *Jews in America*, 52–53.

50. *Ibid.*, 57.

51. Fishman, *Jews of the United States*, 11–14.

52. *Ibid.*, 15–16.

53. *Ibid.*, 27–29.

54. *Ibid.*, 32.

55. Alfred Holt Stone, "Is Race Friction Between Blacks and Whites in the United States Growing and Inevitable?", *American Journal of Sociology* 13 (1908): 676–697.

56. Dimont, *Jews in America*, 162–163.

57. Fishman, *Jews of the United States*, 53.

58. For an excellent discussion of stereotyping and prejudice toward Jews, *see* Feagin, *Racial and Ethnic Relations*.

59. Berman, *The Jews*, 4–5.

60. Thomas Sowell, *Race and Economics* (New York: Longman, 1975), 67.

61. *See*, for example, Dimont, *The Jews in America. See also* Werner Sombart, *Jews and Modern Capitalism*.

62. Light, "Asian Enterprise in America," in *Self-Help in Urban America*, 36.

63. Scott Cummings, ed., *Self-Help in Urban America: Patterns of Minority Business Enterprise*.

64. *Ibid.*, 6–7.

65. Lawrence A. Lovell-Troy, "Clan Structure and Economic Activity: The Class of Greeks in Small Business Enterprise," in *Self-Help in Urban America*, Cummings ed., 60.

66. For an excellent discussion of Greek Americans and their success, *see* Charles C. Moskos, Jr., *Greek Americans* (New Jersey: Prentice Hall, 1980).

67. Lawrence A. Lovell-Troy. "Clan Structure and Economic Activity: The Case of Greeks in Small Business Enterprise," in *Self-Help in Urban America*, Cummings ed., 58–85.

68. *Ibid.*, 60–61.

69. *Ibid.*, 63.

70. *Ibid.*

71. *Ibid.*, 80.

72. *Ibid.*, 85.

73. Ivan H. Light, *Ethnic Enterprise in America* (Berkeley: The University of California Press, 1972).

74. Helen F. Clark, "The Chinese of New York Contrasted with Their Foreign Neighbors," *Century* 53 (November 1896): 110, in Light, *Ethnic Enterprise in America*, 25.

75. See, for example, the work of Light, *Ethnic Enterprise in America*, 1972. pp. 33–34.

76. Patricia Gene Greene and John Sibley Butler, "The Minority Community as a Natural Business Incubator," in *Journal of Business Research* 36 (1996), pp. 51–58.

77. Howard Aldrich, J. Carter, T. P. Jones and D. McEvoy, "From Periphery to Peripheral: The South Asian Petite Bourgeoisie in England," in *Research in Sociology of Work* 2 (1983), pp. 1–32.

78. Greene and Butler, op. cit. John Sibley Butler and Patricia Gene Green, "Entrepreneurship and Wealth Building: From Pakistani/Ismaili Enterprise." In Paul D. Reynolds, et al, *Frontiers of Entrepreneurial Research* (Wellesley Massachusetts: Center for Entrepreneurial Studies, 1997), 242–253.

79. See for example Candance Campbell, "Change Agents in the New Economy: Business Incubators and Economic Development," in *Economic Development Review* 7 (1989): 56–59.

80. Patricia Gene Greene and John Sibley Butler, "The Minority Community as a Natural Business Incubator," p. 55.

81. *Ibid.*

82. *Ibid.*, pp. 55–56.

83. *See*, for example, Light, *Ethnic Enterprise in America*, 33–34.

84. A. Kalleberg and A. Sorensen, "The Sociology of Labor Markets," *The Annual Review of Sociology*, 1979, 5:351–379.

85. Robert T. Averitt, *The Dual Economy: The Dynamics of American Industry Structure* (New York: Norton, 1968).

86. *See*, for example, R. C. Edwards, M. Reich and D. M. Gordon, eds., *Labor Market Segmentation* (Lexington, Mass.: Health, 1975).

87. *Ibid.*, 351.

88. *See*, for example, B. Harrison, *Education, Training, and the Urban Ghetto* (Baltimore: Johns Hopkins University Press, 1972).

89. Piore, 1975.

90. *See* Kenneth L. Wilson and Alejandro Portes, "Immigrant Enclaves: An Analysis of the Labor Market Experiences in Cubans in Miami," *American Journal of Sociology*, 86 (September 1980): 295–319; Kenneth L. Wilson and W. Allen Martin. "Ethnic Enclaves: A Comparison of the Cuban and Black Economies in Miami," *American Journal of Sociology*, 88 (1982): 135–159; Alejandro Portes and L. Bach, *Latin Journey* (Berkeley: University of California Press, 1985).

91. Portes and Bach, *Latin Journey*, 203.

92. Wilson and Martin, "*Ethnic Enclaves*," 139.

93. Portes and Bach, *Latin Journey*.

94. Joan Moore and Harry Pachon, *Hispanics in the United States* (New York: Prentice-Hall, 1985), 35–36.

95. Irving Louis Horowitz, "Military Origins of the Cuban Revolution," *Armed Forces and Society*, no. 4, (August 1974): 402–403.

96. Portes and Bach, *Latin Journey*, 201.

97. *Ibid.*, 205.

98. *Ibid.*, 205–206.

99. *Ibid.*, 207–208.

100. *Ibid.*, 239.

101. Although it is clear that the enclave thesis adds to our understanding of adjustment to America and the ethnic experience, a literature is emerging which questions the significance of enclaves' abilities to provide economic stability for an ethnic group. *See*, for example, Victor Nee and Jimmy M. Sanders, "The Limits of Ethnic Solidarity in The Enclave Economy," *American Sociological Review*, 52(1987): 745–773; *see also* Alejandro Portes and Leif Jensen, "What's An Ethnic enclave? The Case for Conceptual Clarity," *American Sociological Review*, 52(1987): 768–771.

102. Wilson and Martin, 154–155.

103. Donald B. Kraybill and Steven M. Nolt, *Amish Enterprise: From Plows to Profits* (Baltimore: The Johns Hopkins University Press, 1995).

104. For a discussion of Anabaptist thought see J. Denny Weaver, *Becoming Anabaptist: The Origin and Significance of Sixteenth Century Anabaptism* (Scottsdale, Pa: Herald Press, 1987). This discussion follows that found in Kraybill and Nolt, *Amish Enterprise*.

105. Donald B. Kraybill and Steven M. Nolt., p. 6.

106. *Ibid.*, pp. 6–7.

107. *Ibid.*, p. 8.

108. *Ibid.*, p. 9.

109. For a discussion see *ibid.*, p. 20.

110. *Ibid.*, p. 25.

111. *Ibid.*, p. 23.

112. *Ibid.*, p. 41.

113. *Ibid.*, p. 43.

114. *Ibid.*, p. 47.

115. *Ibid.*, pp. 47–48.

116. *Ibid.*, p. 48.

117. *Ibid.*

118. *Ibid.*

119. *Ibid.*, p. 41.

120. Robin Ward and Richard Jenkins, *Ethnic Communities in Business: Strategies for Economic Survival* (Cambridge: Cambridge University Press, 1984).

121. *See* especially Gerald Mars and Robin Ward, "Ethnic Business Development in Britain: Opportunities and Resources," in Ward & Jenkins, *Ethnic Communities*, 1–20; Harold Pollins, "The Development of Jewish Businesses in the United Kingdom," in Ward & Jenkins, 73–89; Frank Reeves and Robin Ward, "West Indian Business in Britain," in Ward & Jenkins, 125–149; Pnina Werbner, "Business on Trust: Pakistani Entrepreneurship in the Manchester Garment Trade," in Ward & Jenkins, 169–189.

122. Roy Simon and Bryce-Laporte, *Sourcebook on The New Immigration: Implications for The United States and The International Community* (New Brunswick, New Jersey: Transaction Books, 1980).

NOTES TO CHAPTER TWO

1. Although the work of the early scholars who addressed business enterprise is sometimes quoted in the modern work of scholars such as Light, they are quoted in a way which is unattached to the major theory that has guided this field of research. These early works on Afro-American scholars should the be starting point and anchor the ideas which have been developed in the area of ethnic entrepreneurship. Not realizing this is the same as arguing that rock-and-roll music started with Elvis Presley and that jazz had its beginning in the music work of Paul Whiteman. For a discussion of the process by which the contribution of blacks have been excluded from the cultural and intellectual arena, *see* Harold Cruse, *The Crisis of The Negro Intellectual*, 1977.

2. Bonacich, "Theory of Middleman Minorities," 583–594.

3. Light, "Asian Enterprise in America," in *Self-Help in Urban America* Cummings, ed., 33.

4. "The Negro in Business," *Ebony*, 18 (1963): 212.

5. Robert H. Kinzer and Edward Sagarin, *The Negro in American Business* (New York: Greenberg Publisher, 1950), 27.

6. Juliet E. K. Walker, "Racism, Slavery, and Free Enterprise: Black Entrepreneurship in the United States Before the Civil War," in *Business History Review*, 60 (Autumn 1986): 333.

7. Joseph A. Pierce, *Negro Business and Business Education* (New York: Harper & Brothers Publishers, 1947).

8. Kinzer and Sagarin, *Negro in American Business*, 30.

9. John Hope Franklin, *From Slavery to Freedom* (New York: Alfred A. Knopf, 1948), quotation taken from Kinzer and Sagarin, *Ibid.*, 32.

10. For a discussion of the experiences of free Afro-Americans *see* Leonard P. Curry, *The Free Black in Urban America 1800–1865* (Chicago: The University of Chicago Press, 1981); Ira Berlin, *Slaves Without Masters* (New York: Pantheon Books, 1974); Kenneth G. Goode, *California's Black Pioneers* (Santa Barbara: McNally & Loftin, Publishers, 1974).

11. Henry M. Minton, M.D., *Early History of Negroes in Business in Philadelphia,* read before The American Historical Society, March, 1913.

12. *Ibid.,* 8–10.

13. *Ibid.,* 6–6.

14. Walker, *Racism, Slavery, and Free Enterprise,* 252.

15. *Ibid.,* 349.

16. *Ibid.,* 11.

17. *Ibid.,* 8.

18. *Ibid.,* 8–9.

19. *Ibid.*

20. Abram H. Harris, *The Negro As Capitalist* (New York: Arno Press, 1936), 9–10.

21. *Ibid.,* 20–21.

22. *Ibid.,* 21–22.

23. *Ibid.,* 22.

24. Light, *Ethnic Enterprise in America* (Berkeley: University of California Press, 1972), 19.

25. *Ibid.,* 21.

26. Harris, *Negro as Capitalist,* 6–7.

27. *Ibid.,* 11–12.

28. *Ibid.*

29. *Ibid.,* 4–5.

30. Walker, *Racism, Slavery, and Free Enterprise,* 354.

31. *Ibid.*

32. Kinzer & Sagarin, *Negro in American Business,* 36.

33. *Ibid.*

34. Harris, *The Negro As Capitalist,* 17.

35. *Ibid.*

36. Walker, *Racism, Slavery, and Free Enterprise,* 364.

37. *Ibid.,* 365.

38. *Ibid.,* 366.

39. Most of this literature has been presented by historians. See especially Juliet E. K. Walker. *Free Frank: A Black Pioneer on the Antebellum Frontier* (Lexington, Kentucky:

University of Kentucky Press, 1983); Gary B. Mills, *The Forgotten People: Cane River's Creoles of Color* (Baton Rouge: Louisiana State University Press, 1977); Leonard P. Curry, *The Free Black in Urban America, 1880–1850: The Shadow of A Dream* (Chicago: The University of Chicago Press, 1981).

40. Pierce, *Negro Business,* 6.

41. Kinzer & Sagarin, *Negro in American Business,* 35–37.

42. William Z. Foster, *The Negro People in American History* (New York: International Publishers, 1954), 56.

43. *Ibid.*

44. Henry D. Spaulding, *Encyclopedia of Black Folklore* (New York: Middle Village, Jonathan David Publishers, 1972), 417.

45. *Ibid.*

46. *Ibid.*

47. Aaron E. Klein, *The Hidden Contributors: Black Scientists and Inventors in America* (New York: Doubleday, 1971).

48. *Ibid.,* 6–9.

49. *Ibid.,* 10.

50. *Ibid.*

51. *Ibid.,* 22–28.

52. *Ibid.,* 28.

53. *Ibid.,* 29–30.

54. *Ibid.,* 37–38.

55. *Ibid.,* 38–39.

56. *Ibid.,* 39.

57. *Ibid.,* 59.

58. *Ibid.*

59. *Ibid.,* 70.

60. *Ibid.*

61. *Ibid.,* 72.

62. *Ibid.,* 72–73.

63. *Ibid.,* 74.

64. William C. Davis, *The Civil War* (Alexandria, Virginia: Time-Life Books, 1983), 9.

65. *Ibid.,* 13–14.

66. *Ibid.,* 15–16.

67. Richard J. Stillman, *Integration of the Negro in the U.S. Armed Forces* (New York: Frederick Praeger, 1968), 9.

68. Dwight W. Hoover, *Understanding Negro History* (Chicago: Quadrangle Books, 1968), 9.

69. Foster, *The Negro People,* 274.

70. *Ibid.,* 286–287.

71. *See,* for example, S. Dale McLemore, *Racial and Ethnic Relations in America* (Boston: Allyn and Bacon, Inc., 1983), 271–281.

72. *Ibid.,* 337.

73. For an excellent discussion, see C. Vann Woodward, *The Strange Career of Jim Crow* (New York: Random House, 1955).

74. W. E. B. Du Bois, *The Souls of Black Folk* (New York: Fawcett Publications, Inc., 1977), 42.

75. Louis R. Harlan, *Booker T. Washington: The Wizard of Tuskegee* (New York: Oxford University Press, 1983).

76. Stokely Carmichael and Charles V. Hamilton, *Black Power: The Politics of Liberation* (New York: Vintage Press, 1967), 125.

77. Booker T. Washington, "The Atlanta Exposition Address," in John Hope Franklin and Isidore Starr, *The Negro in Twentieth Century America: A Reader on the Struggle for Civil Rights* (New York: Vintage Books, 1967), 85–87.

78. *Ibid.,* 88.

79. Booker T. Washington, *The Negro in Business* (Chicago: Hertel, Jenkins & Co., 1907), 14–15.

80. *Ibid.*

81. *Ibid.,* 346.

82. *Ibid.,* 347.

83. W. E. B. Du Bois, *The Philadelphia Negro* (New York: Schocken, 1967), 311–318.

84. *Ibid.,* 26, 31.

85. August Meier, *Negro Thought in America: 1880–1915* (Ann Arbor: The University of Michigan Press, 1966), 125–126.

86. M. S. Stuart, *An Economic Detour* (New York: Wendell Malliett and Company, 1940).

87. Bonacich and Modell, *Economic Basis of Ethnic Solidarity,* 98.

88. Harris, *Negro as Capitalist,* 11.

89. Stuart, *Economic Detour,* xviii–xix.

90. C. Van Woodward, *The Strange Career of Jim Crow* (New York: Random House, 1955); Clarence A. Bacote, "Some Aspects of Negro Life in Georgia, 1880–1908," *Journal of Negro History,* 43 (July 1958): 186–213; John Hope Franklin, "History of Racial Segregation in the United States," *Annals,* 304 (March 1956): 1–9;

and Roger L. Rice, "Residential Segregation by Law, 1910–1911," *Journal of Southern History*, 34 (May 1968): 179–199.

91. Stuart, *Economic Detour,* xxiii.

92. *Ibid.,* xxii–xxi.

93. Bonacich and Modell, *Economic Basis,* 111.

94. *See* especially W. E. B. Du Bois, *The Souls of Black Folk* (New York: Fawcett Publications, 1961), the chapter entitled "Of Mr. Booker T. Washington and Others." For an excellent collection of the major opposition against Washington, see August Meier and Ruderick, *Negro Protest in the Twentieth Century* (Urban: University of Illinois Press, 1976).

95. Bonacich and Modell, *Economic Basis,* 16.

96. E. Franklin Frazier, *Black Bourgeoisie* (New York: Collier Books, 1957), 129–145.

97. See James Boggs, *Racism and the Class Struggle* (New York: Monthly Review Press, 1970); Earl Ofari, *The Myth of Black Capitalism* (New York: Monthly Review Press, 1970); and St. Clair Drake and Horace Clayton, *Black Metropolis* (New York: Harcourt, Brace, 1945).

98. See, for example, Peter Decker, *Fortunes and Failures; White Collar Mobility in Nineteenth Century San Francisco* (Cambridge: 1978); E. Kimbark MacColl, *The Shaping of a City: Business and Politics in Portland, Oregon, 1885–1915* (Portland: University of Oregon Press); Donna R. Gabaccia, *From Sicily to Elizabeth Street: Housing and Social Change Among Italian Immigrants, 1880–1930* (Albany: State University of New York Press, 1984).

NOTES TO CHAPTER THREE

1. Religion has played an important organizing role in ethnic communities. For example, *see* Jack Chen, *The Chinese of America* (New York: Harper & Row, 1980), 120–121; Joe R. Feagin, *Racial and Ethnic Relations* (Englewood Cliffs, New Jersey: Prentice-Hall, 1984); Luciano J. Lorizzo and Salvatore Mondello, *The Italian-Americans* (Boston: Twayne Publishers, 1971); and Dimont, *The Jews In America.*

2. Foster, *The Negro People in American History,* 97–98.

3. Sidney Kaplan, *The Black Presence in the Era of the American Revolution* (Washington D.C.: Smithsonian Institution, 1973), 81.

4. *Ibid.,* 85.

5. Meier, *Negro Thought In America,* 44–45.

6. W. E. B. Du Bois, *Economic Co-Operation Among Negro Americans* (Atlanta: The Atlanta University Press, 1907), 78–81.

7. *Ibid.,* 85.

8. *Ibid.*, 88.

9. Louis R. Harlan. *Separate and Unequal* (New York: Atheneum, 1969), 3.

10. *Ibid.*, 4–5.

11. *Ibid.*, 10–11.

12. *Ibid.*, 10.

13. *Ibid.*

14. *Ibid.*, 11–12.

15. Du Bois, *Economic Co-Operation*, 90.

16. Stuart, *Economic Detour*, 4.

17. *Ibid.*, 7–8.

18. Du Bois, *Economic Co-Operation*, 92–93.

19. *Ibid.*, 92–93.

20. *Ibid.*, 95.

21. *Ibid.*, 96–97.

22. Stuart, *Economic Detour*, 11.

23. *Ibid.*

24. See William Denslow, *10,000 Famous Freemasons* (Missouri: Missouri Lodge of Research, 1957); Ronald Heaton, *The Masonic Membership of the Founding Fathers* (Masonic Service Association, 1974); and Alphonse Cerza, "Masons," in *Encyclopedia Americana* (Danbury Connecticut: Grolier Incorporated, 1980), 18: 432.

25. Du Bois, *Economic Co-Operation*, 22–23.

26. *Ibid.*, 110.

27. *Ibid.*

28. *Ibid.*, 110–111.

29. *Ibid.*, 121–122.

30. *Ibid.*, 122.

31. Stuart, *Economic Detour*, 14–15.

32. *Ibid.*, 12–13.

33. "Report of the Hampton Conference," No. 8, 15–16, 18. Quoted in W. E. B. Du Bois, *Economic Co-Operation*.

34. J. H. Harmon, Jr., Arnett G. Lindsay and Carter G. Woodson, *The Negro As A Business Man* (College Park, Maryland, McGrath Publishing Company: 1929), 97.

35. Stuart, *Economic Detour*, 36.

36. *Ibid.*, 36–37.

37. Stuart, *Economic Detour*, 59–61.

38. *Ibid.*, 36.

39. *Ibid.*, 42–44.

40. *Ibid.*, 46.

41. *Ibid.*, 49–50.

42. Kinzer & Sagarin, *The Negro in American Business.*

43. *Ibid.*, 93.

44. Pierce, *Negro Business,* 126.

45. *Ibid.*, 128–129.

46. *Ibid.*, 134.

47. *Ibid.*, 133–135.

48. *Ibid.*, 140–141.

49. William K. Bell, *A Business Primer for Negros* (New York: William K. Bell, 1948), 185–186.

50. W. J. Kennedy, Jr., "The Negro's Adventure in The Field of Life Insurance," in William K. Bell, 1948, 186.

51. *Ibid.*, 186–187.

52. Light, *Ethnic Enterprise in America,* 48–49.

53. Pierce, *Negro Business,* 150–152.

54. Dave Skidmore, "Bank Failures Hit a Record During 1987," *Austin American-Statesman.* Wednesday, January 6, 1988, C8.

55. Harris, *The Negro As Capitalist,* 22.

56. Mauris Lee Porter Emeka, *Black Banks, Past and Present* (Kansas City, Missouri: 1971), 6.

57. *Ibid.*, 6–7.

58. Richard J. Stillman, *Integration of the Negro in the U.S. Armed Forces* (New York: Frederick Praeger, 1968), 169.

59. Dwight W. Hoover, *Understanding Negro History* (Chicago: Quadrangle Books, 1968), 270.

60. Stillman, *Integration of the Negro,* 11.

61. Walter L. Fleming, *The Freedmen's Savings Bank* (Chapel Hill: University of North Carolina Press, 1927), 20.

62. Du Bois, *Economic Co-Operation,* 137.

63. *Ibid.*

64. Harmon, Jr., Lindsay, and Woodson, 44–45.

65. Washington, *Negro in Business,* 111–112.

66. Harris, *Negro As Capitalist,* 47–48.

67. Other excellent works are Jesse B. Blayton, "The Negro in Banking," *Bankers Magazine.* 133 (December 1936): 511–514; Harry H. Pace, "The Business of Banking Among Negroes," *Crisis* (February 1927): 184–188.

68. *Ibid.*, 59.

69. *Ibid.*, 60.

70. T. Bruce Robb, "Safeguarding the Depositor," *The Annals of the American Academy of Political and Social Science,* Philadelphia: (January 1934) 171: 56–57. Quoted from Mauris Lee Porter Emeka, *Black Banks Past and Present* (Kansas City: 1971).

71. Robert Weidenhammer, "An Analysis of Fifty Bank Families," *The Annals of the American Academy of Political Social Science,* Philadelphia: (1934), 171: 50. See also Emeka, *Black Banks,* 38.

NOTES TO CHAPTER FOUR

1. For an excellent analysis on this point *see* August Meier, "Negro Class Structure in the Age of Booker T. Washington," *Phylon* (Fall 1962): 258–266.

2. Monroe N. Work, *Negro Year Book, 1918–1919* (Tuskegee, Alabama: Tuskegee Normal and Industrial Institute, 1919) 359.

3. William A. Carter, "Negro Main Street As a Symbol of Discrimination," *Phylon* (Fall 1960): 236.

4. *See* "Business in Bronzeville," *Time.* 18, April 1938.

5. Archibald Henderson, *North Carolina: The Old North State and the New* (Chicago: 1941), 440–41.

6. Stephen J. Whitfield, "Commercial Passions: The Southern Jew as Businessman," *American Jewish History,* 1982, 71; 342–357.

7. Thomas D. Clark, "The Post-Civil War Economy in the South," eds. Leonard Dinnerstein and Mary Dale Palsson (Baton Rouge: Louisiana State University Press, 1973) 166.

8. Margaret Levenstein, "African-American Entrepreneurship: The View from the 1910 Census," *Business and Economic History,* v. 24 no. 1, Fall 1995.

9. *Ibid.,* pp. 107-108.

10. *Ibid.,* p. 115.

11. *Ibid.,* p. 108.

12. Juliet E. K. Walker, *The History of Black Business in America: Capitalism, Race, Entrepreneurship.* New York: Simon & Schuster, 1998.

13. See Jonathan Greenberg, *Staking a Claim: Jake Simmons, Jr. and the Making of an African-American Oil Dynasty.* New York: Atheneum, 1990.

14. Juliet E. K. Walker, *The History of Black Business in America: Capitalism, Race, Entrepreneurship.* New York: Simon & Schuster, 1998.

15. A'Lelia Bundles, *On Her Own Ground: The Life and Times of Madam C. J. Walker.* New York: Scribner, 2001.

16. For a discussion see Juliet E. K. Walker, *The History of Black Business in America: Capitalism, Race, Entrepreneurship.* New York: Simon & Schuster, 1998.

17. Washington, *Negro in Business,* 14–15.

18. August Meier, *Negro Thought in America: 1880–1915* (Ann Arbor: The University of Michigan Press, 1966), 114.

19. Meier, *Negro Thought in America,* 125–157.

20. Work, *Negro Year Book,* 132–133.

21. *Ibid.,* 133.

22. Irene Caldwell Hypps, *Changes in Business Attitudes and Activities of The Negro In The United States Since 1619* (Ph.D. Diss. New York University, 1943), 144.

23. *Ibid.,* 145.

24. *Ibid.,* 145–146.

25. *See* Sterling Spero and Abram L. Harris, *The Black Worker* (New York: Columbia University Press, 1931), 50–51.

26. Study summarized in Monroe N. Work, *Negro Year Book* (Tuskegee, Alabama: Tuskegee Institute, 1937–1938), 94.

27. Pierce, *Negro Business.*

28. *Ibid.,* 31.

29. *Ibid.,* 53.

NOTES TO CHAPTER FIVE

1. George Gilder, *The Spirit of Enterprise* (New York: Simon & Schuster, Inc., 1984), 93–114.

2. William Kenneth Boyd, *The Story of Durham* (Durham, North Carolina: Duke University Press, 1927), 277.

3. Booker T. Washington, "Durham, North Carolina: A City of Negro Enterprises," in *Independent,* 70 (March 30, 1911): 642.

4. Emphasis author's.

5. Boyd, *Story of Durham,* 277.

6. E. Franklin Frazier, "Durham: Capital of the Black Middle Class," in *The New Negro* Winold Reiss, ed. (New York: Albert and Charles Boni, 1925) 333.

7. "Wall Street of Negro America," *Ebony,* 4 (September 1949): 19–22.

8. S. Huntington Hobbs, Jr., *North Carolina: An Economic and Social Profile* (Chapel Hill: The University of North Carolina Press, 1958), 52.

9. Helen Edmonds, *The Negro and Fusion Politics in North Carolina* (Chapel Hill: Duke University Press, 1951).

10. Frank Hollowell White, The Economic and Social Development of Negroes in North Carolina Since 1900 (New York University: Ph.D. Diss., 1960), 2.

11. *Ibid.*

12. *Ibid.*

13. Bureau of the Census, *Negro Population, 1790–1915,* 15. Quoted in *Ibid.*

14. C. Horace Hamilton and Francis Henderson, "Migration from North Carolina Farms," *University of North Carolina News Letter,* 89, 24 February 1943. Quoted in *Ibid.*

15. White, *Economic and Social Development,* 89.

16. From an interview with Dr. Eugene A. Evaes, professor at North Carolina Central University, Durham, North Carolina.

17. Claudia P. Roberts, *The Durham Architectural and Historic Inventory* (Durham: The Historic Preservation Society, 1981), 113.

18. *Ibid.,* 114.

19. *Ibid.*

20. Hugh Penn Brinton, *The Negro in Durham: A Study of Adjustment to Town Life* (Chapel Hill: The University of North Carolina at Chapel Hill, Ph.D. Diss., 1930), iv–v.

21. *Ibid.,* vi. An interesting account of the hosiery mill can be found in Chapter Seven. See also Boyd, *Story of Durham.*

22. Brinton, *Negro in Durham,* 141.

23. *Ibid.,* 146.

24. *Ibid.,* 147.

25. Thomas H. Houck, *A Newspaper History of Race Relations in Durham, North Carolina, 1910–1940* (Durham, N.C.: Graduate School of Arts and Sciences, 1941), 31–32.

26. *Ibid.,* 162.

27. Rayford W. Logan, "The Hiatus—A Great Negro Middle-Class," *Southern Workman,* 58: 531–535.

28. Brinton, *Negro in Durham,* 165.

29. Roberts, *Durham Architectural and Historical Inventory,* 114–115.

30. Thomas H. Houck, *A Newspaper History of Race Relations in Durham, North Carolina: 1910–1940* (Masters Thesis: Duke University, 1941).

31. Frazier, "Durham: Capital of the Black Middle Class" in The New Negro, ed. Reiss, 333–334.

32. Walter B. Weare, *Black Business in the New South: A Social History of The North Carolina Mutual Life Insurance Company* (Chicago: University of Illinois Press, 1973), 4–5.

33. William Kenneth Boyd, *The Story of Durham: City of The New South* (Durham, N.C.: Duke University Press, 1927).

34. *Ibid.*, 279.

35. *Ibid.*

36. Weare, *Black Business*, 39–42.

37. Clipping, *Raleigh News and Observer*, 26 May 1899, Carr Papers. Quoted from Weare, *ibid.*, 40.

38. *Ibid.*, 40–41.

39. Boyd, *Story of Durham*, 279–280.

40. *Ibid.*, 278–279.

41. Weare, *Black Business*, 42–43.

42. "Wall Street of Negro America," *Ebony*. (September 1949): 19–22.

43. *Ibid.*

44. *Ibid.*

45. "Durham, North Carolina: A City of Negro Enterprise," in *Independent*. 60, 30 March 1911: 642.

46. *Ibid.*, 644.

47. Boyd, *Story of Durham*, 290.

48. Andrew, R. McCants, *John Merrick A Bibliographical Sketch* (Durham, N.C.: The Seeman Printery, 1920), 50–56.

49. Quoted from Houck, "A Newspaper History of Race Relations in Durham, N.C." 89.

50. *Ibid.*, 82.

51. *The Durham Morning Herald*, 16 September 1927. Quoted from Houck, *Newspaper History*, 81.

52. *Ibid.*, 82.

53. *Ibid.*

54. W. E. B. Du Bois, "The Upbuilding of Black Durham," *World's Work*, 23 (January 1912): 334–338. As quoted in Weare, *Black Business*, 44.

55. *Ibid.*

56. Weare, *Black Business*, 26.

57. Boyd, *Story of Durham*, 286.

58. Albon Holsey, "Pearson: The Brown Duke of Durham," *Opportunity*, (April, 1923): 116.

59. Stuart, *Economic Detour*, 196.

60. *Ibid.*, 196–197.

61. *Ibid.*, 198.

62. *Ibid.*, 197.

63. *Ibid.*, 204.

64. *Ibid.*, 205.

65. *Ibid.*, 205–206.

66. *Ibid.*

67. Weare, *Black Business,* 54–55.

68. Forty-first Annual Statement, North Carolina Mutual Life Insurance Company (Durham, N.C.: December, 1939).

69. *The Whetstone,* Magazine of the North Carolina Mutual Life Insurance Company. Fortieth Anniversary, edition, 1938.

70. Stuart, *Economic Detour,* 210.

71. *Ibid.*, 210–211.

72. Forty-first Annual Statement, *op. cit.* This section also draws from Houck, *Newspaper History, see* especially 64–96.

73. *The Durham Herald,* 18 December 1921. Quoted in Houck, *Newspaper History,* 89.

74. *Ibid.*

75. Weare, *Black Business,* 92.

76. *Ibid.*, 180.

77. *Ibid.,* see especially Chapters Four, Five, and Six.

78. *The Durham Sun,* April 1939, 50th anniversary Edition, Business Section. Also Houck, *Newspaper History,* 88–89.

79. *Ibid.*, 163–164.

80. *Ibid.*, 168.

81. Portes and Bach, *Latin Journey,* 203.

82. Wilson and Portes, "Immigrant Enclaves," 295–319; Wilson and Martin, "Ethnic Enclaves," 135–159; Portes and Bach, *Latin Journey.*

83. Bonacich and Modell, *Economic Basis.*

84. *Black Enterprise,* June 1987, 196, 228, and June 1990, 214–218.

85. *Ibid.*, June 1987, 197–198.

86. The discussion of present day Durham was based on personal conversations and interviews which took place during visits to Durham. See also the following articles that appear in *Agenda: The Alternative Magazine of Critical Issues.* Neighborhood Policy Institute: The National Center For Neighborhood Enterprise. Washington, D.C., Fall, 1990. John Sibley Butler, "Self-help and Adjustment to American Society," 2–6; F. V. Allison, "The Durham Story: 100 Years of Black Enterprise," 7–12; and Larry Hester, "I'll Be My Own Developer: The Story of Phoenix Square," 13–15.

NOTES TO CHAPTER SIX

1. H. Wayne Morgan and Anne Hodges Morgan, *Oklahoma* (New York: W. W. Norton & Company, 1977), 14–18.

2. Patrick J. Blessing, *The Irish and British in Oklahoma* (Norman, Oklahoma: The University of Oklahoma Press, 1980), 27–28.

3. Richard C. Rohrs, *The Germans in Oklahoma* (Norman, Oklahoma: University of Oklahoma Press, 1980), 18–19.

4. Kenny L. Brown, *The Italians in Oklahoma* (Norman, Oklahoma: University of Oklahoma Press, 1980), 14.

5. Henry J. Tobias, *The Jews in Oklahoma* (Norman, Oklahoma: University of Oklahoma Press, 1980), 8–9.

6. For a discussion of these groups *see* Karel D. Bicha, *The Czech in Oklahoma* (Norman, Oklahoma: University of Oklahoma Press, 1980); Richard M. Bernard, *The Poles in Oklahoma* (Norman, Oklahoma: University of Oklahoma Press, 1980).

7. Blessing, *The Irish and British*, 34–35.

8. Tobis, *Jews in Oklahoma*, 53.

9. For an interesting discussion of the different waves of Afro-Americans who were exposed to Oklahoma and the "new world" since the 1500s, see Arthur L. Tolson, *The Black Oklahomans, A History: 1541–1972* (New Orleans: Edwards Printing Company, 1966).

10. *Ibid.*, 19.

11. Duane Gage, "Oklahoma: A Resettlement Area for Indians," in *Chronicles of Oklahoma*. 47, 1969–1970: 286.

12. Wyatt F. Jeltz, "The Relations of Negroes and Choctaw and Chickasaw Indians," in *Journal of Negro History*. 33, 1948; 28–30. Also in Tolson, *Black Oklahomans*, 21.

13. *Ibid.* Quoted from Tolson, *Black Oklahomans*, 22.

14. Colonel Clarence B. Douglas, *The History of Tulsa, Oklahoma. Vol. I* (Chicago: The S. J. Clarke Publishing Company, 1921), 29–30.

15. Tolson, *Black Oklahomans*, 32.

16. John Sibley Butler, *Inequality in the Military: The Black Experience* (Saratoga, California: Century Twenty-One Publishing, 1980), 23.

17. Tolson, *Black Oklahomans*, 38–39.

18. *Ibid.*, 36–37.

19. *Ibid.*, 41.

20. For example, a black convention was held in Kansas in 1882 for the purpose of discussing the massive settlement of blacks in Oklahoma. This convention sent a letter to Congress asking that every third section of land in that territory be reserved for blacks from the South. For a discussion of these issues, see Tolson, *Black Oklahomans*.

21. *See* Mozel C. Hill, "The All-Negro Communities of Oklahoma: The Natural History of a Social Movement," in *Journal of Negro History*. 31 (July 1946): 254–68; William Bittle and Gilbert Geis, "Racial Self-fulfillment and the Rise of an All-Negro Community in Oklahoma," *Phylon*. 17. 1956. 247–60.

22. Tolson, *Black Oklahomans*, 45.

23. Jimmie Lewis Franklin, *The Blacks in Oklahoma* (Norman, OK: University of Oklahoma Press, 1980), 26.

24. *Ibid.*, 23.

25. *Ibid.*, 26–27.

26. *Ibid.*

27. For more on blacks in Oklahoma see *ibid.*

28. Douglas, *History of Tulsa*, 114–154.

29. Scott Ellsworth, *Death in a Promised Land* (Baton Rouge: Louisiana State University Press, 1982), 10–13.

30. Walter White, "The Eruption of Tulsa," *The Nation*, 29 June 1921, 909.

31. Ellsworth, *Death in a Promised Land*, 1–3.

32. *Ibid.*, 1.

33. *Ibid.*, 15–16.

34. For example, see "The Tulsa Race Riots," *The Independent*, 18 June 1921, 646–647; White, "The Eruption of Tulsa," *The Nation*, 909–910.

35. Douglas, *History of Tulsa*, 621.

36. *Ibid.*, 16.

37. R. Halliburton Jr., *The Tulsa Race War of 1921* (San Francisco: R and E Research Associates, 1975), vii.

38. *Ibid.*, 3.

39. Ellsworth, *Death in a Promised Land*, 32.

40. Tulsa *Tribune*, 1 June 1921. Our thanks to Professor Patricia Bell of Oklahoma State University for providing all old newspapers published during the period of the riot.

41. Franklin, *Blacks in Oklahoma*, 32.

42. Halliburton, *Tulsa Race War*, 7.

43. Ellsworth, *Death in a Promised Land*, 24–25.

44. White, "The Eruption of Tulsa," 909.

45. Halliburton, *Tulsa Race War*, 5–6.

46. Ellsworth, *Death in a Promised Land*, 52.

47. Halliburton, *Tulsa Race War*, 4.

48. *Ibid.*, 10.

49. Ellsworth, *Death in a Promised Land*, 55.

50. Halliburton, *Tulsa Race War*, 11.

51. Franklin, *Blacks in Oklahoma*, 33–34.

52. Ellsworth, *Death in a Promised Land*, 57.

53. Douglas, *History of Tulsa*, 623.

54. Tulsa *Daily World* 1 June 1921.

55. Halliburton, *Tulsa Race War*, 12–13.

56. All readings indicate that there is some confusion over the use of planes during the destruction of Greenwood.

57. Ellsworth, *Death in a Promised Land*, 63.

58. Douglas, *History of Tulsa*, 621–622.

59. National Association for the Advancement of Colored People, Oklahoma Riot Victims' Relief and Defense Fund, Box C-162, NAACP Papers, Library of Congress.

60. *Ibid.*

61. White, "The Eruption of Tulsa," 909.

62. *Ibid.*

63. Amy Comstock, "Over There: Another View of the Tulsa Riots," *Survey*, 2 July 1921, 460.

64. Halliburton, *Tulsa Race War*, 29.

65. *Ibid.*, 26–28.

66. Tulsa *Daily World*, 26 June 1921.

67. Douglas, *History of Tulsa*, 322.

68. Weare, *Black Business.*

69. "Good People and Dirty Work," in *The Sociological Eye: Collected Works of Everett Hughes* (Chicago: Aldine, 1971), 87–97.

70. *Ibid.*, 88.

71. *Ibid.*, 89.

72. *Ibid.*

73. *Ibid.*, 90.

74. *Ibid.*

75. "Blood and Oil," in *The Survey*, vol 66, 11 June 1921.

76. White, "The Eruption of Tulsa," 909.

77. Many of the historical events reported in this chapter were related to me by people of the Greenwood Section of Tulsa. I especially thank Shana Miller, Robert Goodwin, Gary Davis, and Lloyd Williams, Jr. Another source for general information in the chapter is a video entitled "The Greenwood Blues," that was produced by 5 Alive Productions of Oklahoma City (1983). The video can be found in the Public Library of the Greenwood section of Tulsa.

NOTES TO CHAPTER SEVEN

1. See especially Light *Ethnic Enterprise*.

2. Frazier, *Black Bourgeoisie*.

3. *Ibid.*, 7.

4. Although Frazier's study is often identified as the seminal work on the black middle class, other works relating to the topic preceded the publication of his book. In 1944, Gunner Myrdal laid out many of the problems addressed by Frazier in chapters 14 and 32 in *An American Dilemma* (New York: 1944). In 1945, St. Clair Drake and Horace R. Clayton published *Black Metropolis: A Study of Negro Life in a Northern City* (New York); in 1937, John Dillard published *Caste and Class in a Southern Town* (New Haven). Although these works deal with similar topics as Frazier, they did not capture and stir the waves of uproar caused by *Black Bourgeioise*.

5. Nathan Hare, *Black Anglo-Saxon* (New York: MacMillan, 1970); Oliver Cox wrote the introduction to this work, see 20.

6. *Ibid.*, 17.

7. William A. Muraskin, *Middle-Class Blacks In A White Society* (Berkeley: University of California Press, 1975).

8. *Ibid.*, 2.

9. For a review of those criticisms, see the preface of Frazier's *Black Bourgeoisie*. He lays out the criticisms and answers them. They range from what people said to him on the street to official publications about his work.

10. Frazier, *Black Bourgeoisie*, 129.

11. Bart Landry, *The New Black Middle Class* (Berkeley: University of California Press, 1987), 212.

12. *Ibid.*

13. Weber, *The Protestant Ethic*, 39.

14. *Ibid.*

15. Bonacich and Modell, *Economic Basis*, 17–18.

16. *Ibid.*

17. Portes and Bach, *Latin Journey*, 38.

18. John Dollard, *Caste and Class in a Southern Town* (New York: Doubleday Anchor Books, 1957), 89.

19. Stephen Birmingham, *Certain People* (Toronto: Little, Brown and Company, 1977), 98.

20. Robert Staples, *Introduction to Black Sociology* (New York: McGraw-Hill, 1976), 192; C. J. Munford, "Social Structure and Black Revolution," *The Black Scholar*, vol. 4 (November–December 1972): 11–23.

21. Carter G. Woodson, *Free Negro Heads of Families in the U.S. in 1830* (Washington D.C.: Vintage Books, 1969), xxxi–xxxii.

22. Birmingham, *Certain People*, 111.

23. E. Franklin Frazier, "The Changing Status of the Negro Family," *Social Forces* 9 (March 1931): 386–393.

24. Charles S. Johnson, *The Negro College Graduate* (Chapel Hill: The University of North Carolina Press, 1938), 75.

25. *Ibid.*, 75–76.

26. *Ibid.*, 76.

27. Otis Dudley Duncan, "Inheritance of Poverty or Inheritance of Race?" in Daniel P. Moynihan, ed., *On Understanding Poverty: Perspectives from the Social Sciences* (New York: Basic Books, 1969).

28. David L. Featherman and Robert M. Hauser, *Opportunity and Change* (New York: Academic Press, 1978).

29. Bonacich and Modell, *Economic Basis*.

30. Sterling D. Spero and Abram L. Harris, *The Black Worker* (New York: Columbia University Press, 1931), 132.

31. James Weldon Johnson, "Harlem: The Cultural Capitol" in Alain Locke, ed., *The New Negro* (Albert and Charles Boni, 1925), 304. Quoted from Harold Cruse, *The Crisis of The Negro Intellectual* (new York: William Morrow & Co., 1968), 21.

32. Alex Haley, *The Autobiography of Malcolm X* (New York: Ballentine Books, 1964), 36.

33. In the classic study of Afro-American college graduates, this southern effect was quite prominent. When southern states and border states were combined, 74.6 percent of all graduates were from this region. The presence of traditional Afro-American schools account for the difference. The western states contributed 2.6 percent of college graduates, and northern states contributed 22.8 percent. These figures represent where Afro-American college graduates lived during the time of the study. When place of birth is taken into consideration, the southern effect becomes stronger. See Charles S. Johnson, *The Negro College Graduate* (Chapel Hill: The University of North Carolina Press, 1938), 22–40.

34. Bart Landry, *The New Black Middle Class* (Berkeley: The University of California Press, 1987), 86.

35. G. Franklin Edwards, "Community and Class Realities: The Ordeal of Change," in *The Negro American* (Boston: Houghton Mifflin Company, 1966), 281.

36. Bonacich and Modell, *Economic Basis*, 41.

37. Minton, *Early History of Negroes in Business in Philadelphia*, read before the American Historical Society, March, 1913, 8.

38. Ofari, *Myth of Black Capitalism*.

39. See also L. Coleman and S. Cook, "The Failures of Minority Capitalism: The Edapco Case," *Phylon*, 37, no. 1, 45–58.

40. Portes and Bach, *Latin Journey*, 38–39.

41. Allan H. Spear, *Black Chicago: The Making of a Negro Ghetto* (Chicago: The University of Chicago Press, 1967), 91.

42. Bonacich and Modell, *Economic Basis*, 46.

43. Eugene P. Foley, "The Negro Business Man: In Search of A Tradition," in *The Negro American*, Talcott Parsons and Kenneth B. Clark, eds. (Boston: Beacon Press, 1965), 561.

44. William Toll, *The Making of an Ethnic Middle Class* (Albany: State University of New York Press, 1982), 5. For a discussion of this point, see Don H. Doyle, *The Social Order of a Frontier Community* (Urbana: The University of Illinois Press, 1978).

45. *Ibid.*, 33.

46. *Ibid.*, 141.

47. Frazier, *Black Bourgeoisie*, 84.

48. *Ibid.*, 76.

49. *Ibid.*, 146–161.

50. Drake and Clayton, *Black Metropolis*, 658–715.

51. Frazier, *Black Bourgeoisie*, 13.

52. Jerry D. Crosby, "Two Hundred Years of Educational Development Through Self-Help, Self-Reliance, and Self-Determination," *The Negro Educational Review* (July–Oct. 1978): 207–208.

53. Bonacich and Modell, *Economic Basis*, 19.

54. *Ibid.*, 86.

55. *Ibid.*, 87.

56. *Ibid.*, 93–94.

57. The literature on the migration of blacks to the North between 1916 and 1917 is plentiful. See Henderson H. Donald, "The Negro Migration of 1916–1918," *Journal of Negro History* (Oct. 1921), 383–498; Charles S. Johnson, "How Much is Migration a Flight from Persecution?" *Opportunity* (Sept. 1923), 272–274; Louise V. Kennedy, *The Negro Peasant Turns Cityward: Effects of Recent Migrations to Northern Cities* (College Park: University of Maryland Press, 1969; Originally published in 1930).

58. Paul C. Coe, "The Nonwhite Population Surge to Our Cities," *Land Economics*, vol. 45, 3 (August 1959): 196–197.

59. See, for example, August Meier and Elliott Rudwick, *From Plantation to Ghetto* (New York: Hill and Wang, 1966); Allan H. Spear, *Black Chicago: The Making of a Negro Ghetto* (Chicago: The University of Chicago Press, 1967); Richard B. Sherman (ed.), *The Negro and the City* (Englewood Cliffs, N.J.: Prentice Hall, 1970).

60. Stanley Lieberson, *A Piece of the Pie* (Berkeley: University of California Press, 1980), 98–99.

61. Karl E. and Alma F. Taeuber, "Is The Negro an Immigrant Group?" *Integrated Education*, vol. 1, no. 3 (June 1963): 25–27; see also the "The Negro As an Immigrant Group: Recent Trends in Racial and Ethnic Segregation in Chicago," *American Journal of Sociology*, 69 (1964): 374–382; see also Alma F. Taeuber and Karl E. Taeuber, "Recent Immigration and Studies of Ethnic Assimilation," *Demography* 4 (1967): 798–808.

62. Patrick D. Moynihan, *The Negro Family: The Case for National Action* (Washington D.C.: Office of Policy Planning and Research, U.S. Department of Labor, 1965).

63. See, for example, Lee Rainwater and William L. Yancey, *The Moynihan Report and the Politics of Controversy* (Cambridge: Massachusetts Institute of Technology Press, 1967).

64. See, for example, James Boggs, "Blacks in the Cities: Agenda for the 1970s," *Black Scholar*, vol. 4, Nov.–Dec. 1972: 50–61; Bradley R. Schiller, *The Economics of Poverty and Discrimination* (Englewood Cliffs, N.J.: Prentice-Hall, 1973); Kenneth B. Clark, *Dark Ghetto: Dilemmas of Social Power* (New York: Harper and Row, 1965).

65. See, for example, Reynolds Farley and Albert I. Hermalin, "Family Stability: A Comparison of Trends Between Blacks and Whites," *American Sociological Review*, vol. 36 (Feb. 1971): 1–17; Frank F. Reissman, "Low-Income Culture: The Strength of the Poor," *Journal of Marriage and the Family*, vol. 26 (Nov. 1964): 417–421; Robert Staples, *The Black Family: Essays and Studies* (Belmont, California: Wadsworth Publishing Company, 1971).

66. Walter R. Allen, "Black Family Research in the United States: A Review Assessment and Extension," *Journal of Comparative Family Studies*, vol. 9 (1978): 167–189.

67. Robert Staples, "Black Family Life and Development," in *Mental Health: A Challenge to the Black Community*, ed. Lawrence E. Gray (Philadelphia: Dorrance).

68. W. E. B. Du Bois, *The Negro American Family* (Atlanta: Atlanta University Press, 1908); E. Franklin Frazier, *The Negro Family in the United States* (Chicago: The University of Chicago Press, 1939). For an excellent review of research on the black family, see Lenwood G. Davis, *The Black Family in The United States: A Selected Bibliography of Annotated Books, Articles, and Dissertations on Black Families in America* (Westport, Connecticut: Greenwood Press, 1978).

69. William Julius Wilson, *The Truly Disadvantaged* (Chicago: The University of Chicago Press, 1987), 55.

70. The following analyses is based on research being done by the author and will appear in a work entitled *The Truly Advantaged of the Disadvantaged: Toward a Theory of the Afro-American Middleman*. Interviews with Afro-Americans based on their parents' adjustment to America are in progress.

71. From interviews for the project in progress entitled *The Impact of Self-Help on Future Generations*. John Sibley Butler, Department of Sociology, The University of Texas at Austin, Austin Texas, 78712.

72. *Ibid.*

73. Daniel C. Thompson, *A Black Elite: A Profile of Graduates of UNCF Colleges* (New York: Greenwood Press, 1986).

74. When Professor Thompson's work was published, I spoke with him extensively about my conceptualization of the Afro-American truncated middleman. Unfortunately, his untimely death prevented the feedback of ideas on the rough draft of this manuscript.

75. Thompson, *Black Elite*, 29–30.

76. *Ibid.*, 29.

77. *Ibid.*, 30.

78. Harriette Pipes McAdoo, "Factors Related to Stability in Upwardly Mobile Black Families, *Journal of Marriage and The Family* (Nov. 1978): 770.

79. Thompson, *Black Elite*, 51.

80. *Ibid.*

81. *Ibid.*, 50–51.

82. Helen S. Astin and Patricia H. Cross, "Black Students in White Institutions," in *Black Students in Higher Education*, ed. Gail E. Thomas (Westport, Connecticut: Greenwood Press, 1981), 36.

83. "Leading B. A. Sources of 1984 Minority Group Doctorate Recipients," *Black Issues in Higher Education* (Dec. 1986): 8.

84. See, for example, Reynolds Farley, *Blacks and Whites* (Massachusetts: Harvard University Press).

85. Gail E. Thomas, "The Effects of Standardized Achievement Test Performance and Family Status on Black-White College Access," in *Black Students in Higher Education*, ed. Gail E. Thomas (Westport, Connecticut: Greenwood Press, 1981).

86. Butler, *The Impact of Self-Help on Future Generations.*

87. For an excellent analysis of organization participation among Afro-Americans, *see* Michael D. Woodard, "Voluntary Association Membership Among Black Americans: The Post-Civil Rights Era," *The Sociological Quarterly*, vol. 28, no. 2: 285–301; and "The Effects of Social Class on Voluntary Association Membership Among Urban Afro-Americans," *Sociological Focus*, vol. 21, no. 1 (Jan. 1988): 67–80.

88. Thompson, *Black Elite*, 107.

89. Woodard, "Volunteer, Association Membership," 285–301.

90. Thompson, *A Black Elite*, 110.

91. Frazier, *Black Bougeoisie*, 84.

92. Pat King, "New Wave Networks: Black Fraternities and Sororities Use Old School Ties to Expand Opportunities and Promote Political Action," *Black Enterprise* (Dec. 1983): 30.

93. Thompson, *Black Elite*, 110.

94. *Ibid.*

95. Landry, *Black Middle Class*, 186.

96. There are very few schools founded for Afro-Americans which are in the northern part of the United States.

97. Thomas Sowell, "Guest in a Strange House."

98. Frank Riessman, *The Culturally Deprived Child* (New York: Harper and Row, 1962). Quoted from Charles E. Silberman, *Crisis in Black and White* (New York: Vintage Book, 1964), 261.

99. *Ibid.*, 261–262.

100. Butler, *Impact of Self-Help on Future Generations*.

101. Sylvester Monroe, "Guest in a Strange House: A Black at Harvard," 45–48. Unknown source.

102. *Ibid.*, 45.

103. *Ibid.*, 48.

104. Thomas Sowell, *Black Education: Myths and Tragedies* (New York: McKay Publishing Co., 1973).

105. Will B. Scott, "Critical Factors for the Survival of First Generation College Blacks," in *Black Students in Higher Education*, ed. Gail B. Thomas, 227.

106. *Ibid.*

107. Landry, *Black Middle Class*.

108. William Julius Wilson, *The Declining Significance of Race* (Chicago: University of Chicago Press, 1980); *The Truly Disadvantaged* (Chicago: The University of Chicago Press, 1987).

109. Thompson, *Black Elite*, 93–125.

110. Landry, *Black Middle Class*, 187, 191.

111. See, for example, Kinzer and Sagarin, *The Negro In American Business* (New York: Greenberg Press, 1950), 24–49.

112. Cruse, *Crisis of the Negro Intellectual*, 309.

113. W. Loyd Warner and Leo Srole, *The Social System of American Ethnic Groups* (New Haven: Yale University Press, 1945).

114. For example, see Robert E. Park, *Race and Culture* (Glencoe, Illinois: Free Press, 1950); Milton M. Gordon, *Assimilation in American Life* (New York: Oxford University Press, 1984); R. A. Schermerhorn, *Comparative Ethnic Relations* (New York: Random House, 1970).

115. For a presentation of the pluralist approach, see Gordon, *Assimilation in American Life*, especially 141–159.

116. *Ibid.*

117. See, for example, Joe R. Feagin, *Racial and Ethnic Relations* (New Jersey: Prentice-Hall, 1984).

118. Lieberson, *Piece of the Pie*, 1980.

119. Manning Marable, *How Capitalism Underdeveloped Black America* (Boston, Mass: South End Press, 1983), 140.

120. For discussions of Marxism see James F. Becker, *Marxian Political Economy* (Cambridge: Cambridge University Press, 1977); Karl Marx, *Capital.*

121. See, for example, Gerson S. Sheer, *Marxist Humanism and Praxis* (New York: Prometheus Books, 1978).

122. Marable, *How Capitalism Underdeveloped Black America*, 255–256.

123. Irving Louis Horowitz, "Disenthralling Sociology," *Society*, vol. 24 (Jan./Feb. 1987): 49.

124. Cruse, *Crises of the Negro Intellectual*, 174.

125. *Ibid.*, 263.

126. The fact that Afro-American Marxist-Leninists claim that any kind of racial solidarity is a diversionary force that leads away from black liberation has been debated in the literature. I think that the best article is entitled "Black Nationalism and Confused Marxist," by Tony Thomas in *Black Liberation and Socialism.* (edited) by Tony Thomas also (New York: Pathfinder Press, 1974).

127. Although the Communist Party in the United States has acted positively on behalf of Afro-Americans, the latter have never shared the same opportunities to become radicalized in industry as have their white counterparts. There exists an interesting literature which proposes to show the importance of the commitment of Marxist-Communists to the Afro-American cause. See, for example, Dan T. Carter, *Scottsboro: A Tragedy of The American South* (Baton Rouge: Louisiana State University Press, 1969); see also Wilson Record, "The Development of the Communist Position in the United States," *Phylon*, 19 (1958), 306–326.

128. For an excellent discussion of these issues, see Harold Cruse, *Rebellion or Revolution* (New York: Morrow Paperback Editions, 1968), 139–155.

129. *Ibid.*, 148.

130. See, for example, B. Denitch, "Is There a New Working Class: A Brief Note On a Large Question," *Dissent* (July–Aug. 1970), 351–355; James D. Wright, "In Search of a New Working Class," *Qualitative Sociology.* (1978/79): 33–57; H. Gintis, "The New Working Class and Revolutionary Youth," *Socialist Revolution*, 1 (May–June, 1970): 13–43.

131. Cruse, *Rebellion or Revolution*, 140.

132. In a recent article Edna Bonacich, who earlier was instrumental in developing middleman theory, analyzes entrepreneurial minorities within a Marxist framework. She argues that these minorities exploit their own members while building their enterprises. But her conclusions are the same "pie in the sky" religious varieties that the Afro-American Marxist viewpoint already discussed generate. While it is an excellent goal to wait for the white working class to become radicalized to save everyone else from capitalism—in reality this working class is quite conservative and anti-minority—the fact is that middleman groups and their offspring, had to survive. The white work-

ing class had no interest in their economic survival, unless, of course, it was at the bottom of the economic ladder and serving their interest. Thus, Bonacich, in her most recent work, falls into the same religious theorizing as others who applied a Marxist framework to race and ethnicity. See Bonacich, "Making It In America: A Social Evaluation of the Ethics of Immigrant Entrepreneurship," *Sociological Perspectives*, 30, no. 4 (October 1987): 446–466.

NOTES TO CHAPTER EIGHT

1. Robert L. Wallace, *Black Wealth Through Black Entrepreneurship.* (Edgewood, MD, Duncan & Duncan, Inc., 1993), pp. 26–27.

2. T.M. Pryor, *Wealth Building: Lessons of Booker T. Washington for a New Black America* (Edgewood MD, Duncan & Duncan, Inc., 1995).

3. *Ibid.*, p. 45.

4. T.M Alexander, *Beyond the Timberline: The Trials and Triumphs of A Black Entrepreneur* (Edgewood, New Jersey: M.E. Duncan & Company, 1992); Jonathan Greenberg's *Staking a Claim: Jake Simmons, Jr. and the Making of an African-American Oil Dynasty* (New York: Atheneum, 1990).

5. Thomas D. Boston, *Affirmative Action and Black Entrepreneurship.* (New York: Routledge, 1999).

6. Karen Starks, *African American Community Well-Being: A Reconsideration of The Contributions of Urban Entrepreneurs* (Dissertation, Clark Atlanta University, Department of Social Work, 1999).

7. John Sibley Butler. "Entrepreneurship and the Advantages of the Inner City: How to Augment the Porter Thesis" *Review of Black Political Economy* Winter, 1996 Volume 24, Nos. 2–3, pp. 39–49.

8. For the relationship between ideology, method and protest, see, for example, August Meier and Elliott Rudwick, *Along The Color Line.* Urbana: University of Illinois Press, 1976; Harold Cruse, *The Crisis of The Negro Intellectual.* New York: Quill, 1984; Stokely Carmichael & Charles V. Hamilton, *Black Power: The Politics of Liberation.* New York: Vintage, 1967; Huey P. Newton, "The Black Panthers," in *Ebony*, XXIV (August, 1969): 102–12.

9. Alphonso Pinkeney, *Black Americans.* New Jersey: Prentice-Hall, 1987, p. 71; see also David L. Featherman and Robert M. Hauser, *Opportunity and Change.* New York: Academic Press, 1978, pp. 313-384; Reynolds Farley, *Blacks and Whites.* Cambridge: Harvard University Press, 1984, pp. 83-90; James E. Blackwell, *The Black Community: Diversity and Utility.* New York: Harper and Row. 1985; Alejandro Portes and Kenneth L. Wilson, "Black-White Differences in Educational Attainment," *American Sociological Review*, 41:(June), 1976, pp. 414–431.

10. Farley, *op. cit.*, p. 50.

11. *Ibid.*, p. 49.

12. Robin W. Williams, Jr., *Mutual Accommodation: Ethnic Conflict and Coopera-tion*. Minneapolis: University of Minnesota Press, 1977, p. 118; see also Albert I. Her-malin and Reynolds Farley, "The Potential for Residential Integration in Cities and Suburbs: Implications for the Busing Controversy," *American Sociological Review* 38, No. 5 (Oct.) 595–610; A. Mead, "The Distribution of Segregation in Atlanta," *Social Forces* 51:1972, pp. 182–92.

13. Williams *op. cit.*, p. 7.

14. J. G. Condran, "Changes in White Attitudes Toward Blacks: 1963–1977," *Public Opinion Quarterly* 43: 463–76.

15. Joe R. Feagin, *Racial and Ethnic Relations*. New Jersey: Englewood Cliff, 1984, pp. 232–233.

16. Farley, *op. cit.*, p. 195.

17. *Ibid.*, pp. 192–206.

18. James S. Coleman, Charles C. Berry and Zahava D. Blum, "White and Black Careers During The First Decade of Labor Force Experience. Part III: Occupational Status and Income Together," *Social Science Research* 1:293–304." 1972.

19. See, for example, John Sibley Butler, "Inequality in the Military: An Exami-nation of Promotion Rates For Black and White Enlisted Men," *American Sociological Review*, etc.

20. Carmichael & Hamilton, *op. cit.*, p. 54.

21. *Ibid.*, p. 53.

22. For a discussion of this process, see John Sibley Butler, "Black Educators in Louisiana: A Question of Survival," *Journal of Negro Education*.

23. Richard B. Freeman, *Black Elite: The New Market for Highly Educated Black Americans*. New York: McGraw-Hill, 1976; Nathan Glazer, *Affirmative Discrimination: Ethnic Inequality and Public Policy*. New York: Basic Books, 1975.

24. William Julius Wilson, *The Declining Significance of Race*. Chicago: University of Chicago Press, 1978.

25. See, for example, Howard F. Stein and Robert F. Hill, *The Ethnic Imperative: Examining the New White Ethnic Movement*. University Park: The Pennsylvania State University Press, 1977.

26. James R. Kluegel and Eliot R. Smith, "Whites' Belief About Blacks' Oppor-tunity," *American Sociological Review* 47: (August):520.

27. Wilson, *op. cit.*, p. 177.

28. Lester Thurow, "Affirmative Action in a Zero-Sum Society," in Ronald Takaki (edited), *From Different Shores: Perspectives on Race and Ethnicity in America*. Oxford: Oxford University Press, 1987. p. 230.

29. Nathan Glazer, *Affirmative Discrimination: Ethnic Inequality and Public Policy*. New York: Basic Books. 1975.

30. Harold Eugene Byrd, *The Black Experience in Big Business*. New York: Exposi-tion Press. 1977. pp. 117–118.

31. *Ibid.*, pp. 124–125.

32. *Ibid.*, p. 124.

33. Edward W. Jones, Jr. "What It's Like To Be A Black Manager," *Harvard Business Review.* (July-August) 1973. pp. 111–112.

34. Patricia Cooper, "Interview: Bayard Rustin," *The Crisis*, March 1985: p. 26.

35. George Gilder, *The Spirit of Enterprise*. New York: Simon & Schuster. 1984, pp. 110–111.

36. Kenneth L. Wilson and Alejandro Portes, "Ethnic Enclaves: A Comparison of the Cuban and Black Economies in Miami," *American Journal of Sociology* 86 (September):pp. 295–319.

37. Max Weber, *The Protestant Ethnic and the Spirit of Capitlaism*. New York: Charles Scribner's Sons. 1968.

38. Robert L. Woodson, "A Legacy of Entrepreneurship," in Robert L. Woodson, (ed.) *On The Road to Economic Freedom.* Washington D.C.: Regnery Gateway, 1987, pp. 1, 3, 23.

39. L. Durham, *Black Capitalism: Critical Issues In Urban Management*. Washington, D.C.: Arthur D. Little and Company, 1970; T. L. Cross, *Black Capitalism*. New York: Atheneum, 1969; Ronald Bailey, *Black Business Enterprise*. New York: Basic Books, 1975.

40. James L. Everett, "An American Revolution is Lined to Entrepreneurs," *Minorities and Women in Business*. September/October, 1985. Comments taken from an interview with D. Bruce Miller, Assistant Secretary for Productivity, Technology, and Innovation, Washington, D.C.

41. Sammuel E. Harris, *Operations Manual for Project Outreach of The National Business League*. Undated. Quoted from William L. Henderson and Larry C. Ledebur, *Economic Disparity: Problems and Strategies for Black America*. New York: Free Press, 1970, p. 108.

42. *Ibid.*, p. 114.

43. Margaret C. Simms, "Black Schools and Black Economic Development," in Gerald F. Whittaker (ed.) *Minorities At The Crossroads*. Ann Arbor: Division of Research, Graduate School of Business Administration, The University of Michigan. p. 103.

44. *Ibid.*, pp. 178–179.

45. Flournoy A. Coles, Jr., "Financial Institutions and Black Entrepreneurship," *Journal of Black Studies*. March 1973. pp. 332–333.

46. Author I. Blaustein and Geoffrey Faaux, *The Star-Spangled Hustle*. Garden City, New York: Doubleday Inc., 1972. p. 71.

47. Although it is plausible that many of the Afro-American businesses today were started by, or became extensions of, those established by their parents, data does not allow us to come to such a conclusion. One of the the major research questions is the relationship between businesses which were established under segregation and those of today vis-a-vis blood lines or kinship.

48. For a discussion of the development of the entrepreneurial economy see Wilson Harrell, *For Entrepreneurs Only: Success Strategies* (New York: Career Press, 1994); William D. Bygrave, "The Entrepreneurial Process," in *The Portable MBA in Entrepreneurship* (New York: John Wiley & Sons, Inc., 1997); Robert C. Kenzer, *Enterprising Southerners: Black Economic Success in North Carolina, 1865-1915* (Charlottesville: University Press of Virginia, 1977).

49. For a discussion see Harrel, *op. cit.*, pp. 29–31.

50. William D. Bygrave, "The Entrepreneurial Process," in *The Portable MBA in Entrepreneurship* (New York: John Wiley & Sons, Inc., 1997), p. 1.

51. U.S. Department of Commerce, Bureau of the Census, "Negro Proprietorship in Retail Business: Negro Proprietorship in Retail Business," Chapter XVII, p. 494, 1920–1932.

52. U.S. Censu Burea, "More than 800,000 U.S. Businesses Owned by African Americans; New York, California, Texas Lead States," Census Bureau Reports. Economics and Statistics Administration, March, 2001.

53. *Ibid.*

54. For a discussion see Thomas D. Boston, *Affirmative Action and Black Entrepreneurship* (New York: Routledge 1999).

55. For a discussion see Timothy Bates, *Race, Self-Employment, and Upward Mobility: An Elusive American Dream* (Baltimore and London: The Johns Hopkins University Press, 1999).

56. Timothy Bates, "Why Are Firms Owned by Asian Immigrants Lagging Behind Black-Owned Businesses,?" in National Journal of Sociology, Volume 10 Number 2, Winter 1996, pp. 27–43.

57. *Ibid.*, p. 27.

58. Timothy Bates, *Race Self-Employment & Upward Mobility: An Elusive American Dream* (Baltimore: The Johns Hopkins University Press, 1998), p. 1. For an evaluation of Bates approach see Alejandro Portes, "A Dissenting View: Pitfalls on Focusing on Relative Returns to Ethnic Enterprise," in *National Journal of Sociology* Vol. 10 Number 2 Winter 1996, pp. 54–47; Patricia G. Greene, "A Call for Conceptual Clarity, *National Journal of Sociology* Vol. 10 Number 2 Winter 1996, pp. 46–49; Margaret A. Johnson, "Understanding Differences between Asian Immigrants and African-Americans: Issues of Conceptualization and Measurement, *National Journal of Sociology* Vol. 10 Number 2 Winter 1996, pp. 50–57; Ivan Light, "Reply: Why are Firms Owned by Asian Immigrants Behind Black-Owned Businesses?," *National Journal of Sociology* Vol. 10 Number 2 Winter 1996, pp. 54–47; 65–71

59. *Ibid.*, p. 13.

60. Min Zhou, *Chinatown: The Socioeconomic Potential of an Urban Enclave* (Philadelphia: Temple University Press, 1992).

61. Thomas D. Boston, *Affirmative Action and Black Entrepreneurship* (New York: Routledge, 1999), p. 70.

62. *Ibid.*, p. 63.

63. For a discussion of all of these programs see *ibid.*, pp. 10–16.

64. The enterprises that he examine were those that were certified by the city's minority business program

65. Boston, *Op. Cit.*, p. 27.

66. Each year *Black Enterprise* publishes its list of top 100 enterprises. The best thing to do is to go the site, www.blackenterprise.com

67. See Table 3.10 in Chapter 3.

68. In millions of dollars to the nearest thousand

69. *Black Enterprise*, June 1988, p. 206.

70. Fred Martin, "Navigating Rough Waters," in *Black Enterprise*. June 1988, p. 206.

71. *Ibid.*, p. 208.

72. see www.blackenterprise.com/SO/pageopen.asp?source=BE1000Tab/banks01.html

73. Don Tapscott, *The Digital Economy: Promise and Peril in the Age of Networked Intelligence* (New York: McGraw-Hill, 1966), pp. 6–9.

74. Wall Street Journal, "Black Entrepreneurship," April 3, sec. R, 1–20," 1992.

75. Derek T. Dingle, "Mining Venture Capital," *Black Enterprise*. October, 1984, 52.

76. *Ibid.*, p. 96.

77. *Ibid.*, p. 52.

78. *Ibid.*

79. There have been overtones to the effect that firms associated with the Federal government would like also become independent. See, for example, Lee Kravitz, "Why SBICs Want to Break From the SBA," *Venture*. October, 1984, p. 56.

80. Timothy M. Bates, *Black Capitalism: A Quantitative Analysis*. New York: Praeger, 1973, p. 67; "Government as Financial Intermediary for Minority Entrepreneurs: An Evaluation," *Journal of Business*. October 1975, p. 557.

81. William L. Scott, "Financial Performance of Minority -Versus Nonminority-Owned Businesses," *Journal of Small Business Management*. January 1983, p. 48.

82. For excellent examples of case studies, see "A Model of Black Success in Business," *Business Week*. April 13, 1974, pp.100–102; "Blacks Who Left Dead-End Jobs to Go It Alone," *Business Week*. February, 1984, pp. 106–108.

83. United States Department of Commerce News, "Two-Thirds of Business Owners Get Started Without Borrowing Capital, " Wednesday, September 16, 1987.

84. Michale D. Woodard, *Black Entrepreneurs in America: Stories of Struggle and Success* (New Jersey: Rutgers University Press, 1997.

85. For a discussion see Timmothy Bates, *Race, Self-Employment: An Illusive American Dream* (Washington, D.C.: The Woodrow Center Press, 1999).

86. Teresa A. Sullivan and Stephen D. McCracken, "Patterns and Rates of Return To Self-Employment." *National Journal of Sociology.* Vol. 2 No. 2. 1988, p. 167.

87. See, for example, George E. Berkner, *Black Capitalism and the Urban Negro.* Tempe: Arizona State University, 1970; Cross, *op. cit.*; Frank Davis, *The Economics of Black Community Development.* Chicago: Markham Publishing Company, 1972; Laird Durham, *Black Capitalism.* Washington, D.C.: Arthur D. Little, Inc., 1970; Eli Ginzberg, (ed.) *Business Leadership and The Negro Crisis.* New York: McGraw-Hill, 1968; John Seder and Berkeley Burrell, *Getting it Together.* New York: Harcourt Brace Javanovich, Inc., 1971; Julia Kay Kilgore, "MESBICs Striving for Fiscal Fitness," *Hispanic Business.* March, 1988, p. 10; Alex Beam, "Why Few Ghetto Factories Are Making It," *Business Week.* February 16, 1987, p. 86; "Lending, Not Giving to Non-Profits," *Nations Cities Weekly,* February, 1984, p. 3.

88. John Sibley Butler and Cedric Herring, "Ethnicity and Entrepreneurship in America: Toward an Explanation of Racial and Ethnic Group Variations in Self-Employment," *Sociological Perspectives* vol. 34, pp. 1, pp. 79–94.

89. For an excellent discussion of this process, along with examples, see Derek T. Dingle, "Venturing Out On Your Own," *Black Enterprise,* August, 1985, pp. 34–38.

90. See, for example, Andrew Brimmer, "Small Business and Economic Development in the Negro Community," in R.W. Bailey (ed.) *Black Business Enterprise: Historical and Contemporary Perspectives.* Basic Books., 1971.

NOTES TO CHAPTER NINE

1. This is, of course, not to say that other groups in America did not have systematic problems. This has been documented in the literature. See Joe R. Feagin, *Racial and Ethnic Relations.* But it is certainly true that no other group in America has had to face forced slavery for hundreds of years and massive amounts of national legislature directed against them.

2. Bart Landry, *The New Black Middle Class.* Berkeley: The University of California Press, 1987.

3. Thomas Sowell, *Race and Economics,* New York: Longman Inc. 1975, 43.

4. Max Weber, *The Protestant Ethic the Spirit of Capitalism.* New York: Charles Scribner's Sons, 19.

5. William Julius Wilson, *The Declining Significance of Race.* Chicago: The University of Chicago Press, 1978.

6. R. Freeman, *The Black Elite: The New Market for Highly Educated Black Americans* (New York: McGraw-Hill, 1976).

7. Sidney Wilhiem, *Who Needs The Negro?* (New York: Transaction Press, 1964).

8. Samuel Yette, *The Choice: The Issue of Black Survival* (New York: 1971).

9. Wilson, *Declining Significance of Race.*

10. In this analysis, the measurement of the primary sector differs from the measurement usually found in sociology and economics. The primary sector is defined as "those Cuban-Americans who work alongside Anglos," and the secondary sector is defined as "those who work with other minority groups." The enclave is defined as "those who work within the ethnic community." See Portes and Bach, *Latin Journey*.

11. *See Reverse Commute*, video presentation of the National Center for Neighborhood Enterprise (Washington, D.C., 1988).

12. *See*, for example, W. Block and M. Walker, *Discrimination, Affirmative Action, and Equal Opportunity* (Vancouver, B.C.: Frazier Institute, 1982); Thomas Sowell, *Civil Rights: Rhetorical or Reality?* (New York: Morrow, 1984); *Markets and Minorities* (New York: Basic Books, 1981).

13. For a discussion of "conservative" logic in race and economics see Thomas D. Boston, *Race, Class & Conservatism* (Boston: Unwin Hyman, 1988).

14. Victor Nee and Jimy Sanders, "The Road to Parity: Determinants of the Socioeconomic Achievements of Asian Americans," in *Ethnicity and Race in the U.S.A.*, ed. Richard D. Alba (London: Routledge & Kegan Paul, 1985), 82.

15. It is also worth noting that the many debates over affirmative action do not recognize the many preferential treatments given to groups that were allowed to find jobs in the developing industrial sector of the country at the turn of the century and beyond. Indeed, it is this early preferential treatment given to some ethnic groups that caused not only middleman types of adjustment, but also reactions such as the Civil Rights Movement. During segregation, it was common knowledge that blacks believed that whites, especially if they were Protestants, were provided opportunities simply because they were white. Thus, the Civil Rights Movement in America, and the creation of business enterprise by middleman groups, can be seen as reactions to preferential treatment received by most Protestant white groups in the marketplace.

16. See, for example, Wilson, *The Truly Disadvantaged* (Chicago: University of Chicago Press, 1988).

17. Robert L. Woodson, "Black America's Legacy of Entrepreneurship," *National Journal of Sociology*, vol. 2, no. 2, 1988: 221.

18. Richard Lacayo, "Between Two Worlds," *Time* (March 1989): 62.

19. Ed. Wiley III, "Entrepreneurial Scholars Tackle Black Agricultural Decline," *Black Issues in Higher Education*, vol. 6, no. 7 (8 June 1989): 10.

20. Edna Bonacich, Ivan Light, and Charles Choy Wong, "Korean Immigrants: Small Business in Los Angeles," in *Source on the New Immigration*, eds. Roy Simon and Bryce La Port (New Jersey: Transaction Books, 1980), 148–165.

21. Colin Leinster, "Black Executives: How They're Doing," *Fortune* (18 January 1988): 109–120.

Bibliography

41st Annual Statement, North Carolina Mutual Life Insurance Company, December, 1939. Durham, North Carolina.

1885–1915. Portland: University of Oregon Press; Donna R. Gabaccia. *From Sicily to Elizabeth Street: Housing and Social Change Among Italian Immigrants, 1880–1930*. Albany: State University of New York Press. 1984.

"A Model of Black Success in Business," *Business Week*. April 13, 1974, pp. 100–102; "Blacks Who Left Dead-End Jobs to Go It Alone," *Business Week*. February, 1984, pp. 106–108. Publishing Company. 1936.

Allen, Walter R. "Black Family Research in the United States: A Review Assessment and Extension." *Journal of Comparative Family Studies*. Vol. 9, 1978. pp. 167–189.

Astin, Helen S. and Patricia H. Cross, "Black Students in White Institutions," in Gail E. Thomas, *Black Students in Higher Education*. (edited). Westport, Connecticut: Greenwood Press., p. 36.

Aldrich, Howard, J. Carter, T.P. Jones and D. McEvoy, From Periphery to Peripheral: The South Asian Petite Bourgeoisie in England, in Research in Sociology of Work 2: 1–32 (1983), pp. 1–32.

Averitt, Robert T. *The Dual Economy: The Dynamics of American Industry Structure*. New York: Norton. 1968.

Bacote, Clarence A. "Some Aspects of Negro Life in Georgia, 1880–1908," *Journal of Negro History*. XLIII (July 1958), 186–213.

Bailey, Ronald. *Black Business Enterprise*. New York: Basic Books, 1975.

Bates, Timothy M. *Black Capitalism: A Quanitative Analysis*. New York: Praeger, 1973, p. 67.

Beam, Alex. "Why Few Ghetto Factories Are Making It," *Business Week*. February 16, 1987.

Becker, Howard, *Man in Reciprocity*. New York: Praeger. 1956.

Becker, James F. *Marxism Political Economy*. Cambridge: 1977.

Bell, William K. *A Business Primer for Negroes*. New York: William K. Bell. 1948.

Berkner, George E. *Black Capitalism and the Urban Negro.* Tempe: Arizona State University, 1970.

Bermant, Chaim. *The Jews.* New York: Times Books.

Bernard, Richard M. *The Poles in Oklahoma. Oklahoma:* University of Oklahoma Press. 1980.

Birmingham, Stephen. *Certain People.* Toronto: Little, Brown and Company, 1977.

Bittle, William and Gilbert Geis, "Racial Self-fulfillment and the Rise of an All-Negro Community in Oklahoma," *Phylon.* XVII. 1956. pp. 247–60.

Black Enterprise, www.blackenterprise.com

Blackwell, James E. *The Black Community: Diversity and Utility.* New York: Harper and Row. 1985.

Blalock, Hubert M., Jr., *Toward a Theory of Minority Group Relations.* New York: John.Wiley & Sons. 1967.

Blaustein, Author I. and Geoffrey Faaux, *The Star-Spangled Hustle.* Garden City New York: Doubleday Inc., 1972.

Blayton, Jesse B. "The Negro in Banking," *Bankers Magazine.* 1936 (December) Vol. 133, pp. 511–514.

Blessing, Patrick J. The Irish and British in Oklahoma. Oklahoma: The University of Oklahoma Press. 1980.

Block, W. and M. Walker, *Discrimination, Affirmative Action, and Equal Opportunity.* Vancouver: British Columbia: Frazier Institute. 1982.

"Blood and Oil," *The Survey.* Vol. XLVI. June 11. 1921.

Boggs, James. "Blacks in the Cities: Agenda for the 1970's," *Black Scholar.* Vol. 4, November-December, 1972, pp. 50–61.

Boggs, James. *Racism and the Class Struggle.* New York: Monthly Review Press, 1970.

Bonacich, Edna and John Modell, *The Economic Basis of Ethnic Solidarity.* Berkeley: The University of California Press, 1980.

Bonacich, Edna, Ivan Light, and Charles Choy Wong, "Korean Immigrant: Small Business in Los Angles," in Roy Simon and Bryce La Port (ed.) *Sourcebook on the New Immigration.* New Jersey: Transaction Books. 1980. pp. 148–165.

Bonacich, Edna. "A Theory of Middleman Minorities." *America Sociological Review* 38 (October) 1972:583–594.

Bonacich, Edna. "Making It In America: A Social Evaluation of the Ethics of Immigrant Entrepreneurship," *Sociological Perspectives* 30 No. 4, October 1987: 446–466.

Boston, Thomas D. *Race, Class & Conservatism.* Boston: Unwin Hyman, 1988.

Boyd, William Kenneth. *The Story of Durham: City of The New South.* Durham, North Carolina: Duke University Press. 1927.

Brimmer, Andrew. "Small Business and Economic Development in the Negro Community," in R.W. Bailey (ed.) *Black Business Enterprise: Historical and Contemporary Perspectives.* Basic Books. 1971.

Brinton, Hugh Penn. *The Negro in Durham: A Study of Adjustment to Town Life.* Ph.D. Thesis: University of North Carolina at Chapel Hill. 1930. pp. iv–v.

Brown, Kenny L. *The Italians in Oklahoma.* Oklahoma: University of Oklahoma Press. 1980.

Bryce-Laporte, Roy Simon. *Sourcebook on The New Immigration: Implications for The United States and The International Community.* New Brunswick, New Jersey: Transaction Books. 1980.

"Business in Bronzeville," *Time.* April 18, 1938.

Bundles, A'Lelia, *On Her Own Ground: The Life and Times of Madam C.J. Walker.* New York: Scribner, 2001.

John Sibley Butler. "Entrepreneurship and the Advantages of the Inner City: How to Augment the Porter Thesis" *Review of Black Political Economy* Winter, 1996 Volume 24, Nos. 2–3, pp. 39–49.

John Sibley Butler and Patricia Gene Green, "Entrepreneurship and Wealth Building: From Pakistani/Ismaili Enterprise." in *Frontiers of Entrepreneurial Research* (Wellesley Massachusetts: Center for Entrepreneurial Studies, 1997), 242–253.

Butler, John Sibley. "Black Educators in Louisiana: A Question of Survival," *Journal of Negro Education.*

Butler, John Sibley. "Inequality in the Military: An Examination of Promotion Rates For Black and White Enlisted Men," *American Sociological Review.*

Butler, John Sibley. *Inequality in the Military: The Black Experience.* Saratoga, California: Century Twenty-One Publishing. 1980.

Butler, John Sibley. *The Truly Advantaged of the Disadvantaged: Toward an Understanding of the Afro-American Middleman.* Unpublished manuscript in progress, Department of Sociology, The University of Texas at Austin, Austin,Texas.

Byrd, Harold Eugene. *The Black Experience in Big Business.* New York: Exposition Press, 1977.

Campbell, Candance. "Change Agents in the New Economy: Business Incubators and Economic Development," in Economic Development Review 7 (1989): 56–59.

Carmichael, Stokely & Charles V. Hamilton, *Black Power: The Politics of Liberation in America.* New York: Vintage Books, 1967.

Carter, Dan T. *Scottsboro: A Tradgedy of The American South.* Baton Rouge: Louisiana State University Press. 1969.

Carter, William A. "Negro Main Street As a Symbol of Discrimination." *Phylon,* Fall, 1960.

Cerza, Alphonse. "Masons," in *Encyclopedia Americana.* Danbury Connecticut: Grolier Incorporated. 1980. Vol. 18. p. 432.

Chen, Jack. *The Chinese of America.* New York: Harper & Row. 1980.

Clark, Helen F. "The Chinese of New York Contrasted with Their Foreign Neighbors," Century 53 (November 1896):110 in Ivan H. Light. *Ethnic Enterprise in America.* Berkeley: University of California Press, 1972, p. 25, 33–34.

Clark, Kenneth B. *Dark Ghetto: Dilemmas of Social Power.* New York: Harper and Row. 1965.

Clark, Thomas D. "The Post-Civil War Economy in the South," in *Jews in the South,* edited by Leonard Dinnerstein and Mary Dale Palsson, Baton Rouge: Louisiana State University Press, 1973.

Coe, Paul C. "The Nonwhite Population Surge to Our Cities," *Land Economics.* Vol XXXXV, Number 3: August, 1959.

Coleman, James. S., Charles C. Berry and Zahava D. Blum, "White and Black Careers During The First Decade of Labor Force Experience. Part III: Occupational Status and Income Together," *Social Science Research* 1: 293–304. 1972.

Coleman, L. and S. Cook, "The Failures of Minority Capitalism: The Edapco Case," *Phylon,* Volume 37, No. 1, pp. 45–58.

Coles, Flournoy. A., Jr. "Financial Institutions and Black Entrepreneurship," *Journal of Black Studies.* March, 1973, pp. 332–333.

Comstock, Amy. "Over There: Another View of the Tulsa Riots," *Survey,* July 2, 1921. p. 460.

Condran, J.G. "Changes in White Attitudes Toward Blacks: 1963–1977," *Public Opinion Quarterly,* 43: 463–76.

Conroy, Hilary. *The Japanese Frontier in Hawaii, 1868–1898.* Berkeley: University of California Press. 1953.

Cooper, Patricia. "Interview: Bayard Rustin," *The Crisis,* March 1985: p. 26.

Crosby, Jerry D. "Two Hundred Years of Educational Development Through Self-Help, Self-Reliance, and Self-Determination," *The Negro Educational Review.* July-October, 1978, pp. 207–208.

Cross, T.L. *Black Capitalism.* New York: Athereum, 1969.

Cruse, Harold. *Rebellion or Revolution.* New York: Morrow Paperback Editions, 1968, pp. 139–155.

Cruse, Harold. *The Crisis of The Negro Intellectual.* New York: Quill, 1984.

Cruse, Harold. *The Crisis of The Negro Intellectual.* New York: William Morrow & Co. 1967.

Cummings, Scott. *Self-Help in Urban American: Patterns of Minority Business Enterprise.* New York: National University Publications. 1980.

Curry, Lenonard P. *The Free Black in Urban America, 1880–1850: The Shadow of A Dream.* Chicago: The University of Chicago Press. 1981.

Davis, Frank. *The Economics of Black Community Development.* Chicago: Markham Publishing Company, 1972.

Davis, Lenwood G. *The Black Family in The United States: A Selected Bibliography of Annotated Books, Articles, and Dissertations on Black Families in America.* Westport Connecticut: Greenwood Press, 1978.

Davis, William C. *The Civil War.* Alexandria, Virginia: Time-Life Books.

Decker, Peter. *Fortunes and Failures; White Collar Mobility in Nineteenth Century San Francisco.* Cambridge: 1978.

Denitch, B. "Is There a New Working Class" A Brief Note On a Large Question." *Dissent.* July-August, 1970. pp. 351–355.

Denslow, William. *10,000 Famous Freemasons.* Missouri: Missouri Lodge of Research. 1957.

Dillard, John. *Caste and Class in a Southern Town.* New Haven, 1937.

Dimont, Max. *The Indestructible Jews.* New York: The World Publishing Company, 1971.

Dimont. Max I. *The Jews in America.* New York: Simon and Schuster. 1980.

Dingle, Derek T. "Mining Venture Capital," *Black Enterprise.* October,1984, 52.

Dingle, Derek, T. "Venturing Out On Your Own," *Black Enterprise*, August, 1985, pp. 34–38.

Dollard, John. *Caste and Class in a Southern Town.* New York: Doubleday Ancor Books, 1957.

Donald, Henderson. H. "The Negro Migration of 1916–1918," *Journal of Negro History.* Oct. 1921.

Douglas, Colonel Clarence B. *The History of Tulsa, Oklahoma. Vol. I.* Chicago: S. J. Clarke Publishing Company. 1921.

Doyle, Don H. *The Social Order of a Frontier Community.* Urbana: The University of Illinois Press, 1978.

Drake, St. Clair and Horace R. Clayton. *Black Metropolis: A Study of Negro Life in a Northern City.* New York, Harcourt Brace, 1945.

Drake, St. Clair and Horace R. Clayton, *Black Metropolis.* New York: Harper & Row, Vol II. Chpt. 22.

Du Bois, W.E.B. *The Philadelphia Negro.* Philadelphia.

Du Bois, W.E.B. *Economic Co-Operation Among Negro Americans.* Atlanta, Georgia: The Atlanta University Press. 1907.

DuBois, W.E.B. *The Negro American Family.* Atlanta: Atlanta University Press. 1908.

DuBois, W.E.B. *The Negro in Business.* Atlanta: Atlanta University. 1898.

DuBois, W.E.B. *The Souls of Black Folk.* New York: Fawcett Publications, Inc.

DuBois, W.E.B. "The Upbuilding of Black Durham," *World's Work*, XXIII January, 1912), 334–338.

Duncan, Otis Dudley. "Inheritance of Poverty or Inheritance of Race?" In Daniel P. Moynihan, ed., *On Understanding Poverty: Perspectives from the Social Sciences.* New York: Basic Books, 1969.

Durham, Laird. *Black Capitalism: Critical Issues In Urgan Management.* Washington, D.C.: Arthur D. Little and Company, 1970.

"Durham, North Carolina: A City of Negro Enterprise," in *Independent*. LX March 30, 1911: p. 642.

Edmonds, Helen. The Negro and Fusion Politics in North Carolina. Chapel Hill: Duke University Press. 1951.

Edwards, G. Franklin. "Community and Class Realities: The Ordeal of Change," in *The Negro American*. Boston: Houghton Mifflin Company, 1966.

Edwards, R. C., M. Reich and D.M. Gordon (eds.) *Labor Market Segmentation*. Lexington, Mass.: Health. 1975.

Ellsworth, Scott. *Death in A Promised Land*. Baton Rouge: Louisiana State University Press. 1982.

Emeka, Mauris Lee Porter. *Black Banks, Past and Present*. Kansas City, Missouri. 1971.

Everett, James L. "An American Revolution is Lined to Entrepreneurs," *Minorities and Women in Business*. September/October, 1985.

Farely, Reynolds and Albert I. Hermalin, "Family Stability: A Comparison of Trends Between Blacks and Whites," *American Sociological Review*. Vol. 36, February, 1971, pp. 1–17.

Farley, Reynolds. *Blacks and Whites*. Cambridge, Massachusetts: Harvard University Press.

Feagin, Joe R. *Racial and Ethnic Relations*. New York: Prentice Hall. 1978.

Feagin, Joe R. *Racial and Ethnic Relations*, Englewood Cliffs, New Jersey: Prentice Hall. 1984.

Featherman, David L. and Robert M. Hauser, *Opportunity and Change*. New York: Academic Press, 1978.

Finkelstein, Louis (ed.) *The Jews: Their History, Culture and Religion*. New York: Harper & Brothers. 1960.

Fishman, Priscilla. (ed.) *The Jews of the United States*. New York: Quadrangle. 1973.

Fleming, Walter L. *The Freedman's Savings Bank: A Chapter in The Economic History of The Negro Race*. Chapel Hill: University of North Carolina Press, 1927.

Foley, Eugene P. "The Negro Business Man: In Search of A Tradition," in Talcott Parsons and Kenneth B. Clark, *The Negro American*. Boston: Beacon Press. 1965.

Foster, William Z. *The Negro People in American History*. New York: International Publishers. 1973.

Foster, William Z. *The Negro People*. New York: International Publishers. 1954.

Franklin, E. Frazier. *The Negro Family in the United States*. Chicago: The University of Chicago Press, 1939.

Franklin, Jimmie Lewis. *The Blacks in Oklahoma*. Norman: University of Oklahoma Press. 1980.

Franklin, John Hope. *From Slavery to Freedom*. New York: Alfred A. Knopf, 1948.

Franklin, John Hope. "History of Racial Segregation in the United States," *Annals*, CCCIV (March 1956). pp. 1–9.

Frazier, E Franklin,. "Durham: Capital of the Black Middle Class," in Winold Reiss (ed.) *The New Negro*. New York: Albert and Charles Boni. 1925.

Frazier, E.Franklin. *Black Bourgeoisie*. New York: Collier Books, 1957.

Frazier, E. Franklin. *Black Bourgeoisie*. New York: Collier Books. 1962.

Frazier, E. Franklin. "The Changing Status of the Negro Family," *Social Forces* 9 (March 1931): 386–393.

Freeman, R. *The Black Elite: The New Market for Highly Educated Black Americans*. New York: McGraw-Hill, 1976.

Gage, Duane. "Oklahoma: A Resettlement Area for Indians," in *Chronicles of Oklahoma*. XLVII. 1969–1970. p. 286.

Gilder, George. *The Spirit of Enterprise*. New York: Simon & Schuster, Inc. 1984.

Gintis, H. "The New Working Class and Revolutionary Youth," *Socialist Revolution* 1 (May-June) pp. 13–43.

Ginzberg, Eli.(ed.) *Business Leadership and The Negro Crisis*. New York: McGraw Hill, 1968.

Glazier, Nathan. *Affirmative Discrimination: Ethnic Inequality and Public Policy*. New York: Basic Books, 1975.

"Good People and Dirty Work," *The Sociological Eye: Collected works of Everett Hughes*. Chicago: Aldine, 1971. pp. 87–97.

Gordon, Milton M. *Assimilation in American Life*. New York: Oxford University Press, 1984.

"Government as Financial Intermediary for Minority Entrepreneurs: An Evaluation," *Journal of Business*. October 1975, p. 557.

Graetz, Heinrich. *The History of the Jews*. Philadelphia: The Jewish Publication Society of America. 1956.

Green, Patricia Gene and John Sibley Butler., "The Minority Community as a Natural Business Incubator," in *Journal of Business Research* 36, 51–58 (1996), pp. 51–58.

Greenberg, Jonathan, *Staking a Claim: Jake Simmons, Jr. and the Making of an African American Oil Dynasty*. New York: Atheneum, 1990.

Haley, Alex. *The Autobiography of Malcolm X*.

Halliburton, R.,Jr., *The Tulsa Race War of 1921*. San Francisco: R and E Research Associates. 1975.

Hamilton, C. Horace and Francis Henderson, "Migration from North Carolina Farms"

Hare, Nathan. *Black Anglo-Saxon*. New York: 1970.

Harlan, Louis R. *Booker T. Washingtpm: The Wizard of Tuskegee*. New York: Oxford University Press.

Harlan, Louis R. *Separate and Unequal.* New York: Atheneum, 1969.

Harmon, J.H., Jr., Arnett G. Lindsay and Carter G. Woodson. *The Negro As A Business Man.* New York: Arno Press, Inc. 1929.

Harmon, J.H., Jr., Arnett G. Lindsay and Carter G. Woodson., *The Negro As A Business Man.* McGrath Publishing Company: College Park, Maryland. 1929.

Harris, Abram L. *The Negro As Capitalist.* McGrath Publishing Company: College Park, Maryland, 1936.

Harris, Sammuel E. *Operations Manual for Project Outreach of The National Business League.* Undated in William L. Henderson and Larry C. Ledebur, *Economic Disparity: Problems and Strategies for Black America.* New York: Free Press, 1970, p. 108.

Harrison, B. *Education, Training, and the Urban Ghetto.* Baltimore: Johns Hopkins

Heaton, Ronald. *The Masonic Membership of the Founding Fathers.* Masonic Service Association. 1974.

Henderson, Archibald. *North Carolina: The Old North State and the New.* Chicago, 1941.

Hermalin, Albert I. and Reynolds Farley, "The Potential for Residential Integration in Cities and Suburbs: Implications for the Busing Controversy," *American Sociological Review* 38, No. 5 (Oct.), 595–610.

Hill, Mozel C. "The All-Negro Communities of Oklahoma: The Natural History of a Social Movement," in *Journal of Negro History.* XXXI (July 1946), pp. 254–68.

Hobbs, S. Huntington, Jr., *North Carolina, An Economic and Social Profile.* Chapel Hill: The University of North Carolina Press. 1958.

Hodson, Randy and Robert Kaufman. "Economic Dualism: A Critical Review." *American Sociological Review.* 47:727–739. 1982.

Holsey, Albon. "Pearson: The Brown Duke of Durham," *Opportunity.* (April, 1923).

Hoover, Dwight W. *Understanding Negro History.* Chicago: Quadrangle Books. 1968.

Horowitz, Irving Louis. "Disenthralling Sociology," in *Society.* Vol. 24.

Horowitz, Irving Louis. "Military Origins of the Cuban Revolution." *Armed Forces and Society.* No.4, August 1974. pp. 402–403.

Houck, Thomas H., *A Newspaper History of Race Relations in Durham, North Carolina. 1910–1940.* Thesis, Graduate School of Arts and Sciences. Duke University, Durham, North Carolina, 1941.

Hypps, Irene Caldwell. *Changes in Business Attitudes and Activities of The Negro In The United States Since 1619.* Ph.D. Dissertation, New York University. 1943.

Interview with Dr. Eugene A. Evaes, Professor at North Carolina Central University, Durham, North Carolina.

Jacobs, Audrey. "Funding Alternatives for Minority Businesses," Unpublished paper, Department of Sociology, The University of Texas, Austin, Texas. January/ February 1987. p. 49.

Jeltz, Wyatt F. "The Relations of Negroes and Choctaw and Chickasaw Indians," in *Journal of Negro History*, XXXII. 1948, pp. 28–30 in Tolson, *op. cit.* p. 22.

Jewish Life in the Middle Ages. New York: Meridan Books, 1958.

Johnson, Charles S. "How Much is Migration a Flight from Persecution?" *Opportunity*. Sept. 1923.

Johnson, Charles S. *The Negro College Graduate*. Chapel Hill: The University of North Carolina Press, 1938.

Johnson, James Weldon. *"Harlem: The Cultural Capitol,"* in Alain Locke (editor), *The New Negro*, 1925, Albert and Charles Boni, p. 304. Quoted from Harold Cruse, *The Crisis of The Negro Intellectual*. New York: William & Morrow & Co. 1968, p. 21.

Jones, Edward W., Jr. "What It's Like To Be A Black Manager," *Harvard Business Review*. (July-August) 1973. pp. 111–112.

Kalleberg, A. and A. Sorensen, "The Sociology of Labor Markets." *The Annual Review of Sociology*. 5:351–379.

Kaplan, Sidney. *The Black Presence in the Era of the American Revolution*. Washington D.C.: Smithsonian Institution. 1973.

Kennedy, Louise V. *The Negro Peasant Turns Cityward: Effects of Recent Migrations to Northern Cities*. College Park: University of Maryland Press, 1969. (Originally published in 1930.)

Kennedy, Mr. W.J., Jr., "The Negro's Adventure in The Field of Life Insurance."

Kilgore, Julia Kay. "MESBICs Striving for Fiscal Fitness," *Hispanic Business*. March, 1988, p. 10.

Kinzer, Robert and Edward Sagarin, *The Negro In American Business*. New York: Greenberg Press, 1950.

Kitano, Harry H.L. *Japanese Americans*. New York: Prentice Hall. 1969.

Klein, Aaron E. *The Hidden Contributors: Black Scientists and Inventors in America*. New York: Doubleday. 1971.

Kluegel, James R. and Eliot R. Smith, "Whites' Belief About Blacks' Opportunity," *American Sociological Review*. 47: (August): 520.

Kluger, Richard. *Simple Justice*. New York: Alfred A. Knopf. 1975.

Kravitz, Lee, "Why SBICs Want to Break From the SBA," *Venture*. October, 1984, p. 56.

Kraybill, Donald B. and Steven M. Nolt, *Amish Enterprise: From Plows to Profits* (Baltimore: The Johns Hopkins University Press, 1995).

Lacayo, Richard. "Between Two Worlds," *Time*. March, 1989, p. 62.

Landry, Bart. *The New Black Middle Class*. Berkeley: The University of California Press. 1987.

"Leading B.A. Sources of 1984 Minority Group Doctorate Recipients," *Black Issues in Higher Education*. December, 1986, p. 8.

Leinster, Colin. "Black Executives: How They're Doing." *Fortune*. January 18, 1988, pp. 109–120.

"Lending, Not Giving to NonProfits," *Nations Cities Weekly*, February, 1984, p. 3.

Levenstein, Margaret. "African-American Entrepreneurship: The View from the 1910 Census," *Business and Economic History*, v. 24 no. 1, Fall 1995, pp. 107–108.

Liberson, Stanley. *A Piece of The Pie*. Berkely: University of California Press, 1980.

Light, Ivan H. *Ethnic Enterprise in America*. Berkeley: The University of California Press. 1972.

Light, Ivan H. "Asian Enterprise in America: Chinese, Japanese, and Koreans in Small Business," in Scott Cummings (ed.) *Self-Help in Urban America: Patterns of Minority Economic Development*. Port Washington, N.Y.: Kennikat Press. 1980, p. 33.

Lindsay, Arnett G. "The Negro in Banking." *Journal of Negro History*. April, 1929.

Logan, Rayford W. "The Hiatus-A Great Negro Middle-Class," *Southern Workman*, LVIII.

Lorizzo, Luciano J. and Salvatore Mondello, *The Italian-Americans*. Boston: Twayne Publishers. 1971.

MacColl, E. Kimbark. *The Shaping of a City: Business and Politics in Portland, Oregon.*

Marable, Manning. *How Capitalism Underdeveloped Black America*. Boston Mass: South End Press.

Mars, Gerald and Robin Ward. "Ethnic Business Development in Britain: Opportunities and Resources," in Ward & Jenkins. pp. 1–20.

Martin, Fred. "Navigating Rough Waters," in *Black Enterprise*. June 1988, p. 206.

Marx, Karl. *Capital*. Volumes I–III. Pelican edition, 1976.

McAdoo, Harriette Pipes. "Factors Related to Stability in Upwardly Mobile Black-Familes. *Journal of Marriage and The Family*. November, 1978.

McCants, Andrew R. *John Merrick A Bibliographical Sketch*. Durham: The Seeman Printery. 1920.

McLemore, S. Dale. *Racial and Ethnic Relations in America*. Boston: Allyn and Bacon, Inc. 1983.

Mead, A. "The Distribution of Segregation in Atlanta," *Social Forces* 51: 1972, pp. 182–92.

Meier, August and Elliott Rudwick, *Along The Color Line*. Urbana: University of Illinois Press, 1976.

Meier, August and Elliott Rudwick, *From Plantation to Ghetto*. New York: Hill and Wang. 1966.

Meier, August. *Negro Thought In America*. Ann Arbor: The University of Michigan. 1980.

Meier, August. *Negro Thought in America: 1880–1915*. Ann Arbor: The University of Michigan Press. 1966.

Melendy, H. Brett. *The Oriental Americans*. New York: Hippocrene Books, Inc. 1972.

Mills, Gary B. *The Forgotten People: Cane River's Creoles of Color*. Baton Rouge: Louisiana State University Press. 1977.

Milton M. Gordon, *Assimilation in American Life*. New York: Oxford University Press, 1946.

Minton, Henry M., M.D. *Early History of Negroes in Business in Philadelphia.*, Read before the American Historical Society, March, 1913.

Modell, John. "Class or Ethnic Solidarity: The Japanese American Company Union," *Pacific Historical Review* 38 May 1969:193–206.

Monroe, Sylvester. "Guest in a Strange House: A Black at Harvard," pp. 45–48. unknown source.

Moore, Joan and Harry Pachon. *Hispanics in the United States*. New York: Prentice Hall. 1985.

Moreland, Lois B.. *White Racism and the Law*. Columbus Ohio: A Bell & Howell Company, 1970.

Morgan, H. Wayne & Anne Hodges Morgan, *Oklahoma*. New York: W.W. Norton & Company. 1977.

Moskos, Charles C., Jr. *Greek Americans*. New Jersey: Prentice Hall. 1980.

Moynihan, Patrick D. *The Negro Family: The Case for National Action*. Washington D.C.: Office of Policy Planning and research, U.S. Department of Labor. 1965.

Munford, C.J. "Social Structure and Black Revolution." *The Black Scholar*. Vol. 4, November–December 1972. pp. 11–23.

Myrdal, Gunner, *An American Dilemma*. New York: 1944.

Newton, Huey P. "The Black Panters," in *Ebony*, XXIV (August, 1969): 102–12.

O'Hare, William. "Embattled Black Businesses," *American Demographics*. April, 1986, p. 28.

Ofari, Earl. *The Myth of Black Capitalsim*. New York: Monthly Review Press, 1970.

Pace, Harry H. "The Business of Banking Among Negroes," *Crisis* 1927 (February).

Park, Robert E. *Race and Culture*. Glencoe, Illionis: Free Press, 1950.

Parrillo, Vincent N. *Strangers To these Shores*. New York: John Wiley & Sons. 1985.

Peterson,William. *Japanese Americans*. New York: Random House, 1971.

Peterson, William. *The New York Times Magazine*. January 9, 1966. p. 20.

Pierce, Joseph A. *Negro Business and Business Education*, New York: Harper & Brothers. 1947.

Pinkeney, Alphonso. *Black Americans*. New Jersey: Prentice-Hall, 1987.

Pollins, Harold. "The Development of Jewish Businesses in the United Kingdom," in Ward & Jenkins, pp. 73–89.

Portes, Alejandro and Kenneth L. Wilson, "Black-White Differences in Educational Attainment," *American Sociological Review*, 41:(June), 1976, pp. 414–431.

Portes, Alejandro and Leif Jensen, "What's An Ethnic enclave? The Case for Conceptual Clarity," *American Sociological Review* 52: 768–771, 1987.

Portes, Alejandro and Robert L. Bach, *Latin Journey*. Berkeley: University of California Press, 1985.

Rainwater, Lee and William L. Yancey, *The Moynihan Report and the Politics of Controversy*. Cambridge: Massachusetts Institute of Technology Press. 1967.

Record, Wilson. "The Development of the Communist Position in the United States," *Phylon*. XIX 1958, pp. 306–26.

Reeves, Frank and Robin Ward, " West Indian Business in Britain," in Ward & Jenkins, *Ethnic Communities in Business: Strategies for Economic Survival*. Cambridge: Cambridge University Press. 1984. pp. 125–149.

Reissman, Frank. "Low-Income Culture: The Strength of the Poor," *Journal of Marriage and the Family*. Vol. 26, November, 1964, pp. 417–421.

"Reverse Comute." Video Presentation. The National Center for Neighborhood Enterprise. Washington, D.C. 1989.

Rhoads, Esther B. "My Experience with the Wartime Relocation of Japanese," in *East Across the Pacific: Historical and Sociological Studies of Japanese Immigranion and Assimilation*, Hilary Conroy and T. Scott Miyakawa (eds.) pp. 131–132. Reprinted in

Rice, Roger L. "Residential Segregation by Law, 1910–1911," *Journal of Southern History*. XXXIV (May 1968). pp. 179–199.

Riessman, Frank. *The Culturally Deprived Child*. New York: Harper & Row, 1962. Quoted from Charles E. Silberman, *Crisis in Black and White*. New York: Vintage Book, 1964, p. 261.

Rivkin, Ellis. *The Shaping of Jewish History*. New York: Charles Scribner's Sons. 1971.

Robb, T. Bruce. "Safeguarding the Depositor." *The Annals of the American Academy of Political and Social Science*. Philadelphia (January 1934), Vol. 171, pp. 56–57. Quoted from Mauris Lee Porter Emeka, *Black Banks Past and Present*. Kansas City. 1971.

Roberts, Claudia P. The Durham Architectural and Historic Inventory. Durham: The Historic Preservation Society. 1981.

Rohrs, Richard C. *The Germans in Oklahoma*. Oklahoma. University of Oklahoma Press. 1980.

Sachar, Abram Leon. *A History of The Jews*. New York: Alfred A. Knopf. 1930.

Sacramento Union, June 18, 1869.

Sanders, Jimy M. and Victor Nee. "The Limits of Ethnic Solidarity in The Enclave Economy," *American Sociological Review* 52:745–773, 1987;

Schermerhorn, R.A. *Comparative and Ethnic Relations*. New York: Random House. 1970.

Schiller, Bradley R. *The Economics of Poverty and Discrimination.* Englewood Cliffs, N.J.: Prentice-Hall, 1973.

Scott, Will B. "Critical Factors for the Survival of First Generation College Blacks," in Gail B. Thomas, Ed., *Black Students in Higher Education.*

Scott, William L. "Financial Performance of Minority-Versus Nonminority-Owned Businesses," *Journal of Small Business Management.* January 1983, p. 48.

Seder, John. and Berkeley Burrell, *Getting it Together.* New York: Harcourt Brace Jovanovich, Inc., 1971.

Sheer, Gerson S. *Marxist Humanism and Praxis.* (edited). New York: Prometheus Books. 1978.

Sherman, Richard B. (ed.), *The Negro and The City.* Englewood Cliffs, N.J.: Prentice Hall, 1970.

Silberman, Charles E. *Crises in Black in White,* pp. 261–262.

Simms, Margaret C. "Black Schools and Black Economic Development," in Gerald F. Whittaker (editor), *Minorities At The Crossroads.* Ann Arbor: Division of Research, Graduate School of Business Administration, The University of Michigan.

Skidmore, Dave. "Bank Failures Hit a Record During 1987," *Austin American Statesman.* Wednesday, January 6, 1988.

Sombart, Werner, *The Jews and Modern Capitalism.* New Jersey: Transaction, Inc. Original material copyright by The Free Press, 1951.

Sombart, Werner. *Jews and Modern Capitalism.* New Brunswick, N.J.: Transaction Books. 1982.

Sowell, Thomas. *Black Education: Myths and Tragedies.* New York: McKay Publishing Co., 1973.

Sowell, Thomas. *Civil Rights: Rhetorica or Reality?* New York: Morrow, 1984.

Sowell, Thomas. *Markets and Minorities.* New York: Basic Books. 1981.

Sowell, Thomas. "Guest in A Strange House."

Sowell, Thomas. *Race and Economics.* New York: Longman Inc. 1975.

Spaulding, Henry D. *Encyclopedia of Black Folklore* New York: Middle Village. Jonathan David Publishers. 1972.

Spear, Allan H. *Black Chicago: The Making of a Negro Ghetto.* Chicago: The University of Chicago Press, 1967.

Spero, Sterling and Abram L. Harris, *The Black Worker.* New York: Columbia University Press. 1931.

Stables, Robert. "Black Family Life and Development," *Mental Health: A Challenge to the Black Community.* edited by Lawrence E. Gray. Philadelphia: Dorrance.

Stables, Robert. *Introduction to Black Sociology.* New York: McGraw-Hill. 1976.

Staples, Robert. *The Black Family: Essays and Studies.* Belmont, California: Wadsworth Publishing Company, 1971.

Starks, Karen. *African American Community Well-Being: A Reconsideration of The Contributions of Urban Entrepreneurs* (Dissertation, Clark Atlanta University, Department of Social Work, 1999).

Starr, Isidore. *The American Negro America.* New York: Vintage Books.

Stein, Howard F. and Robert F. Hill, *The Ethnic Imperative: Examining the New White Ethnic Movement.* University Park: The Pennsylvania State University Press, 1977.

Stillman, Richard J. *Integration of the Negro in the U.S. Armed Forces.* New York: Frederick Praeger. 1968.

Stone, Alfred Holt. "Is Race Friction Between Blacks and Whites in the United States Growing and Inevitable?" *American Journal of Sociology* 13 (1908): pp. 676–697.

Stryker, Sheldon. "Social Structure and Prejudice," *Social Problems* 6 (Spring) 1959. 340–54.

Stuart, M.S. *An Economic Detour: A History of Insurance in the Lives of American Negroes.* New York: Wendell Malliett and Company. 1940.

Sullivan, Teresa A. and Stephen D. McCracken, "Patterns and Rates of Return To Self-Employment." *National Journal of Sociology.* Volume 2 Number 2. 1988, p. 167.

Taeuber, Alma F. and Karl E. "Recent Immigration and Studies of Ethnic Assimilation." *Demography* 4, 1967: 798–808.

Taeuber, Karl E. and Alma F. "Is The Negro an Immigrant Group?" *Integrated Education.* Vol. 1, No. 3, June, 1963.

The Durham Herald, December, 18, 1921

The Durham Sun. 50th Anniversary Edition, Business Section. April 1939.

"The Effects of Social Class on Voluntary Association Membership Among Urban Afro-Americans," *Sociological Focus,* Volume 21 No. 1. January, 1988 pp. 67–80.

"The Negro As an Immigrant Group: Recent Trends in Racial and Ethnic Segregation in Chicago." *American Journal of Sociology.* 69 1964: 374–382.

"The Negro in Business." *Ebony* 18 (1963): p. 212.

"The Tulsa Race Riots," *The Independent.* June 18, 1921. pp. 646–647.

The Whetstone, Magazine of the North Carolina Mutual Life Insurance Company. 40th Anniversary. 1938.

Thomas, Gail E. "The Effects of Standardized Achivement Test Performance and Family Status on Black-White College Access," in Gail E. Thomas, (Edited) *Black Students in Higher Education.* Westport, Connecticut: Greenwood Press, 1981.

Thomas, Tony. "Black Nationalism and Confused Marxist," in *Black Liberation and Socialism.* (edited) by Thomas also. New York: Pathfinder Press.

Thompson, Daniel C. *A Black Elite: A Profile of Graduates of UNCF Colleges.* New York: GreenWood Press, 1986.

Thurow, Lester. "Affirmative Action in a Zero-Sum Society," in Ronald Takaki (ed.), *From Different Shores: Perspectives on Race and Ethnicity in America.* Oxford: Oxford University Press, 1987.

Tobias, Henry J. *The Czech in Oklahoma. Oklahoma.* University of Oklahoma Press. 1980.

Tobias, Henry J. *The Jews in Oklahoma. Oklahoma:* University of Oklahoma Press. 1980.

Toll, William. *The Making of an Ethnic Middle Class.* Albany, New York: State University of New York Press, 1982.

Tolson, Arthur L. *The Black Oklahomans A History: 1541–1972.* New Orleans: Edwards Printing Company. 1966.

Tolson, Arthur L. *The Black Oklahomans.* New Orleans: Edwards Printing Company. 1962.

Tovell-Troy, Lawrence A. "Clan Structure and Economic Activity: The Case of Greeks in Small Business Enterprise," in Scott Cummings (ed.). *Self-Help in Urban America,* Port Washington, N.Y.: Kennikat Press. 1980. p. 60.

Tulsa Daily World, June 1, 1921.

Tulsa Daily World, June 26, 1921.

Tulsa *Tribune,* June 1, 1921.

Turner, Jonathan H. and Edna Bonacich, "Toward a Composite Theory of Middleman Minorities," *Ethnicity* 7:144–158.

U.S. Department of Commerce, *Minority-Owned Businesses: 1969.* Washington, D.C.: Government Printing Office.

United States Department of Commerce News, "Two-Thirds of Business Owners Get Started Without Borrowing Capital, " Wednesday, September 16, 1987. CB87–148.

United States Department of Commerce News: Bureau of The Census, "Black-Owned Businesses up by More than 100,000," Washington D.C. Public release number CB85–177, 1985.

Victor Nee and Jimy Sanders, "The Road to Parity: Determinants of the Socioeconomic achievements of Asian Americans," in Richard D. Alba, *Ethnicity and Race in the U.S.A.* (edited). London: Routledge & Kegan Paul, 1985. p. 82.

Walker, Juliet E.K. *The History of Black Business in America: Capitalism, Race, Entrepreneurship.* New York: Simon & Schuster, 1998.

Walker, Juliet E.K. *Free Frank: A Black Pioneer on the Antebellum Frontier.* Lexington, Kentucky: University of Kentucky Press. 1983.

Walker, Juliet E.K. "Racism, Slavery, and Free Enterprise: Black Entrepreneurship in the United States Before the Civil War," in *Business History Review* 60 (Autumn 1986). p. 333.

"Wall Street of Negro America," *Ebony* 4:19–22. September, 1949.

Ward, Robin and Richard Jenkins. *Ethnic Communities in Business: Strategies for Economic Survival.* Cambridge: Cambridge University Press. 1984.

Warner, W. Loyd and Leo Srole, *The Social System of American Ethnic Groups*. New Haven: Yale University Press.

Washington, Booker T. "Durham North Carolina: A City of Negro Enterprises," in *Independent*. LXX (March 30, 1911).

Washington, Booker T. "The Atlanta Exposition Address." in John Hope Franklin and Washington, Booker T. *The Negro In Business*. Chicago: Hertel, Jenkins & Co. 1907.

Weare, Walter B. *Black Business in the New South: A Social History of the North Carolina Mutual Life Insurance Company*. Chicago: University of Illinois Press. 1973.

Weber, Max. *The Protestant Ethnic and The Spirit of Capitalism*. New York: Charles Scribner's Sons.

Weidenhammer, Robert. "An Analysis of Fifty Bank Failures," *The Annals of the American Academy of Political Social Science*. Philadelphia: (1934), Vol. 171, p. 51.

Werbner, Pnina. "Business on Trust: Pakistani Entrepreneurship in the Manchester Garment Trade," in Ward & Jenkins, *Ethnic Communities in Business: Strategies for Economic Survival*. Cambridge: Cambridge University Press. 1984. pp. 169–189.

White, Frank Hollowell. *The Economic and Social Development of Negroes in North Carolina Since 1900*. Ph.D. Dissertation. 1960. New York University.

White, Walter F. "The Eruption of Tulsa," *The Nation*. June 29, 1921, pp. 909–910.

Whitfield, Stephen J. "Commercial Passions: The Southern Jew as Businessman," *American Jewish History*, 1982, 71.

Williams, Robin W., Jr., *Mutual Accommodation: Ethnic Conflict and Cooperation*. Minneapolis: University of Minnesota Press, 1977.

Wilson, Kenneth L. and Alejandro Portes, "Ethnic Enclaves: A Comparison of the Cuban and Black Economies in Miami," *American Journal of Sociology* 86 (September): 295–319.

Wilson, Kenneth L. and Alejandro Portes. "Immigrant Enclaves: An Analysis of the Labor Market Experiences in Cubans in Miami." *American Journal of Sociology*, 86 (September 1980):295–319.

Wilson, Kenneth L. and W. Allen Martin. "Ethnic Enclaves: A Comparison of the Cuban and Black Economies in Miami." *American Journal of Sociology* 88: 1982. pp. 135–159.

Wilson, William Julius. *The Declining Significance of Race*. Chicago: University of Chicago Press, 1978.

Wilson, William Julius. *The Declining Significance of Race*. Chicago: University of Chicago Press, 1980.

Wilson, William Julius. *The Truly Disadvantaged*. Chicago: The University of Chicago Press, 1987.

Woodard, Michael D. "Voluntary Association Membership Among Black Americans: The Post-Civil Rights Era," *The Sociological Quarterly*, Volume 28, No. 2, pp. 285–301.

Woodson, Carter G. *Free Negro Heads of Families in the U.S. in 1830.* Washington D.C.: Vintage Books, 1969, pp. xxxi–xxxii.

Woodson, Robert L. "A Legacy of Entreprenurship," in Robert L. Woodwon, (edited) *On The Road to Economic Freedom.* Washington D.C.: Regnery Gateway, 1987, pp. 1, 3, 23.

Woodson, Robert L. "Black America's Legacy of Entrepreneurship," *National Journal of Sociology,* Volume 2, Number 2, 1988, p. 221.

Woodward, C. Van. *The Strange Career of Jim Crow.* New York: Random House. 1955.

Woodward, C. Vann. *The Strange Career of Jim Crow.* New York: Oxford University Press.

Work, Monroe N. *Negro Year Book, 1918–1919.* Tuskegee Normal and Industrial Institute, Tuskegee, Alabama.

Work, Monroe N. *Negro Year Book,* Tuskegee: Tuskegee Institute, 1937–1938.

Wright, James D. "In Search of a New Working Class," *Qualitative Sociology.* pp. 33–57.

Zenner, Walter P. "Middleman Minorities in The Syrian Mosaic," *Sociological Perspectives* 30: 400–421. October, 1987.

Index

and class stratification, 184
and Washington Duke, 187–199
and self-help, 188–189. *See also* self-
    help
and successful enterprises, 190–203
and the Commercial and Security
    Company, 192
and the Mechanics and Farmers Bank,
    193, 194
and the North Carolina Mutual Life
    Insurance Company, 185, 197, 199
Blacks in Miami, Florida, 33
Blacks in Tulsa, Oklahoma
    and Greenwood, 215–216, 223,
        225–226, 236–237
    and race riot, 219–229
Boggs, James, 82
Bogle, Robert. See Catering
Bonacich, Edna, 4–7, 13, 23, 41–42, 72,
    77–78, 80, 229, 245, 256, 259,
    264–266
Bourgeoisie, Petit, 5
Boyd, Henry, 50, 179, 186
Boyd, William Kenneth, 176

California Farm Bureau Association, 12
Calvin, 3
Capitalism, Spirit of, 3
Carmichael, Stokely, 296, 299
Castro, Fidel, 30
Carver, George Washington, 277
Catering, 46
Catholic, 34
Chinese, 5–7, 26, 74
    exclusion act, 10
    in Mississippi, 77
Christian, 16–18, 21, 35
Civil Rights Movement, 296, 300, 306,
    333
Civil War, 43, 52, 68, 106, 151, 152, 179,
    240, 264, 341
Clayton, Horace R., 82, 262, 281
Colonialism, 1
Contract Laborers. *See* Japanese
Cox, Oliver, 241–242
Cruse, Harold, 286
Cuban Americans, 30–33, 176, 305

Cummings, Scott, 23

Delaney, Martin, 297
Discrimination, 1, 5, 41, 49, 55,
    117–118, 240
Dollard, John, 247
Douglass, Fredrick, 297
Drake, St. Clair, 82, 262, 281
Du Bois, W.E.B., 42, 70, 74, 137, 179,
    194, 222, 227, 269, 277, 307, 331
Dual Economy Theory, 28
Duke, Washington. *See* Blacks in
    Durham, North Carolina
DuSable, Jean Baptist, 43
Dutch West India Company, 17

Economic Detour 76, 80–82, 151, 181
Economic Stability, 1–2, 23–24
Ellsworth, Scott, 215
Entrepreneurship
    and the collective approach, 23, 25
    sociology of, 1, 41, 83, 133, 327
    Afro-American, 45
    and capitalism, 53
    under slavery, 53
Ethnic Enclave Theory, 28, 31, 202
Ethnic Enterprise, 2

Fleming, Walter L., 139
Forten, James, 46
Frazier, E. F., 82, 176, 179, 182,
    241–244, 257, 260–263, 270,
    277–281, 330
Free Afro-Americans. *See* Free blacks
Free Blacks, 43, 45, 49, 52, 133–134
Freeman, Richard, 300

Gardon, Milton, 287
Garvey, Marcus, 297
Glazer, Nathan, 300
Great Migration, 267
Greek Americans, 4, 24–26
    as a middleman Minority, 23–28

Hamilton, Charles, 299
Harris, Abram, 47–48, 138–140
Hawaii, Migration to by Japanese, 9